D1473593

The C Toolbox

William James Hunt

Addison-Wesley Publishing Company, Inc.
Reading, Massachusetts   Menlo Park, California
Don Mills, Ontario   Wokingham, England   Amsterdam
Sydney   Singapore   Tokyo   Madrid   Bogotá
Santiago   San Juan

Library of Congress Cataloging in Publication Data

Hunt, William James.
  The C toolbox.

  Bibliography: p.
  Includes index.
  1. C (Computer program language) I. Title.
QA76.73.C15H85 1985   001.64'24   85–6171
ISBN 0–201–11111–X

DEFGHIJ-HA-89876
Fourth Printing, December 1986

Cover design by Marshall Henrichs
Text design by Judith Ashkenaz
Set in 10 point Caledonia by Pine Tree Composition, Inc., Lewiston, Maine

To my mother,
whose love has been invaluable
and whose values give me direction

The C Toolbox

Acknowledgments

Several years ago I read *Software Tools* by Kernighan and Plauger. It helped me to understand my years of programming experience. This book is inspired by *Software Tools* and uses a similar approach to systems programming on personal computers.

In the 11 years that I have been a professional programmer, I have learned from many co-workers. Reading programs they had written was an essential part of my education.

My wife, Lesley, has been invaluable in many ways. Her support encouraged me to start writing a book (and to finish it). Her work in serving as editor and guinea pig for the roughest of drafts was vital too. Finally, she volunteered to learn C to be a better guinea pig. Greater love hath no spouse than to learn another programming language.

Contents

Introduction

Anyone who has used a personal computer (PC) with good software such as Lotus's 1–2–3 or Microsoft's Flight Simulator knows that PCs have great potential. However, the best efforts of casual programmers working in BASIC are often very disappointing. There is a wide gap between what average programmers can achieve and what they see professional programmers achieve. This book helps bridge that gap. It presents examples of complete, useful programs and discusses how they were developed.

The programs are mostly utilities or tools programs that make using and programming a PC easier. I chose these programs to illustrate programming techniques and algorithms that are often mysterious to the casual BASIC programmer. The programs also provide a concrete basis for discussing program design, coding, and testing.

The book is also intended to be a showcase for the C language. If your experience is limited to BASIC, learning C (or another good high-level language like Pascal) is a necessary first step for producing high-quality programs. While the book is not a tutorial or primer on C, it provides concrete examples of its use and is a good tool for learning C.

Programs

☐ To learn about programming (and C), you need to write programs. This book provides a good starting point. Each program is simple so that its basic structure is obvious and is accompanied by a full description of what the program does and how it does it. At the same time, the programs are designed to be easy to enhance for better performance. Possible enhancements are discussed for each program, with many modifications that require only 10 to 50 lines of C code to produce useful improvements. This is much more rewarding than having to start from scratch.

To make programs easier to understand and modify, the book uses a subset of C's features. C programs are often written in a cryptic style that makes heavy use of features unique to C. Using these features usually produces only a modest improvement in performance but a heavy penalty in program clarity. This view may be heresy to some C programmers but will prove eminently practical to many others, especially those coming to C from another language. Optimization by using C's special features is discussed in Chapter 9.

The material presented is substantial. If you do not understand a program fully at first reading, that is quite natural. Read first for general understanding, then focus on details as you need them.

The programs are designed to run on the IBM PC under PC-DOS. The nature of the programs requires that some specific environment be selected, and the IBM PC has important advantages:

1. It is widely used and is becoming a standard.
2. It is more accessible than a large computer to many readers.
3. It has a good architecture, satisfactory speed, and can use lots of memory.
4. It has several good C compilers available (see appendix B).

Only a few changes are needed to make the programs run on other computers under the MS-DOS operating system. More changes are needed to make them run under other operating systems, such as CP/M-80, CP/M-86, or UNIX. These changes are largely confined to Chapter 7.

Audience

□ Readers should be familiar with some programming language and with using a PC, especially using a text editor and DOS commands such as DIR and COPY. It is not essential that you have previous experience with C. Programmers with exposure to Pascal, PL/1, or Modula-2 should have little difficulty. Readers with only BASIC experience are likely to find some features of C puzzling; the examples in Chapters 1 and 2 should help. My style of creating code, by stressing clear, readable code over speed, should also help the transition to C.

Available Disk

□ All the programs in the book are available on a disk, ready for editing and compilation. Since manually copying several hundred lines of code is tedious and can result in errors, the disk is the convenient, safe way to work with these programs. Just insert the disk and edit one of the programs.

The programs were tested with many of the available compilers. Operating instructions for compiling and using the programs with various compilers are included on the disk.

The disk includes all the programs in this book plus additional programs. Library functions for scanning a single directory and for scanning a hierarchy of directories are included. These were not included in the book, to keep the book at a manageable size, but it was decided to keep all useful programs on the disk. To acquire the disk, send a check or money order for $20.00 to William James Hunt, Toolbox Disk, P.O. Box 271965, Concord, CA 94527. The last page of this book has an order form.

What You Need

□ You should get a copy of *The C Programming Language* by Brian W. Kernighan and Dennis M. Ritchie (Englewood Cliffs, N.J.: Prentice-Hall, 1978). While the book is not a tutorial or a primer, it is the standard reference on C. You may also want a primer on C; see Appendix D for suggestions. If you are new to C, you should read one of these primers as you go through this book.

You will need free access to an IBM PC or some other computer running the MS-DOS or PC-DOS operating system (Version 2.0 or later). You will neither find programming enjoyable nor the advice in this book useful if you have limited and infrequent access to a PC.

Your computer should have at least 192 K bytes of RAM memory. It should also have either two 320 K/360 K byte floppy disk drives or one floppy and one hard disk. Appendix A gives some hints to make program development faster.

You will need an editor program to enter new programs and to modify existing ones. The EDLIN editor provided with MS-DOS is not recommended for regular use (see Appendix A for alternatives). You also need a good C compiler; Appendix B discusses specific changes required for a number of C compilers.

A few functions in the book are written in assembler language. The program diskette contains these functions in source file format as well as in object module form for several popular compilers. If you have one of these compilers, you will need an assembler only if you modify these source files.

You will need a linker program to build a complete program from separate object files. PC-DOS includes a linker that can be used with several compilers. (Other compiler products include a suitable linker program.)

Compatibility

□ All the programs presented have been tested on the IBM PC, XT, and AT models. The programs have not been tested with the PC jr. but should work if enough memory is present.

Some hardware-specific functions in Chapter 7 may require revisions for new PC hardware. For example, the SCREEN module for fast output to the display screen works for the monochrome and color graphics adapters. New adapters may require changes to refresh buffer addresses and status port numbers.

New releases of C compilers may differ in memory layout or in the names of segments and groups. Calling conventions for functions may also change.

Outline of the Book

□   Chapters 1 and 2 get you started reading and writing C. While they provide a brief introduction in comparison to that of a primer, they illustrate some features and concepts that are important in understanding the rest of the book. Chapter 1 gives examples of short C programs and the steps needed to create and compile them. It shows those parts of C that will be relatively familiar to you. This gives you confidence that C will be easy to understand.

Programming languages are never perfect; Chapter 2 discusses the way we use C to minimize bugs and portability problems. File I/O and bit operations in C are also covered in this chapter. We also develop some tools and start an object library.

Chapter 3 presents the VIEW program. It allows us to browse through text files composed of ASCII characters. VIEW is useful for looking at C source files as well as text files produced by word processors like WordStar. Techniques for simple file input and for interactive keyboard and display usage are demonstrated. Since Chapter 3 is the first chapter to describe a sizeable program, it goes through the program development process in detail. The following chapters do not repeat these basic points. Testing the program on a module-by-module basis is emphasized here.

Chapter 4 develops another tool for examining data files. This FILEDUMP program displays a file's contents in hexadecimal and ASCII formats much like the dump format of the PC-DOS debug program. This provides a way to determine the format of any file without any prior knowledge of its content. Since this program is closely related to the VIEW program of Chapter 3, Chapter 4 shows how to make use of an existing program in developing a new, but related, one. This chapter discusses more aspects of the program development process.

Chapter 5 builds several tools based on sorting algorithms. Two well-known algorithms—the insertion sort and quicksort—are shown and then made into library functions that are usable on any kind of data. These library functions are then used in a simple program to sort lines of ASCII text. Then the technique of merging is used to handle files too large to fit into RAM memory. The initial MERGE program is then generalized so that the type of records to be sorted and the location and type of the keys for sorting are specified when the program is executed.

Chapter 6 builds a BTREE module for indexed access to data files. This module is rather long but provides features such as multiple indexes to a data file, duplicate keys, and variable-length keys. A sample application maintains an index of correspondence documents by name of addressee, date sent, and subject.

Chapter 7 presents the toolkit used in preceding chapters. While C is adequate for almost all our requirements, a few things require assembler language functions. Other modules specific to MS-DOS or the IBM PC are presented in this chapter. Single-key input, screen output, and DOS and BIOS access are among the modules included here.

Chapter 8 presents a terminal emulator program. The special characteristics of a real-time program are discussed—for example, unpredictable input from several sources with data being lost if the program does not keep up with all input. The techniques for handling such problems—polling input status, buffering data to relax timing requirements, and using interrupt-driven input handling—are demonstrated.

Chapter 9 covers a few loose ends—for example, using C's unique features to optimize execution speed and handling critical errors. It also summarizes the design philosophy of the previous chapters.

Appendix A discusses compiling and executing the programs we present. Appendix B lists the C compilers examined and specific changes required for each compiler. Appendix C explains memory models and their relation to the 8088 architecture. A short bibliography in Appendix D provides a starting point for further reading.

Themes

□ Several themes occur throughout the book. They are listed here to help you understand the book's message.

Create Order out of Chaos

The book presents finished, working programs that, I hope, do not contain bugs. It often looks as though such programs sprang forth from my brain in a complete and correct form. That is almost never the case. The process usually involves some dead ends, some backtracking, lots of bugs, and inelegant first tries.

Each chapter presents a topic in orderly way to make it easy to understand. Do not conclude that program development is a perfectly orderly process with uniform progress through each stage, however. Every program in this book was revised several times to make it simpler and more effective.

In spite of these limitations, you should always set goals at each step. Never start writing a program until you define its function. After you complete the program, you may revise the functional specification and rewrite the program. The cardinal sin is to write a program and then figure out what function it performs.

Keep Up Your Morale

Writing computer programs can be very hard on your ego and your morale. You will make errors in design, get the syntax of C statements wrong, and produce lots of very puzzling bugs in your programs. These problems give abundant and painful testimony to your lack of perfection before you finally get a working program. Some people claim to produce working programs without any such problems, but most just have memory lapses.

You can make the programming process much more pleasant if you break the problem into small pieces. Any large project can seem impossible if you do not break it into manageable steps. Write and test programs in small modules so you get some measure of success at frequent intervals. Simplify the design of a large program, and do a smaller prototype first.

Use an Experimental Approach

Reading reference manuals and computer documentation is hard, frustrating work. The information they contain is often ambiguous and incomplete. This is a fact of life for beginners and old-timers alike. The way to cope with bad documentation is to perform an experiment. Writing a short C program to see how a feature actually works is more productive and less frustrating than guessing what a cryptic description in a manual really means.

Tackle such problems one at a time. It is much easier to understand how a feature of C or the operating system works if you try it out in a controlled environment. Writing a sizeable program filled with unverified assumptions about such features makes testing unnecessarily difficult.

Learn by Doing

Do not waste too much time at first studying C. Learn a little and plunge in. Start by reading a C program for general understanding of what it does. Then think of a small improvement you would like to make. You should be able to find enhancements that require adding fewer than ten lines to the program. Concentrate on understanding how your change will affect the program—what has to be changed and how you can accomplish the change using C.

Learn C as you need it. Develop a small working vocabulary of C features, and expand it as needed. You can treat much of C as material to be looked up when you need it, just as you would unfamiliar words.

Copy Techniques from Existing Programs

When you want to do something new, look through this book for examples that do something similar to what you want. After you copy a technique several times, you learn it without effort.

1

A Quick Tour through C

This chapter shows what C programs look like. The short programs shown do not perform useful functions, but they illustrate C's basic features. The book is not a tutorial on C, but this chapter provides a foundation for later chapters. Vocabulary and concepts needed in the rest of the book are also discussed here. More advanced features of C are discussed in later chapters.

There is a lot of similarity between different high-level computer languages. If you are familiar with BASIC, COBOL, PL/1, Pascal, or FORTRAN, you should be able to recognize the purpose of the features introduced and to relate them to the corresponding features in the language you know. If you have no previous experience with C, one of the primers on C listed in Appendix D might make learning the language easier. If you are familiar with C, this chapter can serve as a review. You may also be familiar with the terms and concepts introduced, but the chapter explains how the book uses them.

1.1 HELLO Program: The Structure of C

☐ The first program is very simple; it displays

. hello, world

on the screen. (The program is not an original composition. I took it from Kernighan and Ritchie [1978], hereafter referred to as K & R.) It serves to illustrate the basic structure of a C program and how to convert it into an executable program.

Figure 1.1 lists the program. Line 1 tells the compiler to use the contents of a file named stdio.h as additional input to the compilation. The file stdio.h is normally provided with the compiler product. For now, we consider it as magic we recite in each C program.

Figure 1.1 hello.c

```
1    #include "stdio.h"
2
3    main()
4    {
5      printf("hello,") ;
6      printf(" world") ;
7    }
```

Lines 3 to 7 define a *function* named main. Line 3 establishes the function's name, and lines 4 to 7 describe what it does. This general format is followed for all C functions:

```
name(. . .)
  . . .
  {
  what it does
  }
```

As the ellipses indicate, there may be more text that we have not illustrated or described. C programs are composed of function definitions. Each definition describes what happens when we *call* that function. When we execute the HELLO program, we call the main function. In turn, it may call other functions.

The what-it-does part of a function consists of one or more *statements* (if the function does not do anything, there would be no statements). Lines 5 and 6 in the HELLO program are such statements. Line 5 calls a function named printf. printf displays the message on the screen. When it finishes, it *returns* to the point where it was called. When we call printf, we specify what it is to display. In line 6 we call printf again with a different message. What printf does depends on the information we provide it. This information is called *parameters*, or *arguments*.

The printf function is supplied in the standard C library; we do not have to write it. printf's use should be documented in your C compiler manual. With this documentation, we can use printf without seeing how it is implemented.

The statements illustrated in Figure 1.1 have the form

```
function-name(. . .) ;
```

Later programs show other forms of statements and relate the statements shown here to a more general form.

The arguments we use in lines 5 and 6 are *character string constants*. The format of such a character string constant is

```
"printable characters"
```

Compiling and Executing the HELLO Program

Figures 1.2a–d illustrate the process of preparing the HELLO program on an IBM PC using the Lattice C compiler. While the details depend on the compiler product you use, similar steps for editing, compiling, linking, and executing the programs are followed.

First we type in the C program using a text editor (or a word processor). When we finish typing the program, we store the text entered in a file. Figure 1.2a shows the editing process using the EDLIN editor provided with PC-DOS. EDLIN is used in the illustration since everyone using PC-DOS has it. Any text editor can be used as long as it produces files of ASCII characters without any special formatting information. We refer to the file created as a *source file* since it is the source for the compilation step.

The compiler reads the source file and translates the C program into instructions and data the IBM PC can execute. Figure 1.2b shows the compile process. Typing lc runs the lc.bat batch file that executes two programs, lc1 and lc2. Some C compilers consist of four separate programs, but the overall result in any case is to produce executable instructions and data at the end. By convention, C source files are normally named with a file extension of .c. Some compilers require this naming scheme. The file produced by the compiler is called an *object file*.

The compile step translated the source file into executable form, but there is another step before the program can be executed. The program that we wrote is not complete because it uses the printf library function. The linking step combines our object file with any necessary functions to produce a complete program that is ready to execute. The program is stored in a *run file* named hello.exe (if your compiler package includes a special linker, it may name the run file differently.)

Figure 1.2c shows the linking step. A special object file named cs.obj, supplied with the Lattice C compiler, sets up the environment expected by C functions; it is always the first object file specified in the link command. The last name on the line specifies that the lcs.lib library is to be searched for any library function that hello.obj requires.

Now we are ready to execute the program. Type the name of the program's run file to execute it. Figure 1.2d shows execution of the HELLO program. Note that we need not type the complete file name—the .exe extension is assumed. When we execute hello.exe, we are calling the main function. C expects to find a function named main in every program; when we named our function main, we were saying to the C compiler, "When you execute the program, begin here."

Figure 1.2   hello.fig

```
 1
 2                      Figure 1.2 - Creating and Executing Hello
 3
 4      Figure 1.2a - Using an Editor
 5
 6      D>edlin hello.c
 7      New file
 8      *i
 9          1:*#include "stdio.h"
10          2:*
11          3:*main()
12          4:* {
13          5:*   printf("hello,") ;
14          6:*   printf(" world") ;
15          7:* }
16          8:*^C
17      *e
18
19      D>
20
21      Figure 1.2b - Compiling the Program
22
23      D>lc hello
24
25      D>LC1 hello
26      Lattice C Compiler (Phase 1) V2.00
27      Copyright (C) 1982 by Lattice, Inc.
28
29      D>LC2 hello
30      Lattice C Compiler (Phase 1) V2.00
31      Copyright (C) 1982 by Lattice, Inc.
32      Module size P=0017 D=000E
33
34      Figure 1.2c - Linking the Program
35
36      D>link cs hello , hello , nul , lcs
37
38      IBM Personal Computer Linker
39      Version 2.00 (C) Copyright IBM Corp 1981, 1982, 1983
40
41      D>
42
43      Figure 1.2d - Executing the Program
44
45      D>hello
46      hello, world
47      D>
```

1.2 SUM OF SQUARES Program: Variables, Arithmetic, and Loops

□   The next C program, shown in Figure 1.3a, displays a table of the sum of squares for the numbers from 1 through 11. It illustrates comments, data variables, arithmetic, and some C statement types. Figure 1.3b lists a sample output from this program.

   Line 1 in Figure 1.3a is a comment; it is ignored by the compiler. In C, comments begin with /* characters and end with */ characters. We place such a comment at the beginning of each file with the name of the file and a few words about its purpose. When the source file is listed, the comment identifies what we are listing.

   As in the HELLO program, line 2 brings the stdio.h file into the compilation.

Figure 1.3a   c:sumsq.c

```
 1    /* sumsq.c - print sum of squares table */
 2    #include "stdio.h"
 3
 4    main()
 5     {
 6        int i ;
 7        int sum ;
 8
 9        sum = 0 ;
10        i = 0 ;
11        while( i < 11 )
12          { i = i + 1 ;
13            sum = sum + i*i ;
14            printf(" %d   %d \n",i,sum) ;
15          }
16     }
```

Figure 1.3b   c:sumsq.fig

```
 1    D>sumsq
 2     1   1
 3     2   5
 4     3   14
 5     4   30
 6     5   55
 7     6   91
 8     7   140
 9     8   204
10     9   285
11    10   385
12    11   506
13
14    D>
```

It is a good idea to include this file unless you know that nothing in it is needed in the source file.

Lines 6 and 7 declare *variables* named i and sum. Such *declarations* serve two purposes: (1) They define the variable names and associate them with a data type (here, integer), and (2) they allocate space to store the variable's value. Unlike BASIC and FORTRAN, C expects explicit declarations for data variables. Variable declarations have the following format:

```
data-type    variable-name ;
```

Lines 9 and 10 assign the value zero to i and sum. Note that each *assignment statement* ends with a semicolon. Line 13 has another assignment statement in which the *arithmetic operators*, + and *, are used. In addition to the addition (+) and multiplication (*) operators, C supports subtraction (−) and division (/) operators. All these operators are *binary operators*. They use two *operands*, one in front of the operator and one after it:

```
operand   binary-operator   operand
```

C also has *unary operators* that use a single operand. The unary minus (−) is common to many other languages; unary minus gives the negative of its operand. The following examples show the general format and a use of the unary minus:

```
unary-operator   operand

    − i                    (a unary minus)
```

Since the same operator is used for subtracting and the unary minus, C has a rule for distinguishing these uses. If the − operator has an expression on either side, it is a binary subtraction operator. If not, it is a unary minus.

The format of an assignment statement is

```
where-to-put-it  =  a-value-to-store ;
```

The value to store is an *expression*. Expressions can be single variables or constants or they can involve several operators as in line 13. In our examples we put the expression into a variable. But the where-to-put-it part of the statement could also be an expression with several operators. All that C requires is that the left side define an *address* at which we can store the value.

Lines 11 to 15 are a while statement. It means

Keep executing lines 12 to 15 as long as the value of the variable i is less than 11.

As this explanation suggests, the < operator compares what is on its left to what is on its right. The result—true or false—will be used to control program execution. C provides the usual set of comparison operators:

```
a <    b      True if a is less than b
a < = b       True if a is less than or equal to b
a >    b      True if a is greater than b
a > = b       True if a is greater than or equal to b
a = = b       True if a is equal to b
a !  = b      True if a is not equal to b
```

The format of a while statement is

```
while( condition to be tested )
      statement to be repeated
```

Since we wanted the three statements on lines 12 to 14 to be repeated, we enclosed them in brackets to make a *compound statement*. The entire compound statement is repeated while the condition is true.

Line 14 calls the printf function used in the HELLO program. This time we pass three arguments:

1. A string of characters. The % characters tell printf that a format for data to be printed follows. The d character specifies that an integer value is to be printed in decimal notation. The number is converted into a series of characters, and printf goes back to scanning the character string. Finding the second %d specification, printf looks for a third argument. This argument is converted into a series of characters, and scanning of the character string continues. Since no more % characters are found, the rest of the string is printed, and printf returns.
2. The value of variable i.
3. The value of the variable sum.

We used one argument in the HELLO program and three here. How did printf understand our intentions? The two %d specifications in the string told printf to look for and output two extra arguments.

Line 14 illustrates another format for a statement:

```
function-name(. . .) ;
```

In fact, we can make a C statement with any expression:

```
expression ;
```

The assignments on lines 9 and 10 and the function call on line 14 are examples of C expressions. While C allows assignments and function calls inside more complicated expressions, we keep our uses simple for readability.

The character string in line 14 includes something else new: \n. Some characters we need to output have a special meaning to the C compiler and cannot be used in the string directly. The newline character is one such *control* character. C recognizes a special notation for that character. The backslash character, \, signals that the next character, n, will identify a control character. When we send the newline character out, it causes subsequent output to start on a new line.

1.3 WEATHER Program: Console Input, for Statements, Variable Addresses, and Symbolic Constants

□ The next program (Figure 1.4a) accepts a week's worth of daily temperatures and calculates the average temperature for the week. It also counts the number of days when the temperature was below freezing. A sample run is shown in Figure 1.4b.

The WEATHER program uses several new features of C: the scanf function is used to collect keyboard input; a for statement is used to provide a program loop;

Figure 1.4a   weather.c

```
1    /* weather.c - calculate average temp. and # cold days */
2    #include "stdio.h"
3
4    #define FREEZE    32    /* freezing temperature  */
5
6    main()
7     {
8        int i , temp , ncold ;
9        float sum ;
10
11       printf(" enter temperatures for the week \n");
12       ncold = 0 ;
13       sum = 0 ;
14       for(i=0 ; i < 7 ; i=i+1 )
15         { scanf("%d",&temp) ;
16           sum = sum + temp ;
17           if( temp < FREEZE )
18               ncold = ncold + 1 ;
19         }
20
21       printf(" average temperature was %3.1f \n", sum / 7.0 ) ;
22       printf(" %d days below freezing \n", ncold);
23     }
24
25
26
27
```

Figure 1.4b   weather.fig

```
1    D>weather
2     enter temperatures for the week
3     15 20 32 40 65 72 55
4     average temperature was 42.7
5     2 days below freezing
6
7    D>
```

the address of a variable is passed as an argument; and a symbolic name is defined for a numeric constant.

Line 4 defines the word **FREEZE** as the number 32. The rest of the program will refer to **FREEZE** instead of using the number 32. If we wanted to convert the program to use centigrade temperatures, we would change line 4, leaving the rest of the program unchanged. Although this point is not important for our small example, defining names for numeric constants is a good practice for real programs since a subsequent numeric change will require altering only one line, its definition. Note that there is no semicolon in line 4. The #define statement is not an assignment statement; it means from now on replace the word **FREEZE** by what is on the rest of this line (32).

Line 9 declares sum as a floating point variable. C relies on explicit declarations to identify the type of data to be stored in a variable. In contrast, BASIC expects integer variable names to end in %, while string variable names have $ as the last character.

Lines 14 to 19 show a for *statement.* Its format is

for(do-first ; test-condition ; do-every-time)
    repeat-this-statement

It is a shorthand equivalent of this sequence using the while statement:

do-first ;
while(test-condition)
  { repeat-this-statement
    do-every-time ;
  }

In this case the for statement repeats lines 15 to 19 for i = 0,1,2. . .7. While C allows any expressions in the for statement, the programs in this book have a simple form:

for(variable = starting value ; variable < final value ;
    variable = variable + 1)
    statement

(We use other comparison operators and add or subtract values other than 1.) This use of C's for statement is much like the for statement in BASIC or Pascal.

Line 15 accepts a temperature value from the keyboard. The scanf function works much like printf but is used for input rather than output. The first argument tells scanf how to interpret characters typed at the keyboard. Subsequent arguments tell scanf where to put the data it has collected from the keyboard. When we pass arguments to a called function, we are passing values, not the location where a variable is stored. We use the & operator to give the *address* of the variable temperature. We pass this address to scanf so scanf can store a value there.

Like printf, scanf is a library function provided with the C compiler. However, the C compiler knows nothing about the kinds of arguments that scanf expects. You must remember that printf requires data values as arguments while scanf needs addresses.

printf and scanf are console input/output (I/O) functions. They are intended to communicate with the keyboard and screen of the PC. They perform the same kinds of functions that PRINT and INPUT do in BASIC.

Lines 17 and 18 contain an if statement. Line 17 tests the temperature value just entered to see if it is below freezing. Line 18 is executed only if the condition is true.

Line 16 shows arithmetic with mixed data types: integer and floating point. C has fixed rules for handling arithmetic on mixed data types. You can force conversions of data in cases where the action that C would take is unsatisfactory.

Line 14 uses the integer constant 7 as the limit on the execution of the for loop. In line 21 the floating point constant 7.0 is used to compute the average temperature. While we could have used an integer constant 7 in line 21 and relied on C to convert 7 to a floating point value, it was clearer to choose the right data type ourselves.

Line 21 shows another format for outputting numbers. The %3.1f description says that a floating point number is being supplied as an argument and that it is to be displayed with a decimal point. Three digits are to be printed, then the decimal point and one fraction digit. printf rounds the number to one decimal place before displaying it.

1.4 SORTNUM Program: Arrays, Function Return Values, and Pointers

□   The next program, shown in Figure 1.5a, accepts a list of numbers from the keyboard, sorts them in ascending order, and displays them in this sorted order. The program can sort up to 100 numbers. We signal the end of the input by typing a nonnumeric character instead of a number. Figure 1.5b gives an example of running the program. The program shows several new features: arrays, function return values, and pointers to variables.

Line 7 in Figure 1.5a declares an array of integers. It allocates space for 100

Figure 1.5a   c:sortnum.c

```
 1     /* sortnum.c - sort input numbers */
 2     #include "stdio.h"
 3
 4     main()
 5      {
 6        int i , n , t ;
 7        int a[100] ;
 8
 9        printf(" enter numbers - (type q to stop)");
10        n=0 ;
11        while( scanf("%d",&t) != 0 )
12         { a[n] = t ;
13           n = n + 1 ;
14         }
15
16        sortn(a,n) ;
17
18        for(i=0 ; i < n ; i=i+1 )
19          { printf(" %d",a[i] ) ; }
20      }
21
22
23     sortn(x,nx)        /* put an array of ints into ascending order */
24      int x[] ;         /* the array */
25      int nx ;          /* count of items to sort */
26      {
27        int i , j , pick ;
28
29        for(i=0 ; i < (nx-1) ; i=i+1 )
30          {                     /* find the smallest remaining number */
31            pick = i ;
32            for(j=i+1 ; j < nx ; j=j+1 )
33              { if( x[j] < x[pick] )
34                   pick = j ;/* element x[pick] is smallest so far */
35              }
36            swap( & x[pick] , & x[i] ) ; /* exchange - smallest first */
37          }
38      }
39
40     int swap(p1,p2)           /* swap two numbers */
41      int *p1 ;                /* points to first number */
42      int *p2 ;                /* points to second number */
43      {
44        int temp ;
45
46        temp = *p1 ;
47        *p1 = *p2 ;
48        *p2 = temp ;
49      }
50
```

Figure 1.5b   sortnum.fig

```
1     D>sortnum
2      enter numbers - (type q to stop) 4 6 5 3 2 1 q
3       1 2 3 4 5 6
4      D>
```

integers with indexes from 0 to 99. It is up to us to be sure that we do not refer to any index outside this range. C does not provide any checking for us. Lines 12 and 19 demonstrate how we refer to an element of the array.

Lines 9 to 14 accept input from the keyboard. When the scanf function is called, it *returns* a value: the number of items that were successfully received. The program accepts input until scanf fails to find a number. (scanf is looking for a number; it stops looking when a q or other nonnumeric character is found.)

Line 16 calls a function named sortn. As arguments, we supply the array and the count of numbers read into the array. Lines 23 to 38 define the sortn function. Lines 24 and 25 define the types of arguments that sortn will expect. These declarations are similar to the variable declarations on lines 6 and 7. The array declaration differs in that we need not describe the size of the array passed to sortn; any size array of integers can be used successfully. C treats array arguments differently from ordinary variables. It passes the location of the array, not the value of all its elements.

The numbers are sorted by selection. First, the smallest number is found and placed first. Then the next smallest is selected from what remains and placed second. This process is repeated until only one element of the array remains unselected. Lines 29 to 37 implement this algorithm. Two for loops are used, one nested inside the other. There is nothing special here; the inner for statement is just one of the statements inside the braces marking the body of the outer for statement.

At each step when the smallest remaining number has been selected, the swap function is called to exchange it with the first number in the unsorted area. We pass the addresses of the array elements to be swapped. As in the WEATHER program, we use the address operator & to get these addresses.

In the swap function, lines 41 and 42 define the arguments representing the locations of the numbers to be swapped. The asterisk describes p1 and p2 as pointing to integers rather than being integers. When we refer to the locations of the variables, we also use an asterisk before the pointer argument. We often choose names beginning with *p* for pointers to remind us what they are. Here is an English translation of line 47:

```
*p1 = *p2 ;
```

Take the value of the location pointed to by p2, and store it at the location pointed to by p1.

We will see other uses of pointers later, but the basic lesson is that C allows us to work with addresses of variables as easily as with their values.

1.5 SENTENCE Program: File I/O, Characters, and I/O Redirection

□   Figure 1.6a shows a program that counts the number of sentences in a file. It simply counts the number of times that a period, question mark, or exclamation point occurs. While this may be too simple to be really useful, it provides a first look at

Figure 1.6a   c:sentence.c

```
1     /* sentence.c - count sentences */
2     #include "stdio.h"
3
4     int ns ;
5
6     main()
7       {
8         int c ;
9
10        ns = 0 ;
11                              /* get each character and check it */
12        c = getchar() ;
13        while( c != EOF )
14          { check_end(c) ;
15            c = getchar() ;
16          }
17
18        printf(" %d sentences",ns) ;
19      }
20
21
22    int check_end(ch)     /* check for end-of-sentence char. */
23     int ch ;             /* char to check */
24     {
25       if(   (ch == '.')
26          || (ch == '?')
27          || (ch == '!') )
28             ns = ns + 1 ;
29     }
30
31
32
```

file I/O and character constants. Figure 1.6b shows a sample file and the result of using it.

The program relies on I/O redirection to provide input from a disk file rather than from the keyboard. We examine how it is executed after looking at the program. The overall logic of the program is quite simple. The program gets the first character from the file and checks it to see if it is an end-of-sentence character. If so, it adds one to the count. These two steps are repeated until no more characters remain in the file.

Figure 1.6b   sentence.fig

```
1     D>type test
2     I write short sentences.  I like them.  Do you?
3     I hope you agree!
4
5     D>sentence <test
6      4 sentences
7     D>
```

We use the getchar library function to fetch characters from a file one by one. Like printf and scanf, getchar is provided in the standard C library. It returns the next character in the file each time it is called. getchar needs no arguments passed to it so the function call has the parentheses but no arguments inside.

When no more characters remain, getchar returns a special value, EOF (for end-of-file). This value is normally defined in the stdio.h file provided with the compiler. When getchar returns a character, the value will be between 0 and 255. The EOF value is guaranteed to be different from any of these values (it is often −1). While the size of an integer variable varies for different C compilers, it is always large enough to make EOF distinct from all characters returned by get-char.

Because getchar returns an integer value, we declare the variable c as an integer, not a character. Had we declared it as a character, the EOF value could not be kept distinct from all possible character values. C allows us to look at characters as numeric values and provides automatic conversion of characters to integer values.

Lines 22 to 29 define the function check_end. This function checks the character just read to see if it is an end-of-sentence character. If so, it adds one to the count of sentences found. The if statement used makes several comparisons. The || operator means *or*. The statement on line 28 is executed if the character is a period, question mark, or explanation mark. C also provides an operator meaning *and*: the && operator. We used parentheses around each comparison in lines 25 to 27. C has rules to specify the order of evaluation of several operators in a single expression, but we can control the order of evaluation by enclosing parts of the whole expression in parentheses.

The count of sentences ns is declared outside any function. This allows it to be used in both main and check_end without passing it as a parameter.

The comparisons in lines 25 to 27 use *character constants* for the period, question mark, and exclamation characters. Character constants are written with a single quotation mark before and after the character. We use character constants for single characters and string constants where a series of one or more characters is needed. Section 1.6 discusses the way C represents each kind of constant.

Running Sentence: I/O Redirection

The getchar function is a console I/O function like printf and scanf. DOS 2.0 provides a way to substitute a file for keyboard input. When we execute the SENTENCE program, we follow the program's name with the < character and the name of a file to be used as input. Figure 1.6b illustrates this feature.

C provides another library function, putchar, to output a single character. Its output is normally displayed on the screen but can be redirected to a file. The following program fragment outputs letters of the alphabet; if we execute it with > afile following the program name, the output is placed in a file named afile:

```
...
main( )
  {
   int c ;
   for (c = 'a' ; c < = 'z' ; c = c + 1)
     { putchar(c) ; }
  }
```

Earlier versions of PC-DOS (1.0 and 1.1) did not provide this redirection capability, but most C compilers implemented it independent of DOS. When DOS 2.0 first appeared, the peculiar implementation of redirection in DOS caused program crashes. By now, most C compiler vendors have worked around the shortcomings of the DOS implementation. If your system crashes when you execute this program, check with your compiler vendor about problems with DOS 2.0 I/O redirection.

1.6 REVERSE Program: Character Arrays and Strings, Separate Compilation

□   The program shown in Figure 1.7a tests a phrase to see if it is a palindrome (the same read forward and backward). If the phrase is a palindrome, the program says so, and if not, it prints the reverse of the phrase. REVERSE accepts an entire line of input as the phrase to be tested.

The program demonstrates character arrays and the conventions that C uses for strings. Several library functions for string handling are provided. The program is composed of two source files and provides an example of separate compilation.

Lines 6 and 7 of Figure 1.7a declare two arrays of characters. They store the phrase to be tested and its reverse. The declaration is like that we saw in the SORT-NUM program, but here the types of data are **char** instead of **int**.

Line 9 prompts for a phrase, and line 10 calls the function getstr to collect the phrase from the keyboard. getstr is not defined in the **reverse.c** file, and it is not in the C standard library; it is defined in a separate source file.

There are several reasons for placing the getstr function in a separate source file:

1. getstr can be used in other programs. Collecting a line of keyboard input and storing it in character string form is a general function that may be useful in many programs. If it is placed in a separate source file, it can be used as easily as standard library functions.

2. It is easier to edit and compile small source files. Packaging programs in several small 50-to-100-line source files keeps editing and compilation times down to 30 to 45 seconds.

Figure 1.7a   c:reverse.c

```
 1    /* reverse.c - checks a phrase to see if it is a palindrome */
 2    #include "stdio.h"
 3
 4    main()
 5     {
 6        char phrase[81] ;
 7        char rev_phrase[81] ;
 8
 9        printf("type a phrase : \n");/* prompt for phrase from keybd */
10        getstr(phrase,80) ;            /* and get it */
11
12        do_reverse(phrase,rev_phrase) ; /* construct reversed phrase */
13        if( strcmp(phrase,rev_phrase) == 0 ) /* compare original */
14            printf(" ** palindrome ** ");
15        else printf(" reverse = %s",rev_phrase) ;
16     }
17
18
19    int do_reverse(s1,s2)    /* reverse a string */
20     char s1[] ;              /* the string to be reversed */
21     char s2[] ;              /* place its reverse here */
22     {
23        int i , j ;
24                          /* copy characters starting at end of s1 */
25        i= 0 ;
26        j = strlen(s1) - 1 ; /* find index of last character in s1 */
27        while( j >= 0 )
28          { s2[i] = s1[j] ;
29            i = i + 1 ;
30            j = j - 1 ;
31          }
32        s2[i] = 0 ;              /* mark end of string */
33     }
34
```

3. Testing small single-purpose modules is much easier and more effective than testing whole programs. Modifying programs is also easier when they are composed of small single-purpose modules.

The phrase that **getstr** accepts from the keyboard will be stored in the character array word in the string format C supports. The characters in the word are stored consecutively with a character with the value zero at the end. We have been using string constants in previous programs (HELLO, for example). The C compiler allocates space for them and stores them in this same format. For example, the HELLO string would be stored as

Position	0	1	2	3	4	5	6
Character value	h	e	l	l	o	,	\0

The notation \0 represents a zero (or null) value just as \n represented a newline control character.

The do_reverse function on lines 19 to 33 reverses the word, placing the result into the array provided. It uses the library function, strlen, for string length, to find the end of the string. strlen returns the number of characters in the string, not counting the null value at the end. Since C arrays are indexed starting at zero, a string having n characters has the last character at index n−1.

When all the characters in the string have been copied, the value zero is stored to mark the end of the string. The character constant '\0' could have been used also.

When the reverse of the word has been constructed, line 13 uses the library function strcmp to compare the word and its reverse. C does not support assignments or comparisons on strings, but the library does provide functions to perform several string operations.

Figure 1.7b shows the source file containing the getstr function. It expects two arguments: a character array to hold the word entered and a maximum length to allow. getstr accepts characters from the keyboard using getchar until it receives a newline character or until the array is filled. It also stops if the end of file is reached.

Separate Compilation

Figure 1.7c shows how we build the REVERSE program from two source files. First, each source file is compiled. Then the linker program is run with both object files as inputs. This produces a single executable file. While it is hardly necessary in our example, most useful programs should be split into several source files.

Figure 1.7b   c:getstr.c

```
1    /* getstr.c - get a line of input from keyboard */
2    #include "stdio.h"
3
4    int getstr(s,maxs)          /* get a line of input */
5     char s[] ;                 /* place the input here in string form */
6     int maxs ;                 /* limit on characters allowed */
7     {                          /* returns string length */
8       int i , c ;
9
10      i=0 ;
11      c = getchar() ;                  /* get first character */
12                      /* repeat til full, EOF or end-of-line */
13      while( (i < maxs) && (c != '\n') && ( c != EOF) )
14        { s[i] = c ;                   /* place char in string */
15          i = i + 1 ;                  /* advance char count   */
16          c = getchar() ;              /* and get another character */
17        }
18      s[i] = '\0' ;
19      return( i ) ;                    /* return count of characters */
20    }
```

Figure 1.7c   c:reverse.fig

```
 1
 2
 3
 4     D>lc reverse
 5
 6     D>LC1 reverse
 7     Lattice C Compiler (Phase 1) V2.00
 8     Copyright (C) 1982 by Lattice, Inc.
 9
10     D>LC2 reverse
11     Lattice C Compiler (Phase 2) V2.00
12     Copyright (C) 1982 by Lattice, Inc.
13     Module size P=00A7 D=0031
14
15
16     D>lc getstr
17
18     D>LC1 getstr
19     Lattice C Compiler (Phase 2) V2.00
20     Copyright (C) 1982 by Lattice, Inc.
21
22     D>LC2 getstr
23     Lattice C Compiler (Phase 2) V2.00
24     Copyright (C) 1982 by Lattice, Inc.
25     Module size P=00A7 D=0000
26
27
28
29     D>link cs reverse getstr , reverse , nul , lcs
30
31     IBM Personal Computer Linker
32     Version 2.00 (C) Copyright IBM Corp 1981, 1982, 1983
33
34     D>
35
36
37     D>reverse
38     type a phrase :
39     ana
40      ** palindrome **
41     D>
42
43     D>reverse
44     type a phrase :
45     anvil
46      reverse = livna
47     D>
```

1.7   CURVE Program: Defining Data Types, Using Structures

□   The program in Figure 1.8a grades student work on the curve. It assigns a passing grade to the top 70 percent of the class and fails the bottom 30 percent. It accepts a list of students' names and numerical grades from the keyboard. To keep the pro-

Figure 1.8a   c:curve.c

```
1    /* curve.c - assigns pass/fail grades on a curve system */
2    #include "stdio.h"
3
4    typedef struct           /* definition of student data t*/
5     { char name[30] ;
6       int grade ;
7     } STUDENT ;
8
9    main()
10    {
11       STUDENT class[400] ; /* student data for entire class */
12       int ns ;             /* count of students in the class */
13                /* collect list of students and number grades */
14       int i , cutoff ;
15
16       printf(" number of students: \n");
17       scanf("%d",&ns) ;
18       printf("enter name and grade for each student \n");
19       for( i=0 ; i < ns ; i=i+1 )
20         { scanf("%s %d", class[i].name, & class[i].grade ); }
21
22       sortclass(class,ns) ;
23       cutoff = (ns * 7) / 10  - 1 ;
24       printf("\n");
25       for( i=0 ; i < ns ; i=i+1 )
26         { printf("%-6s %3d", class[i].name, class[i].grade) ;
27           if( i <= cutoff )
28                 printf(" pass \n");
29           else printf(" fail \n");
30         }
31    }
32
33    sortclass(st,nst)        /* sort by numeric grade */
34     STUDENT st[] ;          /* array of student data structures */
35     int     nst ;           /* number of students */
36     {
37       int i , j , pick ;
38
39       for(i=0 ; i < (nst-1) ; i=i+1 )
40         { pick = i ;
41           for(j=i+1 ; j < nst ; j=j+1 )
42             { if( st[j].grade > st[pick].grade )
43                 pick = j ;
44             }
45           swap(& st[i] , & st[pick] ) ;
46         }
47     }
48
49    swap(ps1,ps2)
50     STUDENT *ps1 ;
51     STUDENT *ps2 ;
52     {
53       STUDENT temp ;
54
55       strcpy(temp.name, ps1->name ) ; temp.grade = ps1->grade ;
56       strcpy(ps1->name,ps2->name) ; ps1->grade = ps2->grade ;
57       strcpy(ps2->name,temp.name) ; ps2->grade = temp.grade ;
58     }
```

gram simple, we use single-word names without embedded blanks. It prints out the students' names and a pass/fail grade. The names are ordered by numerical grade—highest first. Figure 1.8b shows a sample run.

The program is similar to the SORTNUM program. First, the names and numerical grades are accepted. Then the names and grades are sorted. The algorithm used is the same one used in the SORTNUM program. Then the sorted list is printed. The word **pass** or **fail** is printed after each name. We use a sorting function much like that in the SORTNUM program; instead of sorting numbers it will sort a list of names and grades.

The program illustrates two new ideas about C: (1) We can define new data types, and (2) we can declare structures composed of several *members* of different types. Lines 4 to 7 in Figure 1.8a define a new data type called **STUDENT**. It is like **int** or **char** data type, but we defined it. This data type has two members: an array of characters for the student's name and an integer variable to hold the number grade. This is an example of a *structure*. A structure is like an array because it may contain more than one member; unlike an array the members may be of different data types, and each has a separate name.

Line 11 declares an array named **class** to hold data for up to 400 students. Each element of the array is a **STUDENT** data structure. Line 12 declares an integer, **ns**, that will record a count of students in the class.

Line 26 shows how the members of the **STUDENT** data structure are referenced. The class variable is an array; when we refer to one student's data, we use an index,

    class[i]

In line 20 we call **scanf** with the addresses of the members of the **STUDENT** structure.

Figure 1.8b   curve.fig

```
 1
 2    D>curve
 3     number of students:
 4    5
 5    enter name and grade for each student
 6    Fred 35
 7    Mary 76
 8    Joe   0
 9    Bill 98
10    Sam  40
11
12    Bill    98 pass
13    Mary    76 pass
14    Sam     40 pass
15    Fred    35 fail
16    Joe      0 fail
17
18    D>
```

The sortclass function in lines 33 to 47 is quite similar to the sort function in the SORTNUM program. The syntax for referencing structures differs from that for integers, but most of the function is unchanged. Chapter 5 develops a sort function that works on all kinds of data. Line 45 passes the addresses of the two array elements that are to be swapped. Note that we pass the address of the whole **student** data; we want to exchange both the student name and the number grade.

The swap function works just like that in the SORTNUM program. The pointers ps1 and ps2 are declared to point to data of the **STUDENT** type instead of to **int** data. The temporary variable is declared to be of type **STUDENT** also. Since most C compilers do not support assignments of whole structures, swap exchanges each member individually. C allows assignments to single variables only; entire structures and arrays cannot appear in assignments. The string copy library function, strcpy, is used to exchange the student name strings. Lines 55 to 57 show the C notation for using pointers to refer to structure members:

pointer->member name

In contrast, the notation,

variable.member name

is used when the variable is declared to be of the structured type.

Line 23 calculates a pass/fail cutoff point; 70 percent of the students pass. Division of integers truncates the result so that the cutoff point is actually below 70 percent unless the class size is divisible by 10.

Note that most C compilers arrange the C program in the PC's memory without help from the programmer. Lattice C and Microsoft C versions 1.0 through 2.0 defined a stack size parameter (_stack) that divides memory between local variables (on the stack) and static and dynamically allocated data. For versions before 2.10, the default value of this parameter is normally ignored. Starting with version 2.10, Lattice C arranges memory so that the default setting will not work whenever a significant amount of local storage is allocated. (By the time you read this, current versions of Lattice C may again operate in a sensible fashion.) The stack size can be specified on the command line when the program is executed as follows:

A>curve = 30000

This value, 30,000 bytes, is appropriate for many of the programs in this book but not all. Some experimentation may be required.

1.8 NOTABS Program: Switch, Break Statements, and More Loops

□ The NOTABS program in Figure 1.9a converts tab characters into strings of space characters. All other input characters are simply output using the putchar library function discussed in Section 1.5. NOTABS keeps track of the column position where the current character would be displayed or printed. Normal characters move this position to the right by one column, and Carriage Return and Line Feed characters move the position to column one. When tab characters are encountered, NOTABS outputs enough tab characters to move the position to the next tab stop.

Figure 1.9a   c:notabs.c

```
1    /* notabs.c - turn tabs into blanks */
2    #include "stdio.h"
3
4    #define TS 8                    /* tab stop interval */
5    int col ;                       /* current column position */
6
7    main()
8      {
9        int c ;
10
11       col = 1 ;
12       while( 1 == 1 )             /* get chars from input */
13         { c = getchar() ;
14           if( c == EOF )          /* until EOF is reached */
15               break ;
16           do_it(c) ;
17         }
18     }
19
20   int do_it(ch)                   /* handle one char */
21     int ch ;                      /* the character */
22     {
23       switch( ch )                /* classify ch */
24         {
25         case '\t' :               /* tab char */
26           do
27             { putchar(' ') ;      /*    put out blanks */
28               col = col + 1 ;
29             } while( (col % TS) !=1);/* until we reach a tab stop */
30           break ;
31         case '\r' :               /* carriage return */
32         case '\n' :               /* or line feed (newline) */
33           putchar( ch ) ;         /*    output it */
34           col = 1 ;               /*    back to column 1 */
35           break ;
36         default :                 /* any other char - assume printable */
37           putchar( ch ) ;         /*    output it */
38           col = col + 1           /*    advance to next column */
39           break ;
40         }
41     }
```

NOTABS illustrates several new features: the modulus operator (%), the break and switch statements, and the do { } while loop.

The main function collects input, one character at a time, using the getchar function discussed earlier. The while loop in lines 12 to 17 stops when getchar returns an EOF value, but it is different from while loops in previous programs. The test in line 12 (1 = = 1) is always true; it never terminates the execution of lines 13 to 16. But the if statement in lines 14 to 15 checks for EOF, and when it is found, the break statement in line 15 terminates the loop.

The do_it function in lines 20 to 41 handles each input character. The switch statement in lines 23 to 40 classifies the character and performs the appropriate action. If statements evaluate an expression as true or false and select from two outcomes, the switch statement allows us to specify more than two outcomes. The format of the switch statement is

```
switch ( expression )
   {
   case value-1 :  /* start here if exp = = this value*/
   some-statements
   break ;        /* terminate the switch statement */
   case value-2 :  /* start here if exp = = this value*/
   some-more-statements
   break ;        /* terminate the switch statement */
   case value-3 :  /* start here if exp = = this value*/
   case value-4 :  /*             or this value */
   more-statements
   break ;        /* terminate the switch statement */
   . . .
   default :       /* start here if no case fits */
   more-statements
   break ;        /* terminate the switch statement */
   }
```

The value specified in each case must be an expression that the compiler can evaluate fully; expressions with constants and multiple operators may appear, but variables may not appear. The cases specify where to start executing C statements; execution will continue until the end of the switch statement or until a break statement is encountered. We use the switch statement in a rigid way: several case labels may share the same starting point (as value-3 and value-4 do), but each case must end with a break statement.

For Carriage Return or Line Feed characters (lines 31 to 35), the character is output and the current position set to column one. For any other characters (lines 36 to 39), the character is output and the current position is advanced.

Lines 25 to 30 handle the case of tab characters. The program outputs space characters and advances the column position until a tab stop is reached. At least one space character is always output. The do { } while loop statement in lines 26 to

29 repeats lines 27 and 28 until the test in line 29 fails. Unlike the while loop already discussed, this loop executes the body once before checking the test condition. The % operator in line 29 divides col by the constant TS, producing the remainder. Tab stops lie at columns 1,9,17. . .(n*8 + 1) so this test checks to see if we have reached a tab stop.

The format of the do{ } while statement is

```
do
    { statements to be repeated
    } while ( condition-to-be-tested ) ;
```

The % operator is a binary operator like the regular division operator. For integers, the division operator produces the quotient truncating any fractional part; the % operator provides the remainder. In other languages the mod operator or function performs the same function as % does in C. The following examples should make its operation clear:

```
1 % 8 is 1
7 % 4 is 3
6 % 3 is 0
```

Our example shows two uses of the break statement, but it can also be used to exit from a for statement or a do{ }while statement. The break statement always refers to the immediately enclosing while, switch, for, or do{ } while statement.

Figure 1.9b shows a sample run with input redirected to the testtabs file and output redirected to the testo file. The output file looks the same when listed but is longer because tabs have been replaced by multiple space characters.

1.9   Summary of Definitions and Concepts

☐   This chapter has introduced some definitions and concepts needed in the rest of the book. Here is a summary of those terms:

Program Preparation

C programs are created in a three-step process. First they are typed into the computer with a text editor. The *source file* produced is given a file name with a .c extension. This source file is read by the *compiler*, producing an *object file*, a translation into instructions understood by the computer being used. This object file (and perhaps others) are read along with a *library* of standard C functions by the *linker*,

Figure 1.9b   c:notabs.fig

```
 1    D>type testtabs
 2    abc
 3            def
 4    12345678901234567890123 4567890
 5    123      9012345 7
 6    1                    7
 7    12       9
 8
 9    D>notabs <testtabs >testo
10
11    D>type testo
12    abc
13            def
14    12345678901234567890123 4567890
15    123      9012345 7
16    1                    7
17    12       9
18
19    D>dir test*
20
21      Volume in drive D has no label
22      Directory of  D:\
23
24    TESTTABS          72    2-12-85   12:10p
25    TESTO             99    2-12-85   12:14p
26            2 File(s)      182272 bytes free
27
28    D>
```

producing an executable problem. This program is executed from DOS by typing the name of the executable file.

Separate Compilation

A C program can be composed of several source files. Each is compiled separately, and the object files produced are combined by the linker into an executable program.

Text Editors

C source files must contain standard ASCII characters, no special formatting characters like those used by several word processing programs. Any text editor or word processor program that produces such files can be used to enter and edit C source files.

Libraries

A library of standard functions is provided with almost all C compilers. C programs that you write can use these functions, and the linker will incorporate those needed into your executable program.

Functions

C programs are composed of *functions*. Function definitions specify what data variables will be created and used and what *statements* will be executed. A single source file may contain more than one of these functions. Functions are *called* to execute them. Executing a C program causes the function named main to be executed.

Variables and Data Types

C provides several types of data: characters, integers, and floating point, for example. Variables must be declared explicitly to tell the compiler their type. Declaring variables allocates space to hold the variable's value and makes its name and type known to the compiler.

Parameters, or Arguments

Functions may expect to be *passed* values when they are called. These *parameters*, or *arguments*, are used by the called function much as variables defined within the function would be.

Arrays and Subscripts, or Indexes

We can define arrays of variables as well as single variables. We refer to one element of the array by number using a *subscript*, or *index*.

Addresses or Pointers

We can find the location of a variable when necessary. This *address*, or *pointer*, can be passed to a function. Variables that contain such addresses can be defined as well.

Console I/O

The C library provides some library functions for input from the *console* (the keyboard and display screen). These functions are a special case of file I/O functions. Using I/O redirection, we are able to perform file input using these console I/O functions.

1.10 Reference

□ Kernighan, Brian W., and Ritchie, Dennis M. *The C Programming Language.* Englewood Cliffs, N.J.: Prentice-Hall, 1978.

2
Adapting C to Our Use

This chapter introduces more features of C and presents some useful tools. It also shows how to improve the readability and portability of C programs. Concrete examples are the basis for discussing C's features. We illustrate our points with a C program and then discuss the new features in general.

2.1 File I/O: Three Programs to Copy Files

☐ The programs in Chapter 1 performed some kind of input or output. Most performed only console I/O, but the SENTENCE program used redirection to read a file. What if we need to accept input from the keyboard and from a file too? The C standard library provides more functions for file I/O. In this section we use these functions to copy the contents of a file. Our program (CCOPY) expects the names of input and output files to be typed on the command line when the program is executed. For example, to copy the file test.in to a new file named test.out, we would type

    copya test.in test.out

in response to the DOS prompt (A>). If the input file does not exist or if the output file can not be created, the program will display a message and exit.

The C library gives us more than one way to accomplish the job, so we show three programs (Figures 2.1a, 2.1b, and 2.1c). The COPYA program in Figure 2.1a uses *buffered file I/O* library functions getc and putc for input and output. They are similar to the getchar and putchar functions used in Chapter 1.

Using getc and putc is somewhat more complicated than using getchar and putchar. Before we can perform any input or output, we must *open* the files. Then, after we finish doing input and output, we must *close* the files.

Our first job in the program is to get the file names typed on the command line following the program name. Most C compilers provide access to the characters typed on the command line (with the DOS prompt) in a standard way.

Figure 2.1a   copya.c

```
1
2     /* copya.c - copy a file with getc/putc    */
3     #include "stdio.h"
4
5     main(argc,argv)
6       int argc ;
7       char *argv[] ;
8       {
9           FILE  *in ,
10                 *out ;
11          int c ;
12          long n ;
13
14          if( argc < 3 )
15            { printf(" USAGE - copy2 input-file output-file \n");
16              exit(1);
17            }
18
19          in  = fopen(argv[1],"r");
20          out = fopen(argv[2],"w");
21          if( (in == NULL) || (out ==NULL) )
22            { printf("can't open a file");
23              exit(0) ;
24            }
25
26          n = 0L ;
27          c = getc(in) ;
28          while( c != EOF )
29            { n = n + 1 ;
30              putc(c,out);
31              c = getc(in) ;
32            } ;
33          fclose(in);
34          fclose(out);
35          printf(" %ld characters copied",n) ;
36      }
```

The line is scanned and broken into words divided by spaces. Each word is stored in string format. The main function receives two parameters: a count of words found (argc) and an array of pointers to those words (argv[ ]). In the UNIX environment the first word (to which argv[0] points) is the program name; since this is not available in the MS-DOS environment, argv[0] points to a dummy value like c.

Lines 6 to 7 show how we declare these arguments. The input and output file names should be pointed to by argv[1] and argv[2]. Lines 19 and 20 pass the addresses of these names to the fopen function. The fopen function returns a value that identifies the file just opened. Subsequent file I/O function calls will present this value as one of the arguments to identify the file to which they apply. These values are pointers to a data type called FILE. Lines 9 and 10 declare two variables to hold these pointer values. The FILE data type is defined in the stdio.h file. We do not have to worry about what that definition is; we just declare *file pointers* as shown.

If the fopen function cannot open the file successfully, it returns a special value, NULL. Like FILE and EOF, NULL is normally defined in stdio.h. We can use NULL as a symbolic constant without being concerned about its definition.

Lines 27 to 32 perform the actual input and output. We use getc and putc almost the same way that we used getchar and putchar in Chapter 1. The difference is that we supply the file pointer as an argument to getc and putc.

After we finish input and output, we *close* the file using the fclose function. This tells the library functions and DOS that we have finished with these files. The library functions and DOS then perform any internal housekeeping needed to complete our I/O operations.

We count the number of characters copied with a *long* variable (n). It is declared in line 12 and used in lines 26, 29, and 35. Long variables are like integers but may be capable of storing larger number than can integers. Line 26 shows a long constant, a number followed by the letter L (or lowercase l). In line 29 we add an integer constant (1) to n. Since long numbers are potentially larger in magnitude than integers, the integer constant is first converted to the long type and then added. Lines 26 and 29 are both correct; we used one to show the form of a long constant and the other to discuss integer to long data conversions.

In line 35 we use printf to display the count of characters. The format specification (%ld) tells printf to expect a long data item rather than an integer. Long data are normally represented in memory differently from integer data. When we pass data to functions, we must be sure that the data type we pass is what the functions expect.

Copying a File with fscanf and fprintf Functions

Just as getchar and putchar had more general analogs for file I/O, the scanf and printf functions have more general forms. The fscanf and fprintf functions work like scanf and printf except that the first argument to each is a file pointer. For example, to read an integer, we would use

```
scanf("%d",&i) ;      or      fscanf(in,"%d",&i) ;
```

Figure 2.1b shows a file copy program written using these functions. Since we just want to read and write single characters, we use the %c format specification rather than %d as in previous programs. This format tells fscanf to collect one character from the file (or fprintf to output one character). We detect the end of the input file when fscanf returns a zero value. The rest of the program is just like the COPY program using getc and putc.

Like scanf and printf, fscanf and fprintf are very versatile. In practice,

Figure 2.1b   copyb.c

```
 1
 2    /* copyb.c - copy a file with fscanf/fprintf   */
 3    #include "stdio.h"
 4
 5    main(argc,argv)
 6     int argc ;
 7     char *argv[] ;
 8     {
 9         FILE   *in ,
10                *out ;
11         char c ;
12         int nr ;
13         long n ;
14
15         if( argc < 3 )
16            { printf(" USAGE - copy2 input-file output-file \n");
17              exit(1);
18            }
19
20         in  = fopen(argv[1],"r");
21         out = fopen(argv[2],"w");
22         if( (in == NULL) || (out ==NULL) )
23            { printf("can't open a file");
24              exit(0) ;
25            }
26
27         n = 0L ;
28         nr = fscanf(in,"%c",&c) ;
29         while( nr > 0 )
30            { n = n + 1 ;
31              fprintf(out,"%c",c);
32              nr = fscanf(in,"%c",&c) ;
33            } ;
34         fclose(in);
35         fclose(out);
36         printf(" %ld characters copied",n) ;
37     }
```

their use would be more appropriate in more complicated formatting tasks. Unlike getc and putc, they can interpret the data and transform them.

The file I/O functions we used in Chapter 1—getchar, putchar, scanf, and printf—are special cases of the file I/O functions just introduced. Since we use console I/O in almost all programs, the C library provides several shortcuts. The console I/O functions use file pointers just like those used in COPYA and COPYB. These file pointers—stdin for keyboard input and stdout for screen output—are defined for us. We do not have to open them before use or close them when we are finished. As a further convenience, the console functions do not require that the file pointer be passed as an argument. getchar and scanf refer to stdin, while putchar and printf refer to stdout.

Copying a File Using read and write Functions

Most C compilers provide another kind of file I/O function. Such functions provide simpler services directly based on the file I/O support provided by MS-DOS. (In the UNIX environment, their *unbuffered* file I/O functions were simply calls to operating system services. Most MS-DOS C compilers provide equivalent services even when the corresponding MS-DOS support differs from that of UNIX.)

The same sequence of function calls is required for unbuffered I/O: first files must be opened, then input and output can be performed, and finally the files are closed. Open files are identified by an integer value called a *file descriptor*. The functions used for unbuffered I/O are different from those used in Figures 2.1a and 2.1b but are parallel. The following table shows the relation of functions:

Purpose	Buffered I/O Function	Unbuffered I/O Function
Open a file	fopen	open or creat
Input data	getc or fscanf	read
Output data	putc or fprintf	write
Close a file	fclose	close

Two functions are provided for opening files: open is used when the file already exists, and creat is used to create a new file. Figure 2.1c shows the COPY program using these functions. read and write can transfer more than one byte; they are normally used to transfer hundreds or thousands of bytes. In the program we transfer 1,024 bytes at a time. (Data are stored on disks in *sectors* of 512 bytes. Operations will be somewhat faster if we transfer data in multiples of 512 bytes when it is convenient. For now, you can accept this without too much thought.) We detect the end of input data when the read function fails to read any data.

The read and write functions are simple in purpose; they transfer data between a file and a data area we specify. As arguments we provide a file descriptor identifying the file, the address of a data area, and a maximum number of bytes to transfer. The data area we provided here was an array; its address is just the name of the array. If we used a single variable or a structure as a data area, we would use the address of the operator before the name of the variable (&c, for example).

Comparing COPY Programs

Figure 2.2 shows elapsed times required to copy a single 30,000-byte file with the three COPY programs. The read/write-based COPY program is fastest, with the getc/putc version a bit slower. The fscanf/fprintf version is much slower—almost three times as long for this test.

Figure 2.1c   copyc.c

```
 1
 2    /* copyc.c - copy a file using read/write  */
 3    #include "stdio.h"
 4
 5    #define NO_FILE    (-1)
 6    #define BUF_SIZE   1024
 7    #define RD_MODE    0
 8    #define WR_MODE    0
 9
10    main(argc,argv)
11     int argc ;
12     char *argv[] ;
13     {
14        int    in ,
15               out ;
16        long n ;
17        char buffer[ BUF_SIZE ] ;
18        int nr ;
19
20        if( argc < 3 )
21          { printf(" USAGE - copy1 input-file output-file \n");
22            exit(1);
23          }
24
25        in = open(argv[1],RD_MODE) ;
26        out = creat(argv[2],WR_MODE) ;
27        if( (in == NO_FILE) || (out == NO_FILE) )
28          { printf("can't open a file");
29            exit(2) ;
30          }
31
32        n = 0L ;
33        nr = read(in,buffer,BUF_SIZE) ;
34        while( nr > 0 )
35          { n = n + nr ;
36            write(out,buffer,nr);
37            nr = read(in,buffer,BUF_SIZE) ;
38          } ;
39        close(in);
40        close(out);
41        printf(" %ld characters copied",n) ;
42     }
```

Figure 2.2   Copy program execution speeds

Program	Time to Copy 30,000 Bytes (seconds)
COPYA (getc/putc)	27
COPYB (fscanf/fprintf)	73
COPYC (read/write)	21

If this read/write version is fastest, what is the point of the other versions? Each set of file I/O functions has a different role to play:

1. The read/write version transferred 1,024 bytes of data in each operation. It is the fastest way to move such large blocks of data. If we change the program to transfer 1 byte of data at a time, it takes 297 seconds. read and write are not intended to transfer single characters efficiently.
2. The getc/putc functions are nearly as fast as read and write but give us convenient access to characters one at a time. For programs like the SENTENCE program in Chapter 1 where we need to look at characters individually, these functions give a practical compromise between execution speed and ease of writing the program.
3. The fscanf and fprintf functions are too slow for simple input and output of characters, but they are appropriate when we need to interpret a character stream as a number or a character string. Such tasks often involve a small volume of data, and the effort of writing the formatting functions is too great for the resulting improvement in speed.

We can think of these three levels of file I/O functions in terms of the grocery business:

1. read and write are like buying groceries wholesale. If you need a thousand loaves and fishes, buy them wholesale and save lots of money. For a single fish, buying wholesale is not practical. read and write deliver data by the freezerful.
2. getc and putc are like buying at a supermarket. You pay more per fish but it is a better way to get the food for tonight's dinner. getc and putc give you data in meal-sized portions.
3. fscanf and fprintf are like eating at a seafood restaurant. It is too expensive to do every night, but when you are hungry right now and do not want to cook, the restaurant is convenient. Think of fscanf and fprintf as serving up data in cooked form.

If we transfer larger amounts of data in each operation, the read and write functions are even faster. Using 8,192-byte transfers (and the binary mode discussed in the next section), COPYC requires about 6 seconds.

2.2 ASCII and Binary Files

□ As is often the case with computers, a few details defy logic but nevertheless must be understood. The C library evolved on the UNIX system, and C's functions were defined to fit well with the file I/O services provided by the UNIX operating system. These services (and conventions used by application programs in the UNIX environment) are somewhat different from those provided by MS-DOS. The means that MS-DOS C compiler libraries provide to resolve these differences is the subject of this section. We must start by identifying how UNIX and MS-DOS file-handling services differ.

UNIX keeps track of file sizes to the byte. UNIX application software and utilities let the operating system tell them when the end of data is reached. While MS-DOS can also record file sizes to the byte, some application software writes data in fixed-sized blocks with a control character (value 26 decimal, called *control-Z*) that marks the end of data. The marker and any data following it are not treated as part of the file's contents. This convention, inherited from the CP/M world, is used only for files composed of character text. These files are often called *ASCII* or *text* files. Files that contain noncharacter data may contain the control-Z value as part of the data; in such *binary* files the control-Z value is not interpreted as the end of the file's contents.

Thus, our first problem is that in the MS-DOS environment, files may be interpreted in two different ways. The choice of these interpretations depends purely on its content—neither MS-DOS nor the C library can make the choice automatically. It is up to us to supply explicit choices when we write C programs for the MS-DOS environment.

In the UNIX environment, application programs and utilities expect lines of text to be marked by a single control character (the ASCII Line Feed character), called *newline* in the UNIX and C documentation. In the MS-DOS environment, text files contain a two-character sequence (Carriage Return followed by Line Feed) to mark the end of each line of text.

To make it easy to use existing C programs, most MS-DOS C compilers provide automatic conversion between the end-of-line sequences expected by existing C programs and those normal in the MS-DOS environment. Such conversions make sense only for files composed of lines of text. As with the end-of-file convention, an explicit choice must be made by the programmer.

Most MS-DOS C compilers provide a method for dealing with this problem. They provide some means for the programmer to specify ASCII or binary modes of operation. The end-of-file and end-of-line choices are lumped into a single choice: ASCII or *binary* mode. In most cases, this choice of operating mode is made when a file is opened. Unfortunately, the means for specifying the operating mode differs for each compiler. We can write portable C programs when each compiler handles this problem differently by providing our own generalized functions in place of fopen, open, and creat. While we must rewrite these functions for each compiler, our application programs can be used unchanged.

Figures 2.3a, 2.3b, and 2.3c are *manual pages* for our functions gfopen, gopen, and gcreat. We use this style of documentation throughout the book. Our functions are used like the functions they replace, but each expects one additional argument: a number specifying ASCII or binary operation. To make programming easier or less error prone, we define symbolic constants for the mode values:

```
#define   ASC_MODE    0
#define   BIN_MODE    1
```

Figure 2.3a   gfopen description

Name

gfopen   open a file for buffered I/O–ASCII or binary

Usage

```
FILE *gfopen ( );
FILE *in;
char filename [65];
int operating_mode;
in = gfopen(filename, "r", operating_mode);
```

Function

gfopen opens a file for buffered I/O. It performs the same function as fopen. Its purpose is to provide a portable way to specify the operating mode (ASCII or binary.) If the compiler does not provide the requested mode, it returns a NULL value.

gfopen calls fopen to open the file. It returns whatever value fopen returns to it. See the documentation for the fopen function supplied with your compiler for more information.

Example

```
FILE *in;
char filename[65];
getstr (filename, 64);                          /* get the file name */
in = gfopen (filename, "r", ASC_MODE );          /* open the file */
if ( in = = NULL )
   { /* can't open the file */
     . . .
```

Notes

Symbolic constants for the ASCII and binary modes are defined in **cminor.h.**

References

Standard library function fopen.

Just as stdio.h contains definitions of symbolic constants used in connection with the standard library, our file, cminor.h, will contain definitions we develop to refine C.

This is our first example of refining C. We can add functions and definitions to make C programs easier to write and more portable. This chapter offers more refinements.

These three functions—gfopen, gopen, and gcreat—will be part of our toolkit, general purpose functions that we develop and use like C library functions.

Figure 2.3b   gopen description

Name

```
gopen        open a file for unbuffered I/O-ASCII or binary
```

Usage

```
int gopen ( ) ;
int in ;
char filename[65] ;
int fmode = 0 ;                              /* 0 = read, 1 = write , . . . */
int operating_mode;
in = gopen (filename, fmode, operating_mode) ;
```

Function

gopen opens a file for unbuffered I/O. It performs the same function as open. Its purpose is to provide a portable way to specify the operating mode (ASCII or binary). If the compiler does not provide the requested mode, it returns a NULL value.

gopen calls open to actually open the file. The first two arguments to gopen will be passed to open. gopen returns whatever value open returns to it.

See the documentation for the open function supplied with your compiler for more information. Requirements for the filename and fmode parameters should be covered there.

Example

```
int in ;
char filename[65] ;
getstr (filename, 64) ;        /* get the file name */
in = gopen (filename, 0, ASC_MODE);        /*open the file */
if ( in < 0 )
   { /* can't open the file */
      . . .
```

Notes

Symbolic constants for the ASCII and binary modes are defined in cminor.h.

References

Standard library function open.

Implementing gfopen for Several Compilers

How do we implement the gfopen function? Until we discuss implementations of gfopen, gopen, and gcreat in detail in Chapter 7, we can use it like a library function without concern for how it is implemented. To convince you that the laws of nature are not being defied, we show three samples of the gfopen function for different compilers.

Figure 2.3c gcreat description

Name

gcreat   create and open a file for unbuffered I/O
                      –ASCII or binary

Usage

```
int gcreat ( ) ;
int in ;
char filename[65] ;
int fmode = 0 ;     /* second argument to creat */
int operating_mode ;
in = gcreat (filename, fmode, operating_mode) ;
```

Function

gcreat opens a file for unbuffered I/O. It performs the same function as **creat**. Its purpose is to provide a portable way to specify the operating mode (ASCII or binary). If the compiler does not provide the requested mode, it returns a NULL value.

    gcreat calls **creat** to actually open the file. The first two arguments to **gcreat** will be passed to **creat**. **gcreat** returns whatever value **creat** returns to it.

    See the documentation on the **creat** function provided with your compiler for more information on using **creat**.

Example

```
int in ;
char filename[65] ;
getstr (filename,64) ;     /* get the file name */
in = gcreat (filename,0,ASC_MODE) ;     /* open the file */
if ( in < 0 )
  { /* can't create the file */
    . . .
```

Notes

Symbolic constants for the ASCII and binary modes are defined in **cminor.h**.

References

Standard library function **creat**.

Figure 2.4a shows an implementation of **gfopen** for the Digital Research Compiler. The library provided with that compiler has two versions of fopen— one for binary mode and one for ASCII mode. We use the value of the operating mode parameter to select the library function.

    Figure 2.4b shows the **gfopen** function for the Computer Innovations C86 compiler. Here, the library function selects the ASCII or binary mode based on an

Figure 2.4a   c:gfopen.drc

```
1    /* gfopen.c - generalized buffered file open function */
2    /*            allows either Binary or ASCII treatment */
3    #include "stdio.h"
4    #include  "cminor.h"
5
6    /* Digital Research version */
7    FILE *gfopen(fn,fmode,ft)
8     char fn[] ;
9     char fmode[] ;
10    int  ft ;
11    {
12       if( ft == BIN_MODE )
13          return( fopenb(fn,fmode) ) ;
14       else return( fopena(fn,fmode) ) ;
15    }
16    /* end of version */
17
18
```

extra character in the file mode string. We append an 'a' or 'b' value to the file mode string based on the value of the operating mode argument specified.

Figure 2.4c shows the implementation for the Lattice C compiler marketed by Lifeboat Associates and Microsoft. Here, the value of an external variable, __fmode, is checked by the fopen function to select the ASCII or binary mode when the file is opened. We save the current value of __fmode and then set it based

Figure 2.4b   c:gfopen.c86

```
1    /* gfopen.c - generalized buffered file open function */
2    /*            allows either Binary or ASCII treatment */
3    #include "stdio.h"
4    #include  "cminor.h"
5
6    /* Computer Innovations version */
7    FILE *fopen() ;
8
9    FILE *gfopen(fn,fmode,ft)
10    char fn[] ;
11    char fmode[] ;
12    int  ft ;
13    {
14       char mode_string[20] ;
15
16       strcpy(mode_string,fmode) ; /* copy input mode string */
17       if( ft == BIN_MODE )
18          strcat(mode_string,"b");
19       return( fopen(fn,mode_string) ) ;
20    }
21    /* end of version */
22
```

Figure 2.4c gfopen.lat

```
 1    /* gfopen.c - generalized buffered file open function */
 2    /*             allows either Binary or ASCII treatment */
 3    #include "stdio.h"
 4    #include  "cminor.h"
 5
 6    /* Lattice C version */
 7    /* (works for either Microsoft or Lifeboat version) */
 8    extern int _fmode ;    /* global binary/ASCII flag */
 9    FILE *gfopen(fn,fmode,ft)
10     char fn[] ;
11     char fmode[] ;
12     int  ft ;
13     {
14         int tmode ;
15         FILE *tfd ;                    /* temporary file ptr */
16
17         tmode = _fmode ;          /* save the flag value */
18         if( ft == BIN_MODE )
19              _fmode = 0x8000 ;   /* open in binary mode */
20         else _fmode = 0 ;        /* "   "  ASCII  mode */
21         tfd = fopen(fn,fmode) ; /* open the file */
22         _fmode = tmode ;    /* restore the flag value */
23         return( tfd ) ;
24     }
25    /* end of version */
26
```

on the value of the operating mode argument. Before we return from gfopen, we restore the value of the _fmode variable. Saving and restoring this variable ensures that our function will not affect normal operation of the library functions.

None of these implementations is difficult to write. If the differences were spread throughout our programs, however, converting them would be a significant headache.

2.3 Bit Operations: Cleaning Up Word Processor Files

□ Many word processing programs store documents in a format similar to that of normal ASCII text files. However, the differences in format often make DOS utilities such as the TYPE and PRINT commands useless on these document files. The CLEAN program shown in Figure 2.5 reads a document file and writes a cleaned-up version acceptable as an ASCII text file. This program uses the gfopen function just discussed and provides an opportunity for exploring C's facilities for operating on bits within data values. CLEAN fixes the major problems with files created with the WordStar program. It should be useful for files produced by other word processors although modifications may be needed.

Figure 2.5   clean.c

```
1    /* clean.c - strip high-order bits & ctrl chars from text file */
2    #include "stdio.h"
3    #include "cminor.h"
4
5    FILE *gfopen() ;
6
7    main(argc,argv)
8     int argc ;                 /* number of command line words */
9     char *argv[] ;             /* pointers to each word */
10    {
11      int c ;
12      FILE *in ;               /* use this file for input */
13      FILE *out ;              /* use this one for output */
14      long nin , nout ;        /* counts of chars in and out */
15
16      if( argc < 3 )           /* be sure command line has enough words */
17        { printf(" USAGE - clean input-file output-file \n");
18          exit(1) ;
19        }
20
21      in = gfopen(argv[1],"r",ASC_MODE) ; /* open input file */
22      if( in == NULL )
23        { printf(" can't open input file - %s \n",argv[1]);
24          exit(2) ;
25        }
26
27      out = gfopen(argv[2],"w",ASC_MODE) ; /* open output file */
28      if( out == NULL )
29        { printf(" can't open output file - %s \n",argv[2]);
30          exit(3) ;
31        }
32
33      nin = 0 ;
34      nout = 0 ;
35      c = getc(in) ;
36      while( c != EOF )              /* get chars until end reached */
37        { nin = nin + 1 ;
38          c = c & 127 ;              /* strip high-order bit */
39          /* now see if it is a non-control char */
40          /* or Carriage Return , Line Feed or Tab */
41          if(  ( (c >= ' ') && (c <= '~') )  || (c == '\n')
42             || (c == '\r') || (c == '\t') || (c == '\f') )
43            { nout = nout + 1 ;     /* good char - output it */
44              putc(c,out) ;
45            }
46          c = getc(in) ;
47        }
48      fclose(in) ;
49      fclose(out) ;
50      printf(" %10ld characters read \n",nin) ;
51      printf(" %10ld characters written \n",nout) ;
52    }
```

CLEAN fixes two problems. First, normal ASCII characters are represented by values from 0 to 127. This requires 7 bits in an 8-bit byte. The 8th bit is set equal to 0 for normal ASCII text. WordStar sets this bit to 1 in some characters to mark formatting information. For example, the last character in each word has this bit set equal to 1. When a DOS utility such as TYPE processes such characters, they appear as special graphic symbols. Here is a diagram of normal versus these special character values:

Bit Number	7	6	5	4	3	2	1	0
Normal ASCII	0	x	x	x	x	x	x	x
Special Characters	1	x	x	x	x	x	x	x

The x's denote bit values that depend on the character stored. Our program must replace the 1 in bit 7 by a 0 to make such characters acceptable to DOS utilities.

Bit 7 is the most significant bit in the character. We refer to it as the *high-order bit*. Since it corresponds to the parity bit used in asynchronous trnsmission, it is sometimes called a *parity bit*.

Second, the document file may contain ASCII control characters that convey special formatting information. For example, WordStar uses a control-B character (value 2) to mark the beginning and end of boldface emphasis. CLEAN removes all control characters except Carriage Return, Line Feed, Tab, and Form Feed.

The overall structure of the CLEAN program is similar to that of the COPYA program in Figure 2.1a. We use the same library functions getc, putc, and fclose for file I/O. Instead of fopen, we use our function gfopen. WordStar uses the control-Z convention to mark the end of data so we specify ASCII mode in opening the file.

As each character is read with getc, we perform two operations on it. In line 38 of Figure 2.5 we set the high-order bit to 0. Then we check the character to see if it should be written out. We compare it to the acceptable control characters and check it against the lowest and highest noncontrol characters. Characters that pass this check are written with putc. At the end of the program we display counts of characters read and written. These counts may not be vital information, but displaying them gives some confirmation that the program ran and processed about the right number of characters.

Line 38 contains new ideas and deserves a full explanation. We have already explained what we want to do, but how does this statement accomplish it? The & operator combines its left and right operands bit by bit to form a result. The value of bit 0 in the result depends only on the values of bit 0 in the two operands, not on the values of bits 1 to 7. The rule that the & operator uses is simple: If a bit is 1 in both operands, it is 1 in the result. Otherwise, the bit is 0 in the result. Here is an example:

Bit Number	Left Operand	Right Operand	Result
7	0	0	0
6	0	1	0
5	1	0	0
4	1	1	1
3	1	0	0
2	1	1	1
1	0	0	0
0	0	1	0

The right operand to & is the constant 127. The individual bits in the number 127 are as follows:

Bit Number	7	6	5	4	3	2	1	0
127	0	1	1	1	1	1	1	1

When we combine the character c just read with 127, the result is as follows:

Bit Number	Character c	Constant 127	Result
7	x	0	0
6	x	1	x
5	x	1	x
4	x	1	x
3	x	1	x
2	x	1	x
1	x	1	x
0	x	1	x

Since bit 7 in the constant 127 is 0, bit 7 in the result must be 0 whatever the value of bit 7 in c. Bits 0 to 6 of 127 are 1 so those bits in the result depend on the corresponding bits in c. The values of bits 0 to 6 in the result will reproduce those bits in c. We store the result back in c. Thus, the effect of this statement is to set bit 7 to 0, leaving the other bits unchanged.

The comparisons in lines 41 and 42 use the escape notation for the control character constants. We have seen \n for newline before; the tab (\t), carriage return (\r), and form feed (\f) notations are new.

2.4 Hexadecimal Notation

☐ The number 127 that we used in the CLEAN program produces the right results, but it looks mysterious at first glance. *Hexadecimal* notation (Hex) often makes more sense than decimal in bit-level operations. Each Hex digit represents a value between 0 and 15; to display these values we use the letters A to F for values 10 through 15. The advantage of hexadecimal notation is that each Hex digit corresponds to 4 bits.

C interprets numbers as hexadecimal constants when they begin with 0x (or 0X). Either uppercase or lowercase letters may be used for the digits A to F.

The constant 127 would have the value 0x7f in hexadecimal notation. The relation between Hex digits and bits is shown by this diagram:

```
Bit Number    7    6    5    4    3    2    1    0
127           0    1    1    1    1    1    1    1
Hex           ------------------    ------------------
Digit                  7                    f
```

As an example of the usefulness of hexadecimal notation, the following table shows the result of line 38 in the CLEAN program (Figure 2.5) for different character values.

Character Value In				Character Value Out		
Decimal		*Hexadecimal*		*Decimal*		*Hexadecimal*
13	or	0D	gives	13	or	0D
141		8D		13		0D
10		0A		10		0A
138		8A		10		0A
32		20		32		20
160		A0		32		20
97		61		97		61
225		E1		97		61

Each pair of rows shows the result for characters with bit 7 equal to 0 and equal to 1. In Hex notation the numbers show that the lower 4 bits are unchanged. A more careful examination would be needed to see that only bit 7 was affected. But in decimal notation there is no obvious relationship.

2.5 More Bit Operations and Macros

□   In addition to the Bitwise AND operator (&) used in the CLEAN program, C has several other bit-level operators. Those that we will be using are the Bitwise OR operator (|), the Bitwise Exclusive OR or XOR operator (∧), and the Not Operator (~). Like the bitwise AND operator, the OR and Exclusive OR operators require two operands. The NOT operator (called the *one's complement* operator in K & R) requires only one operand. Here are word and tabular definitions of what these operators do:

Bitwise OR: Operates in a bit-by-bit manner. If either or both operands has a 1 value for a bit, the corresponding bit is set to 1 in the result. A bit in the result is 0 only if the corresponding bits in both operands are 0.

Bitwise Exclusive OR: Operates in a bit-by-bit manner. Result bits are 0 when both operand bits are 0 or both bits are 1. Result bits are 1 when one operand has a 1 bit and the other has a 0 bit.

Cases	Left Operand	Right Operand	OR Result	AND Result	XOR Result
Both 0	0	0	0	0	0
0/1	0	1	1	0	1
1/0	1	0	1	0	1
1/1	1	1	1	1	0

Bitwise NOT: Operates in a bit-by-bit manner on a single operand. A result bit is 0 when the operand bit is 1 and is 1 when the operand bit is 0.

Cases	Operand	Result
0	0	1
1	1	0

C also provides operators to shift bits right and left within a value. These operators are sometimes useful when several data values are packed within one byte or integer value. We discuss them later when they are used.

Practical Uses of Bit Operations

Bit operations are often difficult to understand even for fairly experienced programmers. This section illustrates a few practical uses and shows how to hide the messy details.

The CLEAN program showed that a common use of bit operations is to force the high-order bit of a character to be 0. This task and the related one of testing to see if the high-order bit is 0 are needed in many character-handling programs. We can use the #define statement to define a *macro* for this operation:

```
#define toascii (a)   ( (a) & 0x7f )
```

We follow the macro's name toascii with parentheses enclosing the parameters. When we use this macro, the parameter a in the definition will be replaced by whatever we place inside the parentheses. These examples show how the macro works:

toascii (c)   means   ((c) & 0x7f)

toascii (buf[i + 1])   means   ((buf[i + 1]) & 0x7f)

In the same way, we can define a macro isascii to test whether the high-order bit of a character is 0:

#define isascii (a)   (((a) & 0x80) = = 0)

In both these macros we use parentheses liberally. This ensures that the macro will work as intended when the parameter is a complicated expression or when the macro is embedded in a complicated expression. Since we will not be looking at the *expansion* of the macro, the extra parentheses do not have any disadvantages.

C does not specify whether character values are to be treated as signed or unsigned values when they are converted to integers. Some compilers treat characters as values from -128 to $+127$, while others view characters as numbers from 0 to 255. If we want to write portable C programs, we often need to force characters to be treated as values from 0 to 255.

On the IBM PC, positive and negative integers are represented in memory as follows:

Bit Number	15	14	13	12	11	10	9	8	7	6	5	4	3	2	1	0
Positive	0	x	x	x	x	x	x	x	x	x	x	x	x	x	x	x
Negative	1	x	x	x	x	x	x	x	x	x	x	x	x	x	x	x

where x indicates that the value of the bit depends on the particular number represented.

The problem with signed or unsigned characters requires quite a bit of explanation. Fortunately, the solution is quite simple. To defeat sign extension, we perform a Bitwise AND operation with the constant, 0xff, as one operand. For example, using the character variable c,

c & 0xff

Since this constant has 1 as the value for its lowest 8 bits and 0s for all higher bits, the result will have bits 0 through 7 unchanged from the variable c. But all higher bits (including the sign bit) will be 0.

We can make a macro for this operation too:

#define tochar(a)   ((a) & 0xff)

If the compiler we are using treats characters as unsigned values, we do not have to do anything to prevent sign extension. In that case, we can change the macro definition in **cminor.h** to be

```
#define tochar(a)    (a)
```

This gives us the best of both worlds: portability without any unnecessary calculations.

Sometimes individual bits in a variable are used to store separate yes/no values. Such *flag bits* are often used by operating systems, and if we use operating system services directly, we need to manipulate such flag bits. These operations must check or change the value of a single bit in a variable independent of the other bits in a word.

Hexadecimal notation is useful for defining constants with single bits equal to 1. The following table gives some examples:

Bit Equal to One	Constant Value
0	0x01
1	0x02
2	0x04
3	0x08
4	0x10
5	0x20
6	0x40
7	0x80

Setting a bit to a 1 value, clearing a bit (setting it to 0), and testing the value of a bit are operations we need. Here are some examples:

Setting bit 7	`c = c | 0x80 ;`
Clearing bit 0	`c = c & ~ 0x01 ;`
Testing bit 6	`if( (c & 0x40) = = 0 ) . . .`

We do not use macros for these operations in this book. If you feel uncomfortable with the bit operators, you can define macros for bit operations.

More Macros

We can define several more macros to make C easier to learn and use. Some are just cosmetic improvements to C syntax, but you may find them easier to use than straight C. They do provide examples of how C can be molded to the individual's preferences.

The equality operator (= =) is a frequent cause of syntax errors. It is natural to use the assignment operator where an equality comparison is intended; since the assignment operator is legal inside expressions, the compiler does not catch this mistake. We can prevent this mistake by defining an English substitute for the = = operator;

```
#define is  = =
```

In a similar way, we can define English equivalents for other operators. The logical operators && and || are good candidates:

```
#define and  &&

#define or   ||
```

Many programming languages have built-in functions for selecting the maximum or minimum of two values. A function to return the absolute value of an expression is also common. C lacks these functions but we can supply equivalents. We could build library functions, but we would need separate functions for **int**, **unsigned**, **long**, and **float** data types. A single set of C macros will work for all numeric data types.

The logic for a maximum function seems simple as shown in the first C fragment that follows. The if . . . else statement does what we want, but we cannot put it inside an expression. The second fragment shows the conditional operator (? . . . :) that can be used inside an expression:

```
if( a < b )
   x = b ;
else x = a ;

(a < b) ? b : a
```

The operation of these operators is parallel to the if statement: The first expression (a logical operation normally) is evaluated. If it is true, the expression following the ? is evaluated and becomes the value of the expression. If it is false, the expression following the : is evaluated and becomes the value of the expression. This operator is not needed in normal C source files, but it is useful in macros like these. You can look at the following macros and then forget about this operator until you need to use it to write more macros.

```
#define   max(a,b)   ( ( (a) < (b) ) ? (b) : (a) )

#define   min(a,b)   ( ( (a) < (b) ) ? (a) : (b) )

#define   abs(x)   ( ( (x) < 0 ) ? −(x) : (x) )
```

Defining Portable Data Types

C provides a good variety of data types: characters, integers, longs, and float data have been used so far. C does not specify the size of these data types. The compiler writer can make choices that are appropriate for that particular environment. It is a practical solution to the problems that differing computer architectures present.

We can use integers for routine purposes where we do not expect very large numbers and longs where we expect large numbers. In some cases however, it is important that we control the way a variable is represented. For example, when we use operating system services, we must use 16-bit values where the operating system expects it.

We can use the typedef statement introduced in Chapter 1 to solve this problem. We define new data types INT16, INT32, and WORD16 for use when the exact size of a variable is important. We define the data types twice, with lowercase and uppercase letters, so you do not have to remember which way they were defined. These definitions are kept in **cminor.h** and can be changed easily to fit the

Figure 2.6 c:cminor.h

```
1   /* cminor.h - enhancements to C syntax */
2
3   /* define file opening modes for gfopen, gopen, gcreat */
4   #define BIN_MODE 0
5   #define ASC_MODE  1
6
7   /* use the following when the compiler treats char as signed */
8   #define tochar(c)  ( (c) & 0xff )
9
10  /* use the following  when char is treated as unsigned  */
11  /* #define tochar(c)   c          */
12
13
14  /* toascii - strip parity bit from a char value */
15  #define toascii(c) ( (c) & 0x7f )
16
17  /* test a char to see whether the high order bit is zero */
18  #define isascii(c) ( ((c) & 0x80) == 0 )
19
20  /* test a char to see if it is printable (ASCII graphic) */
21  #define isgraphic(c)  ( ((c) >= ' ') && ((c) <= '~') )
22
23  /* English for equality comparison operator */
24  #define is  ==
25
26  /* english for logical operators */
27  #define and   &&
28  #define or    ||
29
30  /* portable data types */
31  typedef int        int16 ;      /* signed 16 bit integer */
32  typedef int        INT16 ;      /* signed 16 bit integer */
33  typedef long       int32 ;      /* signed 32 bit integer */
34  typedef long       INT32 ;      /* signed 32 bit integer */
35  typedef unsigned   word16 ;     /* unsigned 16 bit number */
36  typedef unsigned   WORD16 ;     /* unsigned 16 bit number */
37
38  /* maximum, minimum and absolute value macros */
39  #define max(a,b)    (  (a) < (b) ? (b) : (a) )
40  #define min(a,b)    (  (a) < (b) ? (a) : (b) )
41  #define abs(x)      (  (x) < 0   ? - (x) : (x) )
```

computer and compiler we are using. For most MS-DOS C compilers the following definitions are appropriate:

```
typedef int INT16 ;
typedef long INT32 ;
typedef unsigned WORD16 ;
```

Figure 2.6 shows the cminor.h file. We include it for compilation just as we do the stdio.h file. As you can see, it includes all the macros and data type definitions we have developed. Any changes to cminor.h needed for particular compilers are discussed on the program diskette (see introduction).

2.6 Controlling the Order of Evaluation: Operator Precedence

□   What happens when several operators appear in a single C statement? What rules does C use to specify the order in which the operations are carried out? First, operators are assigned a precedence level so that high-precedence operators are evaluated before lower-level operators. Several operators may share the same precedence level; as a tie-breaking rule, a fixed order of evaluation is defined for groups of operators at the same level. (The rule is left to right for some operators and right to left for other operators.)

   In all, there are 15 precedence levels. Twelve of these levels group left to right, and three group right to left. Most books on C discuss the operator precedence table and the grouping rules adequately. However, since we think the rules are too complicated to remember reliably, we provide a simpler approach. The following five-level table shows our precedence rules (highest precedence first):

Type of Operator	*Operators at This Level*	
Primary expression	a[i]	(subscript)
	st.grade	(structure member)
	ps1 – >grade	(pointer to member)
	(x + y)	
Unary operators	! ~ ++ −−	− (minus)
	(type) *	sizeof
Binary operators (multiplication)	* / %	
Binary operators (other than multiplication)	+ − << >>	
	< <= > >=	
	== != & ∧	
	¦ && ¦¦	? : (conditional operator)
Assignment Operators	= += −=	and so on
Comma Operator	,	

We have listed all C's operators in the table for completeness. Some operators not mentioned here are discussed when they are used; others are discussed in Chapter 9 in connection with optimization. A few are not used (the comma operator, for example).

We need some additional rules to make our approach work:

Use parentheses whenever the simplified precedence table does not define the result completely.

Primary expressions group left to right; thus, s[i].name[j] is equivalent to ((s[i]).name) [j]. For other precedence levels we do not rely on grouping rules.

Avoid side effects that depend on the order of evaluation. Do not use the value of a variable in the same statement where its value is changed.

Test everything before using it. Rely on your knowledge of C when you write programs but not when you test them.

Use parentheses whenever the simplified precedence table does not define the result completely.

We cannot change the way C works, but we can simplify the way we use its features.

2.7   Starting a Toolkit

□   We are now ready to start a toolkit. As we identify functions that may be useful in more than one program, we can document them and place them in a library. As we build this toolkit, the effort needed to write programs decreases. The common repetitive parts of the job may already be present in our library. We can develop a few general functions based on the programs in Chapter 1.

The getstr Function

We developed one useful function in chapter one: getstr. Many programs in this book need a function to accept a line of input from the keyboard and store it in a character string. While the standard library function, fgets, performs this function, it places a newline character at the end of the string. It is easy enough to fix this problem, as Figure 1.7b showed.

We already have the getstr function, but we do need some documentation for its use. Figure 2.7 gives a description of getstr and how to use it. We should be able to use getstr based on this information. This *manual page* documentation is similar to that for the CLEAN program; since getstr is a function rather than a complete program, the details we supply are a bit different.

Figure 2.7   getstr description

Name

getstr   get a string (line of input) from the console

Usage

```
int getstr ( ) ;
char s[81] ;
int length, max_length ;
max_length = 80 ;
length = getstr (s,max_length) ;
```

Function

getstr collects a line of input from **stdin** and places it in the character array passed in string format. The newline at the end of the line is not placed in the string. If the input line exceeds the maximum length specified, getstr returns with a maximum length string. getstr also stops if it reaches the end of file.

The length of the string is returned by **getstr**. A value of 0 is returned for a null string.

Example

```
File *in ;
char filename[65] ;
getstr (filename,64) ;        /* get the file name */
in = fopen (filename, "r") ;   /* open the file */
```

Notes

getstr is implemented using standard library functions for buffered I/O. Calls to scanf or getchar are compatible with this function. getstr differs from the library function, fgets, in that the newline character is not placed in the returned string.

References

Standard library functions getchar and fgets.

The movedata Function

The next function for the toolkit, **movedata**, moves data from one location to another. It works for different types of data; all it needs to know is the source and destination addresses and the number of bytes of data to move. Figure 2.8 documents its use.

The movedata function is listed in Figure 2.9. Before we explain the function in detail, we give a *pseudo-code* description of what it is to do:

Repeat for each byte to be copied.
Get a byte from the source location.
Store the byte at the destination location.
Advance the source address to the next byte.
Advance the destination address to the next byte.

Figure 2.8   movedata description

Name

movedata   move a specified number of bytes

Usage

```
int movedata ( ) ;
char to_array [20] ;      /* destination for move */
char from_array [20] ;   /* origin for move */
unsigned nbytes ;         /* number of bytes to move */
nbytes = 20 ;
movedata (to_array,from_array,nbytes) ;
```

Function

movedata moves a specified number of bytes from a source address to a destination address. The bytes to be moved start at the source address and end at the address (source + number of bytes). There is no return value.

Example

```
int old_values [10] ;
int new_values [10] ;
movedata (new_values,old_values,10*sizeof (int)) ;

typedef struct { int year , month , day ; } DATE ;
DATE temp , today ;
movedata(&temp,&today, sizeof(DATE) ) ;
```

Notes

movedata expects addresses as its first and second arguments. With arrays, using the array name passes its address. With single variables or structures, the Address operator (&) is needed. The sizeof function allows the number of bytes to be specified in a portable, fool-proof way.

These examples assume that pointers to all kinds of data share the same representation as pointers to **char.** This is true for most modern computers such as the Intel 8086/8088 (in the IBM PC), Motorola 68000, DEC PDP-11, DEC VAX, and IBM 360 families.

References

The standard library function strcpy for copying strings has similar arguments.

Figure 2.9   c:movedata.c

```
1     /* movedata.c - moves specified number of bytes */
2     #include "stdio.h"
3
4     int movedata(to,from,nbytes)
5       char *to ;                 /* move the data to here */
6       char *from ;               /* move it from here */
7       int nbytes ;               /* number of bytes to move */
8       {
9          while( nbytes > 0 )  /* stop when all bytes are moved */
10            { *to = *from ;    /* move a byte */
11              to = to + 1 ;    /* advance pointers to and from */
12              from = from + 1 ;
13              nbytes = nbytes - 1 ; /* reduce bytes left */
14            }
15        }
16
17
```

We use pseudo-code like this in the rest of the book to show what a program or a function is to do. It helps to define what we want to do before we think about how we can accomplish the job in C. This pseudo-code contains loops (**repeat**, **for**, and **while**) and English sentences for assignments and function calls. We use pseudo-code to show the basic outline of a program and gloss over details.

To accomplish the function the pseudo-code describes, we use two new ideas: (1) We can modify function arguments like variables declared within the function, and (2) we can do arithmetic on pointers.

Line 10 of Figure 2.9 gets a byte from the location pointed to by from and stores it in the location pointed to by to. Lines 11 and 12 advance these pointers to the next source and destination locations. Line 13 reduces the number of bytes by 1 every time the while loop is executed. The following example shows the pointer values at each iteration after the function call movedata(s,"ab",3):

Contents of s	Contents of "ab"	nbytes
? ? ? ?	a b \ 0 ?	3
a ? ? ?	a b \ 0 ?	2
a b ? ?	a b \ 0 ?	1
a b \ 0 ?	a b \ 0 ?	0

Does movedata have any real uses? C does not have any built-in facilities for moving entire arrays or structures, but we can use movedata to do it for us. For example, we could rewrite the swap function in the CURVE program of Chapter 1 using movedata:

```
int swap(p1,p2)
  STUDENT *p1 ;
  STUDENT *p2 ;
  {
    STUDENT temp ;

    movedata(&temp , p1, sizeof(STUDENT) ) ;
    movedata(p1,p2, sizeof(STUDENT) ) ;
    movedata(p2,&temp , sizeof(STUDENT) ) ;
  }
```

Figure 2.10   sindex description

Name

sindex   find a character in a string

Usage

```
int sindex () ;
char c ;              /* character to look for */
char string[20] ;     /* string to search in */
int index ;           /* index of 1st occurrence of char */
index = sindex(c,string) ;
```

Function

sindex searches for the first occurrence of a character in a character string. It returns the index of the first occurrence of the character. Zero is returned when the character is found at the beginning of the string. A return value of -1 indicates that the character was not found.

Example

```
int nv = 0 ;
int c ;
c = getchar () ;
while( c != EOF )         /* count vowels */
  { if( sindex(c,"aeiou") > = 0 )
      nv = nv + 1 ;
    c = getchar () ;
  }
```

Notes

sindex expects a character as its first argument. But since C converts characters to integers when they are passed in a function call, the first argument can be of integer type as well.

The sizeof function we use is provided by C. It returns the size in bytes of the data type passed as an argument. We can use sizeof to avoid having to figure out how many bytes the **STUDENT** structure occupies. This makes our job easier and prevents mistakes in computing the size of a data structure or array.

The sindex Function

Another function that occurs in many programs is that of finding the first occurrence of a character in a string. Figure 2.10 describes such a function. Figure 2.11 lists the source file for sindex. The implementation of sindex is straightforward: if the character is matched, the function returns immediately with the index in the string where the character was found. If the character is not matched, the search stops when the end-of-string marker is found. A value of −1 is returned in that case.

Making a Library

Now that these toolkit functions are documented and implemented, we can compile them and make a library. Figure 2.12 shows the steps we used to compile the functions and start an *object module library*. While these steps are specific to one particular compiler, most compiler products have equivalent capabilities. Now when we use one or more of these functions in a program, we need only specify the

Figure 2.11   c:sindex.c

```
1    /* sindex.c - find first occurence of a char in a string */
2    #include "stdio.h"
3
4    #define FAILURE   -1   /* return value if string not found */
5
6    int sindex(c,s)         /* find char in string - return position */
7     int c ;                /* char to be found */
8     char s[] ;             /* string in which to look for c */
9     {
10       int i ;
11
12       i = 0 ;
13       while( s[i] != '\0' )      /* stop at end of the string */
14         { if( c == s[i] )
15              return( i ) ;       /* c found - return its position */
16           i = i + 1 ;
17         }
18       /* c was not found in s  */
19       return( FAILURE ) ;
20     }
21
```

Figure 2.12   c:library.fig

```
1
2
3                   Starting an Object Module Library
4
5    D>MC1 getstr
6    Microsoft C Compiler   (Phase 1)   V1.04
7    Copyright (C) 1983 by Lattice, Inc./Lifeboat Associates
8
9    D>MC2 getstr
10   Microsoft C Compiler   (Phase 2)   V1.04
11   Copyright (C) 1983 by Lattice, Inc./Lifeboat Associates
12   Module size P=008F D=0000
13
14   D>MC1 movedata
15   Microsoft C Compiler   (Phase 1)   V1.04
16   Copyright (C) 1983 by Lattice, Inc./Lifeboat Associates
17
18   D>MC2 movedata
19   Microsoft C Compiler   (Phase 2)   V1.04
20   Copyright (C) 1983 by Lattice, Inc./Lifeboat Associates
21   Module size P=0027 D=0000
22
23   D>MC1 sindex
24   Microsoft C Compiler   (Phase 1)   V1.04
25   Copyright (C) 1983 by Lattice, Inc./Lifeboat Associates
26
27   D>MC2 sindex
28   Microsoft C Compiler   (Phase 2)   V1.04
29   Copyright (C) 1983 by Lattice, Inc./Lifeboat Associates
30   Module size P=0032 D=0000
31
32   D>lib
33
34      Microsoft Library Manager V1.02
35   (C) Copyright 1981 by Microsoft Inc.
36
37   Library File: toolkit
38   Library does not exist. Create?y
39   Operations: +getstr+movedata+sindex
40   List file:
41
42   D>
```

library name in addition to that of the C standard library. Instead of the command used in Chapter 1 to link the REVERSE program,

```
link c reverse getstr,reverse,nul,mc
```

we can use

```
link c reverse,reverse,nul,toolkit mc
```

We can go further and define a batch file (l.bat) to reduce the typing

```
link c %1 %2 %3 %4 %5 %6 %7 %8 %9,%1,nul,toolkit mc
```

Then we can link a program like REVERSE by typing

```
l reverse
```

A similar batch file can be constructed for most C compilers.

2.8 Summary

□ Chapter 2 discussed more advanced features of C than Chapter 1 did and tailored C to make it easy to use and portable. The chapter also started a toolkit of general purpose functions. We have been laying a foundation for reading, understanding, and modifying real C programs. The rest of the book is devoted to presenting such programs. If you find parts of these programs hard to understand, refer to Chapters 1 and 2 for examples. You should also have a copy of the K & R book handy for reference. Each program is accompanied by an explanation of what the program does. You should use this description of what the program does to understand how the individual C statements do the job.

3
Viewing ASCII Files

This chapter follows the development of a single program from its specification through completion. The program is larger than those introduced in Chapters 1 and 2, and it is the first program intended to perform a useful function rather than just be an appropriate example. Since this is the first real application to be presented, this chapter discusses the development process from beginning through end. Defining the functional specifications for the program, writing pseudo-code, testing the individual parts of the program, and measuring its performance are topics discussed in this chapter.

The program we develop in this chapter, VIEW, is a tool for browsing through text files. It displays a screenful of text at a time and then waits for an input command. Keyboard commands let us navigate about in the file at will. VIEW gives us a way to look at long text files without waiting for a printed listing or wasting paper.

3.1 Specifying the VIEW Program

☐ Before we can design the VIEW program, we need a thorough description of its function. Sometimes we do not know everything about the program's function at this point. For example, we may not know the best form for input commands or output formats. It is still worthwhile to specify what we can and outline the parts that cannot be specified. It is always easier to produce programs to meet a specification than to develop the specifications as we write the program.

We start by discussing what VIEW should do. When we have a good description of its functions, we can write a formal manual page to document its specifications.

VIEW should display one screenful of text and stop automatically. It should then wait for a command describing what it should do next. It should never write so much data that part scrolls off the screen.

VIEW should provide commands for movement in the file in big and little steps: by lines of text, whole screenfuls, or all the way to the beginning or end of the file. We would like to use VIEW as a window into the file—a window that we can move through the file at will. Moving backward should be as easy and as well supported as moving forward.

We want to use familiar commands in VIEW. Since many other programs on the IBM PC use cursor control keys for movement in a file, we would like to use them here. In addition, we want to specify commands by pressing a single key. Pressing return after each command should not be necessary.

We may not use VIEW very often. We would like to reduce the effort of remembering how to use it by displaying a list of commands (and the keys to press) on the screen.

We should be able to use VIEW to examine not only text files but also word processor files. VIEW will use the same techniques that we developed for the CLEAN program; it will ignore the setting of the high-order bit in a character. Most control characters other than tab and newline will be ignored.

Figure 3.1 documents these requirements in a manual page description. As the manual page shows, cursor movement and other commands are consistent with usage in popular application programs. The display format follows the guidelines just discussed; it should describe where you are and what you can do next.

3.2 Pseudo-code for VIEW

□ We have specified what the program as a whole is to do. Now we need to elaborate, describing how the program will work in increasing levels of detail. We use the pseudo-code language described in Chapter 2. We will not worry about writing any C statements until we have broken the problem into many small parts and described the functions of each. We do not consider exception conditions or fine points here but focus on the normal function of the program.

Overall Structure

The program must perform this sequence of steps:

    Find out the name of the file to be used.
    Display the first page of the file.
    Get an input command.
    Execute that command.
    Get another input command (not exit pgm).
    Execute it.
    .
    .

    .
    Get another input command (exit pgm).
    Exit to the operating system.

Figure 3.1   VIEW program description

Name

> view   displays a text file a screenful at a time

Function

VIEW displays a text file on the screen. On entry it displays the first screenful in the file and waits for a command. Single-key commands provide movement in the file by single lines or pages. Commands for movement to the beginning and end of the file are also supported.

The high-order bit of characters in the text file is ignored. Control characters other than line feed and tab are ignored when the file is displayed. A control-Z character in the last 128-byte block of the file is interpreted as the effective end of data.

Usage

From DOS, type VIEW and the name of file to be viewed.

> a>VIEW file-name   or a>VIEW
>   file name:file__name

Inside the VIEW program the following list of single-key commands (you do not need to press return) are recognized:

HOME:	Displays the first page in the file
END:	Displays the last page in the file
PgUp:	Moves backward in the file almost one page
PgDn:	Moves forward in the file almost one page
Down Arrow:	Moves forward in the file by one line
Up Arrow:	Moves backward in the file by one line
Space Bar:	Moves to a position you specify
Escape:	Ends the program and returns to DOS

The program will display three areas on the screen: a heading, the text (16 lines), and a prompt describing input commands.

FILE-sample.txt	*POSITION-0*	*FILE SIZE-750*

---

first line of the page.
*
*
*
16th line of the page.

Type one of these input commands:

HOME	= First Page	↑	= Prev. Line	PgUp	= Prev. Page
END	= Last Page	↓	= Next Line	PgDn	= Next Page
Esc	= Exit Pgm	Space	= Move to Position		

A limitation of VIEW is that it handles long lines poorly.

The program is controlled by input from the keyboard. Our pseudo-code will make that control explicit in its structure.

The program repeats the steps "get an input command" and "execute that command" indefinitely. Our pseudo-code will contain a loop control structure to reflect the function required.

The pseudo-code representing the overall program is as follows:

```
view program—overall function
    get file name
    display the first page of the file

    repeat until an exit command is received
        get the next input command
        execute the command

    close the file
end
```

Some of the individual steps are vague so we describe them in more detail. The order in which the steps are described is somewhat different from their order of appearance in the overall pseudo-code.

Some of the steps can be written down without further explanation:

```
get_the_file_name
    get a file name from the command line
    if( file-name not specified on the command line )
        prompt for the file name
        get a file name from the keyboard
end

get_next_input_command
    display a prompt describing input commands
    get the command from keyboard input
    classify it
end
```

Executing the Input Command

Executing the command requires a bit more detail. Seven commands are defined; we describe the process by a large switch statement with a separate case for each input command. While there may be some steps in common, this will keep the pseudo-code understandable.

```
execute_input_command
  switch( input command )
      {
      case Next Page :
        move forward almost a full page
        display the page
      case Previous Page :
        move backward almost a full page
        display the page
      case First Page :
        move to beginning of file
        display the page
      case Last Page :
        move to end of the file
        move backward a full page
        display the page
      case Move To Position :
        move to specified position in file
        move backward to beginning of line
        display the page
      case Previous Line :
        move backward one line
        display the page
      case Next Line:
        move forward one line
        display the page
      case Exit Program :
        no action needed
      }  /* end of switch statement */
end
```

The move_forward and move_backward functions need more detail as does the display_page function.

Moving Forward/Backward

The move_forward function moves forward in the file, reading characters until it has found the beginning of the *n*th line after the current line. The new position is at the beginning of this line.

```
move_forward(n lines)
        start at the top of the current page
        get the next char from the file
```

```
        repeat until the n-th end-of-line is found
            get the next char from the file
        position after the last end-of-line found
end
```

The move_backward function is similar but it must skip over the end-of-line marker at the beginning of the current line. The final position is at the beginning of the *n*th preceding line.

```
move_backward(n lines)
        start at the top of the current page
        find the beginning of the current line
        get the previous char from the file
        repeat until the n-th end-of-line is found )
            get the previous char from the file
        position after the last end-of-line found
end
```

Diagrams may clarify these functions:

move_forward 2 lines

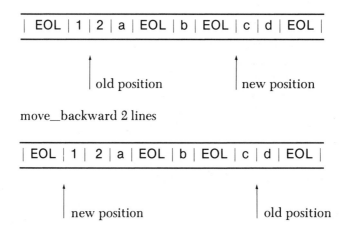

| EOL | 1 | 2 | a | EOL | b | EOL | c | d | EOL |

old position   new position

move_backward 2 lines

| EOL | 1 | 2 | a | EOL | b | EOL | c | d | EOL |

new position   old position

Displaying a Page of Text

Our design displays the entire page of text whatever the input command. For the previous line and next line commands, only part of the screen need be updated. We do not use shortcuts for these commands because we have to display an entire new page for some of them. If we use the same function for all commands, we save the effort of writing functions for the special cases. Our approach is very flexible; new commands can be added without writing special display functions for them. Our version of VIEW is a starting point. It is better strategy to implement it in a quick and simple way. Then our experience with it can guide enhancements. The pseudo-code is straightforward at this level of detail:

```
display_page
        write heading—file name, position in file, file size
        start at the top of the display page
        repeat until a page has been displayed
                get next char from the file
                display a char
end

display_a_char
        if( char is a graphic ASCII char )
                display it
        else if( char is an end of line marker )
                start a new line of text
        else if( char is tab char )
                display a space char
                repeat until we reach a tab stop
                        display a space char
        else ignore other control character
end
```

Important Constants and Data

The most important data used by VIEW are the text file. In addition, however, VIEW needs the file's name, the location of the display page in the file, and the size of the file. We also need to store the type of input command requested and to define constants for the valid input commands. Other information may be needed in the implementation of VIEW, but we can see the need for these data from the pseudo-code alone.

In this case it seems natural to outline the program's logic and let the data required be defined by the logic. In other programs, the data required may be a better starting point.

Exception Conditions

We have ignored exceptions and error conditions in the pseudo-code, which has allowed us to concentrate on the basic structure of the VIEW program. Now we have a framework for identifying some exceptions that VIEW must accommodate.

First, we may reach the end of the file while moving forward in the file or while displaying a page of text. The move_forward function must stop on reaching the end-of-file even if the requested number of lines has not been skipped. The display_page function must fill out the page with blank lines if the end of the file is reached before a full page is displayed.

Second, we may reach the start of the file while moving backward in the file. The move_backward function must handle this exception by stopping early.

Third, the file may contain lines of text that are too long to fit on one line of the display screen. We handle long lines by wrapping them around onto another screen line. The display_page function must allow for such long lines in sensing when a full page has been written. In our first version of the VIEW program, we allow the move_forward and move_backward functions to count lines of text, not lines on the screen. This may produce larger movements than we would like on files with many long lines.

Fourth, keyboard input—a file name, input commands, or a new file position—may be invalid. All input must be fully checked. After invalid input, a warning message should be displayed and new input accepted.

Finally, we may not be able to read the file because of a faulty disk or a hardware problem. We rely on the default critical error handling provided by DOS for now.

We leave the pseudo-code simple and uncluttered, but we must remember these exceptions and ensure that the VIEW program does handle them. We have used the pseudo-code as a design tool. For that purpose we glossed over details that must be addressed in the actual program. Pseudo-code is also useful in the implementation stage. There we include much more detail in the pseudo-code. It is important to keep these stages separated; until the big picture is understood, the details can be confusing.

3.3 Implementing VIEW

☐ The next job is to translate the pseudo-code into a C program that can be executed. Much of this work is now straightforward and can be done immediately. However, we may not know how to implement some functions in C. Thus, we need a combination of research and experiment. The research into the facilities provided by C and our operating system supplies ideas. A short experimental program helps to verify that we understand the facility we want to use.

It may seem inefficient to detour from our objective to write an experimental program, but it often shortens the time to get a working program. It is frequently difficult and time consuming to understand what a new facility does when it is in the middle of a program that you are trying to test.

Reading a File

Before we can write the VIEW program, we need to find out how to read the file and what a typical file's structure is. We have the following requirements:

We want to get a single character at a time.

We want to read characters from the file moving backward as well as moving forward (the normal case).

We must be able to change position within the file. We do not want to be restricted to reading the file sequentially.

We want to get characters from the file without any translation by the operating system or by the file I/O functions we use.

The buffered I/O functions that we saw in Chapter 2 meet most of the following requirements:

The **gfopen** function we developed in Chapter 2 gives us a portable method of opening the file. We use **fclose** to close the file.

The **getc** function reads the next character from the file. Reading a character with **getc** advances our position in the file so that the next call to **getc** will read the following character.

The **fseek** function, not discussed in Chapter 2, allows us to change our position in the file. The new position can be specified relative to the beginning of the file, the end of the file, or the current position in the file. Another function, **ftell**, gives us the current position in the file.

At first glance, ASCII mode appears to be the mode to use. We need to recognize a control-Z as the effective end of the file, and ASCII mode provides this. But the translation of end-of-line markers also provided makes the use of **fseek** unpredictable. The safe course is to use binary mode and recognize control-Z ourselves.

A short data file was prepared with the EDLIN editor supplied with DOS. It consists of two lines, **abc** and **123**. Figure 3.2 shows its creation. The program shown in Figure 3.3 reads this file using the I/O functions just discussed. Figure 3.4 shows the output produced by this program.

Figure 3.2   makefile.fig

```
 1
 2     A>edlin test.dat
 3     New file
 4     *i
 5          1:*abc
 6          2:*123
 7          3:*^C
 8     *e
 9
10     A>dir test.dat
11     TEST      DAT        11    2-01-83    1:14p
12              1 File(s)
13     A>
```

Figure 3.3 expread.c

```
1    /* expread.c - try reading a file */
2    #include "stdio.h"
3    #include "cminor.h"
4
5    long ftell();
6    FILE *gfopen() ;
7    FILE * fp ;               /* file pointer */
8
9     /* modes for fseek */
10   #define BOF_SEEK 0
11   #define REL_SEEK 1
12   #define EOF_SEEK 2
13
14    main()
15    {
16       int  n    ;          /* put fread return value here */
17       int  c    ;          /* put the char read here */
18
19       /* open the file  */
20       fp = gfopen("test.dat","r",BIN_MODE) ;
21       printf("\n gfopen returns - %d \n",fp) ;
22
23       printf("\n position     char    char      position");
24       printf("\n  before      read    value      after\n");
25
26       printf("\n                                       ");
27       printf("   start at beginning of file and read it");
28
29       /* read the file one character at a time */
30       /* stop when we get to the end of the file */
31
32       while( get_and_print() != EOF )
33         { ; }
34
35       printf("\n");
36       printf("\n                                       ");
37       printf("   move to position %2d and read",5) ;
38       fseek(fp,5L,BOF_SEEK);
39       get_and_print();
40
41
42       printf("\n");
43       printf("\n                                       ");
44       printf("   move to position %2d",5) ;
45       fseek(fp,5L,BOF_SEEK);
46       printf("\n                                       ");
47       printf("   then move backward 1 char and read");
48       fseek(fp,-1L,REL_SEEK);
49       get_and_print();
50
51       fclose(fp);
52    }
53
54    int get_and_print()
55    {
```

Figure 3.3   expread.c (continued)

```
56          int c ;
57
58          printf("\n     %21d ",ftell(fp));
59          c = getc(fp);
60          printf("          ");
61          if( isgraphic(c) )
62          printf("     %c",c);
63          else if( c == '\n' )
64              printf("   LF");
65          else if( c == '\r' )
66              printf("   CR");
67          else if( c == EOF )
68              printf("   EOF");
69          else if( c == 26 )
70              printf("ctl-Z");
71          else printf("     ");
72          printf("     %3d",c);
73          printf("          %21d ",ftell(fp));
74          return(c);
75      }
76
```

Figure 3.4   c:expread.fig

```
 1
 2                  Figure 3.4 - Simulated Output from Expread.c
 3
 4
 5       fopen returns - -32765
 6
 7       position       char     char      position
 8        before        read     value      after
 9
10                                                    start at begin. & read
11          0             a       97          1
12          1             b       98          2
13          2             c       99          3
14          3             CR      13          4
15          4             LF      10          5
16          5             1       49          6
17          6             2       50          7
18          7             3       51          8
19          8             CR      13          9
20          9             LF      10         10
21         10           ctl-Z     26         11
22         11            EOF      -1         11
23
24                                                    move to pos. 5 & read
25          5             1       49          6
26
27                                                    move to position  5
28                                                    then back 1 char & read
29          4             LF      10          5
```

The file position before and after each character is read and displayed so that we can understand fully how getc works. The first line in the file (abc) is present and is followed by both an ASCII carriage return character (13 decimal) and an ASCII line feed (10 decimal) character. The second line, 123, is followed by the same 13 and 10 characters with a single control-Z character (26) after that. As described in Section 2.2, this character marks the effective end of the file.

Each line of the file is marked by two characters: a carriage return character (13) followed by a line feed character (10). VIEW can treat the line feed character as the end-of-line marker and ignore the carriage return character. This strategy works for files with carriage return–line feed pairs or for files with only the line feed character. It does not work for files with only a carriage return as an end-of-line marker. Fortunately, the carriage return–line feed marker is the standard in text files in the DOS environment.

Reading a File Backward

The previous section gave an example of reading a file forward one character at a time. Neither the C standard I/O library nor DOS supplies a function to read a file backward. To read it backward we have to synthesize a function from the facilities that are available.

We define a new function, get_previous_char, that is a mirror image of getc. get_previous_char reads one character from the file. It returns the character preceding the file position and moves the file position backward. Successive get_previous_char operations get data from the file in sequence moving backward.

To implement get_previous_char, the raw materials are the file operations getc, fseek, and ftell that the C standard I/O library provides. The following three-step sequence appears to meet our needs. We use the test.dat file from the preceding section to illustrate the steps, starting with the file position equal to 5 as it would be after the statement

    fseek(fp,5,BOF_REL)

The following diagram shows the starting position. Similar diagrams are used in later steps to show the situation after each step.

Start of the file   End of the file

| a | b | c | CR | LF | 1 | 2 | 3 | CR | LF | ctl-Z |

file position

Step 1. Position the file in front of the character we want to read (LF). We do this with

fseek(fp, − 1,CURR_REL)

This positions the file as shown:

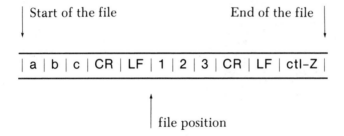

Step 2. Read the character with

c = getc(fp)

The character LF is returned and the file position is advanced:

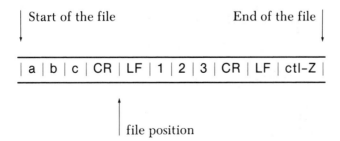

Step 3. Position the file in front of the character just read with

fseek(fp, − 1,CURR_REL)

This leaves the file position less by one character than it was before Step 1.

| a | b | c | CR | LF | 1 | 2 | 3 | CR | LF | ctl–Z |

To continue reading the file backward, we would repeat these three steps: move backward one position (in front of CR), call getc (returns CR), then move backward one position (in front of CR).

The test program in Figure 3.5 checks out our plan. The accompanying output in Figure 3.6 was produced using the two-line file from the previous section. Notice that get_previous_char must first check to see whether the file position is at the beginning of the file. While we could ignore this exception case in working out how get_previous char should work, we had to cover it to produce a working function.

These experiments have demonstrated what a file looks like and how we can build up a new facility for reading a file backward. The examples I chose illustrate a method of solving problems. Reading language reference manuals and operating

Figure 3.5 expback.c

```
1    /* expback.c - try reading a file backward */
2    #include "stdio.h"
3    #include "cminor.h"
4
5    long ftell();
6    FILE *gfopen() ;
7    FILE * fp ;              /* file pointer */
8
9     /* modes for fseek */
10   #define BOF_SEEK 0
11   #define REL_SEEK 1
12   #define EOF_SEEK 2
13
14    /* special return value for beginning of file */
15   #define BOF   (-2)
16
17    main()
18    {
19       int  n    ;         /* put fread return value here */
20
21       /* open the file   */
22       fp = gfopen("test.dat","r",BIN_MODE) ;
23       printf("\n gfopen returns - %d \n",fp) ;
24
25       printf("\n position     char    char     position");
26       printf("\n  before      read    value     after\n");
27
28       printf("\n                                        ");
29       printf("    start at end of file and read backward");
30       fseek(fp,0L,EOF_SEEK);
31
32       /* read the file one character at a time */
33       /* stop when we get to the beginning of the file */
34
35       while( get_and_print() != BOF )
36          { ; }
37
38       printf("\n");
```

Figure 3.5   expback.c (continued)

```
39        printf("\n                                    ");
40        printf("    move to position %2d and read",5) ;
41        fseek(fp,5L,BOF_SEEK);
42        get_and_print();
43
44
45        printf("\n");
46        printf("\n                                    ");
47        printf("    move to position %2d", 5) ;
48        fseek(fp,5L,BOF_SEEK);
49        printf("\n                                    ");
50        printf("    then move backward 1 char and read");
51        fseek(fp,-1L,REL_SEEK);
52        get_and_print();
53
54        fclose(fp);
55    }
56
57    int get_and_print()
58    {
59      int c ;
60
61      printf("\n    %2ld ",ftell(fp));
62      c = get_previous_char();
63      printf("        ");
64      if( isgraphic(c) )
65      printf("    %c",c);
66      else if( c == '\n' )
67          printf("   LF");
68      else if( c == '\r' )
69          printf("   CR");
70      else if( c == EOF )
71          printf("  EOF");
72      else if( c == BOF )
73          printf("  BOF");
74      else if( c == 26 )
75          printf("ctl-Z");
76      else printf("   ");
77      printf("    %3d",c);
78      printf("            %2ld ",ftell(fp));
79      return(c);
80    }
81
82    int get_previous_char()
83    {
84      int c ;
85
86      if( ftell(fp) > 0 )
87        { fseek(fp,-1L,REL_SEEK);
88          c = getc(fp);
89          fseek(fp,-1L,REL_SEEK);
90          return( c ) ;
91        }
92      else return( BOF ) ;
93    }
```

Figure 3.6   c:expback.fig

```
 1              Figure 3.6 - Simulated Output from Expback.c
 2
 3      fopen returns - -32765
 4
 5      position      char    char    position
 6       before       read    value    after
 7
 8                                               start at EOF & read bkwrd
 9         11        ctl-Z     26        10
10         10         LF       10         9
11          9         CR       13         8
12          8          3       51         7
13          7          2       50         6
14          6          1       49         5
15          5         LF       10         4
16          4         CR       13         3
17          3          c       99         2
18          2          b       98         1
19          1          a       97         0
20          0         BOF      -2         0
21
22                                               move to pos.  5 & read
23          5         LF       10         4
24
25                                               move to position  5
26                                               move back 1 char & read
27          4         CR       13         3
```

system manuals is a valuable skill. A little empirical testing often clears up the obscure explanations you find in those manuals.

3.4   The VIEW Program Listing

□   The VIEW program is composed of a number of functions grouped into seven source files, each having a single purpose:

Source File	Functions	Purpose
view.c	main, get_filename	Overall flow of execution
viewget.c	get_cmd, prompt	Input commands
viewexec.c	exec_cmd	Execute a command
viewpos.c	get_pos	Input file position
viewfind.c	move_forward, move_backward, set_top_page	Forward/backward movement by lines of text

Source File	Functions	Purpose
viewdisp.c	display_page , disp_char	Displays file contents
viewio.c	open_file , close_file, set_filesize , move_to, where_now, get_next_char, get_previous_char	Handles file I/O

The following diagram shows the calling relationship of these functions. The functions called by main are indented below it. Below each of these functions are listed the functions they call, indented another level. This indented list of called functions is repeated to more levels until no further function calls occur. When a function occurs more than once, the functions it calls are shown only once.

```
main
    get_filename
        open_file
    get_filesize
    get_cmd
        getkey
        prompt
    exec_cmd
        get_pos
        move_to
        set_top_page
            where_now
        move_forward
            get_next_char
            move_to
            set_top_page
        move_backward
            get_previous_char
            move_to
            set_top_page
        display_page
            move_to
            get_next_char
            disp_char
    close_file
```

Two include files—viewcmds.h and viewparm.h—shown in Figure 3.7 and 3.8, define constants needed in more than one file. viewcmds.h contains the

Figure 3.7 viewcmds.h

```
 1    /* viewcmds.h - definition of codes for input commands */
 2
 3    #define   NEXTPAGE       0
 4    #define   PREVPAGE       1
 5    #define   FIRSTPAGE      2
 6    #define   LASTPAGE       3
 7    #define   MOVETOPOS      4
 8    #define   EXITPGM        5
 9    #define   NEXTLINE       6
10    #define   PREVLINE       7
11    #define   INVALIDCMD     99
12
13
14
```

definitions of allowed input commands, while **viewparm.h** has parameters like the
number of lines to be displayed at a time.

The following sections discuss interesting points in each module of the program. Complete source file listings are included for VIEW and for the programs
presented in later chapters. Most of VIEW's modules correspond closely to one or
more pseudo-code functions, but the I/O module groups all functions that do any
operations on the text file. The order of discussion is somewhat different from that
of Section 3.2.

Figure 3.8 viewparm.h

```
 1
 2
 3    /* viewparm.h - parameters for view program */
 4
 5    /* number of lines in a display page */
 6    #define  PAGE_SIZE      16
 7
 8    /* number of lines of overlap between display pages */
 9    #define  LINES_OVERLAP   2
10
11    /* special return values from get_next_char & get_previous_char */
12    /* to indicate that beginning or end of file has been reached */
13    #define  EOF_MARK       -1
14    #define  BOF_MARK       -2
15
16    /* definition of control char marking the end of a line */
17    #define  END_LINE       10
18
19    /* define success/failure for return codes */
20    #define SUCCESS  1
21    #define FAILURE  0
```

view.c

view.c, shown in Figure 3.9, corresponds to the overall pseudo-code in Section 3.2.
The individual lines of pseudo-code have been translated into calls to C functions.
The declaration of the filename array on line 7 initializes it to a null string.
Lines 15 and 16 copy a command line argument into the file name if there is

Figure 3.9   view.c

```
1     /* view.c -  VIEW program - main function */
2    #include "stdio.h"
3    #include "cminor.h"
4    #include "viewcmds.h"
5    #include "viewparm.h"
6
7    char filename[65] = "" ;
8
9    main(argc,argv)
10     int argc ;
11     char *argv[] ;
12     {
13         int cmd ;                       /* holds current cmd      */
14
15         if( argc >= 2 )                 /* get file name from command */
16           strcpy(filename,argv[1]) ;  /* line (if present) */
17
18         get_filename(filename) ;        /* get file name and open file */
19         set_filesize(ASC_MODE) ;        /* set up file size variable */
20         cmd = FIRSTPAGE ;               /* force display of 1st page */
21
22         while( cmd != EXITPGM )         /* repeat until told to exit */
23           { exec_cmd(cmd);              /* execute the current command */
24             cmd = get_cmd();            /* get the next command */
25           }
26
27         close_file() ;
28     }
29
30
31    int get_filename(fn)                 /* get name of file and open it */
32     char fn[] ;                         /* file name string */
33     {                                   /* filled out by caller */
34         if( strlen(fn) == 0 )
35           { printf("file name:") ;
36             scanf("%s",fn) ;
37           }
38                                         /* open the file (verify name) */
39         while( open_file(fn) == FAILURE )
40           { printf("\n file - %s can not be opened\n",fn);
41             printf("file name:") ;  /* try again */
42             scanf("%s",fn) ;
43           }
44     }
45
```

anything present. The get_filename function validates the file name by calling open_file to open the file. The while loop on lines 39 to 43 repeats the process until a valid file name is received and the file is successfully opened.

The call to the set_filesize function does not correspond to anything in the pseudo-code. It was added because the file I/O functions in viewio.c need to know the location of the effective end-of-data in the file being read.

The pseudo-code specified that the program should display the first page of the file before accepting an input command. Since there is a command to display the first page in the file, the program executes that command immediately, before it accepts an input command. This solution makes the loop on lines 22 to 25 compact and avoids the need for a special function to display the first page of text.

Long, descriptive names are used for variables and functions. While standard C uses only the first eight characters of the name, the extra characters can make the program more understandable to us. It is necessary to make names unique in their first 8 characters to avoid trouble.

viewget.c

get_cmd accepts a single keystroke input and translates it into an input command value. It must act on each keystroke as typed; it cannot wait for a carriage return. In addition, the key pressed must not be echoed on the screen. For most C compilers, the standard console input function getchar fails one or both of these conditions. What can we do? The getkey function in Chapter 7 fits our need. Here we can use getkey just as we would use a C library function. The manual page for getkey and other keyboard input functions shown in Figure 3.10 tells us how to use that function. A header file keyio.h (Figure 3.11) defines symbolic constants for special keys. With this information, we should be able to use getkey without knowing how it is implemented. When we link VIEW, we just include the toolkit object library in addition to the standard library.

The viewget.c file is shown in Figure 3.12. It first displays a prompt message that describes valid input commands and then waits for a key to be pressed. A switch statement (lines 20 to 31) classifies the key in terms of input commands. Since the key pressed may not correspond to a valid command, the process is repeated until a valid command is received.

viewexec.c

This file, shown in Figure 3.13, is a direct translation of the execute_input_command pseudo-code. Each input command is handled by a separate case in a switch statement. It would be possible to shorten the function by combining cases in a clever way, but the savings in program size would be trivial and the cost in clarity significant. As it is written, the exec_cmd has no secrets; a single reading shows exactly what it does for each command.

Figure 3.10   KEYIO description

Name

> getkey   –get one keystroke from the keyboard.
> keypress–check for waiting keystroke.
> keyflush –discard any waiting keystroke input.
> waitcr   –discard keyboard input until CR pressed.

Usage

> int getkey ( ) ;
> int c, input_waiting ;
> c = getkey ( ) ;
> input_waiting = keypress ( ) ;
> keyflush ( ) ;
> waitcr ( ) ;

Function

getkey waits for the next keystroke from the keyboard. It returns an ASCII code (0 to 127) for keys corresponding to ASCII characters and values from 256 up for special keys such as function keys or cursor control keys. These are returned as (256 + extended code), using the extended code described in the PC technical reference manual.

The include file keyio.h defines symbolic constants for the values returned for many special keys.

keypress returns a zero value if no keyboard input is waiting and a nonzero value if some input is waiting. keyflush checks for keyboard input using keypress and discards it using getkey until no more input is waiting. waitcr uses keypress and getkey to discard input until the return key is pressed.

Keyboard input is not echoed by any of these functions. Input is available as soon as a single key is pressed; it is not queued until an entire line has been typed.

Examples

> if(getkey ( ) = = UPARROW)
>   { /* start scrolling up */
>   keyflush( ) ;
>   printf("press a key to stop scrolling\n") ;
>   while(keypress ( ) = = 0)
>   { scroll_up( ) ; }
>   }
>   . . .
> printf(" press return to continue \ n");
> waitcr ( ) ;

References

IBM PC DOS manual, Appendix D. Function call 8.
IBM PC Technical Reference manual, Chapter 3. Character codes and extended codes.

Figure 3.11   keyio.h

```
1
2     /* keyio.h  - definitions of values returned by getkey() */
3
4     /* keypress return values */
5     #define NO_INPUT   0
6     /* non-zero return means there is input waiting */
7
8      /* ASCII control characters */
9
10    #define   ASCNUL       (256+3)
11    #define   ASCBEL       7
12    #define   ASCBS        8
13    #define   ASCTAB       9
14    #define   ASCLF        0xA
15    #define   ASCFF        0xC
16    #define   ASCCR        0xD
17    #define   ASCESC       0x1B
18    #define   ASCDEL       0x7F
19    #define   ASCSPACE     0x20
20
21     /* special keys for IBM PC */
22
23    #define   HOMEKEY      (256+71)
24    #define   BACKTAB      (256+15)
25    #define   UPARROW      (256+72)
26    #define   LEFTARROW    (256+75)
27    #define   RIGHTARROW   (256+77)
28    #define   ENDKEY       (256+79)
29    #define   DOWNARROW    (256+80)
30    #define   PGUPKEY      (256+73)
31    #define   PGDNKEY      (256+81)
32    #define   INSERTKEY    (256+82)
33    #define   DELETEKEY    (256+83)
34    #define   CTLPRTSC     (256+114)
35    #define   CTLLARROW    (256+115)
36    #define   CTLRARROW    (256+116)
37    #define   CTLEND       (256+117)
38    #define   CTLPGDN      (256+118)
39    #define   CTLHOME      (256+119)
40    #define   CTLPGUP      (256+132)
41
42    /* function key codes */
43    #define   F1KEY        (256+59)
44    #define   F11KEY       (256+84)
45    #define   F21KEY       (256+94)
46    #define   F31KEY       (256+104)
47
48    /* alt-key + number key (top row) */
49    #define   ALT1KEY      (256+120)
```

Figure 3.12   viewget.c

```
1     /* viewget.c - get_cmd function - get an input command  */
2     #include "stdio.h"
3     #include "cminor.h"
4     #include "viewcmds.h"
5     #include "viewparm.h"
6
7     /* definitions of key values returned by getkey */
8     #include "keyio.h"
9
10    int get_cmd()         /* get next input command from keyboard */
11     {                    /* returns the command type entered */
12        int key ;         /* holds the keyboard input value */
13                          /* ( see keyio.h ) for values */
14        int cmd ;         /* holds the command type value */
15
16        prompt() ;            /* display prompts */
17        cmd = INVALIDCMD;    /* get next keyboard input */
18        while( cmd == INVALIDCMD )
19          { key = getkey() ;/* get next keyboard input */
20           switch( key )    /* classify the key pressed */
21               {
22               case PGDNKEY : cmd = NEXTPAGE       ;break;
23               case PGUPKEY : cmd = PREVPAGE       ;break;
24               case ASCESC  : cmd = EXITPGM        ;break;
25               case ' '     : cmd = MOVETOPOS      ;break;
26               case HOMEKEY : cmd = FIRSTPAGE      ;break;
27               case ENDKEY  : cmd = LASTPAGE       ;break;
28               case UPARROW : cmd = PREVLINE       ;break;
29               case DOWNARROW : cmd = NEXTLINE     ;break;
30               default      : cmd = INVALIDCMD     ;
31               } /* end of switch stmt */
32          }
33        return(cmd) ;
34     }
35
36    int prompt()             /* display prompts */
37     {
38    #define  UP_A  24         /* displays up arrow */
39    #define  DN_A  25         /* displays down arrow */
40
41        printf(  "\n        Type one of these Input Commands");
42        printf(  "\n HOME  = First Page      ");
43        printf(  "  %c    = Previous Line    ",UP_A);
44        printf(     "PG UP = Previous Page ");
45        printf(  "\n END   = Last  Page      ");
46        printf(  "  %c    = Next Line        ",DN_A);
47        printf(     "PG DN = Next Page ");
48        printf(  "\n ESC   = Exit Pgm        ");
49        printf(     "SPACE = Move to position ");
50     }
```

Figure 3.13   viewexec.c

```
1   /* viewexec.c file - executes one input command  */
2   #include "stdio.h"
3   #include "viewcmds.h"
4   #include "viewparm.h"
5   extern long filesize ;              /* position of effective eof */
6
7   int exec_cmd(cmd)                   /* execute input command */
8    int cmd ;                          /* value of command to execute */
9   {
10        long new_pos , get_pos() ;
11
12        switch( cmd )  {
13          case PREVPAGE  :            /* move backward to last page */
14               move_backward(PAGE_SIZE - LINES_OVERLAP) ;
15               display_page() ;
16               break;
17          case NEXTPAGE  :            /* move forward to next page */
18               move_forward(PAGE_SIZE - LINES_OVERLAP);
19               display_page() ;
20               break;
21          case EXITPGM :
22               break;
23          case MOVETOPOS :
24               new_pos = get_pos() ;  /* get new file position */
25               move_to(new_pos) ;     /* move to specified position */
26               set_top_page() ;       /* make it top_of_page for now */
27               move_backward(0);      /* move to start of this line */
28               display_page() ;
29               break;
30          case FIRSTPAGE  :
31               move_to(0L);           /* move to beginning of file */
32               set_top_page() ;       /* make it the top of the page */
33               display_page() ;
34               break;
35          case LASTPAGE  :
36               move_to(filesize) ;          /* move to end of file */
37               set_top_page() ;             /* make it top of page */
38               move_backward(PAGE_SIZE);   /* put eof at bottom */
39               display_page() ;
40               break;
41          case  PREVLINE :
42               move_backward(1) ;     /* move back one line */
43               display_page() ;
44               break;
45          case  NEXTLINE :
46               move_forward(1);       /* move forward one line */
47               display_page() ;
48               break;
49        }
50    }
```

The filesize variable is used to move to the end of the file. It is defined and allocated storage in the viewio.c source file. Here we declare it with the extern storage class. This tells the compiler that it is defined in some other file and allocated storage there. Note that we still must describe the variable's data type.

The MOVETOPOS command accepts a new file position from the keyboard. After exec_cmd moves to this new file position, it adjusts the position so the display page starts at the beginning of a line. This is treated as a special case (zero lines) by move_backward.

exec_cmd uses other functions to do all the work. This keeps the viewexec.c file manageable in size and makes it easier to use the same C statements for several input commands.

viewpos.c

Figure 3.14 shows the viewpos.c file. It accepts a new file position from the keyboard. In this case, we can use a standard library function—scanf—for getting the position. We want each digit to be echoed as typed, and we want to wait until a full line of input is typed. The basic function of get_pos is simple and would require only two lines C statements:

```
printf(" \ n new file position:");
scanf("%ld",&pos);
```

As Figure 3.14 shows, making get_pos usable and bulletproof requires a lot more effort. It must check that scanf found a number (line 14), that the number is not negative (line 18), and that it is not greater than the size of the file (line 22). If the new position passes these tests, get_pos returns it (line 29). If any test fails, a warning message is displayed and the prompt displayed again. The while loop from lines 12 to 31 repeats the process until get_pos can return a successful value. Note that the condition tested by the while loop (1 = = 1) is always true; line 29 exits from the loop and from get_pos when a valid position is found.

scanf stops processing characters as soon as the end of the number is found. Calls to flush_line ensure that the next call to scanf will start with a new line of input. This is done for valid input as well as invalid input.

viewfind.c

The viewfind.c file, shown in Figure 3.15, contains the move_forward and move_backward functions. These functions use the get_next_char and get_previous_char functions to do the file-reading operations. This keeps the movement functions small and simple and allows us to implement the file-reading operations as we choose without affecting these functions.

Figure 3.14   viewpos.c

```
1    /* viewpos.c - collect new file position from keyboard  */
2    #include "stdio.h"
3    #include "cminor.h"
4    extern long filesize ;            /* use to validate new position */
5
6    long get_pos()                    /* return new file position */
7    {
8        long pos ;
9
10       /* get a new position from the keyboard and validate it */
11       /* if it is not valid, repeat the process */
12       while( 1 == 1 )
13         { printf("\n new file position: ");
14           if( scanf("%ld",&pos) == 0 )
15             { printf("\n file position must be numeric") ;
16               flush_line() ;
17             }
18           else if( pos < 0L )   /* got a number - check its range */
19             { printf("\n file position must be >= zero");
20               flush_line() ;
21             }
22           else if( pos > filesize )
23             { printf("\n file position must be <=");
24               printf(" %ld",filesize) ;
25               flush_line() ;
26             }
27           else                     /* valid file position */
28             { flush_line() ;        /* get rid of rest of this line */
29               return( pos ) ;       /* return this new position */
30             }
31         }
32    }
33
34
35   int flush_line()
36   {
37       char c ;
38
39       scanf("%c",&c) ;
40       while( c != '\n' )
41         { scanf("%c",&c) ; }
42   }
```

Special return values tell us when we reach the beginning or end of the file. When these values are found, the position is marked as the top of the page, and the function returns to the caller. While testing for these exception conditions could have been built into the while loop, using a separate test and an immediate return statement seems a simpler solution. The details of detecting the beginning or end of the file are hidden in get_next_char and get_previous_char.

The set_top_page function is called by move_forward and move_ backward and by exec_cmd to make wherever we are now the new top of the display page. The corresponding variable top_of_page is declared in

Figure 3.15   viewfind.c

```
1      /* viewfind.c file - moves to new positions in the file */
2      #include "stdio.h"
3      #include "cminor.h"
4      #include "viewparm.h"
5      long top_of_page ;   /* position in file of top of display page */
6      long where_now() ;            /* returns current file position */
7
8      int move_forward(nlines)         /* move forward n lines */
9       int nlines ;                    /* number of lines to move */
10     {
11        int c ;                       /* hold chars read here */
12
13        move_to(top_of_page) ;        /* start at top of page */
14        while( nlines > 0 )
15           { c = get_next_char() ;
16             if( c  == END_LINE )     /* check for end of line */
17                nlines = nlines - 1 ;
18             if( c == EOF_MARK )      /* check for end of file */
19                { set_top_page() ;    /* yes - mark as top of page */
20                  return ;            /* and exit */
21                }
22           }
23        set_top_page() ;              /* mark this as top of page */
24     }
25
26     int move_backward(nlines)        /* move backward n lines */
27     int nlines ;                     /* number of lines to move */
28     {                                /* (zero = start of this line) */
29        int c ;                       /* hold char here */
30
31        move_to(top_of_page) ;        /* start at top of page */
32        nlines = nlines + 1 ;         /* add one for current line */
33        while( nlines > 0 )
34           { c = get_previous_char();
35             if( c  == END_LINE )
36                nlines = nlines - 1 ;
37             if( c == BOF_MARK )      /* check for BOF */
38                { set_top_page() ;    /* yes - mark as top of page */
39                  return ;            /* and exit */
40                }
41           }
42                                      /* we're before an end_line */
43        get_next_char() ;             /* move past it */
44        set_top_page() ;              /* mark as top of page */
45     }
46
47     int set_top_page()
48     {
49        top_of_page = where_now() ;
50     }
```

viewfind.c. It is defined outside set_top_page so that its value will be retained after set_top_page returns to its caller. The value of top_of_page is also used by exec_cmd and display_page. There it is declared as

    extern long top_of_page ;

viewdisp.c

Figure 3.16 shows the display_page and disp_char functions. The page is displayed using regular printf and putc functions. Since the C library functions do not provide us with a way to find out how many lines of text have been displayed, we keep track ourselves. The row and column variables are updated when a character is displayed. disp_char also uses the column variable to position the cursor when a tab character must be displayed.

display_page displays the file's name, the position in the file of the top of the page, and the file's size. All these variables are defined in other source files so they are declared in lines 8 to 10 to be extern.

display_page may find the end of the file before it displays a full page. Handling this exception is easy: the loop on lines 33 to 37 ends when a full page is

Figure 3.16   viewdisp.c

```
1    /* viewdisp.c file - display current page of file */
2    #include "stdio.h"
3    #include "cminor.h"
4    #include "viewparm.h"
5
6    #define TAB_WIDTH      8
7    #define PAGE_WIDTH     80
8    extern char    filename[] ;
9    extern long    filesize ;          /* size of file in bytes */
10   extern long    top_of_page;        /* file position of top of page */
11   int   row ;                        /* current line of page */
12   int   col ;                        /* current column of page */
13
14     display_page()
15     {
16        int c ;                       /* hold the character here */
17        int i ;                       /* counter for loop */
18
19        move_to(top_of_page);         /* start at top of the page */
20                                      /* write a header line */
21        printf("\n FILE - %s     POSITION - %ld     FILE SIZE - %ld \n",
22        filename,top_of_page,filesize);
23
24                                      /* write a border line of dashes */
25        for( i=1 ; i <= 80 ; i = i + 1 )
26            { putchar('-'); }
```

Figure 3.16   viewdisp.c (continued)

```
27
28          /* get chars from file until we've written (PAGE_SIZE) lines */
29          /* or we've reached the end of the file */
30          row = 1 ;                      /* starting row & column values */
31          col = 1 ;
32          c = get_next_char() ;
33          while( ( row <= PAGE_SIZE ) && ( c != EOF_MARK ) )
34              {                          /* write til end of page or file */
35              disp_char(c) ;             /* display current character */
36              c = get_next_char() ;      /* and get another one */
37              }
38
39          while( row <= PAGE_SIZE )   /* pad out page if eof reached */
40              { putchar('\n'); row = row + 1 ; }
41
42                                         /* write a border line of dashes */
43          for( i=1 ; i <= 80 ; i = i + 1 )
44              { putchar('-'); }
45
46      }
47
48
49
50
51      int disp_char(c)                  /* display one char */
52                                        /* and update row and column */
53      int c ;                           /* value of char to write */
54      {
55          /* classify the character and handle accordingly */
56
57          if( isgraphic(c) )
58              { putchar(c);             /* display ASCII graphic char */
59              col = col + 1 ;           /* advance column number */
60              if( col > PAGE_WIDTH )    /* check for wrap-around */
61                  { row = row + 1 ;     /*    y - advance row no   */
62                  col = 1 ;             /*     and set column to first col*/
63                  }
64              }
65          else if( c == END_LINE )
66              { putchar('\n') ;         /* end_line char - force new line */
67              row = row + 1 ;           /* advance row no. */
68              col = 1 ;                 /* set column back to first col */
69              }
70          else if( c == '\t' )
71              {
72              do                        /* tab - expand it */
73                  { putchar(' ');       /* print spaces      */
74                  col = col + 1 ;       /* and advance column no. */
75                  if( col > PAGE_WIDTH )  /* checking for wrap-around */
76                      { row = row + 1 ;
77                      col = 1 ;
78                      }
79                  } while( ( col % TAB_WIDTH ) != 1 ) ; /* until tab stop */
80              }
81      }
```

displayed or when the end-of-file is reached. Lines 39 and 40 then pad out the
displayed page if fewer than PAGE_SIZE lines have been written.

Tab stops are fixed at every eighth column, starting at column one. The division remainder operator, %, is used in line 79 to check for a tab stop. The do { }
while loop in lines 72 to 79 executes the body of the loop before testing, ensuring
that at least one space character is displayed.

viewio.c

The viewio.c file in Figure 3.17 groups all operations on the data file. It uses standard I/O library functions for actual I/O, but it keeps these details private to this

Figure 3.17   viewio.c

```
 1    /* viewio.c file - I/O module for VIEW program */
 2    #include "stdio.h"
 3    #include "cminor.h"
 4    #include "viewparm.h"
 5
 6    /* fseek mode definitions */
 7    #define   CURRENT_REL    1         /* relative to current position */
 8    #define   EOF_REL        2         /* relative to end of the file */
 9    #define   BOF_REL        0         /* relative to beginning of file */
10
11    #define   CTL_Z         26         /* marks EOF in some text files */
12
13    FILE *fp ;                         /* file pointer for text file */
14    long filesize ;                    /* size of the file in bytes */
15    long int ftell() ;
16    FILE *gfopen() ;
17
18    int open_file(fn)                  /* open a file */
19     char fn[] ;                       /* file name string */
20     {                                 /* return success or failure */
21        fp = gfopen(fn,"r",BIN_MODE) ;
22        if(fp != NULL)
23             return(SUCCESS) ;
24        else return( FAILURE ) ;
25     }
26
27
28    int set_filesize(chk_ctlz)                /* set up file size */
29     int chk_ctlz ;                    /* if =ASC_MODE check for control-Z */
30     {
31        long back ;
32        int c ;
33
34        fseek(fp,0L,EOF_REL) ;  /* get size of file */
35        filesize = ftell(fp) ;
36
37        if( chk_ctlz != ASC_MODE )  /* control-Z checking needed ? */
38             return ;
39
40        /* check last 128 byte block for a CTL-Z */
41        back = filesize % 128 ;    /* how far back to start of block? */
```

Figure 3.17   viewio.c (continued)

```
42          if( (back == 0) && (filesize > 0) )  /* if at start of block ,*/
43              back = 128 ;                      /*     last block is full */
44          fseek(fp, filesize - back ,BOF_REL);
45          c = getc(fp);
46          while( c != EOF )
47            { if( c == CTL_Z )           /* look for control-Z */
48                { filesize = ftell(fp) - 1 ;
49                  return ;          /* found - adjust file size and exit */
50                }
51              c = getc(fp);
52            }
53      }
54
55  int move_to(new_pos)                /* move to specified position */
56   long new_pos ;
57   {
58       fseek(fp,new_pos,BOF_REL);
59   }
60
61  long where_now()                    /* return current position */
62   {
63      return( ftell(fp) ) ;
64   }
65
66
67  int get_next_char()               /* get char at file position */
68   {
69       char c ;
70
71       if( ftell(fp) == filesize ) /* are we at end of file ? */
72           return( EOF_MARK ) ;     /*  y - return end file mark */
73       else                         /* no - get next char */
74         { c = getc(fp);            /* get a char */
75           return( toascii(c) ) ; /* force char to ascii, return it */
76         }
77   }
78
79
80  int get_previous_char()            /* read the char in front of */
81   {                                 /* current file position */
82       char c ;
83
84       if( ftell(fp) != 0L )            /* check for begin. file */
85         { fseek(fp,-1L,CURRENT_REL);  /* back up one char */
86           c = getc(fp);               /* read a char*/
87                                   /* back up in front of char read*/
88           fseek(fp,-1L,CURRENT_REL) ;
89           return( toascii(c) ) ;      /* force to be ascii */
90         }                             /* and return the char */
91       else return(BOF_MARK) ;
92   }
93
94
95  int close_file()
96   {
97       fclose(fp) ;
98   }
```

file. We can change the way we read the data file without making an impact on other parts of the program. This lets us fix bugs or make enhancements without causing problems in the rest of the program.

The open_file function, lines 18 to 25, just hides the details of opening a file from its caller. Since it returns an integer success/failure value, the caller does not need to know whether a buffered file pointer or a file descriptor for unbuffered I/O is used. The success or failure of open_file is used by its caller to validate the file name. Opening the file would have been necessary before the file was read, and doing it in get_filename serves the need for validating the file name. Note that the file is opened in the binary mode as discussed in section 3.3.

The set_filesize function finds out how big the operating system thinks the file is. It then checks for the presence of a control-Z character (26) in the last 128-byte block of the file. The file size used will correspond to the position of this character if one is present. This allows movement in the file to behave sensibly when the control-Z end-of-file convention is used. We have confined the details of end-of-file conventions to this single function. The rest of the I/O module uses the file size value to specify the end of the file.

The move_to and where_now functions hide the details of using fseek and ftell from other parts of the VIEW program. move_to and where_now let us get or set the current file position, but we rely on the library functions to keep track of this file position.

The get_next_char and get_previous_char functions use fseek and ftell to change or to determine the current position in the file. get_previous_char is implemented just as in the experimental program in section 3.3.

3.5   Testing VIEW

□   The real purpose of testing is to raise our level of confidence that the program is correct. That means that we must explicitly test the program for each case in which we expect its behavior to be different.

We take a methodical approach and test each function separately. We verify its operation before we put the program together. This requirement means extra work before the testing can begin, but it has several advantages:

> We can test each function thoroughly. When we finish testing a function, we have confidence that it works.
> Each test is well controlled. When a function fails a test, we can usually fix the problem immediately. In the usual approach to testing, the hardest job is often to understand what the program is doing when it does not appear to work correctly.
> Test data are easy to construct. We can test display functions without placing the test data into files. Constructing test data is often a difficult job in the usual way of testing. The result is often that testing is not comprehensive.

The following sections discuss the testing of each function: what we test and how we test. We group the tests by source files; the functions in a single source file cannot be separated so we test them together. For each source file tested, we list a test program that exercises the file and presents a sample test run. To save space, the test runs have been condensed. They may not show the testing of all functions in a source file or all cases that must be tested, but they should give a feeling for what you see when the test programs are executed.

Testing view.c

The main function is mostly calls to other functions: get_filename, set_filesize, get_cmd, exec_cmd, and close_file. We verify that these are called in the right sequence and with the right arguments. We expect the main to keep calling get_cmd and exec_cmd until get_cmd returns an exit program command.

It is important that we understand what we are trying to prove before we begin testing. The specifications we made for the program, the pseudo-code, and the source listing are useful in deciding what to test and what to expect.

We test main using special versions of the functions it calls. These contain printf statements to tell us when they are called. Parameters received are displayed, and any values to be returned will be accepted from the keyboard. Such dummy versions of functions are often called *stubs*. Figure 3.18a shows the stubs we use to test main.

Since the get_filename function is in the view.c source file with main, we cannot replace it by a stub function. The way we package functions in source files affects our flexibility in testing. In this case, get_filename is short and simple so testing main and get_filename at the same time is not a problem. The file with the stub functions includes one—open_file—needed by get_filename. We compile both view.c and testmain.c and link them together:

```
link cs view testmain,view,nul
```

We expect results like the following:

```
get_filename called
set_filesize called ( with ASC_MODE )
exec_cmd called (with a FIRSTPAGE cmd )
get_cmd called ( we specify a command )
exec_cmd called (with the cmd we specified to get_cmd)
    .
    .
    .
get_cmd called ( we specify an EXITPGM command )
close_file called
program terminates
```

Figure 3.18a   testmain.c

```
1     /* testmain.c - test view.c (main function) */
2     #include "stdio.h"
3     #include "cminor.h"
4
5     int open_file(fn)
6      char fn[] ;
7      {
8          int ret ;
9          printf("\n open_file called - fn= %s\n",fn);
10         printf("return code:");
11         scanf("%d",&ret);
12         return(ret);
13     }
14
15
16    int set_filesize(chk_ctlz)
17     int chk_ctlz ;
18     {
19         printf("\n set_filesize called - chk_ctlz = %d \n",chk_ctlz);
20     }
21
22    int get_cmd()
23     {
24         int cmd ;
25         printf("\n get_cmd called\n");
26         printf("cmd:");
27         scanf("%d",&cmd);
28         return(cmd);
29     }
30
31    int exec_cmd(cmd)
32     int cmd ;
33     {
34         printf("\n execcmd called\n");
35         printf("cmd= %d  \n",cmd);
36     }
37
38    int close_file()
39     {
40         printf("\n close_file called\n");
41     }
42
43
44
```

We can run this test without adding any special testing statements to main. Figure 3.18b shows the test run. This test run tested the program with a valid file name. We should also test the program with an invalid file name and with no file name typed on the command line.

Figure 3.18b   testmain.fig

```
 1
 2    D>view abcdef
 3
 4     open_file called - fn= abcdef
 5    return code:
 6     set_filesize called - chk_ctlz = 1
 7
 8     execcmd called
 9    cmd= 2
10
11     get_cmd called
12    cmd: 0
13     execcmd called
14    cmd= 0
15
16     get_cmd called
17    cmd: 1
18     execcmd called
19    cmd= 1
20
21     get_cmd called
22    cmd: 2
23     execcmd called
24    cmd= 2
25
26     get_cmd called
27    cmd: 3
28     execcmd called
29    cmd= 3
30
31     get_cmd called
32    cmd: 4
33     execcmd called
34    cmd= 4
35
36     get_cmd called
37    cmd: 6
38     execcmd called
39    cmd= 6
40
41     get_cmd called
42    cmd: 7
43     execcmd called
44    cmd= 7
45
46     get_cmd called
47    cmd: 5
48     close_file called
49    D>
```

Testing viewget.c

To test the viewget.c file, we revise the stub file, removing the dummy get_cmd function (Figure 3.19a). Since the main function now works, we can use it in testing get_cmd. main calls get_cmd and then exec_cmd. The dummy exec_cmd function in the stub file displays the command it receives. This serves to tell us what value get_cmd returned to main.

Should we use the real getkey function or a stub function? In this case we chose to use the real function. Had using the real getkey function made the test more difficult, we might have chosen to run the test first with a stub getkey function.

We can now compile this revised file and link:

link cs view viewget testget,view,nul,toolkit

Since we are using the getkey function from the toolkit, we need to include the toolkit object library in the linking step.

Figure 3.19a   testget.c

```
1      /* testget.c - test viewget.c (get_cmd function) */
2     #include "stdio.h"
3     #include "cminor.h"
4
5     int open_file(fn)
6      char fn[] ;
7      {
8          int ret ;
9          printf("\n open_file called - fn= %s\n",fn);
10         printf("return code:");
11         scanf("%d",&ret);
12         return(ret);
13     }
14
15
16    int set_filesize(chk_ctlz)
17     int chk_ctlz ;
18     {
19         printf("\n set_filesize called - chk_ctlz = %d \n",chk_ctlz);
20     }
21
22    int exec_cmd(cmd)
23     int cmd ;
24     {
25         printf("\n execcmd called\n");
26         printf("cmd= %d   \n",cmd);
27     }
28
29    int close_file()
30     {
31         printf("\n close_file called\n");
32     }
```

We should type all valid commands to getkey and try the invalid keys as well. What do we expect to see? The output should look about like the previous test. Instead of the line get_cmd called and the prompt for a return value, we should see a prompt describing the valid input commands. But the sequence of events should be the same. When keys that do not correspond to valid commands are pressed, the program should just wait for further input. Figure 3.19b shows results from a test run. To shorten the listing, several of the prompting messages are replaced by ellipsis marks (. . .).

Testing viewexec.c

The procedure we used to test get_cmd is also useful for testing the exec_cmd function. We edit the stub file again, removing the dummy exec_cmd function. The real exec_cmd function calls a number of new functions (move_backward, move_forward, display_page, set_top_page, move_to, and get_pos) so we add stub versions to this file. The new test file is shown in Figure 3.20a. This technique of starting with the main function and successively replacing stubs by the actual functions is called *top-down* testing. If we continue using this technique until the whole program is tested, we wind up with the entire program working together. This method of testing may not always be practical to carry out, but it is often useful.

The exec_cmd function does not do anything but make a series of function calls. We want to verify that exec_cmd makes the right series of function calls for each input command. The messages from the stub functions should allow us to demonstrate this. Figure 3.20b lists output from a test run. To keep it brief, we suppressed even more of the prompting messages from get_cmd.

Testing viewpos.c

We could test the viewpos.c source file with the same top-down testing method we have been discussing. We need only delete the get_pos function from the test program source file. However, it would be hard to interpret the resulting test because of all the messages from dummy functions. This difficulty illustrates a problem with top-down testing: as more real functions replace stubs, it becomes difficult to design tests that are both thorough and concise. Figure 3.21 shows an alternative for testing viewpos.c. This program stands alone; we do not need any of the functions already tested. We just link this file with the viewpos.obj file and run the test.

The basic function of get_pos is simple so we list only the exceptions that must be tested without showing any test runs:

1.   The keyboard input may be nonnumeric.
2.   The input value may be negative.

Figure 3.19b   testget.fig

```
 1    D>view abc
 2
 3     open_file called - fn= abc
 4    return code:
 5     set_filesize called - chk_ctlz = 1
 6
 7     execcmd called
 8    cmd= 2
 9
10            Type one of these Input Commands
11    HOME  = First Page      PG UP = Previous Page
12    END   = Last  Page      PG DN = Next Page
13    ↑     = Previous Line    ESC   = Exit Pgm
14    ↓     = Next Line        SPACE = Move to position
15    [ PgDn key pressed ]
16     execcmd called
17    cmd= 0
18
19            Type one of these Input Commands
20    HOME  = First Page      PG UP = Previous Page
21    END   = Last  Page      PG DN = Next Page
22    ↑     = Previous Line    ESC   = Exit Pgm
23    ↓     = Next Line        SPACE = Move to position
24    [ PgUp key pressed ]
25     execcmd called
26    cmd= 1
27
28            Type one of these Input Commands
29    HOME  = First Page      PG UP = Previous Page
30    END   = Last  Page      PG DN = Next Page
31    ↑     = Previous Line    ESC   = Exit Pgm
32    ↓     = Next Line        SPACE = Move to position
33    [ Home key pressed ]
34     execcmd called
35    cmd= 2
36    ...
37    cmd= 3
38    ...
39    cmd= 4
40    ...
41    cmd= 6
42    ...
43    cmd= 7
44    ...
45    cmd= 2
46            Type one of these Input Commands
47    HOME  = First Page      PG UP = Previous Page
48    END   = Last  Page      PG DN = Next Page
49    ↑     = Previous Line    ESC   = Exit Pgm
50    ↓     = Next Line        SPACE = Move to position
51    [ Esc key pressed ]
52     close_file called
53    D>
```

Figure 3.20a   testexec.c

```
1       /* testexec.c - test viewexec.c (exec_cmd function) */
2      #include "stdio.h"
3      #include "cminor.h"
4      long filesize ;
5
6      int open_file(fn)
7       char fn[] ;
8       {
9          int ret ;
10         printf("\n open_file called - fn= %s\n",fn);
11         printf("return code:");
12         scanf("%d",&ret);
13         return(ret);
14      }
15
16
17     int set_filesize(chk_ctlz)
18      int chk_ctlz ;
19      {
20         printf("\n set_filesize called - chk_ctlz = %d \n",chk_ctlz);
21         printf(" file size:");
22         scanf("%ld",&filesize) ;
23      }
24
25     int close_file()
26      {
27         printf("\n close_file called\n");
28      }
29
30     int move_backward(nlines)
31      int nlines ;
32      {
33         printf("\n move_backward called nlines= %d ",nlines);
34      }
35
36     int move_forward(nlines)
37      int nlines ;
38      {
39         printf("\n move_forward called nlines= %d ",nlines);
40      }
41
42     int display_page()
43      {
44         printf("\n display_page called ");
45      }
46
47
48     int set_top_page()
49      {
50         printf("\n set_top_page called ");
51      }
52
53
54     int move_to(pos)
55      long pos ;
```

Figure 3.20a testexec.c (continued)

```
56      {
57          printf("\n move_to called  - pos= %ld ",pos);
58      }
59
60
61  long get_pos()
62      {
63          long pos ;
64
65          printf(" \n get_pos called ");
66          printf("\n new position:");
67          scanf("%ld",&pos) ;
68          return( pos) ;
69      }
```

3. The input value may be larger than the file size.

4. A second value may be typed on the same line. get_pos must ensure that these characters are discarded.

We must check that get_pos recognizes these exceptions and recovers properly. It is also wise to try both small and large values for the file size and file position to ensure that the long number variables are handled correctly. Finally, the *boundary* values zero and the file size should be tried as file positions.

The file I/O functions that we wrote require actual files as input. Building suitable files is a new element in the testing process. Most of the testing can be done with a small file like the one created in Section 3.3. However, we should also test with a large file to show errors in handling large file position values. (The C library functions handle file size and file position as long data type values. A likely error would be to treat them as integer values. Since integers are stored as 16-bit signed values with a maximum value of 32,767 in most IBM PC implementations of C, a file of about 40,000 characters would provide a valid check for this type of error.)

Testing viewfind.c

Next we test the functions in the viewfind.c source file: move_forward, move_backward, and set_top_page. The top-down method is not very convenient for this test; thus, we use a standalone test program, shown in Figure 3.22a, like that suggested for the get_pos function. We supply a main function that calls the functions to be tested and stubs for any functions the functions in viewfind.c call.

The set_top_page function is used by move_forward and move_backward so we test it first. Its role is to set the variable top_of_page. Before we call set_top_page, we place a recognizable value in top_of_page. We must

Figure 3.20b   testexec.fig

```
 1    D>view abc
 2     open_file called - fn= abc
 3    return code:1
 4     set_filesize called - chk_ctlz = 1
 5     file size:2000
 6
 7     move_to called  - pos= 0
 8     ...
 9              Type one of these Input Commands
10    HOME   = First Page      PG UP = Previous Page
11    END    = Last  Page      PG DN = Next Page
12     ↑     = Previous Line   ESC   = Exit Pgm
13     ↓     = Next Line       SPACE = Move to position
14    [ PgDn Key Pressed ]
15    move_forward called nlines= 14
16    display_page called
17    ...
18    [ PgUp Key Pressed ]
19    move_backward called nlines= 14
20    display_page called
21    ...
22    [ Home Key Pressed ]
23    move_to called  - pos= 0
24    set_top_page called
25    display_page called
26    ...
27    [ Space Bar Pressed ]
28    move_to called  - pos= 2000
29    set_top_page called
30    move_backward called nlines= 16
31    display_page called
32    ...
33    [ Space Bar Pressed ]
34    get_pos called
35    new position:50
36    move_to called  - pos= 50
37    set_top_page called
38    move_backward called nlines= 0
39    display_page called
40    ...
41    [ Down Arrow Key Pressed ]
42    move_forward called nlines= 1
43    display_page called
44    ...
45    [ Down Arrow Key Pressed ]
46    move_backward called nlines= 1
47    display_page called
48    ...
49     close_file called
50    D>
```

Figure 3.21   testpos.c

```
1      /* testpos.c - test viewpos.c (get_pos function) */
2      #include "stdio.h"
3      #include "cminor.h"
4      #include "viewcmds.h"
5      #include "viewparm.h"
6      long filesize ;
7      long get_pos() ;
8
9      main()
10     {
11         int cmd ;                        /* holds current cmd     */
12         long pos ;
13
14         printf("\n\n testing get_pos\n");
15         printf("file size:");
16         scanf("%s",&filesize) ;
17         pos = get_pos() ;
18         while( pos != 999 )
19            { printf(" get_pos = %ld \n",pos) ;
20              pos = get_pos() ;
21            }
22     }
23
```

Figure 3.22a   testfind.c

```
1    /* testfind.c - test viewfind.c (move_forward & move_backward) */
2    #include "stdio.h"
3    extern long top_of_page ;
4    long pos ;
5
6    main()
7    {
8        int c ;
9        int n ;
10       char s[81];
11
12      printf("\n testing set_top_page \n");
13      top_of_page = -999L ;
14      pos = 7 ;
15      printf("\n before call - top_of_page = %ld",top_of_page);
16      set_top_page() ;
17      printf("\n after call - top_of_page = %ld",top_of_page);
18      printf("\n");
19
20
21      printf("\n test move forward ");
```

Figure 3.22a   testfind.c (continued)

```
22        while( 1 == 1 )
23          { printf("\n nlines:"); scanf("%d",&n);
24            if( n < 0 )
25                break ;
26            move_forward(n) ;
27            printf("\n top_of_page = %ld",top_of_page);
28          }
29
30
31        printf("\n test move_backward ");
32        while( 1 == 1 )
33          { printf("\n nlines:"); scanf("%d",&n);
34            if( n < 0 )
35                break ;
36            move_backward(n) ;
37            printf("\n top_of_page = %ld",top_of_page);
38          }
39    }
40
41
42
43    get_next_char()
44    {
45       int c ;
46       printf("\n get next char called");
47       pos = pos + 1 ;
48       printf("  - return(decimal):");
49       scanf("%d",&c);
50       return(c) ;
51    }
52
53    get_previous_char()
54    {
55       int c ;
56       printf("\n get previous char called");
57       pos = pos - 1 ;
58       printf("  - return(decimal):");
59       scanf("%d",&c);
60       return(c);
61    }
62
63    move_to(p)
64    long p ;
65    {
66       pos = p ;
67       printf("\n move to called -  position = %ld",pos);
68
69    }
70
71    long where_now()
72    {
73       return( pos ) ;
74    }
75
76
```

ensure that a call to set_top_page really changes the variable, not just that the value after a call looks right.

The key to testing move_forward and move_backward is the stub functions for get_next_char and get_previous_char. These functions accept return values from the keyboard, not from a data file. This gives us the flexibility to test thoroughly. Constructing one or more data files to test move_forward and move_backward completely would take a lot of effort.

There are several special cases to be tested for move_forward: end-of-file, one line and more than one line, lines with only the end-of-line character, and end-of-line as the first character found. Testing move_backward is similar but zero lines is an additional case to be treated. A sample test run is shown in Figure 3.22b.

Figure 3.22b **testfind.fig**

```
 1    D>testfind
 2
 3    testing set_top_page
 4
 5    before call - top_of_page = -999
 6    after call - top_of_page = 7
 7
 8    test move_forward
 9    nlines:0
10    move_to called -  position = 0
11    top_of_page = 0
12    nlines:1
13    move_to called -  position = 0
14    get_next_char called  - return(decimal):2
15    get_next_char called  - return(decimal):3
16    get_next_char called  - return(decimal):10
17    top_of_page = 3
18    nlines:2
19    move_to called -  position = 3
20    get_next_char called  - return(decimal):1
21    get_next_char called  - return(decimal):10
22    get_next_char called  - return(decimal):2
23    get_next_char called  - return(decimal):10
24    top_of_page = 7
25    nlines:1
26    move_to called -  position = 7
27    get_next_char called  - return(decimal):2
28    get_next_char called  - return(decimal):-1
29    top_of_page = 9
30    nlines:-1
31    test move_backward
32    nlines:0
33    move_to called -  position = 9
34    get_previous_char called  - return(decimal):10
35    get_next_char called  - return(decimal):10
36    top_of_page = 9
37    nlines:0
38    move_to called -  position = 9
39    get_previous_char called  - return(decimal):1
```

Figure 3.22b   testfind.fig (continued)

```
40    get previous char called   - return(decimal):10
41    get next char called   - return(decimal):10
42    top_of_page = 8
43    nlines:1
44    move to called -   position = 8
45    get previous char called   - return(decimal):1
46    get previous char called   - return(decimal):10
47    get previous char called   - return(decimal):2
48    get previous char called   - return(decimal):3
49    get previous char called   - return(decimal):10
50    get next char called   - return(decimal):10
51    top_of_page = 4
52    nlines:1
53    move to called -   position = 4
54    get previous char called   - return(decimal):-2
55    top_of_page = 3
56    nlines:-1
57    D>
```

Testing viewdisp.c

Figure 3.23a shows another standalone test program. It tests first disp_char and then display_page. display_page depends on disp_char for updating row and column variables. It is wise to make sure that disp_char works correctly before we tackle display_page. This test illustrates a weakness with top-down testing: functions like disp_char are tested after the functions that call them. Testing the lower functions before those that call them is called *bottom-up* testing.

Figure 3.23b shows part of a test run. The part shown checks disp_char. As with viewfind.c we supply characters interactively. We also control the row and column values before each character. For each test we are concerned with two results: what is displayed on the screen and how the row and column variables are changed. We must try a variety of cases for disp_char: normal and control characters and tab characters at tab stops and off them. We also test the behavior when column 80 is reached for normal characters, end-of-line, and tab characters.

Once the disp_char function works correctly, we are ready to test the display_page function. (These test results are not shown in Figure 3.23b. However, you should be able to follow the test program.) We are interested in two cases: one in which a full page is displayed without reaching the end of file and one in which the end-of-file is reached before a full page is displayed. The expected outcome is that exactly 16 lines are displayed on the screen in each case.

Since display_page writes to the screen, our testing output interferes with normal output. The solution is to run one test to see that the loops in display_page work correctly. For this test we use get_next_char to display the current row and column values and to accept the character value from the keyboard. Then we test display_page with no test output to check the layout on the screen. Even

Figure 3.23a   testdisp.c

```
1    /* testdisp.c - test viewdisp.c (display_page and disp_char) */
2    #include "stdio.h"
3    #include "cminor.h"
4    #include "viewparm.h"
5
6    char filename[81] ;
7    char s[256] ;
8    extern int row,col ;
9    long filesize ;
10   long top_of_page ;
11   int ix ;                 /* index into char string */
12   int silent ;             /* flag for get_next_char */
13
14    /* test viewdisp module */
15    main()
16    {
17       int c ;
18       char a ;
19       int i ;
20
21       printf("\n testing disp_char");
22       while( 1 == 1 )
23          {
24          printf("\n char (decimal):");
25          scanf("%d",&c);
26          if( c == -1 ) break ;
27          printf("\n col:");
28          scanf("%d",&col);
29          printf("\n row:");
30          scanf("%d",&row);
31          printf("\n12345678901234567890\n");
32
33          for( i=1 ; i < col ; i= i + 1 )
34             {
35             printf(">");
36             }
37          disp_char(c) ;
38          printf("<  row= %d  col= %d \n",row,col);
39          }
40
41       printf("\n\n testing display_page \n");
42
43       strcpy(filename,"< file name >") ;
44       top_of_page = 333000000 ;
45       filesize = 444000000 ;
46
47       silent = 0 ;
48       printf("\n  show get_next_char calls\n");
49       display_page() ;
50
51
52       printf("\n test with get_next_char silent\n");
53       silent = 1 ;
54       printf("\ntest with full page-no output from get_next_char\n");
55       strcpy(s,"1234567890");
```

Figure 3.23a   testdisp.c (continued)

```
56      ix = 0 ;
57      display_page() ;
58      scanf("%c%c",&a,&a) ;              /* pause before next test */
59      printf("\ntest with eof in 3rd line-no get_next_char out.\n");
60      strcpy(s,"1\n2\n\f");
61      ix = 0 ;
62      display_page() ;
63   }
64
65
66   int get_next_char()
67   {
68      int c ;
69
70      if( silent == 0 )
71        { printf("\n get_next_char called\n") ;
72          printf("\n row= %d   col= %d \n",row,col);
73          printf("value to return:");
74          scanf("%d",&c);
75          return(c);
76        }
77      else if( s[ix] == '\0' )   /* at end of string */
78        { ix = 0 ;               /* start over in string */
79          return( '\n' ) ;       /* and return Newline char */
80        }
81      else                       /* not at end of string return char */
82        { c = tochar( s[ix] ) ;
83          ix = ix + 1 ;
84          if( c == '\f' ) c = EOF_MARK ;
85          return( c ) ;
86        }
87   }
88
89   int move_to(pos)
90   long pos ;
91   {
92      printf("\n move_to called - position = %ld \n",pos) ;
93   }
```

this test does not correspond fully to the screen layout expected from the final program; we are missing the input prompts written by get_cmd.

Testing viewio.c

We packaged all the file access functions into the viewio.c source file. This allowed us to test the rest of the VIEW program without creating any special data files for testing. But in testing viewio.c we cannot avoid actual file I/O.

The file I/O functions we wrote require actual files as input. Building suitable files is a new element in the testing process. Most of the testing can be done with a

Figure 3.23b   c:testdisp.fig

```
 1    D>testdisp
 2
 3     testing disp_char
 4     char (decimal):32
 5     col:1
 6     row:1
 7    12345678901234567890
 8     <  row= 1  col= 2
 9
10     char (decimal):48
11     col:79
12     row:2
13    12345678901234567890
14    >>>>>>>>>>>>>>>>>>>>>>>>>>>>>>>>>>>>>>>>>>>>>>>>>>>>>>>>>>>>>>>>>0<
15      row= 1  col= 80
16
17     char (decimal):97
18     col:80
19     row:3
20    12345678901234567890
21    >>>>>>>>>>>>>>>>>>>>>>>>>>>>>>>>>>>>>>>>>>>>>>>>>>>>>>>>>>>>>>>>>>>a
22    <  row= 3  col= 1
23
24     char (decimal):1
25     col:2
26     row:2
27    12345678901234567890
28    ><  row= 2  col= 2
29
30     char (decimal):10
31     col:3
32     row:3
33    12345678901234567890
34    >>
35    <  row= 4  col= 1
36
37     char (decimal):13
38     col:4
39     row:4
40    12345678901234567890
41    >>><  row= 4  col= 4
42
43     char (decimal):127
44     col:5
45     row:5
46    12345678901234567890
47    >>>><  row= 5  col= 5
48
49     char (decimal):9
50     col:1
51     row:1
52    12345678901234567890
53          <  row= 1  col= 9
54
55     char (decimal):9
```

Figure 3.23b   c:testdisp.fig (continued)

```
56    col:8
57    row:2
58    12345678901234567890
59    >>>>>>> <  row= 2  col= 9
60
61    char (decimal):9
62    col:79
63    row:3
64    12345678901234567890
65    >>>>>>>>>>>>>>>>>>>>>>>>>>>>>>>>>>>>>>>>>>>>>>>>>>>>>>>>>>>>>>
66    <  row= 4  col= 1
67
68    char (decimal):9
69    col:80
70    row:5
71    12345678901234567890
72    >>>>>>>>>>>>>>>>>>>>>>>>>>>>>>>>>>>>>>>>>>>>>>>>>>>>>>>>>>>>>>
73    <  row= 5  col= 1
74
75    char (decimal):-1
76    ...
77    D>
```

small file like the one created in Section 3.3. However, we should also test with a large file of 40,000 or more characters to ensure that the long values for the file's size and the file position are handled correctly.

Figure 3.24a shows our test program, and Figure 3.24b shows test results. As in the previous sections, we use a standalone program. We call the functions in viewio.c directly and display results after the calls to get clear test results.

The tests are fairly simple. All the functions except open_file require that the data file be opened and a file pointer identify it. So we start with open_file. Since the other functions also require that the filesize variable be set properly, set_filesize is tested next. As each function is tested, it can be used to aid testing the other functions. The move_to and where_now functions are useful in this way.

Testing Summary

We have covered testing the individual functions in VIEW thoroughly. More topics to discuss include testing the program as a whole, building test data files, and tracking down bugs exposed by testing. The next chapter continues the discussion.

The test programs that we wrote have lasting value; we will not throw them away as soon as the VIEW program works. Bugs often turn up later and these testing tools will help find them. Successful programs evolve with enhancements

Figure 3.24a   testio.c

```
1     /* testio.c - test viewio.c */
2     #include "stdio.h"
3     #include "cminor.h"
4     #include "viewparm.h"
5
6     extern FILE *fp ;
7     extern long filesize ;
8     long ftell() ;
9     long where_now() ;
10
11    main()
12      {
13        long pos ;
14        int c , i ;
15        char fn[65] ;
16
17        printf("\n testing I/O module\n");
18
19        printf("\n file name:");
20        scanf("%s",fn) ;
21        printf(" open_file = %d ",open_file(fn) ) ;
22        printf("\n fp = %x ",fp);
23
24        printf("\n\n calling set_filesize");
25        filesize = -1L ;
26        set_filesize(ASC_MODE);
27        printf("\n filesize= %ld  \n",filesize);
28
29        pos = 3  ;
30        printf("\n move_to %ld",pos);
31        move_to(pos) ;
32        printf("\n where_ now = %ld  next char is %d  ftell=%ld\n",
33        where_now() , get_next_char() ,ftell(fp) );
34        printf("\n where_ now = %ld  next char is %d   ftell=%ld\n",
35        where_now() , get_next_char() , ftell(fp) );
36        pos = 1  ;
37        move_to(pos) ;
38        printf("\n move_to %ld",pos);
39        printf("\n where_ now = %ld  next char is %d ftell=%ld\n",
40        where_now() , get_next_char() ,ftell(fp) );
41
42        scanf("%c%c",&c,&c);   /* pause here */
43
44        /* test  get next char */
45        move_to(0L) ; /* start at beginning of file */
46        printf("\n test get next char - sequential reads \n ") ;
47        c = get_next_char() ;
48        i = 0;
49        while( c != EOF_MARK )
50          { printf(" c=%d ",c);
51            c = get_next_char() ;
52            i = i + 1 ;
53            if( i > 100 )
54                 break ;
55          }
```

Figure 3.24a   testio.c (continued)

```
56        printf("\n eof reached - c=%d \n",c);
57        scanf("%c%c",&c,&c);   /* pause here */
58
59
60        move_to(filesize) ;   /* start at end of file */
61        printf("\n test get next char - at eof \n ") ;
62        for(i=0 ; i < 10 ; i=i+1)
63          { printf("  c=%d ",get_next_char() ) ; }
64        printf("\n thru  \n");
65        scanf("%c%c",&c,&c);   /* pause here */
66
67
68        /* test  get previous char */
69        printf("\n test get previous char \n ") ;
70        i = 0 ;
71        c = get_previous_char() ;
72        while( c != BOF_MARK )
73          { printf("  c=%d ",c);
74            c = get_previous_char() ;
75            i = i + 1 ;
76            if( i > 100 )
77                break ;
78          }
79        printf("\n bof reached - c=%d \n",c);
80        scanf("%c%c",&c,&c);   /* pause here */
81
82        move_to(0L) ;
83        printf("\n test get previous char - at BOF \n ") ;
84        for(i=0 ; i < 10 ; i=i+1)
85          { printf("  c=%d ",get_previous_char() ) ; }
86        printf("\n thru  \n");
87
88        close_file() ;
89     }
```

added as practical use suggests them. These enhancements need testing to ensure that they do what was intended and do not interfere with the rest of the program. Without available test programs, there is an irresistible temptation to bypass thorough testing of enhancements. With the test programs, it is easy to modify them and run new tests.

The VIEW program went through several revisions to make it simple and clear in structure. The test programs evolved along with VIEW and made the revision process much easier.

We have presented a methodical approach to testing programs. Each step is small and fairly quick. It produces steady progress and gives positive feedback at short intervals. The problem is that we set out to write one program and wound up writing several more. You may feel that even if it is the best way to do the job, it is too much work to be practical. The following paragraphs give reasons why it is the quicker and easier way to produce useful programs.

Figure 3.24b   testio.fig

```
 1    D>testio
 2
 3      testing I/O module
 4
 5      file name:test.dat
 6      open_file = 1
 7      fp = 2E0
 8
 9      calling set_filesize
10      filesize= 10
11
12      move_to 3
13      where_now = 3   next char is 13   ftell=4
14
15      where_now = 4   next char os 10   ftell=5
16
17      move_to 1
18      where_now = 1   next char is 98 ftell=2
19
20    test get next char - sequential reads
21      c=97   c=98   c=99   c=13   c=10   c=49   c=50   c=51   c=13   c=10
22    eof reached - c=-1
23
24
25    test get next char - at eof
26      c=-1    c=-1    c=-1    c=-1 ...
27    thru
28
29    test get previous char
30      c=10   c=13   c=51   c=50   c=49   c=10   c=13   c=99   c=98   c=97
31    bof reached - c=-2
32
33    test get previous char - at bof
34      c=-2    c=-2    c=-2    c=-2   ...
35    thru
36
37    D>
38
```

The usual method of testing is to add a few printf statements at key points in the program and run the whole program. Each time the program does something wrong, you must figure out what it is doing and then try to pinpoint the cause of the problem. This usually requires adding some new printf statements and running the program again.

Since the printf statements intrude on the normal operation of the program, they are usually removed when the bug is found. When the next bug is found, some new printf statements are inserted, and the detective work begins again. After the program is believed to work, the printf statements are removed. When enhancements are made, some fresh printf statements are inserted, and the testing process starts from scratch.

Our methodological approach to testing does require some support from the computer and its software. It requires that editing, compiling, and linking a 50-to-100-line program be quick and easy (no more than 1 to 2 minutes). Access to the computer for at least an hour or more a day is also necessary. The language used must allow separate compilation and must support modular programs composed of many small functions. Fortunately, using C on a PC meets these requirements.

3.6 Measuring the Performance of VIEW

□ Now that the VIEW program works correctly, we can see how well it performs. Since VIEW is an interactive program, we want to know how long it takes to respond to an input command. We can use a stopwatch to time the interval from pressing a key for an input command until the updating of the screen has been completed. The following table shows our results:

Operation	Time
View file-name	9 seconds
Next page	9
Previous page	15
First page	12
Last page	15
Move to character 20,000	9
Next line	8
Previous line	8
Exit to DOS	1

These results were measured for a file of about 60K bytes on a floppy disk. The results also depend on the compiler (Lattice C version 2.01 with DOS 2.0 library) and the operating system used (DOS 2.0 with 12 I/O buffers.)

The next step is to find out how different parts of the program are contributing to the overall response time. We can collect this information by modifying the programs we used earlier for testing. For example, Figure 3.25 shows a program to measure the performance of the display_page function. As we did in the testing of VIEW, we replace functions by stub functions. This allows us to measure the speed of a function like display_page independent of the real get_next_char function.

Some parts of VIEW need no measurements; they are used only on entry or

Figure 3.25 *perfdisp.c*

```
1     /* perfdisp.c - measure the performance of disp_page */
2     #include "stdio.h"
3
4     char filename[81] ;
5     char s[2500] ;
6     extern int row,col ;
7     long filesize ;
8     long top_of_page ;
9     int ix ;
10
11    main()
12     {
13       int  j  , ll ;
14       char c;
15
16       /* initialize filename , top_of_page and filesize */
17       strcpy(filename,"< file name >");
18       top_of_page = 3000 ;
19       filesize = 123456789 ;
20
21       /* build list of chars to be displayed */
22       printf("\n line length:");
23       scanf("%d",&ll);
24       for( j=0 ; j < ll ; j = j + 1 )
25         { s[j] = ' '+ j  ; }
26       s[ll] = '\0' ;
27
28       /* set up a standing start */
29       printf("\n press enter to start");
30       scanf("%c%c",&c,&c);
31
32       /* display the page 10 times for accuracy */
33       for( j=1 ; j <= 10 ; j = j + 1 )
34         {  display_page() ; }
35
36       printf("\n ** thru **");
37     }
38
39     int get_next_char()
40     {
41       if( s[ix] == '\0' )
42         { ix = 0 ;
43            return('\n') ;
44         }
45       else
46         { ix = ix + 1 ;
47            return( s[ix-1] ) ;
48         }
49     }
50
51
52     int move_to(pos)
53     long pos ;
54     {
55        ix = 0 ;
56     }
```

exit. Others are executed once and perform only a few statements. The following table shows timings for functions that might be contributing to response time:

Operation	Time
display_page	
10 char lines	2.5 seconds
20 char lines	3.2
40 char lines	4.9
80 char lines	8.0
get_cmd	1.3
move_forward(16 lines)	
40 char lines	0.06
80 char lines	0.12
move_backward(16 lines)	
40 char lines	0.06
80 char lines	0.12
get_next_char(16 lines)	
40 char lines	1.2
80 char lines	2.3
get_previous_char(16 lines)	
40 char lines	12.2
80 char lines	24.3

These figures give us a roadmap to follow if we want to improve the performance of the VIEW program. For example, we can see that making the move_forward function faster would have little effect on overall performance. The display_page and get_previous_char functions are both candidates for improvement. Measurement is a much better guide than guesswork because it allows us to concentrate our efforts where they will be fruitful.

Conclusions about the problem areas may be different for your compiler and environment. You should run similar tests for your system to guide your enhancements to VIEW. The program diskette package contains the measurement programs used to make the preceding table.

3.7   Enhancing VIEW

□   The VIEW program meets the functional specification we defined for it. That specification was kept simple to allow the program to be small and to have a clear structure. There is room for enhancements, however; the more useful a program is, the more enhancements come to mind. Some possibilities are discussed in the following sections.

Better Performance

VIEW takes too long to respond to an input command. More rapid execution of the input command would make the program more pleasant to use. The performance measurements show us where we can speed up the program. In the Lattice C implementation, there are two areas for improvement.

First, the get_previous_char function is much slower than get_next_char. The difference is the calls to fseek in get_previous_char. The implementation of buffered I/O functions in the Lattice C library makes getc quite fast and fseek much slower. This is reasonable in general but not good for VIEW. One alternative is to use the read library function and implement our own buffering scheme.

Displaying the page of text on the screen is another area for improvement. Further performance measurements suggest that the limitation is mostly due to the speed of output through the operating system's standard output services. The screen-writing functions from the toolkit of Chapter 7 could be used to avoid this bottleneck. Chapter 4 enhances another file display program to use direct screen updating.

Different End-of-Line Conventions

Some text files may contain a single carriage return character (13) to mark the end of a line of text. A way to accommodate such files would make VIEW more useful.

We could define an option on the command line to select an end-of-line marker character other than line feed. A better approach would be to modify view-find.c and viewdisp.c to recognize either a carriage return, a line feed, or both as an end-of-line marker. This would add some complication but might make VIEW applicable for more text files.

Long Lines of Test

VIEW handles files with an occasional line a little longer than 80 columns in an acceptable way. But it would not be satisfactory for files with many long lines or lines that were much longer than 80 columns.

As a possible improvement, we could move forward and backward in the file in terms of lines of the screen.

Moving forward in the file would require that we keep track of the current row and column as we moved forward in the file. This would be similar to the logic of the disp_char function.

Moving backward would require an extra step. We would have to find the beginning of the previous line and then move forward in that line, keeping track of the current row and column. The search for the beginning of the line would be limited to some maximum number of characters to prevent looking through an entire file when no end-of-line character is present.

Suppressing Scrolling

When a new command is entered and the screen updated, the screen is scrolled upward as each new line is written. This is distracting, especially when a single line movement is involved. Reducing the amount of extraneous motion would make VIEW more pleasant to use. Erasing the screen and positioning the cursor at the top of the screen is one way to accomplish this.

Adding Search Commands

Additional commands to search forward or backward in the file for a string of characters would make VIEW more useful on large files. This would require changes in several places. New constants would be added to viewparm.h and new cases added to get_cmd to recognize these commands. exec_cmd would also need cases for these commands. Finally, functions to perform the search operations would be needed. While we do not implement this enhancement here, we present pseudo-code for the search operations.

Pseudo-code for String Searches

```
exec_cmd case for forward search
        get string from keyboard
        search forward
        move backward half a page
        (puts string in middle of page)
        display the new page

search_forward for a string(s)
        start at top of page
        repeat until first char matched
                get next char from file
                compare to 1st char of string
        remember this position
        repeat until no match or end of string
                get next char from file
                compare to next char in string
```

```
restore remembered position
if entire string matched
        make top_of_page
        return to caller
(if matching failed, we will try again)
```

Searching backward is similar with a few obvious differences in detail, such as looking for the last character in the string instead of the first.

4
Dumping Files in Hexadecimal Notation

The VIEW program presented in Chapter 3 interprets a file as a sequence of ASCII characters. It is a useful tool for looking at ASCII text files. Sometimes we need a tool for looking at a file on a lower level. For example, if we need to read a file created by a program such as WordStar, dBase II, or Lotus 1-2-3, we need to find out exactly how the file is formatted. Such products rarely provide adequate documentation of file formats; it is usually up to us to figure out how the file is formatted. Once we understand the structure of a file, writing a C program to read it is usually feasible. We need a tool that shows every byte in a file, whether it represents a control character, a printable ASCII character, or any other possible 8-bit pattern (such as part of an integer).

The FILEDUMP program (FD) developed in this chapter serves this purpose. It displays the contents of a file in two formats: hexadecimal and a modified ASCII format. This kind of dump program is common on large systems. Software products with this function are also available for the IBM PC. FD is traditional in the kind of dump format it displays; there is no need for a unique approach.

4.1 Specifying the FILEDUMP Program

☐ We already have one program, VIEW, to display a file interactively. Much of the design (and the C source files) are applicable to the FD program. This can save time in implementing FD, and it makes good use of our experience with VIEW. We use the same input commands and the same keys to invoke them as in VIEW.

The only part of the specification that must be changed from that for VIEW is the display format. Since we can copy the display format from existing utilities (such as the MS-DOS debugger), we can specify FD without much creative effort. Figure 4.1 describes FD. There is only one creative element: We display interesting

Figure 4.1   FD program description

Name

fd   displays a file in hex form a screenful at a time

Function

FD displays the contents of a data file on the screen. Data are displayed byte by byte in hexadecimal form and as ASCII characters. On entry it displays the first screenful in the file and waits for a command. Single-key commands provide movement in the file by single lines or pages. Commands for movement to the beginning and end of the file are also provided.

Bytes are displayed as two hexidecimal digits and as ASCII characters. Bytes that correspond to ASCII graphic characters are displayed. Carriage return, line feed, and control-Z are displayed as special symbols (paragraph sign, down arrow, and a left arrowhead). Other byte values are displayed as a block graphic symbol.

Usage

From DOS, type FD and the name of file to be viewed.

a>FD file–name   or   a>FD
file name:file–name

Inside FD, the following list of single-key commands (you do not need to press return) are recognized:

HOME   Displays the first page in the file
END   Displays the last page in the file
PgUp   Moves backward in the file almost one page
PgDn   Moves forward in the file almost one page
Down Arrow   Moves forward in the file by one line
Up Arrow   Moves backward in the file by one line
Space Bar   Moves to a position you specify
Escape   Ends the program and returns to DOS

The program displays three areas on the screen: a heading, the data (16 lines with 16 bytes per line), and a prompt describing the input commands.

FILE-sample.txt	POSITION-0	FILE SIZE-750

0000 ¦ 41 32 48 97 0D 0A 1A 8D . . .   ¦ A 2 . . .
0016 . . .
.
.
.

Type one of these Input Commands

HOME	= First Page	↑	= Prev. Line	PG UP	= Prev. Page
END	= Last Page	↓	= Next Line	PG DN	= Next Page
Esc	= Exit Pgm	Space	= Move to Position		

control characters such as carriage return, line feed, and control-Z as special IBM PC graphic symbols. This will help us see the line structure in text files.

There are a few minor choices to be made. For example, instead of the two lines of overlap between pages in VIEW, FD has no overlap. FD displays a fixed number of bytes on each line; 16 bytes fit comfortably in 80 columns.

Our choice of hexadecimal notation for displaying byte values follows many other dump programs, but it has clear justifications over using decimal notation:

1. Hexadecimal requires two digits per byte against 3 for decimal.
2. A 2-byte integer value can be read easily. You just put the hexadecimal digits for each byte together. For example, the byte values 0x12 followed by 0x34 are the integer 0x3412. (On the 8088, the least significant byte is stored first.) In contrast, the decimal byte values 12 followed by 34 correspond to the integer value 34*256 + 12, or 8716.
3. The relation between ASCII characters and hexadecimal values is useful in deciphering bytes. Values from 00 through 1F are ASCII control characters, while values from 20 through 7E are graphic (printable) characters. Values from 80 through FF have the high-order bit set. For example, the value 0D is a carriage return while 8D is a carriage return with the high-order bit set.

So you can accept our choice of hexadecimal notation on faith or believe our reasons. You can even modify the program to display bytes values as you wish.

4.2 Pseudo-code for FILEDUMP

□   In designing FD, we have a different job than we did in designing VIEW. We have decided to make FD similar to the VIEW program. We can go through the pseudo-code for VIEW and identify differences in FD's design:

Overall structure: No difference.
Getting a file name: No difference.
Getting an input command: No difference.
Executing an input command: Movement in the file can still be described in lines and pages, but they are fixed in length in FD.
Moving forward/backward: Fixed size lines.
Displaying a page: Each byte is displayed twice, once in hexadecimal and once in ASCII form.

We ignore the differences between VIEW and FD in all but the moving forward/backward function and the display page function. The revised pseudo-code for moving forward and backward is made simpler by the fixed line size in FD as shown:

```
move_forward(n lines)
        move the file position forward (n*line_size) characters
end

Move_backward(n lines)
        move the file position backward (n*line_size) characters
end
```

The display_page function differs more from that in VIEW. For every line of data, there are several separate activities—for example, displaying the corresponding file position and displaying bytes in hexadecimal and in ASCII. So display_page is organized around lines of text rather than single characters. The following pseudo-code shows this organization:

```
display_page
        write heading—file name, position in file
        and file size

        for each of page_size lines
                read a line of data
                display the line of data
end

display_line
        display starting position of line
        for each of 16 bytes of data
                display in Hex format
        for each of 16 bytes of data
                display in ASCII form
end

display_in_ASCII_form
        if( char is a graphic ASCII char )
                display it
        else if( char is Carriage Return char )
                display as CR graphic
        else if( char is Line Feed )
                display as LF graphic
        else if( char is CTL-Z char )
                display as CTL-Z graphic
        else display as non-printable graphic
end
```

FD requires the same constants and data as VIEW. Many of the same exceptions apply—reaching the beginning or end of the file, for example.

4.3   The FILEDUMP Program Listing

□   FD is structured just as VIEW was. The following diagram of function calls differs only in the display_page function:

```
main
        get_filename
        set_filesize
        get_cmd
                getkey
                prompt
        exec_cmd
                move_forward
                        move_to
                        set_top_page
                                where_now
                move_backward
                        move_to
                        set_top_page
                move_to
                get_pos
                display_page
                        read_line
                        prtline
                                disp_char
```

The functions are grouped in source files in much the same way also. The new source files are named fdxxxx.c in this case, but the groupings are the same:

Source File	Functions	Purpose
fd.c	main,get_filename	Overall flow
viewget.c	get_cmd, prompt	Input commands
fdexec.c	exec_cmd	Execute commands
viewpos.c	get_pos	Input file position
fdfind.c	move_forward	Move display
	move_backward	page
	set_top_page	
fddisp.c	display_page	Display page
	prtline	
	disp_char	
fdio.c	open_file,close_file	
	set_filesize	Handles file I/O
	move_to, where_now	
	read_line	

Two header files, viewcmds.h and fdparm.h, are used in FD. Since FD uses the same commands as VIEW used, the viewcmds.h file can be used with changes. The fdparm.h file shown in Figure 4.2 is based on viewparm.h. The constant specifying the number of lines of overlap between old and new pages is changed to 0. In addition, a new parameter, LINE_SIZE, specifies the number of bytes displayed on each line.

The file, fd.c, in Figure 4.3 is based on view.c. There are two changes: fdparm.h is included instead of viewparm.h, and set_filesize is called with binary mode specified instead of ASCII mode. In FD we do not interpret control-Z in a special way. set_filesize should not adjust the file size based on the presence of a control-Z in the file.

The fdexec.c file is not shown. The only change to viewexec.c is to include fdparm.h instead of viewparm.h.

Since FD uses the same input commands and the same way of accepting a new file position, files viewget.c and viewpos.c need not be changed. In fact, they need not be recompiled. We just link object files viewget.obj and viewpos.obj with the new object files.

fdfind.c File

The functions in fdfind.c (Figure 4.4) are different from those in viewfind.c. In FD, the definition of a line is very simple: 16 bytes. The move_forward and

Figure 4.2 fdparm.h

```
1     /* fdparm.h - parameters for FD program */
2
3     /* number of lines in a display page */
4     #define   PAGE_SIZE       16
5
6     /* number of bytes per line */
7     #define LINE_SIZE         16
8
9     /* number of lines of overlap between display pages */
10    #define   LINES_OVERLAP    0
11
12    /* special return values from get_next_char & get_previous_char */
13    /* to indicate that beginning or end of file has been reached */
14    #define   EOF_MARK        -1
15    #define   BOF_MARK        -2
16
17    /* definition of control char marking the end of a line */
18    #define   END_LINE        10
19
20    /* define success/failure for return codes */
21    #define SUCCESS  1
22    #define FAILURE  0
```

Figure 4.3   fd.c

```
1    /* fd.c -  FD program - main function */
2    #include "stdio.h"
3    #include "cminor.h"
4    #include "viewcmds.h"
5    #include "fdparm.h"
6
7    char filename[65] = "" ;
8
9    main(argc,argv)
10    int argc ;
11    char *argv[] ;
12    {
13       int cmd ;                        /* holds current cmd      */
14
15       if( argc >= 2 )                  /* get file name from command */
16         strcpy(filename,argv[1]) ;  /* line (if present) */
17
18       get_filename(filename) ;        /* get file name and open file */
19       set_filesize(BIN_MODE) ;        /* set up file size variable */
20       cmd = FIRSTPAGE ;               /* force display of 1st page */
21
22       while( cmd != EXITPGM )         /* repeat until told to exit */
23         { exec_cmd(cmd);             /* execute the current command */
24           cmd = get_cmd();           /* get the next command */
25         }
26
27       close_file() ;
28    }
29
30
31    int get_filename(fn)               /* get name of file and open it */
32    char fn[] ;                        /* file name string */
33    {                                  /* filled out by caller */
34       if( strlen(fn) == 0 )
35         { printf("file name:") ;
36           scanf("%s",fn) ;
37         }
38                                       /* open the file (verify name) */
39       while( open_file(fn) == FAILURE )
40         { printf("\n file - %s can not be opened\n",fn);
41           printf("file name:") ;  /* try again */
42           scanf("%s",fn) ;
43         }
44    }
45
```

Figure 4.4 fdfind.c

```
 1      /* fdfind.c file - find module: moves to new positions in file */
 2    #include "stdio.h"
 3    #include "cminor.h"
 4    #include "fdparm.h"
 5
 6    long top_of_page ;         /* file position of top of display page */
 7    extern long filesize ;        /* length of file in bytes */
 8    long where_now() ;
 9
10    int move_forward(nlines)
11     int nlines ;                  /* number of lines to move */
12     {
13        long new_pos ;
14
15        new_pos = top_of_page + (nlines*LINE_SIZE) ;
16        if( new_pos > filesize)
17            new_pos = filesize ;
18        move_to(new_pos) ;         /* start at top of page */
19        set_top_page() ;           /* make this new top of display page */
20     }
21
22
23    int move_backward(nlines)
24     int nlines ;                  /* number of lines to move */
25     {                             /* zero lines = start of current line */
26        long new_pos ;
27
28        new_pos = top_of_page - (nlines*LINE_SIZE) ;
29        if( new_pos < 0L )
30            new_pos = 0L ;
31        move_to(new_pos) ;         /* start at top of page */
32        set_top_page() ;           /* make this new top of display page */
33     }
34
35
36    int set_top_page()
37     {
38        top_of_page = where_now() ;
39     }
40
```

move_backward functions do not have to look at the contents of the file. Handling the beginning- and end-of-file exception cases is also simple; we test the new file position to see that it is between zero and the file size.

fddisp.c File

The display_page function in Figure 4.5 has a structure similar to that of its namesake in the VIEW program. It displays a heading, uses prtline to display each line of data, and pads out the page if end-of-file is reached before a full page is

Figure 4.5   fddisp.c

```
1    /* fddisp.c file - display_page: display current page of file */
2    #include "stdio.h"
3    #include "cminor.h"
4    #include "fdparm.h"
5
6    extern char    filename[] ;
7    extern long    filesize ;              /* size of file in bytes */
8    extern long    top_of_page;         /* file position of top of page */
9
10   /* special symbols to represent CR, LF, CTL-Z & other ctl chars */
11   #define PRT_CR   20
12   #define PRT_LF   25
13   #define PRT_CTLZ 17
14   #define PRT_OTHER 22
15   #define ASC_CTLZ   26
16
17   int  row ;                             /* current line of page */
18   long start ;
19
20   int display_page()
21     {
22       char block[ LINE_SIZE ] ;
23       int  nbytes  ;
24       int i ;                            /* index for loops   */
25
26       move_to(top_of_page);              /* start at top of the page */
27                                          /* write a header line */
28       printf("\n FILE - %s    POSITION - %ld    FILE SIZE - %ld \n",
29       filename,top_of_page,filesize);
30
31                                          /* write a border line of dashes */
32       for( i=1 ; i <= 80 ; i = i + 1 )
33          { putchar('-'); }
34
35       /* get chars from file until we've written (PAGE_SIZE) lines */
36       /* or we've reached the end of the file */
37       row = 1 ;                          /* starting row values */
38       start = top_of_page ;
39       while( row <= PAGE_SIZE  )
40          { nbytes = read_line(block,LINE_SIZE) ;
41            if( nbytes <= 0 )
42               break ;
43            prtline(block,nbytes) ;
44            start = start + nbytes ;
45            row = row + 1 ;
46          }
47
48       while( row <= PAGE_SIZE )      /* pad out page if eof reached */
49          { putchar('\n'); row = row + 1 ; }
50
51                                          /* write border line of dashes */
52       for( i=1 ; i <= 80 ; i = i + 1 )
53          { putchar('-'); }
54     }
55
```

Figure 4.5   fddisp.c (continued)

```
56
57    int prtline(block,nbytes)                /* prints one line */
58    char block[] ;
59    int  nbytes ;
60    {
61        int i ;
62
63        printf("%81d  | ",start) ;        /* print file pos. */
64        for(i=0 ; i < LINE_SIZE ; i=i+1)/* print bytes in Hex. */
65          { if ( i < nbytes )
66                printf("%02x ",( tochar(block[i]) ) ) ;
67            else printf("   ") ;            /* out of data - fill in */
68          }
69
70        printf("| ") ;
71
72        for(i=0; i < nbytes ; i = i+1 ) /* display in ASCII form */
73          { disp_char( tochar(block[i]) ) ; }
74        putchar('\n');
75    }
76
77
78    int disp_char(c)                         /* display one char in ASCII */
79    int c ;                                  /* value of char to display */
80    {
81        /* classify the character and handle accordingly */
82
83        if( isgraphic(c) )
84            ;                                /* ASCII graphic - display it */
85        else if( c == '\n' )
86            c = PRT_LF ;                     /* newline (LF) - display symbol */
87        else if( c == '\r' )
88            c = PRT_CR ;                     /* Carr. Return - display symbol */
89        else if ( c == ASC_CTLZ )
90            c = PRT_CTLZ ;                   /* CTL-Z - display symbol */
91        else c = PRT_OTHER ;                 /* other char - display symbol */
92
93        putchar(c) ;
94    }
```

displayed. Lines of dashes separate the data from the heading line and the input command prompts to be written by prompt. Once again we use the structure established for VIEW, keeping the changes to a few lower-level functions.

The display_page function reads one line of data at a time. Since each byte of data will be used twice—once for the hexadecimal format display and once for the ASCII format display—it is convenient to read the whole line first. When we are near the end of the file, the read_line function may read less than a full line of data.

The prtline function displays one line of data. If less than a full line of data is present, prtline fills the space with blanks instead of displayed data. This preserves the column alignment of the ASCII format display regardless of the number of bytes of data present.

The disp_char function displays a single character in a modified ASCII form. Non-ASCII graphic characters are displayed using special symbols available on the IBM PC display. Carriage return, line feed, and control-Z characters are displayed with the symbols ¶, ↓ and ◄, while other nongraphic characters are displayed as the symbol ■.

fdio.c File

The fdio.c file in Figure 4.6 is similar to the viewio.c file (see Figure 3.17). Only the read_line function has been added. The read_line function reads the number of bytes requested (using the getc library function) unless the end-of-file is reached first. In either case, it returns the number of bytes read.

In the VIEW program, bytes were interpreted as ASCII characters. get_next_char and get_previous_char forced the high-order bit of each character returned to 0. FD displays byte values as they exist in the file. So read_line returns characters without altering the high-order bit.

Although the functions get_next_char and get_previous_char are not used in FD, we left them in fdio.c. These functions do not add much to the size of the program, and they might be useful for enhancements to FD.

Figure 4.6   fdio.c

```
1    /* fdio.c file - I/O module for FD program */
2    #include "stdio.h"
3    #include "cminor.h"
4    #include "fdparm.h"
5
6    /* fseek mode definitions */
7    #define  CURRENT_REL   1          /* relative to current position */
8    #define  EOF_REL       2          /* relative to end of the file */
9    #define  BOF_REL       0          /* relative to beginning of file */
10
11   #define  CTL_Z        26          /* marks EOF in some text files */
12
13   FILE *fp ;                 /* file pointer for text file */
14   long filesize ;              /* size of the file in bytes */
15   long int ftell() ;
16   FILE *gfopen() ;
17
18   int open_file(fn)                /* open a file */
19    char fn[] ;                     /* file name string */
```

Figure 4.6   fdio.c (continued)

```
20    {                                         /* return success or failure */
21        fp = gfopen(fn,"r",BIN_MODE) ;
22        if(fp != NULL)
23            return(SUCCESS) ;
24        else return( FAILURE ) ;
25    }
26
27
28    int set_filesize(chk_ctlz)                /* set up file size */
29     int chk_ctlz ;                 /* if =ASC_MODE check for control-Z */
30    {
31        long pos ;
32        int c ;
33
34        fseek(fp,0L,EOF_REL) ;   /* get size of file */
35        filesize = ftell(fp) ;
36
37        if( chk_ctlz != ASC_MODE )  /* control-Z checking needed ? */
38            return ;
39
40        /* check last 128 byte block for a CTL-Z */
41        pos = filesize - (filesize % 128) ;
42        fseek(fp, pos ,BOF_REL);
43        c = getc(fp);
44        while( c != EOF )
45          { if( c == CTL_Z )           /* look for control-Z */
46               { filesize = ftell(fp) - 1 ;
47                 return ;              /* found - adjust file size & exit */
48               }
49            c = getc(fp);
50          }
51    }
52
53
54
55     int move_to(new_pos)                   /* move to specified position */
56     long new_pos ;
57     {
58         fseek(fp,new_pos,BOF_REL);
59     }
60
61    long where_now()                       /* return current position */
62    {
63        return( ftell(fp) ) ;
64    }
65
66
67    int get_next_char()               /* get char at file position */
68    {
69        char c ;
70
71        if( ftell(fp) == filesize )    /* are we at end of file ? */
72            return( EOF_MARK ) ;    /*    y - return our end file mark */
73        else                       /* no - get next char */
74          { c = getc(fp);                /* get a char */
```

Figure 4.6 fdio.c (continued)

```
75                    return( toascii(c) ) ; /* force char to ascii, return it */
76             }
77       }
78
79
80   int get_previous_char()        /* read the char in front of */
81   {                              /* current file position */
82       char c ;
83
84       if( ftell(fp) != 0L )              /* check for begin. file */
85           { fseek(fp,-1L,CURRENT_REL);  /* back up one char */
86             c = getc(fp);               /* read a char*/
87                                  /*  back up in front of char read */
88             fseek(fp,-1L,CURRENT_REL) ;
89             return( toascii(c) ) ;       /* force to be ascii */
90           }                              /* and return the char */
91       else return(BOF_MARK) ;
92   }
93
94
95   int close_file()
96   {
97       fclose(fp) ;
98   }
99
100
101  int read_line(buf,nread)      /* read a one line of characters */
102   char buf[] ;                 /* put the data here */
103   int nread ;                  /* maximum number of bytes to read */
104  {
105      int i , c ;
106
107      i = 0 ;
108      for( i=0 ; i < nread ; i=i+1 )
109          {
110             c = getc(fp) ;
111             if( c == EOF )
112                 break ;
113             buf[i] = c ;
114          }
115      return( i ) ;                /* return number of chars read */
116  }
117
```

4.4 Testing FILEDUMP

□ Testing the individual source files of FD is much the same as it was for the VIEW program. There are a few new functions in FD for which we need additional tests, but the process is the same. However, some aspects of testing were not covered in the preceding chapter. While we covered testing individual modules in detail, we did not discuss integrating the modules and testing the entire program.

What do we test after the modules operate correctly? There may be mistakes in naming functions and global variables. Linking all the object files together makes such mistakes appear as unresolved references or as duplicate names. Most linkers can produce a listing showing public names and the module where they appeared. Careful reading of this listing and of the source files usually locates the problem.

Different modules may have conflicts in the use of function arguments or return values. Where we have tested groups of functions together in a top-down way, these problems have already been checked. For functions where the calling function and the called function have not been tested together, we need to verify that they work together. Sometimes we can do this by observing the behavior of the program without adding any special testing functions. In other cases, we need to insert statements for testing in the source files. To test the interface between the fdfind.c and fdio.c modules, we might add testing statements like the following to display arguments passed to move_to and values returned by where_now:

```
. . .
/* ??? */     printf(" calling move_to %ld \n",new_pos);
move_to(new_pos) ;
. . .
top_of_page = where_now( ) ;
/* ??? */     printf(" where_now returns %ld \n",top_of_page);
```

In the fdio.c source file, corresponding statements would show the arguments received and the values to be returned. When FD is compiled and executed with these versions of fdfind.c and fdio.c, we can verify that these function calls work correctly.

These testing statements present a problem: We want them present for testing but not when we use the program. As is often the case with such problems, there are several partially satisfactory answers. In the example shown, the testing statements are marked by a comment, /* ??? */, on the same line. This makes it easy to find and delete them when we finish testing. Of course, we will need them again when enhancements are made. Instead of deleting them after testing, we could enclose them in comments as in

```
/*     printf(" calling move_to %ld \n",new_pos) ; */
```

We can also use the C preprocessor to skip the testing statements,

```
#ifdef TEST_SWITCH
    printf(" calling move_to %ld \n",new_pos);
#endif
```

To get a version of the module with the testing statements present, we would define the identifier TEST_SWITCH at the beginning of the source file:

```
#define TEST_SWITCH 1
```

If TEST_SWITCH is not defined, the testing statements would not be part of the compiled module. Clear, understandable listings are important in this book; we thus omit such testing statements from the source files.

After we link the entire program and verify the function call interfaces, bugs may still exist. Assumptions made in one part of the program may be inconsistent with those made in another part of the program. To find such bugs, we run the program with a variety of files. By this time the program usually works fairly well, and our confidence in it rises rapidly. It is important to remain suspicious and alert in using the program at first. The program's output probably looks plausible, but we must make the effort to verify that it really is correct.

Getting good test data is one part of the problem. Small files such as the test.dat file created in Section 3.3 are convenient for module testing. We also need to test our programs with large files. Good test data files should meet three criteria: (1) They should cover all cases; (2) we must understand exactly what they contain; and (3) they must help us decipher the test results easily. Existing files are easy to use, but they do not meet these criteria very well. Writing a short program to generate test data is often the best solution. Figure 4.7 shows a program to generate test data for FD. We specify the size of the file we want. It generates all 256 possi-

Figure 4.7   gendata.c

```
1    /* gendata.c - generate test data for FD program */
2    #include "stdio.h"
3    #include "cminor.h"
4
5    FILE *gfopen() ;
6
7    main(argc,argv)
8     int argc ;
9     char *argv[] ;
10   {
11       long nc , i ;
12       char b ;
13       FILE *fp ;
14
15       if( argc < 2 ) exit(1) ;
16       fp = gfopen(argv[1],"w",BIN_MODE) ;
17       if( fp == NULL ) exit(2) ;
18
19       printf("number of characters:");
20       scanf("%ld",&nc) ;
21
22       for(i=0 ; i<nc ; i=i+1)
23         { b = i ;
24            putc(b,fp) ;
25         }
26       fclose(fp) ;
27   }
```

ble byte values. Since the value of a byte is related to its position (position modulo 256), we can check movement in the file quite easily. In addition, the regular pattern of the data makes it easier to spot bugs.

Chapter 3 did not discuss testing VIEW as a whole, but the methods we have just discussed apply there too. Figure 4.8 shows a program to generate a text file for testing VIEW. The line numbers identify position in the file, and the fixed line size helps in translating a line number into a byte position.

When we test a program, we often need a second opinion—an independent way of doing the same thing. For example, the DOS TYPE command provides another way to display a text file. We can use it as an independent check on VIEW. The DOS DEBUG command can provide a similar check on the operation of FD. Once FD is operating correctly, it can be used to check other programs that read files.

Figure 4.8   gendata2.c

```
 1    /* gendata2.c - generate test data for VIEW program */
 2    #include "stdio.h"
 3    #include "cminor.h"
 4
 5    FILE *gfopen() ;
 6
 7    main(argc,argv)
 8     int argc ;
 9     char *argv[] ;
10     {
11         long nc , i , nl ;
12         char s[100] ;
13         FILE *fp ;
14
15         if( argc < 2 ) exit(1) ;
16         fp = gfopen(argv[1],"w",BIN_MODE) ;
17         if( fp == NULL ) exit(2) ;
18
19         printf("number of chars /line:");
20         scanf("%ld",&nl) ;
21         nl = nl - 8 ;                   /* allow for line no. and CR/LF */
22         for(i=0 ; i< nl ; i=i+1)      /* set up string for line */
23            { s[i] = ' ' + i ; }
24         s[i] = '\0' ;
25
26         printf("number of lines:");
27         scanf("%ld",&nc) ;
28
29         for(i=0 ; i<nc ; i=i+1)
30            { fprintf(fp,"%5ld %s\r\n",i,s) ; }
31         fclose(fp) ;
32     }
```

4.5   FILEDUMP's Performance

□   As for FD, response times for input commands are the important quantities to measure. The results are a bit different from those for VIEW: All the commands (except the exit command) take 10 to 11 seconds to execute. Another look at the FD source files gives the reason: In FD the move_forward and move_backward functions do a little arithmetic rather than scanning the file as in VIEW. The measurements on individual functions in the following table show that displaying the page of data and, to a lesser extent, writing the prompt message are responsible for the overall response times. (The time for display_page includes prtline, but a dummy function is used in place of read_line.)

Function	Speed
get_cmd	1.3 seconds
move_forward/backward	<0.1
display_page	8.0
read_line	0.1
prtline	8.0

Results are similar to those for VIEW. Since the page to be displayed is only 256 bytes rather than up to 1,280 bytes as for VIEW, the time needed to read a page from the file is less. However, the time required to display the page is somewhat longer. The result clearly shows that if we want to improve performance, we must concentrate on the display module.

4.6   Enhancements

□   Most of the enhancements that we identified for the VIEW program also apply to FD. Here we add a few ideas specific to FD.

Updating the File

Sometimes we would like to change something in the file after we examine it. We could extend FD to allow us to change the value of bytes in the file.

This enhancement requires some major design decisions. Should insertion and deletion be supported or just overwriting existing bytes? How will new data be entered? What changes are needed to input commands and display format? Will the display and file be updated as each byte is entered? Will changes modify the original file or a copy?

Hexadecimal Input for a File Position

Sometimes it is convenient to specify a file position using hexadecimal notation. We could modify the get_pos function to accept a file position in hexadecimal or decimal notation. The convention for hexadecimal notation used in C source files—0x preceding hexadecimal digits—could be used to distinguish it from decimal input.

We might also want the file position, the file size, and the starting position for each line to be displayed in hexadecimal. This suggests another alternative: a command to select decimal or hexadecimal for both input and output.

4.7   Improving FILEDUMP's Performance

□   FD takes about 10 seconds to respond to an input command. We would like to reduce that time to 1 to 2 seconds. While we may be disappointed that our first version of FD is slow, we have a working program; all we have to worry about now is making it faster. The performance measurements in Section 4.5 point us to the display module and prtline in particular. We start there and try to find out what in the display module is causing the slow response.

Levels of I/O Functions

Instead of making further measurements on the display module, we explore how console I/O works. When we call printf or putchar to display something, several layers of software are invoked. The following table shows how printf and putchar calls use lower levels:

Level	*Sample Function*
Formatting	printf
Buffered I/O	putchar
Unbuffered I/O	write
DOS console I/O	DOS function code 2
or file I/O	function code 0x40
BIOS video I/O	write_tty
Direct screen write	—

Each level makes use of the lower levels to update the screen. With so many levels of software involved, it is not surprising that the performance of printf or putchar is disappointing. The IBM PC is simply not fast enough to hide this overhead.

Measuring I/O Performance

We can perform an experiment to see where the bottlenecks are. Figure 4.9 shows a program to measure the putchar function. By substituting functions to access other levels of I/O functions directly, we can compare performance at each level. The following table gives results with the equivalent to putchar:

Level	Function Used	Time for 2,000 characters
Formatting	printf("%02x ",c)	11 seconds
Buffered I/O	putchar(c)	10
Unbuffered I/O	write(1,&c,1)	10
DOS console I/O	DOS function call 2	5
or file I/O	function call 0x40	9
BIOS video I/O	vid__tc(c)	3
Screen write	scn__wc(c,&sc)	0.4

The functions vid__tc and scn__wc are from the toolkit in Chapter 7. The DOS function calls 2 and 0x40 are performed with the dos2call function from the same chapter.

The results are surprising and encouraging. We should be able to improve the display module by writing directly to the screen. Further experiments give us more information: Writing a line feed character or scrolling the screen takes 13 times as long as writing a normal character at the BIOS level.

Figure 4.9   expio.c

```
1    /* expio.c - test console I/O performance */
2    #include "stdio.h"
3    #include "cminor.h"
4
5    main()
6      {
7         int it , i , c ;
8         char b ;
9
10        printf("\n char value (decimal):") ;
11        scanf("%d",&c) ;
12        printf("\n no. chars to write:") ;
13        scanf("%d",&it) ;
14
15        for( i=1; i <= it ; i=i+1)
16           { putchar(c) ;  }
17        printf("\n ** thru ** \n");
18
19      }
```

Modifying FD

Now we are ready to work on FD. The toolkit in Chapter 7 provides two functions for writing directly to the PC's screen: The scn_wc function writes a single character, and the scn_ws writes a character string. Our approach is simple: We replace calls to putchar by calls to scn_wc and calls to printf by calls to scn_ws. The examples show sample replacements:

putchar (c);   to   scn_wc(c, &sc) ;

printf("¦ ") ;   to   scn_ws("¦ ", &sc) ;

or

printf("%02x ",c);   to   sprintf(s, "%02x ",c) ;
                                   scn_ws(s, &sc) ;

The sprintf library function performs the same formatting operations as printf. It places the resulting characters (in string format) in the character array passed as the first argument. As the examples suggest, the screen-writing functions expect as a second argument the address of a structure. This structure is defined by the data type SCN_DATA in the header file scn.h (also from Chapter 7). We need to include this header file and to declare a variable (sc) of type SCN_DATA. Before we use scn_wc or scn_ws, we must call scn_init to initialize the data in sc. The structure sc also contains the location on the screen where characters will be written. Calls to scn_pos set the row and column to be written next.

The screen-writing functions are limited in the services they provide. They do not recognize control characters such as carriage return or newline, and they do not perform scrolling. Instead of outputting '\n' characters in putchar or printf statements, we have to call scn_pos to move to a new line.

Figure 4.10 shows the modified source file fdedisp3.c. The prompt function has been moved from the viewget.c source file into the display module. Screen-writing functions replace printf statements here as well as in display_page, prtline, and disp_char. Before the page is displayed, line 30 uses another toolkit function, vid_clr_scn, to erase the screen.

After the page has been displayed, line 62 sets the cursor position on row 19 of the screen. The prompt function sets the cursor position to row 24 after the input prompts have been written. This ensures that the get_pos function, which still uses the printf function, will place its output on the correct line.

The init-disp function on lines 140 to 143 initializes the screen data structure. A call to this function is added to the main function. Figures 4.11 and 4.12 (see pages 142–143) show the modified source files—fde.c, containing main, and fdeget.c, from which the prompt function was removed.

The modifications were made in three stages. First, prtline and disp_char were updated. Next, the display_page function was changed. Finally prompt

Figure 4.10   fdedisp3.c

```
1    /* fdedisp.c file - enhanced display_page function */
2    #include "stdio.h"
3    #include "cminor.h"
4    #include "fdparm.h"
5    #include "scn.h"
6
7    extern char    filename[] ;
8    extern long    filesize ;          /* size of file in bytes */
9    extern long    top_of_page;        /* file position of top of page */
10
11   /* special symbols to represent CR, LF, CTL-Z & other ctl chars */
12   #define PRT_CR   20
13   #define PRT_LF   25
14   #define PRT_CTLZ 17
15   #define PRT_OTHER 22
16   #define ASC_CTLZ  26
17
18   int  row ;                         /* current line of page */
19   long start ;
20   SCN_DATA sc ;
21
22   int display_page()
23    {
24       char block[ LINE_SIZE ] ;
25       int  nbytes  ;
26       int i ;                        /* index for loops  */
27       int srow , scol ;
28       char s[81] ;
29
30       vid_clr_scn(0,24) ;
31       scn_pos(&sc,0,0) ;             /* set screen write pos. */
32                                      /* write border line of dashes */
33       move_to(top_of_page);         /* start at top of the page */
34                                      /* write a header line */
35       sprintf(s," FILE - %s   POSITION - %ld   FILE SIZE - %ld ",
36       filename,top_of_page,filesize);
37       scn_ws(s,&sc) ;
38       scn_pos(&sc,1,0) ;
39       for( i=1 ; i <= 80 ; i = i + 1 )
40          { scn_wc('-',& sc); }
41       /* get chars from file until we've written (PAGE_SIZE) lines */
42       /* or we've reached the end of the file */
43       row = 1 ;                      /* starting row values */
44       start = top_of_page ;
45       while( row <= PAGE_SIZE  )
46          { nbytes = read_line(block,LINE_SIZE) ;
47             if( nbytes <= 0 )
48                break ;
49             scn_pos(&sc,row+1,0) ;
50             prtline(block,nbytes) ;
51             start = start + nbytes ;
52             row = row + 1 ;
53          }
54
55
```

Figure 4.10 fdedisp3.c (continued)

```
56                                      /* write border line of dashes */
57         scn_pos(&sc,18,0) ;          /* set screen write pos. */
58                                      /* write border line of dashes */
59         for( i=1 ; i <= 80 ; i = i + 1 )
60             { scn_wc('-',& sc); }
61         scn_pos(19,0) ;
62         vid_set_cur(19,0) ;
63     }
64  char hex[] = "0123456789ABCDEF" ;
65
66  int prtline(block,nbytes)               /* prints one line */
67   char block[] ;
68   int  nbytes ;
69   {
70         int i ;
71         int t ;
72         char s[81] ;
73
74         sprintf(s,"%8ld | ",start) ;        /* print file pos. */
75         scn_ws(s,&sc) ;
76
77         for(i=0 ; i < LINE_SIZE ; i=i+1)/* print bytes in Hex. */
78             { if ( i < nbytes )
79                 { t = ( block[i]  >> 4 ) & 0xf ;
80                   scn_wc( hex[t] , &sc ) ;
81                   t = block[i] & 0xf ;
82                   scn_wc( hex[t] , &sc ) ;
83                   scn_wc( ' ' , &sc ) ;
84                 }
85               else scn_ws("   ",&sc) ;        /* out of data - fill in */
86             }
87
88         scn_ws("| ", &sc) ;
89
90         for(i=0; i < nbytes ; i = i+1 ) /* display in ASCII form */
91             { disp_char( tochar(block[i]) ) ; }
92     }
93
94
95  int disp_char(c)                    /* display one char in ASCII */
96   int c ;                            /* value of char to display */
97   {
98         /* classify the character and handle accordingly */
99
100        if( isgraphic(c) )
101            ;                        /* ASCII graphic - just display */
102        else if( c == '\n' )
103            c = PRT_LF ;             /* newline (LF) - display symbol */
104        else if( c == '\r' )
105            c = PRT_CR ;             /* Carr. Return - display symbol */
106        else if ( c == ASC_CTLZ )
107            c = PRT_CTLZ ;           /* CTL-Z - display symbol */
108        else c = PRT_OTHER ;         /* other char - display symbol */
109
110        scn_wc(c , &sc) ;
```

Figure 4.10   fdedisp3.c (continued)

```
111     }
112
113
114     int prompt()               /* display prompts */
115     {
116     #define  UP_A   24          /* displays up arrow */
117     #define  DN_A   25          /* displays down arrow */
118        char s[81] ;
119
120        scn_pos( &sc , 20 , 0 ) ;
121        scn_ws( "              Type one of these Input Commands" , & sc );
122        scn_pos( &sc , 21 , 0 ) ;
123        scn_ws( " HOME  = First Page        " , & sc );
124        sprintf(s,   "  %c   = Previous Line   ",UP_A);
125        scn_ws( s , & sc ) ;
126        scn_ws(    "PG UP = Previous Page " , & sc );
127        scn_pos( &sc , 22 , 0 ) ;
128        scn_ws( " END   = Last  Page        " , & sc );
129        sprintf(s,   "  %c   = Next Line        ",DN_A);
130        scn_ws( s , & sc ) ;
131        scn_ws(    "PG DN = Next Page " , & sc );
132        scn_pos( &sc , 23 , 0 ) ;
133        scn_ws( " ESC   = Exit Pgm        " , & sc );
134        scn_ws(    "SPACE = Move to position " , &sc );
135        scn_pos( &sc , 24 , 0 ) ;
136        vid_set_cur( 24 , 0 ) ;
137     }
138
139
140     int init_disp()
141     {
142        scn_init(&sc) ;
143     }
```

was modified to use scn_ws. The first step lowers response time from 10 to 4 seconds. The second step gives an improvement to 2 seconds. The final version has a response time of about 1 second. While the original FD program was slow and unpleasant to use, the enhanced version is fun to use.

These enhancements apply to VIEW as well. Bypassing layers of I/O functions and writing directly to the screen are often necessary for really fast response. While it makes the program less portable, it also makes the program more pleasant to use.

4.8 Summary

□ From VIEW, we developed another interactive program—FD—for examining files. Enhancing FD for better performance gave us insight into the workings of

Figure 4.11   fde.c

```
1    /* fd.c -  FD program - main function */
2    #include "stdio.h"
3    #include "cminor.h"
4    #include "viewcmds.h"
5    #include "fdparm.h"
6
7    char filename[65] = "" ;
8
9    main(argc,argv)
10    int argc ;
11    char *argv[] ;
12    {
13        int cmd ;                       /* holds current cmd      */
14
15        if( argc >= 2 )                 /* get file name from command */
16          strcpy(filename,argv[1]) ;    /* line (if present) */
17
18        init_disp() ;                   /* initialize for display */
19        get_filename(filename) ;        /* get file name & open file */
20        set_filesize(BIN_MODE) ;        /* set up file size variable */
21        cmd = FIRSTPAGE ;               /* force display of 1st page */
22
23        while( cmd != EXITPGM )         /* repeat until told to exit */
24          { exec_cmd(cmd);              /* execute current command */
25            cmd = get_cmd();            /* get the next command */
26          }
27
28        close_file() ;
29    }
30
31
32    int get_filename(fn)                /* get name of file & open it */
33    char fn[] ;                         /* file name string */
34    {                                   /* filled out by caller */
35        if( strlen(fn) == 0 )
36          { printf("file name:") ;
37            scanf("%s",fn) ;
38          }
39                                        /* open file (verify name) */
40        while( open_file(fn) == FAILURE )
41          { printf("\n file - %s can not be opened\n",fn);
42            printf("file name:") ;      /* try again */
43            scanf("%s",fn) ;
44          }
45    }
46
```

Figure 4.12 c:fdeget.c

```
1      /* fdeget.c - get_cmd function - get an input command   */
2    #include "stdio.h"
3    #include "cminor.h"
4    #include "viewcmds.h"
5    #include "fdparm.h"
6
7    /* definitions of key values returned by getkey */
8    #include "keyio.h"
9
10   int get_cmd()              /* get next input command from keyboard */
11     {                        /* returns the command type entered */
12       int key ;              /* holds the keyboard input value */
13                              /* ( see keyio.h ) for values */
14       int cmd ;              /* holds the command type value */
15
16       prompt() ;             /* display prompts */
17       cmd = INVALIDCMD;      /* get next keyboard input */
18       while( cmd == INVALIDCMD )
19         { key = getkey() ;/* get next keyboard input */
20           switch( key )     /* classify the key pressed */
21             {
22             case PGDNKEY : cmd = NEXTPAGE      ;break;
23             case PGUPKEY : cmd = PREVPAGE      ;break;
24             case ASCESC  : cmd = EXITPGM       ;break;
25             case ' '     : cmd = MOVETOPOS     ;break;
26             case HOMEKEY : cmd = FIRSTPAGE     ;break;
27             case ENDKEY  : cmd = LASTPAGE      ;break;
28             case UPARROW : cmd = PREVLINE      ;break;
29             case DOWNARROW : cmd = NEXTLINE    ;break;
30             default      : cmd = INVALIDCMD    ;
31             } /* end of switch stmt */
32         }
33       return(cmd) ;
34     }
35
```

console I/O and an example of direct screen output. This knowledge can be applied to other interactive programs.

The enhanced program performs a useful function and does it well enough to be usable. Snooping around in data files made by commercial software such as WordStar, dBase II, or Lotus 1-2-3 is fun and educational too. FD is also a practical tool to help in debugging and testing file-oriented programs.

5
Tools for Sorting

This chapter builds several general purpose tools based on sorting algorithms. While two complete programs are presented, the point of the chapter is to develop general purpose sort modules for use in your programs. Sorting data is a common requirement in many applications, yet many programmers do not have the training or confidence to write sort functions. The modules we present allow you to concentrate on your application. Even if enhancements to the sort modules are necessary, starting with correct, working functions is much easier than starting from scratch.

Sorting algorithms have been a favorite topic for computer science research since computers were first developed. The subject allowed virtuoso feats of mathematical analysis, and the extensive use of sorting programs showed that there were practical benefits. This combination of practical applications and elegant mathematics attracted lots of work and gave us many very useful algorithms. Our job is to put some of these algorithms to good use. We start with programs to sort arrays of integers to illustrate the algorithms, but we develop the algorithms further to produce good tools: modules that can be used without modification for sorting different kinds of data.

There are two kinds of sorting problems: those where all the data fit into RAM memory at once and those where they do not. The chapter begins with algorithms for the first case, *internal sorting*, and develops them into general purpose tools. The second part of the chapter adds the algorithms needed for the second case, *external sorting*. A general sort/merge program that works for different types of files is presented at the end of the chapter.

5.1 Internal Sorting Algorithms: Insertion and Quicksort

Insertion Sorting: A Simple Algorithm

There are many different algorithms for sorting data. To start, we look at a simple one, insertion sorting. This technique is based on the way a bridge player sorts his or her cards. The player picks up one card at a time and inserts it at the proper position in the set of cards already picked up. Our algorithm sorts an array of integers, using the same method. The following diagrams show insertion sorting on an array of four integers (ascending order is chosen for the example, but the algorithm is applicable to descending order, too). When we begin the process, the sorted area consists of only the first element. When we finish, it includes all elements of the array:

Before sorting

—unsorted—

| 4 | 3 | 1 | 6 |

↑ element to insert next

After inserting
second element

—sorted — unsorted —

| 3 | 4 | 1 | 6 |

↑ element to
insert next

After inserting
third element

— sorted   — unsorted

| 1 | 3 | 4 | 6 |

↑ element to
insert next

After inserting
fourth element

—sorted—

| 1 | 3 | 4 | 6 |

Pseudo-code

The pseudo-code to describe the insertion sort is simple and compact:

```
insert
    repeat for each element from the second through last
        compare to sorted elements to find where
        to insert it.
        move sorted elements to make room for this one.
        insert it in order.
    end
```

The **insert** function is shown in Figure 5.1. It is written as a function to be called with any size array of integers. The array elements are indexed as 0 through na-1. The loop on lines 11 to 20 starts with element 1, the second in the array.

Figure 5.1   c:inserti.c

```
1    /* inserti.c - insertion sort for an array of integers */
2    #include "stdio.h"
3
4    int insert(a,na)
5      int a[] ;                /* array of integers to be sorted */
6      int na  ;                /* number of integers to be sorted */
7      {
8        int i , j ;            /* indices for loops */
9        int temp ;             /* holds one element of array temporarily */
10
11       for( i=1 ; i < na ; i = i + 1 )
12          { /* insert the i-th element into the sorted array */
13            temp = a[i] ;
14            j = i - 1 ;
15            while( (j >= 0) && (temp < a[j]) )
16               { a[j+1] = a[j] ;
17                 j = j - 1 ;
18               }
19            a[j+1] = temp ;
20          }
21     }
```

Notice that the inner loop on lines 15 to 18 combines two functions: It compares elements to the one being inserted to find where it belongs and moves elements upward to make room for this element. Line 19 inserts the new element when its proper place has been found.

There are some details that affect the performance of **insert**. The function, as written, requires little extra memory—two loop indexes and a temporary variable for the element being inserted. The inner loop begins comparing elements just below the element being inserted; this ensures that the loop will end immediately if the array is already in order. If we had started the inner loop at element 0, it would terminate only when all the sorted elements had been compared.

Simply examining the algorithm can supply some information about performance. For example, we can see that the best case occurs when the array is already in order. In that case, inserting each element requires a single comparison and no movement of elements already sorted. So an array of n elements would require $(n-1)$ comparisons. An array with elements in reverse order would require comparisons to every element already sorted. The total number of comparisons would be about $(n*n/2)$. For randomly ordered data, each element would be compared to about half the elements already sorted. This total is about $(n*n/4)$ comparisons.

If you would like to test your skills, here are two optional questions to consider:

Questions

1. The inner loop contains two tests that must be performed for each iteration. How could the test for the beginning of the array be eliminated? (Hint—What if a a[0] was reserved for a dummy element?)

2. The algorithm works best for an array that is already sorted. How could it be re-written to perform best on an array that is in reverse order?

Quicksort: A Faster Algorithm

The insertion sort function is simple but not very fast for sorting large arrays. We need a better sorting algorithm. The quicksort algorithm invented by C. A. R. Hoare (1962) is a little more complicated to describe and to program but is very fast for sorting large arrays.

Quicksort is based on the idea of partitioning the array so that all elements in one subarray are less than or equal to all the elements in the second subarray. In practice, we pick a test value and rearrange the array so that all the elements in one subarray are less than or equal to that value, while those in the other subarray are greater than or equal to the value. This practice reduces the size of the sorting problem because we need only to sort the two partitions individually. We apply the same partitioning process to each subarray separately. As each subarray is partitioned, we partition its parts. One large sorting problem is replaced by a series of smaller and simpler problems. Following is the overall pseudo-code:

```
qsort
    select a test value
    partition the array using the test value
    sort the left subarray with quicksort
    sort the right subarray with quicksort
end
```

We use the physically middle element of the array as the test value (we discuss this choice later).

The partitioning is simple. We compare each element to a test value to decide in which partition it belongs. We start at the left and right ends of the array and scan toward the middle. On the left we stop the scan when we find an element that belongs in the right partition. We stop the right scan when we find an element that belongs in the left partition. Then we exchange the two elements and continue the scans just past the exchanged elements. The process ends when the two scans meet. We show the pseudo-code first as a series of steps and then with a loop:

```
partition an array with a test value
    start with left scan index at array[0]
    and right index at array[n]
    scan from left for element > = test value
    scan from right for element < = test value
    exchange elements
    move left index right one element
    move right index left one element
    scan from left for element > = test value
```

```
        scan from right for element < = test value
        exchange elements
        . . .
        scan from left for element > = test value
        scan from right for element < = test value
        ( scans meet and the process ends )
end


partition an array with a test value (with loop)
        start with left scan index at array[0]
        and right index at array[n]
        repeat until scans meet
                scan from left for element > = test value
                scan from right for element < = test value
                exchange elements
                move left index right one element
                move right index left one element
end
```

We demonstrate the partitioning process on the following six-element array. We use the third element (whose value is 4) as the test value so that the left subarray contains values less than or equal to 4 and the right subarray contains values greater than or equal to 4.

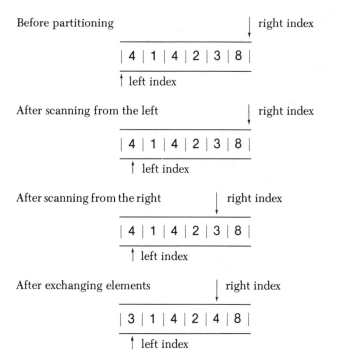

Before partitioning | right index

    | 4 | 1 | 4 | 2 | 3 | 8 |
    ↑ left index

After scanning from the left | right index

    | 4 | 1 | 4 | 2 | 3 | 8 |
    ↑ left index

After scanning from the right | right index

    | 4 | 1 | 4 | 2 | 3 | 8 |
    ↑ left index

After exchanging elements | right index

    | 3 | 1 | 4 | 2 | 4 | 8 |
    ↑ left index

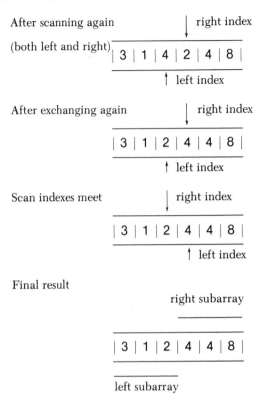

After scanning again

(both left and right)

right index

| 3 | 1 | 4 | 2 | 4 | 8 |

↑ left index

After exchanging again

right index

| 3 | 1 | 2 | 4 | 4 | 8 |

↑ left index

Scan indexes meet

right index

| 3 | 1 | 2 | 4 | 4 | 8 |

↑ left index

Final result

right subarray

| 3 | 1 | 2 | 4 | 4 | 8 |

left subarray

Figure 5.2 lists qsort, a quicksort function for sorting an array of integers. It performs the function described by the pseudo-code, but the scanning loops in lines 22 and 24 have been rearranged for faster execution. Lines 35 to 42 use qsort to sort the partitioned subarrays. qsort expects the address of an array as its first parameter. For the left subarray, this is just the address of the array. For the right subarray, it is the address of the first element in the subarray, a[i].

The qsort function is *recursive;* that is, it calls itself to sort the two subarrays it produces. The test in line 14 stops this recursion when a subarray of one element is produced. Each call to qsort produces a different *activation* with its own arguments and local variables. Recursion may seem to be a complicated concept, but it allows us to write a program that corresponds closely to our pseudo-code.

Each recursive call consumes some memory for local variables, arguments, and housekeeping information. If the partitioning process works unevenly, up to (n−1) recursive calls might be needed to complete the sort. For large arrays (say, 1,000 to 5,000), this process might exhaust available memory. qsort avoids this problem by sorting the smaller partition first. This limits the number of recursive calls to about log(n) base 2.

Several subtle details in the qsort function deserve more attention. For example, selecting the middle element as the test value rather than the first element makes qsort work better for data that are already in order. A check to see if the

Figure 5.2   c:qsorti.c

```
1    /* qsorti.c - performs a quicksort on an array of integers */
2    #include "stdio.h"
3    #include "cminor.h"
4
5    int qsort(a,na)
6     int a[] ;                /* array of integers to be sorted */
7     int na  ;                /* number of elements to be sorted */
8     {
9        int i , j ;           /* indices for loops */
10       int temp ;            /* temporary storage for element */
11       int nr ;              /* number elements in right partition */
12       int part ;            /* element chosen as partition value */
13
14       if( na < 2  )
15           return ;
16
17       part = a[na/2] ;      /* pick middle element for partition */
18
19       i = -1 ; j = na ;
20       while( 1 == 1 )
21         { /* find first element to move right */
22           do { i = i + 1 ; } while( a[i] < part ) ;
23
24           /* find first element to move left */
25           do { j = j - 1 ; } while( a[j] > part ) ;
26
27           if( i >= j )             /* have the boundaries met ? */
28               break ;              /*    yes - through paritioning */
29
30           /* swap i and j elements */
31           temp = a[i] ;  a[i] = a[j] ; a[j] = temp ;
32         }
33
34       nr = na - i ;
35       if( i < (na/2) )             /* now deal with each partition */
36         { qsort( a , i ) ;         /* sort left side  */
37           qsort( &(a[i]),nr);      /* sort right side */
38         }
39       else
40         { qsort( &(a[i]),nr);      /* sort right side */
41           qsort( a , i ) ;         /* sort left side  */
42         }
43    }
```

scans have met is placed in the middle of the loop to avoid duplicating statements. The initialization of left and right indexes in line 19 and the do { } while loops in lines 22 and 25 remove the need for extra statements to advance the indexes after an exchange.

Quicksort performs best when the array is partitioned into two subarrays of equal size at each step. An initial array of n elements would produce subarrays of n/2, n/4, . . . down to 1 element in approximately log(n), base 2 steps. Approximately n comparisons are required at each step. (Although the arrays being partitioned get smaller at each step, they get more numerous.) The total number of comparisons would be proportional to (n*Log(n)).

The quicksort algorithm performs worst when it partitions the array unevenly at each step. When one partition always contains a single element, (n-1) steps are required. In this case the total number of comparisons is proportional to (n*n). Fortunately, the worst case is quite rare. For large arrays, almost all arrangements of elements are sorted quite efficiently.

Special cases such as data that are already in order or that are in reverse order are important. An array with all elements equal is another important case. For these situations, qsort produces best case results.

For the venturesome among you, here are several more questions:

Questions

1. The scanning loops in lines 22 and 24 use the sentinel idea. They do not check for the end of the array. Do the loops as written always stop? (The first time each scan must stop when the element chosen as a test value is reached if not before. What happens on the next scan?)

   Would the qsort still work if the tests in lines 22 and 24 were changed to a[i]< = part and a[j]> = part?

2. In our example partitioning a six-element array, the result was two sub-arrays with three elements each. What would happen when the three element sub-array {3 1 6} is partitioned?

3. Work through the special cases to see how quicksort works. What if we used the first or last element of each partition instead of the middle one?

5.2 Generalizing the Internal Sort Functions: memsort

□ Both sorting algorithms can be applied to any kinds of data. However, the C functions we presented are specific; they work only for arrays of integers. We need general purpose functions that will sort any kinds of data—even character strings of varying length. We could use Figures 5.1 and 5.2 as models for writing sort functions for other types of data, but what we really want is general functions that we can compile and put into an object module along with other toolkit functions. Most textbook discussions stop short of this goal; demonstrating the algorithms is enough for the authors. Since our purpose is producing practical tools, we start with algorithms and produce good tools. Fortunately, C has the features we need to make general purpose sort functions.

The revised functions are shown in Figures 5.3 and 5.4. The quicksort function has been named memsort to avoid possible conflicts with functions in the C library. Most of the changes are common to both insert.c and memsort.c and can be discussed together.

Figure 5.3   c:insert.c

```
1    /* insert.c - insertion sort function */
2    /* uses pointers to actual data elements and a compare function */
3    #include "stdio.h"
4
5    int insert(pa,na,pcomp)
6     char *pa[] ;        /* array of pointers to elements to be sorted */
7     int na  ;                   /* number of elements to be sorted */
8     int (*pcomp) () ;           /* pointer to compare function */
9     {
10      int i ;                /* indices for loops */
11      int j ;                /*   for inner loop - optimize */
12      char *ptemp;           /* temporary storage for one pointer */
13
14      for( i=1 ; i < na ; i = i + 1 )
15         { /* insert the i-th element into the sorted array */
16           ptemp = pa[i] ;
17           j = i - 1;
18           while( (j >= 0) && ( (*pcomp)(ptemp,pa[j]) <= 0 ) )
19              { pa[j+1] = pa[j] ;
20                j = j - 1 ;
21              }
22           pa[j+1] = ptemp ;
23         }
24    }
```

Instead of passing the array of elements to be sorted, we can pass an array of pointers to the data. Now the sort functions reference and move pointers to the data, not the data. The sort functions also receive an additional argument: the address of a function to perform comparisons of elements. When the sort function needs to compare two elements, it calls this function with pointers to the two elements as arguments. Line 18 of Figure 5.3 and lines 27 and 30 of Figure 5.4 show these function calls. (The syntax for declaring and using this function pointer is strange and hard to remember. You will not need it often, so just copy a working example when you need to use a function pointer.)

The compare function must return an integer value less than 0 if the first element should precede the second. It must return values equal to 0 when the elements are equal and a value greater than 0 when the first element is larger than the second.

The memsort function combines the best features of both quicksort and insertion sort algorithms. It uses the quicksort algorithm for large sorts and the insertion algorithm for small ones where it is faster. Figure 5.5 shows a manual page description for memsort. The test program in Figure 5.6 illustrates the use of memsort. Lines 29 to 33 show a compare function for integer data. Line 22 shows how the function's address is passed to memsort. Since the function name is referenced without parentheses, the declaration in line 3 is needed to tell the C compiler that icomp is a function.

Figure 5.4   c:memsort.c

```
1    /* memsort.c - performs a quicksort with an array of pointers */
2    /* and a caller-supplied compare function */
3    #include "stdio.h"
4    #include "cminor.h"
5
6    #define LIMIT 8          /* crossover point for insertion sort */
7
8    int memsort(pa,na,pcomp)
9     char *pa[] ;             /* array of pointers to data to be sorted */
10    int na  ;                /* number of elements to be sorted */
11    int (*pcomp) () ;        /* pointer to compare function */
12    {
13       int i,j ;             /* indices for loops */
14       char  *ptemp ;        /* temporary storage for one pointer */
15       int   nr ;            /* number elements in right partition */
16       char  *ppart ;  /* pointer to element used as partition value */
17
18       if( na < LIMIT )   /* use insert sort for small partitions */
19          { insert(pa,na,pcomp) ;
20            return ;
21          }
22
23       ppart = pa[na/2] ;  /* pick middle element for partition */
24       i = -1 ; j = na ;
25       while( 1 == 1 )
26          { /* find first element to move right */
27            do { i = i + 1 ; } while( (*pcomp)(pa[i],ppart) < 0 ) ;
28
29            /* find first element to move left */
30            do { j = j - 1 ; } while( (*pcomp)(pa[j],ppart) > 0 ) ;
31
32            if( i >= j )                /* have the boundaries met ? */
33                break ;                 /*    yes - through paritioning */
34
35            /* swap i and j elements */
36            ptemp = pa[i] ;  pa[i] = pa[j] ; pa[j] = ptemp ;
37          }
38
39
40       nr = na - i ;
41       if( i < (na/2) )                 /* now deal with each partition */
42          { memsort( pa , i , pcomp) ;         /* sort left side  */
43            memsort(&(pa[i]),nr,pcomp);/* sort right side */
44          }
45       else
46          { memsort(&(pa[i]),nr,pcomp);/* sort right side */
47            memsort( pa , i , pcomp) ;          /* sort left side  */
48          }
49    }
```

Figure 5.5   memsort function description

Name

    memsort   sorts data in memory

Usage

```
int na ;                        /* number of elements to be sorted */
int a[10] ;                     /* data to be sorted */
int *pa[10] ;                   /* pointers to the data */
int intcomp () ;                /* compares two integers */
memsort(pa,na,intcomp) ;
```

Function

memsort sorts data in memory using the quicksort and insertion algorithms. memsort can be used for almost any kind of data. It expects to receive an array of pointers to the data to be sorted and the address of a function to compare two elements. memsort rearranges the pointers to the data rather than rearranging the data.

Example

```
int na = 10 ;
int a[10] ;                     /* assume data is already in a[ ] */
int *pa[10] ;
int intcomp() ;
for (i=0 ; i< na ; i=i+1)       /* set up pointers for sort */
    { pa[i] = & a[i] ; }
memsort(pa,na,intcomp) ;
for (i=0 ; i< 10 ; i=i+1)       /* display sorted results */
    { printf (" %d",*pa[i]) ; }
...

int intcomp(p1,p2)              /* sort function */
int *p1 ;                       /* points to first integer */
int *p2 ;                       /* points to second integer */
{
    return ( *p1-*p2 ) ;
}
```

Notes

The compare function should expect two arguments—pointers to two data elements. It should return a positive integer if the first element is greater than the second element. It should return a 0 value when the elements are equal and a negative value if the first element is less than the second. In more general terms, a positive value means that the first element follows the second in the desired sort order. A negative value means that the first element should precede the second.

The quicksort algorithm is very fast ($n*\log n$ time dependence) for almost all cases. However, a worst case arrangement of data can produce slow sorting ($n*n$ dependence).

Figure 5.6   c:testmem.c

```
1    /* testmem.c - test memsort.c */
2    #include "stdio.h"
3    int icomp() ;
4
5    main()
6      {
7         int i , n ;
8         int a[100] ;
9         int *pa[100] ;
10
11        for(i=0 ; i<100 ; i=i+1 )
12          { a[i] = -i ;
13             pa[i] = & a[i] ;
14          }
15
16        printf(" enter numbers to sort (type q to end) \n");
17        n = 0 ;
18        while( scanf("%d",& a[n]) != 0 )
19          { n = n + 1 ; }
20
21        printf(" pa=%x   na=%d   & icomp=%x \n",pa,n,icomp) ;
22        memsort(pa,n,icomp) ;
23
24        printf(" after memsort \n");
25        for(i=0 ; i<= n ; i=i+1 )
26          { printf(" %3d",*pa[i] ) ; }
27      }
28
29   icomp(p1,p2)
30     int *p1 , *p2 ;
31     {
32        return( *p1 - *p2 ) ;
33     }
```

One more round of optional questions follows so that you can self-test your knowledge.

Questions

1. How would you sort data into descending order using the sort function? (Write a suitable compare function.)

2. Memsort is much more useful than the integer sort functions. But using function calls for comparing elements increases execution time. How much is the penalty? The next section gives benchmark results using memsort to sort arrays of integers. Run the same tests with quicksort to measure the penalty.

The program in Figure 5.6 takes a shortcut in using memsort. The pointer array is described as pointers to integers in the main function but as pointers to

Figure 5.7   Internal sort performance

Array size	10	100	(time in seconds) 1,000	2,000	5,000
Ordered data					
insert	0.0020	0.022	0.20	0.42	1
memsort	0.0034	0.064	1.04	2.3	6.2
Reversed data					
insert	0.0074	0.69	68	272	—
memsort	0.0037	0.067	1.1	2.3	6.4
Disordered data					
insert	0.0055	0.36	35	141	—
memsort	0.0061	0.11	1.5	3.2	9.2

characters in memsort, assuming that these two types of pointers occupy the same amount of memory. While this is true for most computers and C compilers (including 8086 and 8088 computers), it might not be valid in some environments.

The problem with our shortcut is more theoretical than real. Similar problems occur with the use of C library functions such as read and write. We will continue to use such shortcuts throughout this book.

5.3   Performance Analysis of memsort

□   Figure 5.7 shows some performance results using insert and memsort to sort arrays of integers. The results in the figure refer to a single execution of the qsort function; enough iterations were run to permit accurate timing. The tests were run with three kinds of data: ordered, reverse ordered, and disordered data with many duplications. The following function was used to generate the disordered data:

```
long nxt = 13 ;
disorder(a,n)
  int a[ ] ;
  int n ;
  {
    int i ;
    for(i = 0 ; i < n ; i = i + 1)
      { nxt = nxt * 1220703125L ;
        a[i] = nxt % 13 ;
      }
  }
```

The figure's results show about what we expect: memsort is fast for all sizes and all kinds of data. memsort is fast enough for many applications. The insertion sort is adequate for small arrays but terrible for large arrays. The exception is when the data are in order (or nearly so); then insert is even faster than memsort.

5.4   Enhancements to memsort

□   **More Generality**

To use memsort, we have to build an array of pointers to the data. Sometimes this task is convenient, but in some cases it is extra work. The UNIX C library has a quicksort function used as follows:

```
char a[ ] ;                  /*data to be sorted */
int na ;                     /* number of elements */
int width ;              /* size of an element in bytes */
int comp ( );                /* compare function */
qsort(a,na,width,comp) ;
```

This function is more flexible than our memsort function. To sort an array of integers, we would use the UNIX qsort function as follows:

```
qsort(a,na, sizeof(int),icomp) ;
```

with

```
icomp(pa1,pa2)
int *pa1 , *pa2 ;
{
    return( *pa1 − *pa2 ) ;
}
```

No array of pointers is required. But to sort a set of variable-length character strings with pointers to them in pa we would use

```
qsort(pa,na,sizeof(char *),strcmp) ;
```

Our memsort function is less flexible than this, but it allows a simpler, more easily explained implementation. If your C compiler library includes a function like the UNIX qsort, you might wish to use it instead of our memsort function.

Better Performance

The references for this chapter in Appendix D contain ideas for improving the quicksort algorithm. In addition, Chapter 9 discusses optimizations to the C code for qsort.

5.5   An Application: Sorting Lines of Text

□   Now that we have tools for sorting data, we can put them to use in an application: sorting lines in a text file. Such a program would be useful for sorting a list of names, but it gives us an opportunity to illustrate a real program using memsort. In addition, it provides an introduction to sorting *records* in data files. By records we mean the units of data to be compared and rearranged. In this case the records are lines of ASCII text. However, the same logic applies to other types of data files as well.

The SORTTEXT program reads a text file into a storage area, sorts the individual lines of text, and writes the sorted lines of text to an output file. A manual page description is shown in Figure 5.8.

Pseudo-code

The pseudo-code for this program is as follows:

```
sort text file
      read lines of text into memory
      sort lines of text in memory
      write sorted lines to output file
end

read lines of text into memory
      get 1st line
      repeat until end–of–file reached
            place line in free part of storage area
            set up a pointer to the line of text
            update info on free space in storage area
            get another line of text
end

write sorted lines to output file
      open output file
      repeat for each line of text
            get pointer to next sorted line of text
            output the line of text
end
```

Figure 5.8   SORTTEXT program description

Name

sorttext – sorts a text file (lines of ASCII characters)

Usage

a > sorttext input-file output-file

Description

SORTTEXT reads a file of ASCII text and sorts it. The entire line is used as the sorting key with the normal ASCII collation sequence. Control-Z is recognized as the effective end-of-file.

Limitations

Lines longer than 500 characters are split into two or more lines. Files longer than about 20K characters cannot be sorted by the current version of the program.

Some variables that will be needed include an area for storing lines of text, a pointer or index to mark the free space in the area, an array of pointers to the lines of text, and a count of lines of text read in.

The pseudo-code ignores some problems. For example, the program may not be able to open either the input or the output file; the text file may be too large to fit into the storage area; the file may contain a line too long to be handled as a unit. Our program must allow for these problems.

SORTTEXT Source Files

The SORTTEXT program is shown in Figures 5.9 through 5.13. The sorttext.h file in Figure 5.9 defines constants needed in the source files. Sizes for the text storage area and the pointer array are placed here to make changes convenient. We also define symbolic names for values returned by the fillarea function here.

Figure 5.9   c:sorttext.h

```
1    /* sorttext.h - constants for sorttext program */
2
3    #define SSIZE    20000              /* size of storage area for text */
4    #define MAX_REC   2000              /* max number of records */
5    #define MAX_RSIZE 500               /* max. size for a record */
6
7    /* return values for fillarea */
8    #define NOT_EOF      0              /* end-of-file not reached */
9    #define AT_EOF       1              /* end-of-file reached */
```

The following diagram shows the structure of SORTTEXT. The functions follow the preceding pseudo-code. We discuss the program one source file at a time, with the file containing the main function first.

```
main
    dosort
        do_open
        initfill
        fillarea
            getrec
                getl
        memsort
        do_close
        outfile
            putrec
                putl
        do_open
        do_close
```

sorttext.c

The file, sorttext.c (Figure 5.10), contains the main function. It checks to be sure that two file names were specified on the command line and calls dosort to sort the file. dosort follows the overall pseudo-code presented earlier. It uses the fillarea function to read the text file and set up the pointer array. memsort sorts the lines of text, and outfile writes them in sorted order. sorttext.c provides the overall structure for the process; the details of each step are hidden in other source files.

Lines of text are stored as character strings and are compared with the C library function, strcmp.

fillarea.c

The fillarea.c file in Figure 5.11 reads the text file line by line and stores it in the area passed as an argument. As each line is read, a pointer to it is stored in the pointer array. The process can end in one of two ways: The end-of-file may be reached, or the storage space for the text (or the pointer array) may be exhausted. The two return statements on lines 26 and 38 reflect these conditions by returning different values.

A separate function, initfill, reads the first record from the input file. When fillarea is called, it expects a record to be waiting in the rarea character array. We could have fillarea read a record upon entry. SORTTEXT exits if fillarea does not reach the end of the input file. If we call fillarea again instead of exiting, fillarea would already have a record in rarea—the record that would not fit into the

Figure 5.10   c:sorttext.c

```
1      /* sorttext.c - sort a text file (lines of ASCII characters) */
2      #include  "stdio.h"
3      #include  "cminor.h"
4      #include "sorttext.h"
5
6      int strcmp() ;             /* string compare function */
7      FILE *do_open() ;          /* opens file and checks for errors */
8
9      main(argc,argv)
10       int argc ;      /* number of words in command line */
11       char *argv[] ;/* pointers to each word */
12       {
13           /* check to see that file names were specified */
14           if( argc < 3 )
15             { printf(" need file names \n");
16               printf(" USAGE:  sortfile  input-file   output-file \n");
17               exit(1);
18             }
19
20           dosort(argv[1],argv[2]) ;    /* do the sort */
21       }
22
23
24     int dosort(fromfile,tofile)
25       char fromfile[] ;               /* input for sort */
26       char tofile[] ;                 /* put the output here */
27       {
28           int  nrec ;
29           char sarea[ SSIZE ] ;        /* storage area for text lines */
30           char *p[ MAX_REC ] ;         /* pointers to lines of text */
31           FILE *infile ;               /* input file */
32
33           infile = do_open(fromfile,"r") ;  /* open input file */
34           initfill(infile) ;                /* initialize for fillarea */
35                                             /* read text file in storage area */
36           if( fillarea(sarea,SSIZE,p,MAX_REC,&nrec,infile) != AT_EOF)
37             { printf("file too large") ;
38               exit(3) ;
39             }
40           do_close(infile,fromfile) ;
41
42           memsort(p,nrec,strcmp) ;   /* sort using string compare fun. */
43           outfile(p,nrec,tofile) ;    /* write sorted lines out */
44       }
```

Figure 5.11   c:fillarea.c

```
1     /* fillarea.c - fill sort area with records */
2     #include "stdio.h"
3     #include "sorttext.h"
4
5     int rsize ;                     /* size of record found */
6     char rarea[ MAX_RSIZE ] ;   /* storage for one record */
7
8     int fillarea(area,asize,p,psize,pnp,infile)
9      char area[] ;                  /* address of storage area for strings */
10     int  asize ;                   /* size of the area */
11     char *p[] ;                    /* store pointers to records here */
12     int psize ;                    /* size of p[] - (max. no. records) */
13     int  *pnp ;                    /* store no. of records at this loc. */
14     FILE *infile ;                 /* input file */
15     {
16        int nrec ;                  /* counter for number of records found */
17        unsigned start ;            /* index of first free byte in area[] */
18
19        start = 0 ;                 /* free space at area[0] */
20        nrec  = 0 ;                 /* no records yet */
21
22        while( rsize > 0 )          /* stop at end-of-file */
23          {                         /* check for room */
24            if(   ( (start+rsize) > asize )  || ( nrec >= psize ) )
25              { *pnp = nrec ;
26                return( NOT_EOF ) ;
27              }
28                                    /* copy record to storage area */
29            movedata( & area[start] , rarea,rsize) ;
30
31            p[nrec] = & area[start]; /* store pointer to record */
32            nrec = nrec + 1 ;        /* count it */
33            start = start + rsize ;  /* move start past this record */
34                                     /* get next record */
35            rsize = getrec(rarea,MAX_RSIZE,infile) ;
36          } ;
37        *pnp = nrec ;
38        return( AT_EOF ) ;
39     }
40
41
42     initfill(infile)         /* called first time to read first record */
43      FILE *infile ;
44      {
45        rsize = getrec(rarea,MAX_RSIZE,infile) ;
46      }
47
```

storage space remaining in the first call. Therefore, reading another record in fillarea would be incorrect, while our method works.

outfile.c

Figure 5.12 shows the outfile.c source file. outfile uses the pointer array reordered by memsort to write the text lines in sorted order.

sortio.c

The sortio.c file in Figure 5.13 contains I/O functions used by other source files. The do_open and do_close functions use the gfopen function described in Chapters 2 and 8 and the fclose library function to open and close files. Since input files may contain a control-Z character to mark the end of data, we select ASCII mode.

Functions in other source files call the getrec and putrec functions to read and write records. In SORTTEXT these records are just lines of text. But getrec and putrec hide the definition of a file record from the rest of the program. This allows the fillarea and outfile functions to be useful for all kinds of data. Section 5.8 provides for more record types.

Figure 5.12   c:outfile.c

```
1    /* outfile.c - write out sorted file */
2    #include "stdio.h"
3    #include "sorttext.h"
4
5    FILE *do_open() ;
6
7    int outfile(prec,nrec,oname)
8     char *prec[] ;                    /* array of pointers to records */
9     int nrec ;                        /* number of records to be output */
10    char oname[] ;                    /* output file name */
11    {
12      int i ;
13      FILE     *ofile ;               /* output runs to this file */
14
15      ofile = do_open(oname,"w");     /* open output merge file */
16
17      for(i=0 ; i < nrec ; i=i+1 )    /* write records in sorted order */
18        { putrec(prec[i],ofile); }    /* output one record */
19
20      do_close(ofile,oname) ;         /* close the file */
21    }
22
23
```

Figure 5.13   c:sortio.c

```
1    /* sortio.c - I/O functions for sorttext program */
2    /* do_open , do_close , getrec , putrec */
3    #include "stdio.h"
4    #include "cminor.h"
5
6    FILE *gfopen() ;
7
8
9    FILE *do_open(fname,fmode)         /* open file & check for errors */
10     char fname[] ;                   /* file name */
11     char fmode[] ;                   /* read/write/append mode */
12     {                                /* return a file pointer */
13        FILE *fd ;
14
15        fd = gfopen(fname,fmode,ASC_MODE) ;
16        if( fd == NULL )
17          { printf("\n can't open file - %s \n",fname);
18            exit( 8 ) ;
19          }
20        return( fd ) ;
21     }
22
23     int do_close(fd,fname)           /* close file & check for errors */
24      FILE *fd ;                      /* file pointer */
25      char fname[] ;                  /* name of file being closed */
26      {
27        if( fclose(fd) < 0 )
28          { printf("\n can't close file - %s \n",fname);
29            exit( 10 ) ;
30          }
31      }
32
33     int getrec(rec,maxr,fd)
34      char rec[] ;                    /* put it here in string form */
35      int maxr ;                      /* maximum length permitted */
36      FILE *fd ;                      /* file pointer for input file */
37      {                               /* returns no. chars used in rec */
38        return( getl(rec,maxr,fd));   /* let getl do the work */
39      }
40
41
42     int putrec(rec,fd)               /* output one record */
43      char rec[] ;                    /* the record to output */
44      FILE *fd ;                      /* output file pointer */
45      {
46        return( putl(rec,fd) ) ;      /* use putl to do line output */
47      }
48
49
50     /* **************************** line oriented functions */
51
52     int getl(s,maxs,fd)              /* get one line from input file */
53      char s[] ;                      /* put it here in string form */
54      int maxs ;                      /* maximum length permitted */
55      FILE *fd ;                      /* file pointer for input file */
```

Figure 5.13   c:sortio.c (continued)

```
56      {                                    /* getl returns no. chars used in s */
57                                           /* (or -1 if EOF reached) */
58          int i ;
59                                           /* get next line of input */
60          if( fgets(s,maxs-1,fd) == NULL )
61              return( -1 ) ;               /* EOF - return special length value */
62
63          i = strlen(s) ;                  /* get string length */
64          if( s[i-1] != '\n' )             /* see if a new-line is present */
65              { s[i] =     '\n' ;          /*   n - append one */
66                s[i+1] = '\0' ;            /* restore end-of-string marker */
67                i = i + 1 ;                /* adjust string length */
68              }
69                                           /* return length of line */
70          return(i+1) ;                    /* count the '\0' at end too */
71      }
72
73
74
75  int putl(s,fd)                           /* output one line of text */
76  char s[] ;                               /* line to output in string form */
77  FILE *fd ;                               /* output file pointer */
78  {
79      return( fputs(s,fd) ) ;              /* use fputs library function */
80  }
```

getl and putl read and write lines of text using the C library functions fgets and fputs. The fgets function normally returns a line of text in C string format with a newline character at the end. But if it fills the array provided (a line longer than maxs−1 characters), it will return without a newline character in the string. This also occurs if the last line in the file does not have a newline before the end-of-file. getl checks for this condition and adds a newline if it is not already present.

SORTTEXT is a small program, but we have spread it over five source files. This procedure keeps each source file simple and focused on one level of detail. It also provides a foundation for continued development. The next sections build on this version of SORTTEXT to develop programs for external sorting.

5.6   External Sorting Algorithms

□   The SORTTEXT program makes good use of the memsort function, but it is limited to files that fit into the storage area available. When all the data are in RAM memory, any element can be accessed in a few microseconds. When the data are in a disk file, this access takes many milliseconds. memsort relies on free access to every element being sorted. We need an algorithm that fits the limitations of disk file access. The merge algorithm meets our needs; it will be the basis for *external sorting* programs.

The merge algorithm combines two or more sorted files (or arrays) to produce a single sorted file. The process can be described as follows:

1. Get the first record from each file.
2. Select the record with the lowest key.
3. Place it in the output file.
4. Replace the record with the next from the same input file.
5. Repeat steps 2 to 4 until all input files are exhausted.

We can illustrate the process with two arrays of integers:

Before merging

| Output Array | 1 4 | ——— | Input Array 1 |
| ——————— | 2 3 7 | ——— | Input Array 2 |

After first element selected

| Output Array | 4 | ——— | Input Array 1 |
| 1 ——————— | 2 3 7 | ——— | Input Array 2 |

After second element selected

| Output Array | 4 | ——— | Input Array 1 |
| 1 2 ——————— | 3 7 | ——— | Input Array 2 |

After third element selected

| Output Array | 4 | ——— | Input Array 1 |
| 1 2 3 ——— | 7 | ——— | Input Array 2 |

After fourth and fifth elements selected

| Output Array | ——————— | Input Array 1 |
| 1 2 3 4 7 | ——————— | Input Array 2 |

The merge algorithm works well with data stored on floppy or hard disks. Only one record at a time is required from each input file, and records are retrieved sequentially. This limits the amount of RAM memory needed and allows efficient disk I/O operations. The merge algorithm is the heart of the program. We need an initial step to prepare sorted *runs*. Then we use the merge process to combine these runs into fewer but longer runs.

Pseudo-code for External Sort

Now we can write pseudo-code for this external sort. The overall pseudo-code follows the explanation just given:

```
main function
        build sorted runs
        merge runs
        copy final merged result to output file
end
```

Building runs is much like the SORTTEXT program. We read records from the input file until a storage area is filled. Then we sort the records (with memsort) and write them to an output file. Each batch of records sorted together is one run. We repeat this process until the entire input file has been read.

```
build runs
        until all of input file read
                fill storage area with records
                sort records
                output sorted records
end
```

Filling the storage area with records is unchanged from the SORTTEXT program. The fillarea function in Section 5.5 can be used unchanged.

The merge process is carried out in passes. On each pass, the existing runs are combined into new, longer runs. Limits such as the amount of RAM memory available or the number of files open at a time limit the number of runs that can be combined in one step. For example, if this limit were four runs at a time, twenty initial runs would be combined into five runs on the first pass. Those five runs would be combined into two on pass two. Pass three would combine these two into a single run, ending the merging process. The following pseudo-code performs this iteration.

```
do merges
        repeat until a single run is produced
                merge existing runs into longer runs
end
```

The next level of detail describes a single pass of the merge process. Here, the existing runs are grouped into sets of M runs each. Each set is merged into a single new run.

```
merge existing runs
        repeat until all existing runs merged
                select the next M runs
                merge M runs
end
```

Merging a single set of runs into one new run is shown here:

```
merge M runs
        get 1st record from each run
        start output run in pointer array
        repeat until all M runs are exhausted
                pick lowest record
                put in output run
                get replacement record from same input run
end
```

Data Structures

Choosing a way to store runs is the main decision to be made. We choose the simplest way: each run is stored in a separate file. In the merge part of the program, we will be using two sets of runs. One already exists and will be input to each iteration of the merging algorithm. The other is the output runs being created. Naming and keeping track of these files storing runs is a significant part of the algorithm. At the end of each iteration of the merge, the runs just created become input for the next iteration. The old runs are no longer needed, and those files can be deleted.

The two parts of the process need different data structures. Forming runs is similar to the first version of **sorttext**. We need a storage area for an entire run and an array of pointers. It requires two files—one for the original input file and one for the run being written out. Merging runs requires M open files for input runs and one open file for the run being created.

Exceptions

The same exceptions that we met in the SORTTEXT program must be handled here. Input and output file names may be missing or invalid. We may run out of room on a disk while writing a scratch file or the final output file. Long lines of text may exceed the size of the area we reserve for storing a record. We also want the program to handle small files efficiently—if the first stage produces only one run, it should write directly to the final output file, bypassing the merge stage.

5.7 MERGEl Source Files

□ Since this is the first program based on the merge algorithm, we refer to it as
MERGE1. Much of the SORTTEXT program can be used or modified for
MERGE1. Three files—fillarea.c, outfile.c, and sortio.c—can be used without
change. We do not show these files again or discuss them further.

merge1.h

The header file, merge1.h, shown in Figure 5.14, is only slightly changed from
those in the SORTTEXT program. Two definitions were added to those in sort-
text.h: The maximum number of runs to merge is defined, and the MDATA data
structure used by two functions in the merge stage is declared.

merge1.c

The merge1.c file in Figure 5.15 is based on sorttext.c. The main function checks
for input and output file names and uses dosort to control the stages of the merge
process. In sorttext.c, the dosort function contains more detail. Since the
MERGE1 program has two stages, the details of the first stage are moved to a
separate source file (formruns.c) to keep the structure of the program clear.

Figure 5.14   c:merge1.h

```
 1    /* merge1.h - constants and data types for merge1 program */
 2
 3    /* constants for 1st stage - forming runs */
 4    #define SSIZE    20000          /* size of storage area for text */
 5    #define MAX_REC  2000           /* max number of records */
 6    #define MAX_RSIZE 500           /* max. size for a record */
 7
 8    /* return values for fillarea */
 9    #define NOT_EOF     0           /* end-of-file not reached */
10    #define AT_EOF      1           /* end-of-file reached */
11
12    /* merge constants and data */
13
14    #define MAX_MERGE   4           /* no. of runs to merge at a time */
15
16    typedef struct                  /* merge data for one input run */
17      { FILE *inf ;                 /* file pointer */
18        char *pbuf ;                /* address of record buffer */
19      } MDATA ;
```

Figure 5.15   c:merge1.c

```
1    /* merge1.c - external sort for a text file  */
2    #include  "stdio.h"
3    #include  "cminor.h"
4    #include "merge1.h"
5
6    int (*compfun) () ;             /* address of compare function */
7    int strcmp() ;                  /* library string compare function */
8    char scra[68] = "scra";         /* prefixes for scratch file names */
9    char scrb[68] = "scrb";
10
11   main(argc,argv)
12    int argc ;                     /* number of words in command line */
13    char *argv[] ;                 /* pointers to each word */
14    {
15       /* check to see that file names were specified */
16       if( argc < 3 )
17         { printf(" need file names \n");
18            printf(" USAGE:  merge1 input-file   output-file \n");
19            exit(1);
20         }
21       compfun = strcmp ;          /* use string compare function */
22       dosort(argv[1],argv[2]) ;
23    }
24
25
26   int dosort(fromfile,tofile)
27    char fromfile[] ;              /* input for sort */
28    char tofile[] ;                /* put the output here */
29    {
30       int  nruns ;
31                                   /* form runs from input file */
32       nruns = formruns(fromfile,scra,tofile) ;
33                                   /* now merge runs */
34       domerge(scra,scrb,tofile,nruns) ;
35    }
```

Following is the pattern of function calls in the MERGE1 program:

```
main
    dosort
        formruns
            do_open
            initfill
            fillarea
               getrec
                    getl
            memsort
            do_close
```

```
                    mkname
                    outfile
                      do_open
                      putrec
                         put1
                      do_close
                      domerge
                    dopass
                      swap_str
                      dopass
                        mkname
                        do_open
                        do_close
                        smerge
                           getrec
                           putrec
                           resort
                           memsort
                      delfile
```

formruns.c

The formruns.c file shown in Figure 5.16 controls building initial runs from the input file. It is similar to the **dosort** function in the SORTTEXT program. In that program, failing to read the entire input file into memory is an error, causing the program to exit immediately. In MERGE1, it just means that we must repeat the loop to form another run.

Line 29 calls **memsort** to sort each run. Although MERGE1 always uses the strcmp string compare function, we wrote **formruns** to be more general. It uses a compare function address stored in a global variable—**compfun**. The **main** function in merge1.c places the address of **strcmp** in this variable. The next program, MERGE2, uses a different compare function by placing another address into compfun.

Lines 31 to 33 create a file name for the run being output. For a small file that can be sorted in memory, the file name used is that specified for the final output. In the normal case, **mkfile** creates a unique name (like **scra001**), using the run number and the scratch file prefix.

domerge.c

The **domerge** function in Figure 5.17 controls the merging phase of the program. It not only follows the pseudo-code described earlier but also deals with two special

Figure 5.16 c:formruns.c

```
1    /* formruns.c - form initial runs from input file */
2    #include "stdio.h"
3    #include  "cminor.h"
4    #include "merge1.h"
5
6
7    extern int (*compfun) () ;        /* address of compare function */
8
9    FILE *do_open() ;                 /* opens file & checks for errors */
10
11   int formruns(fromfile,scr,tofile)
12    char fromfile[] ;                /* input file name */
13    char scr[] ;                     /* scratch file name prefix */
14    char tofile[] ;                  /* put the output here */
15    {
16       int irun , nrec , ret ;
17       char sarea[ SSIZE ] ;         /* storage area for text lines */
18       char *p[ MAX_REC ] ;          /* pointers to lines of text */
19       FILE *infile ;                /* input file */
20       char oname[68] ;              /* build scratch file names here */
21
22       infile = do_open(fromfile,"r") ;  /* open input file */
23
24       initfill(infile) ;            /* initialize for fillarea */
25       irun = 0 ;
26       do
27          {                          /* read text file into storage area */
28            ret = fillarea(sarea,SSIZE,p,MAX_REC,&nrec,infile) ;
29            memsort(p,nrec,compfun); /* sort using compare function */
30                                     /* now write out sorted lines */
31            if( (ret != AT_EOF) || (irun > 0) )
32               mkname(oname,scr,irun) ; /* use scratch file */
33            else strcpy(oname,tofile) ; /* one run -use output file */
34            outfile(p,nrec,oname) ;
35            irun = irun + 1 ;
36          } while( ret != AT_EOF ) ;
37
38       do_close(infile,fromfile) ;
39       return( irun ) ;
40    }
```

cases. First, it returns without any merging activity if **formruns** produced only one run (and wrote it directly to the output file). Second, when a merge pass involves **MAX_MERGE** or fewer input runs, there will be only one output run. **domerge** substitutes the file name for the final output in place of the scratch file prefix. This eliminates the separate step of copying the run to the output file.

domerge swaps the scratch file name prefixes at the end of each pass of the merge. Thus, the files written in one pass become the input for the next pass.

Figure 5.17   c:domerge.c

```
1     /* domerge.c - merge part of external sort */
2     #include "stdio.h"
3     #include "merge1.h"
4
5
6     int domerge(scra,scrb,tofile,nruns)
7       char scra[] ;                  /* input scratch files on 1st pass */
8       char scrb[] ;                  /* output scratch files on 1st pass */
9       char tofile[] ;                /* put final output here */
10      int nruns ;                    /* number of runs on 1st pass */
11      {
12
13          while( nruns > 1 )
14            { if( nruns <= MAX_MERGE ) .
15                  strcpy(scrb,tofile) ; /* last pass, output to tofile */
16              nruns = dopass(scra,scrb,nruns);/* do a merge pass */
17              swap_str(scra,scrb) ;             /* swap input and output */
18            }
19      }
20
```

dopass.c

dopass (Figure 5.18) performs a single pass of the merge process. It accepts as input arguments file name prefixes for input and output files. dopass keeps track of input and output run numbers, building unique file names for the corresponding files. It opens and closes these files, calling smerge to merge each set of input runs into one output run.

dopass builds file names to open the files and later rebuilds them to close the files. It passes the file pointers to smerge for the output file and the set of input files. The file pointers for input filew are stored in an array of structures along with the address of a buffer to hold one record for that input file. The MDATA data type in the merge1.h data file (see Figure 5.14) defines the structure used.

Normally, dopass uses mkname to create file names, but on the last pass where there are MAX_MERGE or fewer input runs, it uses the file name prefix as is (in this case, domerge has passed the final output file's name).

smerge.c

The smerge function (Figure 5.19) performs the actual merge. Its logic is that of the pseudo-code: Read the first record from each run; sort them; output the first record and replace it with the next from the same input run; repeat until all runs are exhausted.

smerge uses the memsort function to sort the initial records and resort to put each new record into its place. To make the process simple, the mergecmp

Figure 5.18   c:dopass.c

```
1    /* dopass.c - do 1 pass of merge process */
2    #include "stdio.h"
3    #include "merge1.h"
4    FILE *do_open() ;
5
6    int dopass(scrin,scrout,nruns_in)
7     char scrin[] ;
8     char scrout[] ;
9     int nruns_in ;
10    {
11        int first , nruns_out ;
12        int m ;                      /* order of the merge */
13        int i ;
14        char oname[68] , inname[68] ;
15        MDATA md[ MAX_MERGE ] ;   /* file pointer & pointer to buffer */
16        FILE *outf ;                 /* output file */
17        char buf[ MAX_MERGE ] [ MAX_RSIZE ] ; /* store records here */
18
19        nruns_out = 0 ;
20        for( first = 0 ; first < nruns_in ; first= first+MAX_MERGE)
21           {
22            m = nruns_in - first ;
23            if( m > MAX_MERGE )
24                m = MAX_MERGE ;
25
26            /* open output file */
27            if( nruns_in <= MAX_MERGE )      /* final pass ? */
28                    strcpy( oname , scrout ) ;/*   y - use name as is */
29            else   mkname(oname,scrout,nruns_out) ;
30            outf = do_open(oname,"w");
31
32            /* open input files  */
33            for( i=0 ; i < m ; i=i+1 )
34                { mkname(inname,scrin, first + i ) ;
35                  md[i].inf =  do_open(inname,"r");
36                  md[i].pbuf = & buf[i] [0] ;
37                }
38            smerge(  md , m , outf ) ; /* merge these files */
39
40            /* close and delete input files */
41            for( i=0 ; i < m ; i=i+1 )
42                { mkname(inname,scrin,first + i) ;
43                  do_close( md[i].inf,inname ) ;
44                  delfile(inname) ;
45                }
46            do_close(outf,oname) ;
47            nruns_out = nruns_out + 1 ;
48           }
49        return( nruns_out ) ;
50    }
```

Figure 5.19   c:smerge.c

```
1    /* smerge.c - do a single merge making 1 output run */
2    #include "stdio.h"
3    #include "merge1.h"
4
5    int mergecmp() ;                    /* declare function before ref. */
6    FILE *do_open() ;
7    extern int (*compfun) () ;          /* address of compare function */
8
9    int smerge(md,m,outf)
10     MDATA   md[] ;                    /* file ptr and buffer addresses */
11     int     m ;
12     FILE    *outf ;
13     {
14         int i ;
15         MDATA *prec[ MAX_MERGE ] ;
16                                        /* set up pointers to merge data */
17                                        /* & get a record from each run */
18         for( i=0 ; i < m ; i=i+1 )
19            { prec[i] = & md[i]   ;
20              getrec(prec[i]->pbuf,MAX_RSIZE,prec[i]->inf) ;
21            } ;
22         memsort(prec,m,mergecmp) ;     /* sort them (descending order) */
23
24         while( m > 0 )                 /* repeat until all runs exhausted */
25            {                           /* write out rec. with lowest key */
26              putrec(prec[m-1]->pbuf ,outf ) ;
27                                        /* and read another from same run */
28              if( getrec(prec[m-1]->pbuf,MAX_RSIZE,prec[m-1]->inf) <= 0 )
29                  m = m - 1 ;
30              else resort(prec,m,mergecmp) ;
31            }
32     }
33
34    int mergecmp(p1,p2)                 /* compare function */
35     MDATA *p1 ;                        /* pointers to merge data */
36     MDATA *p2 ;
37     {
38                                        /* compare strings in buffer areas */
39                                        /* reverse sign for descending sort */
40        return( - (*compfun)(p1->pbuf,p2->pbuf) ) ;
41     }
42
```

function reverses the order of the sort; the first record in sort order is pointed to by prec[m−1]. This may look strange but it simplifies resorting the records. It also makes handling the end of an input run easy: just decrease the number of elements being sorted.

Notice that the pointer array passed to **memsort** points to the MDATA structure for an input run rather than to the record. **mergecmp** uses these pointers to get the addresses of the records. **mergecmp** adds some overhead to comparing records. But since it is called at most (m−1) times per record, this inefficiency is swamped by the far greater number of comparisons made by formruns and the time needed to read and write files.

As in the formruns function, smerge takes the compare function address from the global variable compfun. We could have passed compfun to formruns and smerge as a function argument, but this would require passing it through domerge and dopass as well. Using a global variable allows domerge and dopass to be simpler.

resort.c

Figure 5.20 shows the resort function. It works like the insert function; it inserts the last element into the array. Since insert.c already exists and has been tested, writing resort is easy.

util.c

The util.c file in Figure 5.21 contains utility functions: swap_str, mkname, and defile. swap_str swaps two character strings using the string copy library function. It is not general; it is intended for use with file name strings only.

mkname builds file names using a prefix and a run number. The sprintf

Figure 5.20   c:resort.c

```
1    /* resort.c - resort after last element of array replaced */
2    /* uses pointers to actual data elements and a compare function */
3    #include "stdio.h"
4
5    int resort(pa,na,pcomp)
6     char *pa[] ;         /* array of pointers to elements to be sorted */
7     int na  ;               /* number of elements to be sorted */
8     int (*pcomp) () ;       /* pointer to compare function */
9     {
10       int i , j ;          /* indices for loops */
11       char *ptemp ;        /* temporary storage for one pointer */
12
13
14       /* insert the last element into the sorted array */
15           i = na - 1 ;     /* last element */
16           ptemp = pa[i] ;
17           j = i - 1;
18           while( (j >= 0) && (*pcomp)(ptemp,pa[j]) < 0 )
19             { pa[j+1] = pa[j] ;
20               j = j - 1 ;
21             }
22           pa[j+1] = ptemp ;
23     }
```

Figure 5.21   c:util.c

```
1    /* util.c - utility functions needed by merge programs */
2    #include "stdio.h"
3    #include "cminor.h"
4
5    int swap_str(s1,s2)              /* swap two strings */
6      char s1[] ;
7      char s2[] ;
8      {
9          char t[68] ;                /* scratch space for one string */
10
11         strcpy(t,s1) ;              /* exchange strings */
12         strcpy(s1,s2) ;            /* assumes that there is room */
13         strcpy(s2,t) ;
14     }
15
16                                    /* make up a scratch file name */
17   int mkname(file_name,prefix,run_no)
18     char file_name[] ;            /* store the file name here */
19     char prefix[] ;               /* something like "scra" */
20     int run_no ;                  /* append this number to prefix */
21     {
22         sprintf(file_name,"%s.%03d",prefix,run_no) ;
23     }
24
25
26   delfile(file_spec)              /* delete a file */
27     char file_spec[] ;
28     {
29         unlink(file_spec) ;
30     }
```

function performs formatting like printf but puts the result into an array as a character string.

At the end of each pass of the merge, the scratch files used as input are deleted. The delfile function uses a C library function, unlink, to delete a file. Calling delfile in the MERGE1 program isolates our application from the C library function. Some C compilers might not provide the unlink function in the library. In that case, we could implement delfile using the dos2call function from Chapter 7. But the rest of our program would not be affected.

Program Structure

It may seem simpler to use fewer functions and fewer source files than we did for MERGE1. Certainly, the number of keystrokes to type it could be reduced as could the number of files to compile and link. But we kept functions and source files short and simple; each function dealt with a single level of detail. For example, domerge handled the repeating of merge passes and the switching of I/O file names. dopass managed run numbers and file names on one merge pass. smerge performed one merge operation. Combining these functions into one large file would make the logic of the program less clear and less amenable to enhancement.

5.8 MERGE2: A Generalized External Sort Program

□ We have a working program for sorting large text files. Our next step is to generalize it for other kinds of files. This is somewhat like generalizing the mem-sort function. But instead of a library function that is linked with an application program, we want a standalone program. We want to specify the types of data to be sorted when we execute the program. We need to specify the type of record—fixed-length data or variable-length lines of text. We also need to specify the field to be used for the comparison—its data type, its offset from the beginning of the record, its length, and whether it is to be in ascending or descending order. To make MERGE2 more general, we allow more than one key field to be specified. Figure 5.22 is a manual page description of such a program.

What do we need to change to produce such a program? First, we need data to describe the file being sorted. Then we need a compare function that accepts this sort specification. Finally, we need more general I/O functions.

5.9 MERGE2 Source Files

□ sortcomp.h

The header file, sortcomp.h (Figure 5.23), defines constants and data types needed to specify key fields. The SORTKEY data type defines the data needed for each key field. These are the types of data: whether to sort in ascending or descending order, where the key begins in each record, and its length. Symbolic constants are defined for the key type and the sort order.

sortspec.h

Figure 5.24 lists the sortspec.h header file. The SORTSPEC data type defines file and record type constants needed by the I/O module. The ASC_MODE and BIN_MODE constants in cminor.h are the values expected for the ftype variable.

sortcomp.c

The sortcomp function shown in Figure 5.25 compares two records. It loops over the key fields defined by getspec. It returns as soon as a comparison shows

Figure 5.22   MERGE2 program description

Name

merge 2 – general sort/merge program for large data files

Description

MERGE2 sorts an input file based on specified file, record, and key field descriptions. It uses the memsort library function to sort initial runs that are merged to give a final sorted output file. Default specs are ASCII file, lines of text with the entire line as a key and ascending order.

Scratch files are placed on the default drive. Space must be available for two copies of the input file.

Usage

A>Merge2 input_file output_file sort_specs

All sort specifications begin with a dash (–). A letter following identifies a specification. Some parameters may be expected after this letter. Specifications recognized are

Specification	Letter	Parameters
File Type		
ASCII	a	——
Binary	b	——
Record Type		
Fixed record	r	Length in bytes
Lines of text (variable)	l	——
Sort keys	k	Data type
		Sort order
		a = ascending
		d = descending
		Starting offset in bytes
		(0 = beginning)
		Field length (for char or str only)

Parameters are separated by commas. Specifications are written without spaces inside. Specifications are separated by blanks. Data types are identified by a single character—integer (i), character field (c), character string (s), long (l), and float (f). Up to ten key fields may be specified, most significant first.

Example

A>merge2 test.in test.out –a –r20 –ki,a,2,1 –ka,d,10,6

This sorts test.in (an ASCII file with 20 byte records), creating test.out. An integer at offset 2 (ascending order) and a character field 6 bytes long at offset 10 (descending order) are the sort keys.

Figure 5.23   c:sortcomp.h

```
1    /* sortcomp.h - define constants & data type for compare funct. */
2    #define MAX_KEYS  10            /* maximum number of keys allowed */
3
4                                    /* sort order constants */
5    #define ASCENDING   1
6    #define DESCENDING -1
7
8                                    /* key types */
9    #define  int16_key      0       /* 16 bit long integer */
10   #define  char_key       1       /* char field (uses klength) */
11   #define  string_key     2       /* char string ('\0' at end) */
12   #define  int32_key      3       /* 32 bit long integer */
13   #define  float_key      4       /* floating point data */
14
15
16   typedef struct                  /* data to define one key field */
17     {
18       int ktype ;                 /* type of field */
19       int kstart ;                /* starting offset of field */
20       int klength ;               /* field length */
21       int korder ;                /* sort order (ascending/desc.) */
22     } SORTKEY ;
23
24   /* The source file including this header file should */
25   /* declare these variables              */
26   /* int nkeys ;                          */
27   /* SORTKEY KEYS[MAX_KEY] ;   or         */
28   /* extern  SORTKEY keys[] ;             */
29
```

Figure 5.24   c:sortspec.h

```
1    /* sortspec.h - defines sort spec data structure */
2
3    typedef struct
4    { int  (*pget) () ;             /* holds address of get rec. fun. */
5      int  (*pput) () ;             /*   "       "      " put rec. fun. */
6      int  (*pcomp) () ;            /*   "       "      " compare  fun. */
7      int  ftype ;                  /* file type (ASCII / binary ) */
8      int  rec_size ;               /* record size */
9    } SORTSPEC ;
10
11   /* declare the following variable in the source file */
12   /* SORTSPEC sspec ;   or        */
13   /* extern SORTSPEC sspec ;      */
14
```

Figure 5.25   c:sortcomp.c

```
 1    /* sortcomp.c - data driven compare function */
 2    #include "stdio.h"
 3    #include "cminor.h"
 4    #include "sortcomp.h"
 5
 6    extern int nkeys ;        /* number of key fields to compare */
 7    extern SORTKEY keys[] ; /* array of sort field definitions */
 8
 9    /* define pointer types for data type conversion */
10    typedef int16 *PINT ;
11    typedef int32 *PLONG ;
12    typedef float *PFLOAT ;
13
14    int sortcomp(p1,p2)        /* compares records   */
15     char *p1 ;                /* pointer to first data record */
16     char *p2 ;                /* pointer to second data record */
17     {
18        int i ;
19        SORTKEY  *p ;
20        char *pt1 ,
21             *pt2 ;
22        int ichar ;
23
24        p = keys ;                    /* point to first sort key desc. */
25        for( i=0 ; i < nkeys ; i = i + 1 )
26           { pt1 = p1 + p->kstart ;   /* get starting addresses of */
27             pt2 = p2 + p->kstart ;   /* fields in the two records */
28             switch( p->ktype )
29                {
30                case int16_key :
31                    if( *(PINT)pt1 != *(PINT)pt2 )
32                       { if( *(PINT)pt1 > *(PINT)pt2 )
33                            return( p->korder ) ;
34                          else return( - p->korder ) ;
35                       }
36                    break ;
37                case char_key :
38                    ichar = p->klength ;
39                    while( ichar > 0 )
40                       { if( *pt1 != *pt2 )
41                            { if( *pt1 > *pt2 )
42                                return( p->korder ) ;
43                                else return( - p->korder ) ;
44                            }
45                         pt1 = pt1+1 ; pt2=pt2+1; ichar=ichar-1 ;
46                       } ;
47                    break ;
48               case string_key :
49                    ichar = p->klength ;
50                    while( ichar > 0 )
51                       { if( *pt1 != *pt2 )
52                            { if( *pt1 > *pt2 )
53                                return( p->korder ) ;
54                                else return( - p->korder ) ;
55                            }
```

Figure 5.25   c:sortcomp.c (continued)

```
56                        if( *pt1 == '\0' )
57                            break ;
58                        pt1 = pt1+1 ; pt2=pt2+1; ichar=ichar-1 ;
59                        } ;
60                    break ;
61                case int32_key :
62                    if( *(PLONG)pt1 != *(PLONG)pt2 )
63                        { if( *(PLONG)pt1 > *(PLONG)pt2 )
64                            return( p->korder ) ;
65                        else return( - p->korder ) ;
66                        }
67                    break ;
68                case float_key :
69                    if( *(PFLOAT)pt1 != *(PFLOAT)pt2 )
70                        {
71                        if( (*((float *)pt1)) > (*((float *)pt2)) )
72                            return( p->korder ) ;
73                        else  return( - p->korder ) ;
74                        }
75                    break ;
76                }
77        p = p + 1 ;                  /* point to next sort field desc. */
78        }
79                                     /* all keys were equal */
80    return( 0 ) ;                    /* return "equal to" result */
81    }
```

inequality. The sort order for the key is used in the **return** statement to produce ascending or descending order.

The following pseudo-code shows the function's logic in a compact form:

```
compare function
      repeat for each key field
            compute the starting addresses of the key fields
            select the type of data to compare
                  do compare for the data type
                  if not equal
                        return result (reversed if descending order)
            return equal if all keys are equal
      end
```

Character string and array types are several bytes long. For these key types, the comparison is repeated for each character.

sortcomp contains a few optimizations. Instead of referring to the sort key specification using array notation (**key[i].ktype**, for example), a pointer to the SORTKEY data type is used. It is initialized on line 24 to point to the first key's specification. At the end of the loop over keys, line 77 advances **p** to point to the next key's specification. The comparisons for integer, long, and float data contain an assumption—namely, that alignment restrictions on integers and larger data types are not important. This is valid on computers based on the Intel 8086/8088 family of microprocessors. It would not be valid on computers using the Motorola 68000 microprocessor. In that case, the key fields should be moved to local variables of the correct data type and then compared. For example, line 31 would be replaced by

```
movedata(&i1,pt1,sizeof(int16)) ;
movedata(&i2,pt2,sizeof(int16)) ;
if( i1 != i2 )
```

where i1 and i2 are declared as int16 variables.

sortio2.c

The I/O functions used in the SORTTEXT and MERGE1 programs need some changes. The sortio2.c file shown in Figure 5.26 shows these changes. The do_open function opens files in ASCII or binary mode based on the file type in the sspec structure. In the same way, the getrec and putrec functions use sspec to select line or fixed-length read and write functions.

The functions getr and putr have been added for reading and writing fixed-length records. They use the C library functions fread and fwrite with extra checking for errors.

getspec.c

Figure 5.27 shows the getspec.c source file. Its job is to scan the command line, looking for specifications of file type, record type, or sort keys. Each valid specification must begin with a dash followed by a letter identifying what is being specified. The getspec function's structure reflects its job: a loop over words in the

Figure 5.26   c:sortio2.c

```
1    /* sortio2.c - I/O functions for MERGE2 program */
2    /* do_open , do_close , getrec , putrec */
3    #include "stdio.h"
4    #include "cminor.h"
5    #include "sortspec.h"
6
7    extern SORTSPEC sspec ;              /* has function addresses and */
8                                        /* other sort spec. info */
9    FILE *gfopen() ;
```

Figure 5.26   c:sortio2.c (continued)

```
10
11      FILE *do_open(fname,fmode)        /* open file & check for errors */
12       char fname[] ;                   /* file name */
13       char fmode[] ;                   /* read/write/append mode */
14      {                                 /* return a file pointer */
15          FILE *fd ;
16
17          fd = gfopen(fname,fmode,sspec.ftype) ;
18          if( fd == NULL )
19            { printf("\n can't open file - %s \n",fname);
20              exit( 8 ) ;
21            }
22          return( fd ) ;
23      }
24
25
26      int do_close(fd,fname)            /* close file & check for errors */
27       FILE *fd ;                       /* file pointer */
28       char fname[] ;                   /* name of file being closed */
29      {
30          if( fclose(fd) < 0 )
31            { printf("\n can't close file - %s \n",fname);
32              exit( 10 ) ;
33            }
34      }
35
36
37      int getrec(rec,maxr,fd)           /* get a record  */
38       char rec[] ;                     /* put it here in string form */
39       int maxr ;                       /* maximum length permitted */
40       FILE *fd ;                       /* file pointer for input file */
41      {                                 /* returns no. chars used in rec */
42          return( (*sspec.pget)(rec,maxr,fd));/* use named get fun. */
43      }
44
45      int putrec(rec,fd)                /* output one record */
46       char rec[] ;                     /* the record to output */
47       FILE *fd ;                       /* output file pointer */
48      {
49          return( (*sspec.pput)(rec,fd) ) ;/* use specified put fun. */
50      }
51
52      /* ************************** line oriented functions */
53
54      int getl(s,maxs,fd)               /* get one line from input file */
55       char s[] ;                       /* put it here in string form */
56       int maxs ;                       /* maximum length permitted */
57       FILE *fd ;                       /* file pointer for input file */
58      {                                 /* getl returns no. chars used in s */
59                                        /* (or -1 if EOF reached) */
60          int i ;
61                                        /* get next line of input */
62          if( fgets(s,maxs-1,fd) == NULL )
63             return( -1 ) ;             /* EOF - return special length value */
64
```

Figure 5.26 c:sortio2.c (continued)

```
65        i = strlen(s) ;              /* get string length */
66        if( s[i-1] != '\n' )         /* see if a new-line is present */
67          { s[i] =    '\n' ;         /*   n - append one */
68            s[i+1] = '\0' ;          /* restore end-of-string marker */
69            i = i + 1 ;              /* adjust string length */
70          }
71                                     /* return length of line */
72        return(i+1) ;                /* count the '\0' at end too */
73      }
74
75    int putl(s,fd)                   /* output one line of text */
76     char s[] ;                      /* line to output in string form */
77     FILE *fd ;                      /* output file pointer */
78     {
79        return( fputs(s,fd) ) ;      /* use fputs library function */
80     }
81
82
83    /* **************************** fixed length record functions */
84
85    #define BYTE_SIZE  1              /*  fread/fwrite element size */
86
87    int getr(rec,maxr,fd)            /* get a fixed length record */
88     char rec[] ;                    /* the record is here */
89     int maxr ;                      /* dummy size value */
90     FILE *fd ;                      /* file stream pointer */
91     {
92        int nr  ;                    /* number of bytes read */
93
94        nr = fread(rec,BYTE_SIZE,sspec.rec_size,fd) ;
95                                    /* check for partial record */
96        if( (nr > 0 ) && (nr < sspec.rec_size) )
97          { /* partial record */
98            printf("\n partial record at %ld \n",ftell(fd));
99            exit(2) ;
100          }
101        return( nr ) ;
102     }
103
104
105   int putr(rec,fd)                 /* putput a fixed length record */
106    char rec[] ;                    /* store the record here */
107    FILE *fd ;                      /* file stream pointer */
108    {
109       int nw  ;
110
111       nw = fwrite(rec,BYTE_SIZE,sspec.rec_size,fd) ;
112                          /* check that entire record is written */
113       if( nw != sspec.rec_size )
114         { /* output problem */
115           printf("\n write error at %ld \n",ftell(fd));
116           exit(3) ;
117         }
118       return( nw ) ;
119    }
```

Figure 5.27   c:getspec.c

```
1    /* getspec.c - get sort file spec from cmd line */
2    #include "stdio.h"
3    #include "cminor.h"
4    #include "sortcomp.h"
5    #include "merge1.h"
6    #include "sortspec.h"
7
8    int nkeys ;                    /* number of sort keys defined */
9    SORTKEY keys[MAX_KEYS] ;       /* data to describe the sort keys */
10   SORTSPEC sspec ;              /* sort spec. info - fun. addresses */
11
12   /* declare functions before we use their addresses */
13   int getl() , getr() , putl() , putr() , sortcomp() ;
14
15   getspec(argc,argv)
16    int argc ;
17    char *argv[] ;
18    {
19       int i ;
20       char *p ;
21
22       /* set up defaults for file type , record type & sort fields */
23       sspec.ftype = ASC_MODE ;
24       sspec.pget  =  getl ;
25       sspec.pput  =  putl ;
26       sspec.pcomp =  sortcomp ;
27       sspec.rec_size = MAX_RSIZE ;
28       nkeys = 0 ;
29
30       for( i=3 ; i < argc ; i=i+1 )
31          {
32             p = argv[i] ;
33             if( *p == '-' )        /* check for dash */
34                 dospec(p+1) ;      /* move past dash, get this spec. */
35             else err_msg("bad option format \n");
36          }
37       if( nkeys == 0 )            /* use char string as default key */
38            addkey(string_key,ASCENDING,0,sspec.rec_size) ;
39    }
40
41
42
43   int dospec(p)                  /* classify and process one spec. */
44    char *p ;                     /* points to spec. char (and parms) */
45    {
46       switch( *p )               /* classify the next char */
47          {
48          case 'r' :               /* fixed length records */
49            sspec.pget  = getr ;
50            sspec.pput  = putr ;
51            p = p + 1 ;            /* move past 'r' */
52                                   /* and get record size */
53            sspec.rec_size = -1 ;  /* use invalid size to ensure */
54            sscanf(p,"%d",&sspec.rec_size) ; /* that sscanf reads it */
55            if(   (sspec.rec_size < 0 )  /* validate record size */
```

Figure 5.27   c:getspec.c (continued)

```
 56                  || ( sspec.rec_size > MAX_RSIZE ) )
 57                   err_msg(" bad record size field \n") ;
 58              break ;
 59          case 'l' :                       /* records are text lines */
 60            sspec.pget  = getl ;
 61            sspec.pput  = putl ;
 62            break ;
 63          case 'a' :                       /* ASCII file - check for CTL-Z */
 64            sspec.ftype = ASC_MODE ;
 65            break ;
 66          case 'b' :               /* binary file - no check for CTL-Z */
 67            sspec.ftype = BIN_MODE ;
 68            break ;
 69          case 'k' :               /* key field spec. */
 70            if( nkeys == MAX_KEYS )
 71                err_msg("too many sort keys \n");
 72            p = p +1 ;                  /* move past the 'k' */
 73            getkparm(p) ;               /* get and check key parms. */
 74            break ;
 75          default :
 76            err_msg("bad option \n");
 77            break ;
 78          }
 79      }
 80
 81
 82
 83   int getkparm(word)                    /* collect and verify key info */
 84    char word[] ;                        /* string with the parms */
 85    {
 86      int kt , ko , ks , kl , n ;
 87      char tc , oc ;
 88                                        /* get parms from cmd. line word */
 89      kl = -1 ;
 90      sscanf(word,"%c,%c,%d,%d",&tc, &oc, &ks, &kl);
 91      if( kl == -1 )
 92          err_msg("not enough info in key field\n");
 93                                        /* convert and check field type */
 94      kt = sindex( tc,"icslf") ;
 95      if( kt < 0 )
 96          err_msg("bad key field type \n") ;
 97
 98      if( oc == 'a' )                    /* convert and check sort order */
 99          ko = ASCENDING ;
100      else if( oc == 'd')
101          ko = DESCENDING ;
102      else err_msg("bad key field order \n") ;
103
104                                        /* check starting offset */
105      if( (ks < 0) || (ks > sspec.rec_size) )
106          err_msg("bad key field offset \n");
107                                        /* check field length */
108      if( (kl <= 0) || ( (ks + kl) > sspec.rec_size) )
109          err_msg("bad key field length \n");
110      addkey(kt,ko,ks,kl) ;
```

Figure 5.27   c:getspec.c (continued)

```
111      }
112
113
114      int addkey(itype,iorder,ioffset,ilength)
115       int itype , iorder , ioffset , ilength ;
116       {
117         keys[nkeys].ktype    = itype ;
118         keys[nkeys].korder   = iorder ;
119         keys[nkeys].kstart   = ioffset ;
120         keys[nkeys].klength  = ilength ;
121         nkeys = nkeys + 1 ;
122       }
123
124      int err_msg(s)
125       char s[] ;
126       {
127         printf("%s \n",s);
128         exit(10) ;
129       }
130
131
```

command line and a call to dospec to collect and validate each specification. getspec.c is rather long; its work is spread over several functions, each focused on a single level of detail.

The dospec function classifies the character following the dash using a switch statement. For the 'r' and 'k' specifications, some additional parameters are required. The pointer to the command line word is advanced past the specification character, and the sscanf function is used to get the parameters. sscanf performs the same input formatting as scanf but uses a character string as input. An invalid value is placed in the last parameter before calling sscanf. If sscanf does not get all the input parameters, the validation process will detect the error.

If an invalid parameter or bad format is detected, an error message is displayed and the program aborts. All the input is validated so that invalid or missing specifications do not produce mysterious behavior.

getspec has defaults for all specifications. Some are assigned at the beginning (lines 23 to 28). The default sort key field choice—a character string starting at offset zero—is applied after the command line has been scanned and no sort key field found (line 38).

merge2.c

The merge2.c main function requires a revision, as shown in Figure 5.28. A call to getspec is added (line 23). Then the sort function address is copied from sspec.pcomp to the compfun variable that formruns and smerge expect.

Figure 5.28   c:merge2.c

```
1     /* merge2.c - generalized external sort */
2     #include  "stdio.h"
3     #include  "cminor.h"
4     #include  "merge1.h"
5     #include  "sortspec.h"
6
7     int (*compfun) () ;          /* store address of compare fun. here */
8     extern SORTSPEC  sspec ;     /* sort spec. filled out by getspec */
9
10    char scra[68] = "scra";      /* prefixes for scratch file names */
11    char scrb[68] = "scrb";
12
13    main(argc,argv)
14     int argc ;                  /* number of words in command line */
15     char *argv[] ;              /* pointers to each word */
16     {
17        /* check to see that file names were specified */
18        if( argc < 3 )
19          { printf(" need file names \n");
20             printf(" USAGE: merge1  input-file   output-file \n");
21             exit(1);
22          }
23        getspec(argc,argv) ;        /* get sort specification from */
24                                    /* the command line */
25        compfun = sspec.pcomp ;     /* set up compare function addr. */
26        dosort(argv[1],argv[2]) ;   /* do the sort */
27     }
28
29
30    int dosort(fromfile,tofile)
31     char fromfile[] ;            /* input for sort */
32     char tofile[] ;              /* put the output here */
33     {
34        int  nruns ;
35                                    /* form runs from input file */
36        nruns = formruns(fromfile,scra,tofile) ;
37                                    /* now merge runs */
38        domerge(scra,scrb,tofile,nruns) ;
39     }
```

5.10 Measuring MERGE2's Performance

□   The following table shows the time required to sort three text files with MERGE2. The files contained lines 40 characters long. They were sorted using ASCII file type and line-oriented I/O. I/O files were assigned to one floppy disk and the scratch files to a second disk.

File Size (bytes)	Number of Merge Passes	Sort Time (seconds)
20,000	0	24
50,000	1	181
100,000	2	490
150,000	2	746

Next, timing statements were placed in **formruns** and **domerge** to show how long the program spent in each major function. The **timer** function described in Chapter 7 was used to display elapsed times between these points. In previous programs we measured each function separately. Here, interaction between reading and writing files makes it easier to get valid results by inserting timing statements. The following results are for the 50,000-byte file:

Activity	Time Spent (seconds)
Forming Runs	
Filling storage area	23
Calling **memsort**	7
Writing initial runs	38
Total	68
Merge pass	116

The results show that both forming initial runs and merging them are time consuming. Within the **formruns** function, reading and writing records takes most of the total time.

5.II Enhancing MERGE2

□ The MERGE2 program is useful as it stands, but there are many potential enhancements. Following are some we have identified.

A Better User Interface

The **getspec** function is rather unforgiving, and the format for indicating **sort** specifications is not easy to remember and use. Perhaps an interactive method for collecting the **sort** specification could be used when the command line does not contain a specification (or contains an invalid one.)

Handling Large Files

Sorting large data files causes extra difficulties. Finding disk space for the input, output, and scratch files may be a problem. We might take scratch file name prefixes as additional input. This would allow scratch files to be stored on some drive other than the default drive. In addition, the two sets of files (scrannn and scrbnnn in MERGE2) could be stored on two separate drives.

Sorting large files on a diskette-based system causes an additional problem. Using two drives, MERGE2 can sort files up to half the capacity of a diskette. With modifications, MERGE2 could sort files as large as the capacity of one floppy disk. But to do so on a computer system with two disk drives requires some swapping of diskettes during the sorting process. MERGE2 needs to pause and prompt for diskette changes to make this swap feasible. The following example shows the placement of files and the prompting in a two-drive system.

PROMPTS/Inputs	Contents of Drive A	Contents of Drive B
A > merge a:infile b:outfile		
	infile	?
(formruns is ready to write runs)		
INSERT SCRATCH DISK IN DRIVE B: THEN PRESS RETURN		
	infile	scra written
(dopass opens 1st file for output runs)		
INSERT SCRATCH DISK IN DRIVE A: THEN PRESS RETURN		
	scrb written	scra read
. . .		
(dopass starts the last pass)		
INSERT OUTPUT DISK IN DRIVE B: THEN PRESS RETURN		
	scrb read	outfile written

What if the last pass begins with the input runs on drive B where we want the output file? Since MERGE2's user cannot easily predict which drive will be convenient for the last pass of the merge, we should accept a file name specification like *:outfile to allow MERGE2 to use the most convenient drive for the output file.

This extra input and the prompting are necessary to handle large files on floppy disks but are unnecessary for smaller files. MERGE2 should check the size of the input file and the amount of space available on the drives specified. If the diskettes currently in the drives have enough room, the pauses and prompts for diskette changes could be skipped.

The putl function issues a message and aborts MERGE2 if the drive used runs out of room. It would be much more convenient if MERGE2 could check the disk space before beginning the sorting process.

In a system with a large-capacity hard disk, these enhancements might be irrelevant. This points out the advantage of developing a simple version of MERGE2 first. You can select enhancements relevant to your needs and avoid those that just add complication.

Handling More Data Types

MERGE2 handles fixed-length records and variable-length lines of text. Some data files with variable-length records might not fit either category. Other data files might contain key fields that are not handled by MERGE2. Adding support for more types of data is easy to do; the getspec function must recognize the new specification. If a new record type is added, new record I/O functions will be needed. For new key field types, more cases must be added to the compare function.

Data files created by software packages such as dBASEII often contain extra data at the beginning or end of the file. Sorting such files requires that MERGE2 bypass those header and trailer areas in the input file.

Better Performance

MERGE2 takes too long to sort large files. Enhancements can improve performance in three different ways.

The first bottleneck in MERGE2 is the use of buffered I/O functions (fgets, fputs, fread, and fwrite, for example). These library functions are usually designed for general purpose use. They use buffers too small for fast I/O with large files and are normally optimized for single-character input and output. Substituting an optimized buffered I/O module for the library functions cut sort times in half in our tests. (The buffered I/O functions used are included on the program diskette available for this book.)

The second bottleneck is the small size of the storage area used in the formruns function. The 20,000-byte size was chosen to make sure that it works well with all C compilers. A larger storage area would reduce the number of merging passes needed for large files.

Some C compilers provide a choice of options for code generation. They usually have a *big* or *large* model that allows up to 1 megabyte of data. But the size of a single array is normally restricted to 64K bytes. Thus, using more than 64K for storage would require modifying fillarea to use two or more areas.

The compare function used in MERGE2 does much more work than the simple integer comparison function or the strcmp library function. There are two ways to improve this aspect of performance. When a single-key field is specified, a simpler compare function could be used instead of sortcomp. Another approach is to compile the compare function before running the sort. We could use the list of key fields in the keys array to produce a compare function that has the data types, offsets, and lengths of key fields built into the function.

Commercial sort/merge programs on large computer systems use such a technique to achieve maximum speed. They are often called *sort generators* since they create the compare function when they are executed.

More Flexibility

MERGE2 is inflexible in several ways. The sizes of storage areas and the number of runs to merge are both compiled into the program. MERGE2 should determine these constants for itself at run time to make best use of available memory.

Adapting MERGE2 to new record or key field types requires changing the program. Bypassing header information in the input file would also require program changes. Commercial sort/merge packages meet this problem with two modes of use. They can be run as standalone programs like MERGE2, but they can also be called as library functions from another program. In this mode they allow the caller to specify function addresses for processing header and trailer data and for reading and writing data.

Refining the Algorithms

MERGE2 was written with simplicity as the major criterion. A number of refinements can improve performance and remove restrictions at the expense of a more complicated program. One example is the use of a separate file for each run. The operating system places a limit on the number of files that can reside in some directories. We could write all output runs from **formruns** or from a single merge pass to a single file. We would keep track of the starting file position for each run.

Using the low-level **read** and **write** functions with our own buffering has been discussed. In the **formruns** functions the entire storage area could be filled with one or more calls to read. Then we could scan the data in the storage area, recording the starting location of each record. This would remove the need to move data into the storage area a record at a time. It would also remove the storage area for a single record from **fillarea** and eliminate the limitation on record size there.

5.12 Summary

□ We now have some tools for sorting data. The **memsort** and **insert** functions are general purpose library functions, while SORTTEXT and MERGE2 are complete programs. In addition, they should take the mystery out of developing your own sorting programs.

Our discussion focused on practical tools for sorting. We did not analyze the algorithms we used or present alternatives. Sorting algorithms have long been a favorite topic in computer science textbooks and research reports. While there is too much emphasis on theory rather than practice, the literature on sorting is invaluable as a source of algorithms and ideas. The references in Appendix D provide a starting point.

5.13   Reference

□   Hoare, C. A. R. *"Quicksort." Comp. J.* 5, no. 1 (1962): 10–15.

6

BTREE: An Indexed File Module

The previous chapter discussed sorting data both in RAM memory and in large files. Putting whole data files in order is a common requirement in applications programs. This chapter discusses another common requirement: keeping files indexed so that a single record can be retrieved based on a key value rather than its position in a file. A common complaint about C is that it lacks built-in facilities for keyed access to data files. The module we develop here provides the basic support for indexing data files.

Our module is based on the B-Tree algorithm, but our emphasis is on producing a practical tool rather than illustrating a famous algorithm. Space limitations and the need to explain the source code have forced some simplifications. Addressing practical problems normally left as exercises for the reader led to other deviations from a pure B-Tree algorithm. Finally, since B-Trees have been discussed by a number of authors, there are differences in their published descriptions.

The module we develop is not a complete program; it is a set of functions to be called from an application program. No amount of documentation of such a module substitutes for an example of use, so we present an application to demonstrate the BTREE module's use. The application is very simple, but it should give a feel for applying BTREE to real problems.

6.1 Developing the Concepts

☐ Understanding the problem of keyed access to data records in disk files and the concepts behind the B-Tree algorithm is a necessary first step. Without this understanding, you will not understand the source code we present or the possible applications for it. Thus, we develop concepts first and then present a concrete application of those concepts.

☐ *197*

We used the term *keyed access* already; now we define it. DOS supports random access to data in disk files. You specify a numeric position in a file (using lseek) and then read or write at that location. But with keyed access, we supply a key value and read or write a record that corresponds to that key value. For example, in a mailing list application we might store and retrieve records based on a name. To implement keyed access, we need an index that relates keys to data records. When a key is presented, we search the index and return the location of the data record that contains that key value.

Our focus in this chapter is on searching files, but we can start by looking at the function in Figure 6.1. This function makes a linear search of an array of integers in RAM memory. How can we apply this algorithm to searching an index? Instead of an array of integers, we might search an array of index entries. Figure 6.2a shows such an index and the data file to which it points. Each index entry might have the following structure:

```
typedef struct
    { long rptr ; /* file position of the data record */
      char key[KMAX]; /* key value for the data record */
    } index_entry ;
```

This structure is certainly simple, but what if the index is too large to fit into RAM memory? One solution might be to place the index in a file (perhaps separate from the file containing data records) and read it sequentially each time a search is performed. Unfortunately, this method is quite slow and impractical for sizable index files. We can already see, however, that storing the index in a disk file is

Figure 6.1 lsearch.c

```
1    /* lsearch.c - search an ordered array of integers for a value */
2    #include "stdio.h"
3
4    int lsearch(target,a,na,pwhere) /* search an array for a value */
5     int target ;                    /* look for this value */
6     int a[] ;                       /* the array to search */
7     int na ;                        /* size of the array */
8     int *pwhere ;                   /* store ending subscript here */
9     {
10        int i , ret ;
11
12        for(i=0 ; i<na ; i=i+1)     /* scan each element in array */
13          { ret = a[i] - target ;   /* compare target to array element */
14            if( ret == 0 )          /* we're thru if it matches */
15                break ;
16          }
17        *pwhere = i ;               /* record where the search ended */
18        return( ret ) ;             /* return result of last compare */
19     }
```

Figure 6.2 Indexing files

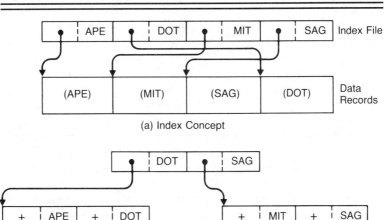

(a) Index Concept

(b) Indexing the Index

necessary and that minimizing the amount of file I/O required for a search is an important goal for a good solution.

The idea that opens the door to a solution is a simple one: Make a small index to the main index. The diagram in Figure 6.2b illustrates the idea. (The data records and pointers to them are not shown in Figure 6.2b or the diagrams that follow. Those pointers are represented by a + character in the diagrams.) We start by searching the small index. The result of that search tells us what part of the large index to search.

Each entry in the small index contains a pointer to a section of the large index and the last key in that section. We search the small index until we find a key that is greater than or equal to the search value. We extract the corresponding pointer and search the section to which it points. Searching the index in Figure 6.2b for the key value **MIT** would require the following steps:

1. Search the small index. The second entry (whose key is **SAG**) is the first entry whose key is greater than or equal to **MIT**. Extract the corresponding pointer to the second block of the large index.
2. Read this block of the large index.
3. Search this block for a key with value **MIT**. The first entry matches this value so the record pointer value identifies the corresponding data record.

Once we have the basic idea, we can develop it further. We can use as many levels of indexes as needed. To minimize the amount of index file I/O, we can organize the indexes in blocks of a fixed size. Each entry in an upper level then points to a single block on the next level of the index. The first level always contains a single block. We can structure each level in the same way and use the same functions to manage·all levels.

This structure of indexes is often called a *tree*. The top level of the tree where we start a search is called the *root*, and the lowest level (which points to data records) is called the *leaf* level. Individual blocks are sometimes called *nodes*. Index trees are usually pictured with the root level at the top, in contrast to nature's trees. (Lots of things about computers appear to defy nature.) We refer to levels as *upper* or *higher* in the direction of the root and *lower* in the direction of the leaf level. B-Trees have special rules about how the blocks are maintained. The important rule is that all blocks except the root block are kept at least half-full.

We have discussed only searching indexes, but in practice we need to add and remove entries. These operations are more complicated than searching; the method we use is specified by the B-Tree algorithm.

In the normal case, inserting a new entry in an index file is easy: we find the position where it belongs and insert the entry into the leaf level block. But what if the leaf level block does not have room for the entry? Then we split the block, moving half the entries into a new block. We then insert an entry pointing to the new block into the index block at the next higher level. Figure 6.3 shows a tree before and after inserting an entry with the key **APE**. Figure 6.4 shows how the tree splits when another entry is added. Since the higher-level index block is also full, it is also split. Thus, an insertion may cause adjustments to several levels of index blocks. If the process causes the root block to be split, a new level is added to the tree that becomes the root level.

Deleting an entry starts with removing it from the leaf level block. If that leaves the block empty, the entry at the next level that pointed to the block is

Figure 6.3   Index insertions

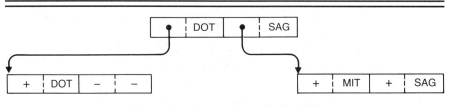

(a) Before Inserting an Entry with Key APE

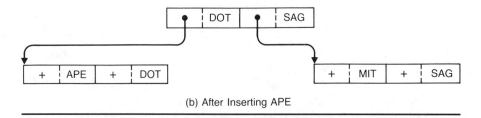

(b) After Inserting APE

Figure 6.4   After inserting BIG (and splitting a block)

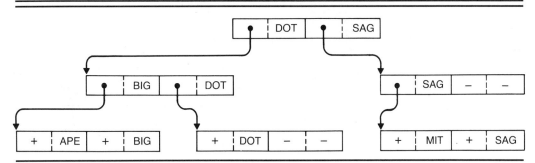

removed. If a deletion leaves a block less than half-full, we try to combine it with the block to its left or right. To keep it simple, we look for neighbors in the next level block. Thus, the leaf level block with the key DOT in Figure 6.4 has no right neighbor by this definition. When two blocks are combined, one is no longer needed and the entry at the next level that points to it is removed. Like insertions, deletions may affect several levels of indexes. Figure 6.5 shows two deletions; the second deletion results in two blocks being combined. Deletions may leave only one entry in the root level block; in that case the root block is no longer needed and the lower level block can become the new root block.

Inserting new entries may require additional index blocks. Deleting entries may free blocks that are empty or have been combined. A scheme for allocating and freeing blocks in index files is needed to support these insertions and deletions.

Splitting and combining blocks destroys any relation between the location of a block in a file and that of its neighbors in the tree. Our original picture of a file with index entries in order from the beginning to the end of the file is not accurate any more. The correct picture is of a tree with a pointer to the root level. From there we just follow the record pointers from one index level to another.

6.2   Functional Specifications for a BTREE Module

□   We know that a BTREE module should provide functions for searching for key values and for inserting and deleting keys. We also know that the purpose of the index is to return a pointer to a data record. However, we need to define some additional capabilities before we can produce a functional specification for our BTREE module.

Our examples have assumed that the keys are char strings. A practical module must accept any kinds of data as keys. In addition, we should allow keys to vary in length from one entry to another. We solve this problem by letting the ap-

Figure 6.5   Index deletions

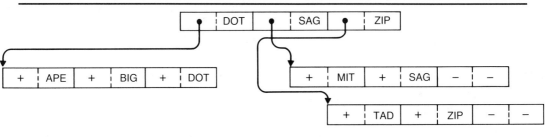

(a) Before Deleting APE

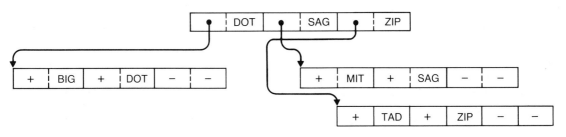

(b) After Deleting APE

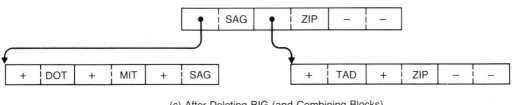

(c) After Deleting BIG (and Combining Blocks)

plication program that uses the BTREE module supply functions that compare entries and find the size of an entry.

The same key value may occur in more than one data record. We allow the same key value to be present in more than one entry, but we require that the combination of a key and the record pointer in an entry be unique.

We may also want to retrieve index entries sequentially. For example, we might want to start at the first entry in an index and get each subsequent entry until the end is reached. To do this we need to keep track of our current position within the index. Then we can provide functions to move forward and backward in the index. In Figure 6.6 we have located the key **BIG**. The current position at each level of the index is underscored.

Figure 6.6   Current position

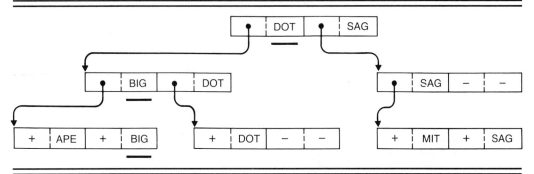

Our goal is to provide a flexible tool that is useful in a wide variety of applications. To accomplish this we provide low-level functions like inserting an entry at the current position in an index. It is up to the application program to ensure that using these functions does not upset the ordering of entries by key value. Our BTREE module also leaves the management of data records up to the application; it just stores and retrieves record pointers that can be interpreted by the application program. Figure 6.7 documents the BTREE module to be presented in the rest of the chapter.

6.3   BTREE Pseudo-code

□   The following pseudo-code describes the normal cases and some exception cases. We discuss more exceptions at the end of the section.

The find_ix function starts at the root level and moves down to the leaf level, searching an index block at each level. The search at the leaf level tells us if the key was found in the index. Searches at higher levels just direct the choice of a block on the next lower level.

```
find_ix
        start at the root block
        for each level starting at the root
             retrieve current index block
             search that block for the target key
             extract record ptr. for next level
        return success/failure of the leaf level search
end
```

We have already shown a function (see Figure 6.1) to search an array of integers; searching a single index block would require the same logic. New entries are inserted, starting at the leaf level. If an index block must be split, new entries must

Figure 6.7   BTREE index module

Name

BTREE – A module for disk-file based indexing

Function

The BTREE module provides functions for creating and using disk files to store index entries. Each entry consists of a record location and a key value. Keys may vary in length, and key values may be duplicated in different entries. The application program using the BTREE module supplies functions to compare keys and to find the size of an entry. The btree.h data structure supplies data structure and constant definitions for use with BTREE. Functions for searching for a specific key and for inserting and deleting entries are provided. A current position in the index is maintained, and functions are provided for moving through the index sequentially. More than one index can be opened and used at a time. Most BTREE functions expect the address of an index file descriptor as an input argument to identify the index file to be used.

Use of each function in the module is described following:

```
char name[65] = "c:\zip.ix" ;
long ixsize = 20000 ;
IX_DESC ixd ;
ENTRY entry ;
int compare ( ) ;   /* compares two entry keys */
int size ( ) ;        /* returns the size of an entry */
creatix(name, ixsize , & dummy_entry , dummy_size) ;
```

creatix creates an index file of the specified size. It returns −1 if the file could not be created. The calling function must supply a dummy entry whose key has the maximum possible value. This dummy key value can not be used in other entries. The size of the dummy entry must also be supplied.

```
removeix(name) ;
```

removeix deletes the index file.

```
openix(name, & ixd , compare , size) ;
```

openix opens an existing index file. It returns −1 if unsuccessful. The addresses of functions to compare entry keys and to get the size of an entry are additional arguments.

```
closeix( & ixd ) ;
```

closeix closes an index file that has previously been opened.

```
go_first( & ixd ) ;
go_last( & ixd ) ;
```

go_first sets the current position in an index to the beginning of the file. go_last sets the position at the end of the index.

```
get_next( & entry , & ixd ) ;
get_prev ( & entry , & ixd ) ;
get_current ( & entry , & ixd ) ;
```

get_next advances the current position in an index file. The new current entry is copied into the address identified by the first argument. get_previous moves the current position backward and copies the new current entry. get_current copies the entry at the current position and leaves the current position unchanged.

```
find_ix( & entry, & ixd ) ;
find_exact( & entry, & ixd ) ;
```

find_ix locates the first entry with a key value greater than or equal to the key specified by the first argument. A return value of 0 indicates that a key equal to that specified was found. If the specified key was found, the record pointer is stored in the entry. The find_exact function searches for an entry in the index file with the specified key and record pointer.

```
insert_ix( & entry , & ixd ) ;
find_ins( & entry , & ixd ) ;
```

insert_ix adds the entry specified in the index in front of the current position in the index. After the insertion, the current position is beyond the inserted entry. A returned value of IX_FAIL indicates that the insertion failed. find_ins verifies that the entry is not in the index file already and establishes the proper position before performing the insertion. It inserts new entries following all existing entries with the same key.

```
delete_ix( & ixd ) ;
find_del( & entry , & ixd ) ;
```

delete_ix removes the entry at the current position in the index. After the deletion, the current position is in front of the entry following the deleted one. A returned value of IX_FAIL indicates that the deletion failed. The find_del function locates the entry described by the first argument and deletes it if it is present.

Usage

See the doccreat.c, docindex.c, and docscan.c programs for examples of use.

Notes

Up to four levels of indexes are allowed with index blocks of 1,024 bytes. These limits are set by constants in btree.h. The module can be recompiled if other values seem more appropriate.

The maximum number of entries allowed depends on the average length of keys used (K in the following formula). Four bytes are required for the record position that accompanies each key. A rough formula for the worst case might be

$$\# \text{ records } = 2 * ((1024 / 2) / (K+4)) ** 4$$

With keys 20 bytes long, this would be $2 * 20**4$ or 320,000 records.

be inserted in higher-level indexes. Inserting entries at higher levels requires the same logic as inserting at the leaf level so we need describe the process only once:

```
insert entry into a specified level
      retrieve current block for this level
      if enough room for new entry
          insert entry to block
      else
          split the block into two blocks
          allocate space for new block
          update both blocks in index file
          insert an entry in higher index for new block
end
```

Like inserting, deleting entries starts at the leaf level. Deletions of entries from higher-level indexes may be required if the leaf level block becomes empty or is combined with its neighbor. And like insertion, a single process applies to leaf level and higher-level deletions.

```
delete current entry at specified level
      retrieve current block for this level
      remove current entry from block
      if block is empty and not the root level
          delete the block's entry on higher level
      if less than half full and not the root level
          compress with adjacent blocks
      else update the block
end
```

Deleting entries is a messy process with lots of exception cases. Our pseudo-code shows two exceptions; others are discussed later. We want the pseudo-code to show the basic structure of the BTREE module even if some important details must be omitted. Compressing the current block with adjacent ones is an important part of the B-Tree algorithm and requires a pseudo-code description.

```
compress adjacent blocks
      retrieve the block to the left
      if(it exists and the combined size < = 1 block )
          combine blocks into the current block
          delete higher level entry for left neighbor
          update the current block
      else
          retrieve block to the right
          if(block exists and combined size < = 1 block)
              combine blocks into right neighbor
              delete higher level entry for current block
              update the right neighbor block
end
```

The get_next and get_previous functions take the current position in the index and move forward or backward. They start at the leaf level and use the upper-level index if they run out of the current block at the leaf level. As for insertion and deletion, a single process works for all index levels:

```
move_to_next_entry on specified level
        retrieve current index block for this level
        advance to next entry
        if( at end of block )
            move to next entry on upper level
            retrieve block pointed to by upper level
            set position at first entry in block
        return record pointer at current position
end
```

```
move_to_previous_entry on specified level
        retrieve current index block for this level
        move back to previous entry
        if( at beginning of block already )
            move to previous entry on upper level
            retrieve block pointed to by upper level
            set position at last entry in block
        return record pointer at current position
end
```

The go_first and go_last functions set a new current position at the beginning or end of the index. They start at the root level and work down to the leaf level.

```
go_first
        start with root block
        for each level from root to leaf
            retrieve this block
            make this block current for this level
            make first entry current
            save record pointer for next level
end
```

```
go_last
        start with root block
        for each level from root to leaf
            retrieve this block
            make this block current for this level
            make last entry current
            save record pointer for next level
end
```

The openix function is analogous to the fopen and open library functions. creatix and closeix are analogous to the creat and close library functions.

```
openix
      open index file
      set up context describing the index file
      go_first
end

closeix
      save context information
      close index file
end

creatix
      create index file
      create an initial tree structure
      allocate free blocks in file
end
```

6.4 Exceptions and Design Choices

□   Our pseudo-code handles some exceptions, and we can remove others with good design choices. The pseudo-code did not handle cases where an index was empty or where a search key was greater than all entries in an index. Insertions that required adding a level to the tree and deletions that required removing a level were not handled either. But simple restrictions remove these and other exception cases. We place a dummy entry (with the highest possible key value) in the index when it is created. This ensures that the index is never empty and that searches never go past the last key in the index. In addition, we build a tree of maximum height when the index is created. The initial tree structure contains one leaf level block with the dummy entry. Each higher-level index will contain one entry with the dummy key and a record pointer to the lone block on the next lower level. We can avoid increasing or reducing the height of the index tree.

The choice of a maximum height for a B-Tree is tied to the choice of a block size. As we shall see, however, trees with three or four levels can hold a large number of records.

There are several factors to be balanced in choosing a size for an index block. A large value minimizes the height of the tree and thus the number of I/O operations for a given number of records. But large block sizes require more RAM memory to store blocks being referenced. In addition, blocks larger than the units in which DOS allocates disk space to files may be fragmented, resulting in slower file I/O performance. Blocks should be a multiple of the disk sector size. This allows blocks to be aligned on sector boundaries for faster I/O. Sector sizes are normally 512 bytes for disks formatted for DOS, and allocation units vary from 512 bytes to 4 Kbytes for different kinds of disks. As we will see later, the BTREE package requires space to hold about nine blocks in memory at one time.

The index tree becomes full when no more entries can be added without increasing the tree's height beyond the maximum we allow. At that point the root level index is full, and lower-level index blocks must be at least half-full. The following formula gives the minimum capacity (worse case) of an l-level index tree where index entries are e bytes long on the average and blocks are b bytes long:

$$\text{\# entries in tree} = (b/e) * (b/2e)**(l-1)$$

The following table shows index capacity for block sizes of 512 and 1,024 bytes, with an average entry size of 50 bytes—the worst case capacity of a BTREE index:

Tree Height	*Block Size*	
	20	*50*
1	10	20
2	50	200
3	250	2,000
4	1,250	20,000

For smaller entry sizes the capacity of an index is much larger (for 20-byte entries, a three-level index with 1,024 blocks holds over 31,000 entries). But since we want the BTREE module to be a general purpose tool, we choose conservative values of 1,024 bytes for the block size and 4 for the maximum tree height.

In addition to the index blocks, we must store some context information about the index file: The location of the root block is one such item. It is convenient to store this information at the beginning of the index file. While only a few bytes of data are required, we must start index blocks at byte 1,024 to keep index blocks aligned on sector (and allocation unit) boundaries.

6.5 BTREE Listings

□ The BTREE module is a large one with a number of source files. The files are introduced and discussed, starting with low-level functions and ending with the top-level functions that are called from application programs. The diagram of the hierarchy of function calls should provide a roadmap for fitting the pieces together. BTREE is not a complete program but a group of functions to be called from an applications program. For this reason, each top-level function has its own hierarchy.

```
find_ix
    call
    go_last
    find_level
     retrieve_block
            chk_cache
            get_cache
            put_cache
            read_block
                    read_if
            find_block
            call
            next_entry
        find_level   *
    copy_current
        retrieve_block
        copy_entry
            mover

insert_ix
    ins_level
        retrieve_block
            ins_block
                copy_entry
                moveup
                    mover
                update_block
                    chk_cache
                    put_cache
                    write_block
                        write_if
        split
            combine
                moveup
                mover
            ins_block
                . . .
            scan_blk
            next_entry
            get_block
                get_free
                    read_if
            copy_entry
            update_block
```

```
    ins_level       *
    mover
    put_free
            scrub_cache
            write_free
                    clr_mem
                    write_block
            next_ix
                . . .
next_ix
    . . .

delete_ix
    copy_current
    del_level
        retrieve_block
        del_block
            movedown
                mover
        put_free
        del_level    *
        copy_current
        first_ix
            . . .
        fix_last
            copy_entry
            replace_entry
                retrieve_block
                del_block
                ins_block
                split
                    . . .
                update_block
                replace_entry    *
    update_block
    compress
            neighbor
                retrieve_block
                next_entry
                prev_entry
            combine
            update_block
            last_ix
                del_level    *
```

get_next
  next_ix
    retrieve_block
    next_entry
    next_ix   *
  copy_current

get_previous
  last_ix
    retrieve_block
    prev_entry
      scan_blk
    last_ix   *
    last_entry
      scan_blk
  copy_current

get_current
  copy_current

go_first
  first_ix
    retrieve_block
    first_ix   *

go_last
  final_ix
    retrieve_block
    last_entry
    final_ix   *

openix
  open_if
  read_if

init_bio
    init_cache
  go_first

closeix
  write_if
  close_if

creatix
  creat_if
  clr_mem
  mover
  write_block
  wrt_dum
    mover
    write_block
  make_free
    write_free
  closeix

removeix
  (no calls to other BTREE functions)

find_exact
  copy_entry
  find_ix
  get_next

find_ins
  find_exact
  insert_ix

find_del
  find_exact
  delete_ix

We listed the calls made by each function just once. For example, the first time retrieve_block occurs in the diagram, we list every function it calls. Recursive calls are marked with an asterisk.

In reading the BTREE source files, you should keep in mind the relation between index blocks stored in the index file and variables of type **BLOCK**. Index blocks in RAM memory in such variables are mirror images of blocks stored in the file or working (scratch) copies being referenced and perhaps updated.

btree.h

The header file shown in Figure 6.8 defines constants and data types needed in application programs that use the BTREE module. These definitions are also needed within the BTREE module. btree.h defines success and failure codes returned by BTREE functions. The RECPOS data type is defined for record pointers with a null value, NULLREC.

The ENTRY data type is used to pass keys and record pointers to the BTREE module and to receive them back. We do not know the actual data type or key length, but we define a dummy array of 100 characters. This dummy array serves as a place holder so we can get the address of the start of the key field. When we declare an ENTRY variable for scratch space, the 100-byte key field provides enough space for any key.

Lines 17 to 27 in Figure 6.8 define the format of an index block. While this structure is not used by the application, it is used in the IX_DESC data structure described later. To simplify the BTREE module, we used the same structure for index blocks stored in the index file and for copies in RAM memory. All the members of the BLOCK structure are not needed in each case, but the cost in wasted disk space is quite small.

The brec member serves two purposes. For free blocks in the file, it points to the next free block. For blocks in RAM memory, it identifies the location in the index file where the block belongs. The lvl member identifies the index level on which a block is used. Values of 0 through (MAX_LEVELS−1) correspond to leaf through root level, while the special value FREE_LEVEL identifies free blocks.

The entries member serves as a dummy place holder; entries are stored here. The size of the member is adjusted to make the BLOCK structure be exactly 1,024 bytes long. The bend member contains the number of bytes actually used in the entries field. It can also be interpreted as the offset of the first unused byte in the block.

The file also defines two data structures whose contents describe an index file. The IX_DISK structure contains permanent data that are stored in the index file between uses of the file. Its members point to the root block and the first free block; when we open an index file, we need this information to make sense of the file.

The IX_DESC structure contains the same information, with additional members needed for an index that is in use. The ixfile member contains a file descriptor for read and write calls. Addresses of compare and entry size functions are also stored here. The current position in the index is stored in the pos array of structures—a current block record pointer and a location within the block for each index level. Space to store recently used blocks is also provided within the structure.

The application program does not need to know about or use the fields in these descriptor data structures, but we can simplify the BTREE module by letting the application program allocate space for index descriptors. Most calls to BTREE functions contain a pointer to a descriptor structure.

Figure 6.8   btree.h

```
1    /* btree.h - data structures and constants for BTREE module */
2    #define EOIX        (-2)    /* return value for end-of-index */
3    #define IX_FAIL     (-1)    /* return value for failed operation */
4    #define IX_OK        0      /* return value for success */
5
6    typedef long RECPOS ;       /* file pos. of index block/data rec. */
7    #define NULLREC     (-1L)   /* special value for a RECPOS */
8
9    #define MAXKEY       100        /* maximum lebgth of a key */
10
11   typedef struct             /* entry format in index */
12    { RECPOS rptr ;            /* points to lower level */
13      char    key[MAXKEY] ;    /* start of key value */
14                               /* (actual data type unknown) */
15    } ENTRY ;
16
17   #define IXB_SIZE     1024   /* no. bytes in a block (on disk) */
18           /* IXB_SPACE = IXB_SIZE - sizeof(int)*2 - sizeof(long) */
19   #define IXB_SPACE    1016   /* no. bytes of entry space in block */
20
21   typedef struct             /* index block format */
22    { RECPOS brec ;            /* index file location of block */
23                               /* or location of next free block */
24      int bend ;               /* first unused location in block */
25      int lvl ;                /* records level no. (-1 = free) */
26      char entries[IXB_SPACE] ;   /* space for entries */
27    } BLOCK ;
28
29   #define MAX_LEVELS    4        /* four index levels permitted */
30
31   typedef struct             /* disk-file index descriptor */
32    { int nl ;                 /* number of index levels */
33      RECPOS rb ;              /* location of root block in file */
34      RECPOS ff ;              /* location of first free block */
35      ENTRY dume ;             /* dummy entry */
36    } IX_DISK ;
37
38   typedef struct             /* in-memory index descriptor */
39    { int ixfile ;             /* descriptor for open index file */
40      struct
41       { RECPOS cblock ;        /* current block number */
42         int coffset ;          /* current offset within block */
43       } pos[ MAX_LEVELS ] ;
44      int (*pcomp) () ;        /* address of compare function */
45      int (*psize) () ;        /* address of entry size function */
46      BLOCK  cache[ MAX_LEVELS] ;   /* cache for current blocks */
47      IX_DISK dx ;             /* disk resident stuff */
48    } IX_DESC ;
```

bt_macro.h

Figure 6.9 lists another header file whose definitions are needed only within the BTREE module. C source code that makes extensive use of pointers and dummy data types can be difficult to understand. The macros in lines 7 to 18 hide the details, keeping the source code looking fairly normal. C's syntax for calling a function whose address is in a variable is awkward, so the call macro substitutes a form whose meaning is obvious. Since we do not want to remember whether we defined it with capital letters, we defined CALL as well. Calls to the entry size function occur frequently in the BTREE module, so the ENT_SIZE macro abbreviates that expression further.

Forming the address of an entry within a block is another common requirement. The ENT_ADR macro hides the type conversions needed to add an offset to a pointer to a block. Although the expression looks complicated, most C compilers generate a single addition instruction (with a load and store instruction).

The CB and CO macros provide shorthand for references to the current block and current offset. They can be used on the left or right side of assignment statements.

The variable pci occurs in several of these macros. It is explained in the next section.

Several constants that are passed as arguments between functions inside the BTREE module are also defined in this file.

Figure 6.9   bt_macro.h

```
 1    /*bt_macro.h - macros, constants, data types for BTREE internals*/
 2
 3    #define CURR   1                    /* getting current block */
 4    #define NOT_CURR 0                  /* getting non-current block */
 5
 6                                        /* call a function using a ptr */
 7    #define CALL(pfun)     (* (pfun) )
 8    #define call(pfun)     (* (pfun) )
 9
10                             /* get address of entry in a block */
11    #define ENT_ADR(pb,off) ((ENTRY *)( (char *)(& (pb)->entries)+off))
12
13                             /* get size of an entry */
14    #define ENT_SIZE(pe)    (*(pci->psize)) (pe)
15
16                             /* current position macros */
17    #define CB(l)   ( pci->pos[l].cblock )
18    #define CO(l)   ( pci->pos[l].coffset )
19
20    #define FREE_LEVEL  (-1)           /* marks a block as free */
21
22                                        /* arguments for neighbor() */
23    #define LEFTN       (-1)           /* request left neighbor */
24    #define RIGHTN       1             /* request right neighbor */
```

bt_space.c

The source file shown in Figure 6.10 defines some global variables used throughout BTREE. In a large module like BTREE, it is convenient to declare and allocate space for all global variables in a single source file that contains no functions. Then all the source files that reference these variables can declare them with the **extern** storage class. The global variable pci is used within BTREE to address the descriptor structure for the BTREE operation underway. This avoids the need to pass that address as an argument in all function calls within the BTREE module.

The spare_block variable is used within BTREE whenever scratch space is needed for an extra index block.

The split_size and comb_size variables establish thresholds for splitting a full block or combining a less than half-full block. In normal use these variables are initialized to be the block size for splitting and half the block size for combining. But for testing, we can set these variables to much smaller values, allowing us to test exception conditions more easily.

The variable pci occurs in several of these macros. It is a global variable used within BTREE that contains the address of the descriptor structure for the BTREE operation underway.

bt_low2.c

The source file in Figure 6.11 provides some low-level tools for working with index entries in blocks. These tools hide the details of dealing with variable-length entries whose data type we do not know. The next_entry function moves forward past the entry at the specified offset, while the prev_entry function moves backward.

Figure 6.10 bt_space.c

```
1    /* bt_space.c - declares some global variables */
2    #include "stdio.h"
3    #include "btree.h"
4    #include "bt_macro.h"
5
6    IX_DESC *pci ;                    /* refers to index descriptor */
7                                      /* for current function call */
8
9    BLOCK spare_block ;               /* scratch block for splits and */
10                                     /* compressing */
11
12   int split_size = IXB_SPACE ;     /* split block when it contains */
13                                     /* more than this many bytes */
14
15   int comb_size = (IXB_SPACE/2); /* combine block when it contains */
16                                     /* fewer than this many bytes */
```

Figure 6.11   bt_low2.c

```
1     /* bt_low2.c - low level functions for BTREE module */
2     #include "stdio.h"
3     #include "btree.h"
4     #include "bt_macro.h"
5
6     extern IX_DESC *pci ;
7
8     int prev_entry(pb,off)              /* back up one entry */
9      BLOCK *pb ;
10     int off ;
11     {
12         if( off <= 0 )                 /* at start of block ? */
13             return( -1 ) ;             /*   yes - can't back up */
14         off = scan_blk(pb,off) ;       /* find previous entry */
15         return( off ) ;
16     }
17
18     int next_entry(pb,off)             /* go forward one entry */
19      BLOCK *pb ;
20     int off ;
21     {
22         if( off >= pb->bend )                  /* at end of block ? */
23             return( -1 ) ;             /*   yes - can't move fwd */
24         off = off + ENT_SIZE(ENT_ADR(pb,off)) ; /* move past entry */
25         if( off >= pb->bend )                  /* at end of block ? */
26             return( -1 ) ;             /*   yes - no entry here */
27         return( off ) ;
28     }
29
30
31     int copy_entry(to,from)            /* copy an entry */
32      ENTRY *to ;                       /* to this address */
33      ENTRY *from ;                     /* from this address */
34     {
35         int ne ;
36
37         ne = ENT_SIZE(from) ;          /* get the entry's size */
38         mover(to,from,ne) ;            /* move that many bytes */
39     }
40
41
42     int scan_blk(pb,n)                 /* find offset of last entry */
43      BLOCK *pb ;                       /* in this block */
44     int n ;                           /* starting before this position */
45     {
46         int i , last ;
47
48         i = 0 ; last = 0 ;
49         while( i < n )                 /* repeat until position reached */
50             { last = i ;               /* save where we are now */
51               i = i + ENT_SIZE( ENT_ADR(pb,i) ); /* move past entry */
52             }
53         return( last ) ;               /* return last offset < n */
54     }
55
```

Figure 6.11   bt_low2.c (continued)

```
56
57    int last_entry(pb)                /* find last entry in a block */
58    BLOCK *pb ;                        /* the block */
59    {
60                                       /* scan for offset of last entry */
61        return( scan_blk(pb,pb->bend) ) ;  /* and return the offset */
62    }
```

Both functions return the new offset or −1 if the end or beginning of the block was reached. The last_entry function finds the offset of the last entry in a block.

Moving forward from an offset is easy: We just get the size of the entry at that offset and add it to get the new offset. Moving backward is a bit more difficult since we cannot find the size of the previous entry directly. We have to start at the beginning of the block and move forward until we reach the specified offset. The last entry found before this point is the previous entry. The scan_blk function provides this scanning.

The copy_entry function copies a single entry. It assumes that the destination area is large enough to hold an entry.

The functions in this source file remove some of the disadvantages of working with variable-length entries. The cost is extra source code and some extra execution time, but it keeps the rest of the BTREE module simple and understandable.

bt_file.c

Figure 6.12 lists functions that do file I/O operations on index files. This hides our use of C library functions for unbuffered I/O from the rest of the BTREE module.

A file position is specified for each operation, and a seek call precedes a read or write. There is no relation between the order of reads and writes and the file position specified. Random rather than sequential I/O is required for index files.

Note that the gopen function is used instead of open to make BTREE usable with any C compiler.

bt_util.c

Figure 6.13 shows utility functions to support BTREE. The clr_mem function sets a memory area to a specified value (0, for example). It is used to clear the entry storage part of a block before writing it to disk. The mover function copies a specified number of bytes from one memory area to another. It is based on the movedata function in Chapter 2, but it handles the case where the origin and destination areas overlap.

Figure 6.12   bt_file.c

```
1    /* bt_file.c - file I/O for BTREE module */
2    #include "stdio.h"
3    #include "cminor.h"
4    #include "btree.h"
5    #include "bt_macro.h"
6
7    #define BOF_REL 0
8    #define WR_MODE 1
9    #define RW_MODE 2
10
11   extern IX_DESC *pci ;
12
13   int creat_if(fn)                      /* create a file */
14    char fn[];
15    {
16        return( gcreat(fn,WR_MODE,BIN_MODE) ) ;
17    }
18
19   int read_if(start,buf,nrd)
20    RECPOS start ;
21    char buf[] ;
22    int nrd ;
23    {
24        lseek(pci->ixfile,start,BOF_REL) ;
25        return( read(pci->ixfile,buf,nrd) ) ;
26    }
27
28   int write_if(start,buf,nwrt)
29    RECPOS start ;
30    char buf[] ;
31    int nwrt ;
32    {
33        lseek(pci->ixfile,start,BOF_REL) ;
34        return( write(pci->ixfile,buf,nwrt) ) ;
35    }
36
37   int close_if()              /* close an index file */
38    {
39        return( close(pci->ixfile) );
40    }
41
42   int open_if(fn)                      /* open an index file */
43    char fn[] ;
44    {
45        return ( gopen(fn,RW_MODE,BIN_MODE) ) ;
46    }
```

Figure 6.13   bt_util.c

```
1      /* bt_util.c - utility functions for BTREE */
2      #include "stdio.h"
3
4      int clr_mem(p,c,n)              /* clear a memory area */
5       char *p ;                      /* start of the memory area */
6       int c ;                        /* value to write there */
7       int n ;                        /* number of bytes to clear */
8       {
9           while( n > 0 )
10              { *p = c ;             /* clear current location */
11                p = p + 1 ;          /* advance pointer */
12                n = n - 1 ;          /* reduce byte count */
13              }
14      }
15
16
17      int mover(to,from,nbytes)/* moves bytes allowing for overlap */
18       char *to ;                     /* move the data to here */
19       char *from ;                   /* move it from here */
20       int nbytes ;                   /* number of bytes to move */
21       {
22          if( from > to )
23             {
24              while( nbytes > 0 )     /* stop when all bytes are moved */
25                 { *to = *from ;      /* move a byte */
26                   to = to + 1 ;      /* advance pointers to and from */
27                   from = from + 1 ;
28                   nbytes = nbytes - 1 ; /* reduce bytes left */
29                 }
30             }
31          else
32             { to = to + nbytes - 1 ;  /* point to end of areas */
33               from = from + nbytes - 1 ;
34               while( nbytes > 0 )     /* stop when all bytes are moved */
35                 { *to = *from ;       /* move a byte */
36                   to = to - 1 ;       /* advance pointers to and from */
37                   from = from - 1 ;
38                   nbytes = nbytes - 1 ; /* reduce bytes left */
39                 }
40             }
41      }
42
43
```

bt_free.c

As we discussed in Section 6.3, insertions and deletions require support for allocating and freeing space in the index file. The source file in Figure 6.14 manages a list of free index blocks.

The **dx.ff** variable stores the address of the first free block. That block in the file points to the next free block. The list ends when a free block contains a pointer with the **NULLREC** value.

Figure 6.14 bt_free.c

```
1    /* bt_free.c - maintain list of free index blocks */
2    #include "stdio.h"
3    #include "btree.h"
4    #include "bt_macro.h"
5
6    #define FREE_LEVEL (-1)          /* marks a block as free */
7    extern IX_DESC *pci ;
8    extern BLOCK spare_block ;
9
10   int make_free(fstart,filesize)  /* set up the free block chain */
11    RECPOS fstart ;                /* first free block */
12    RECPOS filesize ;              /* size of the index file */
13    {
14       BLOCK *pb ;
15       RECPOS r ;
16       pb = & spare_block ;        /* scratch block */
17       pci->dx.ff = NULLREC ;      /* no blocks free to start */
18       for(r= fstart ; r < filesize ; r = r + IXB_SIZE)
19         { write_free(r,pb) ; }
20    }
21
22
23
24   RECPOS get_free()               /* grab a free block for use */
25    {
26       RECPOS r , rt ;
27
28       r = pci->dx.ff ;            /* get location of first free block */
29       if( r != NULLREC )          /* is there one ? */
30         { read_if(r,&rt,sizeof(RECPOS));/* yes - find where it */
31           pci->dx.ff = rt ;       /*   points & make it the 1st free */
32         }
33       return( r ) ;
34    }
35
36
37   int write_free(r,pb)            /* write out a free block */
38    RECPOS r ;                     /* record number of block to free */
39    BLOCK *pb ;                    /* use this as scratch space */
40    {
41       pb->lvl = FREE_LEVEL ;      /* mark block as free */
42       clr_mem(&pb->entries,0,IXB_SPACE) ; /* zero out the block */
43       pb->brec = pci->dx.ff ;     /* point to current 1st free block */
44       write_block(r,pb) ;         /* write the free block */
45       pci->dx.ff = r ;            /* make this block the first free */
46    }
```

When an index file is created, the make_free function creates a list of free blocks. It receives the record position where the free list starts and the total size of the file. The file size specified may not be an exact multiple of 1,024 bytes, so make_free stops when the file's size equals or exceeds the specified size. Writing the free blocks serves two purposes: It links the free blocks into a list, and it forces DOS to allocate space for the file.

The final free list links the blocks in reverse order; the last block in the file is the first on the free list. This order is easy to implement but might reduce disk I/O efficiency in some cases. Note also that we did not check for failure of the write operations.

The get_free function allocates the first free block. It reads that block to get the pointer to the next free block. This next block becomes the new first free block. The put_free function performs the opposite function—namely, it returns a block to the free list. Before we write the free block, we set the level member to the FREE_LEVEL value and clear the entry storage area. Clearing this area is not necessary for BTREE's function, but it makes examining an index file with the FILEDUMP program a bit easier.

blockio.c **and** bt_cache.c

The functions in Figures 6.15 and 6.16 provide input and output of index blocks. They implement a simple scheme of cache buffering to reduce the number of actual disk reads. The retrieve_block function gets index blocks from the cache or from the index file.

Blocks that are at the current position are likely to be referenced again, so we cache only those blocks. Note that we rely on the calling function to tell us the level on which the block is to be used and whether it is to be a current block.

The update_block function puts updated copies of blocks back in the file. It immediately writes each update to the file. (This is often called a *write-through* cache strategy.) An alternate strategy would be to hold updated blocks in the cache and write them to the file only when they are replaced in the cache. Our method is simple to explain and is an effective starting point.

The information in the cache buffers must be kept consistent with the corresponding blocks in the file. When we initialize the BTREE module, we set the cache to show that no valid blocks are present. When we update blocks, we also update the cache if that block is present. When a block is freed, the put_free function ensures that the cache does not contain out-of-date information about the block.

read_block and write_block functions read and write index blocks directly. They bypass the cache.

The cache functions in Figure 6.16 implement the caching. The cache method is simple: We allocate space for one block at each index level and keep the current block there. Cache buffers are allocated in the descriptor so each open index file has its own set.

Figure 6.15   blockio.c

```
1     /* blockio.c - retrieve/update index blocks */
2     #include "stdio.h"
3     #include "btree.h"
4     #include "bt_macro.h"
5
6     extern IX_DESC *pci ;
7     extern BLOCK spare_block ;
8     RECPOS get_free() ;
9
10    int init_bio()                   /* initialize blockio */
11    {
12        init_cache() ;               /* init. cache buffers */
13    }
14
15
16    int retrieve_block(l,r,pb,current)
17                                     /* retrieve an index block */
18    int l ;                          /* index level for this block */
19    RECPOS r ;                       /* block's location in index file */
20    BLOCK *pb ;                      /* put it here */
21    int current ;                    /* =1, put in cache */
22    {
23
24
25        if( chk_cache(l,r) != 0 )    /* look in cache first */
26            get_cache(l,r,pb) ;      /*    there - get it */
27        else
28          { read_block(r,pb);        /*    not there - read it */
29            pb->brec = r ;
30            pb->lvl  = l ;
31            if( current )            /*    current block for level l? */
32                put_cache(l,pb) ;    /*        yes - put in the cache */
33          }
34        return( IX_OK ) ;
35    }
36
37
38    int update_block(pb)             /* update an index block in file */
39    BLOCK *pb ;                      /* address of index block */
40    {
41        if( chk_cache(pb->lvl,pb->brec) != 0 )
42            put_cache(pb->lvl,pb) ;
43        write_block(pb->brec,pb) ;
44    }
45
46    int get_block(l,pb)              /* allocate and set up a block */
47                                     /* retrieve an index block */
48    int l ;                          /* index level for this block */
49    BLOCK *pb ;                      /* put it here */
50    {
51        RECPOS r ;
52
53        r = get_free() ;             /* allocate disk block */
54        if( r == NULLREC )
55            return( IX_FAIL ) ;
```

Figure 6.15   blockio.c (continued)

```
56
57        pb->brec = r ;                    /* record block's file position */
58        pb->lvl  = 1 ;                    /* and its level */
59        return( IX_OK ) ;
60    }
61
62    int put_free(pb)                       /* return block to the free list */
63    BLOCK *pb ;
64    {
65
66        scrub_cache(pb->brec) ;        /* remove from cache */
67        pb->lvl = FREE_LEVEL ;         /* mark as free */
68        write_free(pb->brec,pb) ;
69    }
70
71    int read_block(r,pb)               /* read an index block */
72    RECPOS r ;                         /* block's location in index file */
73    BLOCK *pb ;                        /* store the block here */
74    {
75        int ret ;
76
77        ret = read_if(r,pb, sizeof(BLOCK) ) ;
78        return( ret ) ;
79    }
80
81
82    int write_block(r,pb)              /* write an index block */
83    RECPOS r ;                         /* block's location in index file */
84    BLOCK *pb ;                        /* the data to write */
85    {
86        int ret ;
87
88        ret = write_if(r,pb, sizeof(BLOCK) ) ;
89        return( ret ) ;
90    }
```

Figure 6.16   bt_cache.c

```
1     /* bt_cache.c - cache index blocks to cut Disk I/O   */
2     /* this version handles only a single open index file */
3     #include "stdio.h"
4     #include "btree.h"
5     #include "bt_macro.h"
6
7     extern IX_DESC *pci ;
8
9     int init_cache()                          /* initialize blockio cache */
10    {
11        int l ;
12
```

Figure 6.16   bt_cache.c (continued)

```
13          for(l=0 ; l < MAX_LEVELS ; l=l+1)
14            { pci->cache[l].brec = NULLREC;    /* nothing in memory yet */
15            }
16      }
17
18
19    int chk_cache(l,r)               /* check cache for an index block */
20     int l ;                         /* index level for this block */
21     RECPOS r ;                      /* block's location in index file */
22     {
23         BLOCK *pb ;
24
25         if( pci->cache[l].brec != r )
26             return( 0 ) ;
27         return( 1 ) ;
28     }
29
30
31    int get_cache(l,r,to)            /* get a block from the cache */
32     int l ;                         /* index level for this block */
33     RECPOS r ;                      /* block's location in index file */
34     BLOCK *to ;                     /* if found, copy it here */
35     {
36         BLOCK *pb ;
37
38         if( pci->cache[l].brec != r )
39             return( 0 ) ;
40         pb = & pci->cache[l] ;
41         mover(to,pb, sizeof(BLOCK) ) ; /* copy it */
42         pb->brec = r ;
43         return( 1 ) ;
44     }
45
46
47    int put_cache(l,pb)             /* write an index block back to file */
48     int l ;
49     BLOCK *pb ;                     /* address of index block */
50     {
51         BLOCK *to ;
52
53         to = & pci->cache[l] ;
54         mover(to,pb,sizeof(BLOCK) ) ; /* copy whole block */
55     }
56
57
58    int scrub_cache(r)                  /* remove a block from the cache */
59     RECPOS r ;                         /* the block's file position */
60     {                                  /*  = RECPOS scrubs all levels */
61         int l ;
62                                        /* search the cache */
63         for(l=0 ; l<pci->dx.nl ; l=l+1)
64            { if( (r == NULLREC)  || (r == pci->cache[l].brec) )
65                 pci->cache[l].brec = NULLREC ;
66            }
67     }
```

Our organization is quite modular. blockio.c hides the presence of caching from the rest of the BTREE module. The details of the caching method are confined to the bt_cache.c source file. This makes it easy to enhance the caching scheme without introducing bugs in the rest of the module.

openix.c

The source file in Figure 6.17 groups the functions for opening and closing index files. The openix function opens an index file and prepares it for use. It reads the

Figure 6.17   openix.c

```
 1    /* openix.c - open / close an index file */
 2    #include "stdio.h"
 3    #include "cminor.h"
 4    #include "btree.h"
 5    #include "bt_macro.h"
 6
 7    extern IX_DESC *pci ;
 8    RECPOS wrt_dum() ;
 9
10    int openix(name,pix,cfun,sfun)  /* open an existing index file */
11      char name[] ;                 /* file name */
12      IX_DESC *pix ;                /* control block for index */
13      int (*cfun) () ;              /* address of compare function */
14      int (*sfun) () ;              /* address of entry size function */
15      {
16          int ret ;
17
18          pci = pix ;
19          ret = open_if(name) ;
20          if( ret < 0 )              /* check for failure to create file */
21              return( IX_FAIL ) ;
22          pci->ixfile = ret ;
23          read_if(0L,&pix->dx, sizeof(IX_DISK) ) ;
24          pci->pcomp = cfun ;        /* record address of compare fun. */
25          pci->psize = sfun ;        /* and of entry size function. */
26          init_bio() ;               /* initialize block I/O */
27          go_first(pix) ;            /* position at start of file */
28          return( IX_OK ) ;
29      }
30
31
32    int closeix(pix)                 /* close an index file */
33      IX_DESC *pix ;                 /* index descriptor */
34      {
35          pci = pix ;
36          write_if(0L,&pci->dx, sizeof(IX_DISK) ) ;
37          close_if() ;               /* close the index file */
38      }
39
40
41    int creatix(name,filesize,pdum,ndum) /* create a new index file */
42      char name[] ;                       /* name of the file */
```

Figure 6.17 openix.c (continued)

```
43    long filesize ;                   /* size of the file */
44    ENTRY *pdum ;                      /* dummy entry for EOF */
45    int ndum ;                         /* size of dummy entry */
46    {
47        BLOCK b ;
48        IX_DESC ixd ;
49        int ret ;
50
51        pci = & ixd ;
52        ret = creat_if(name) ;
53        if( ret < 0 )                  /* check for failure to create file */
54            return( IX_FAIL ) ;
55        ixd.ixfile = ret ;
56        ixd.dx.nl = MAX_LEVELS ;       /* all levels present */
57        mover(&ixd.dx.dume,pdum,ndum) ;
58        clr_mem(&b,0,IXB_SIZE) ;       /* make a block of zeros */
59        write_block(0L,&b) ;           /* write it at BOF */
60                                       /* set up index block for each level */
61                                       /* and record location of root block */
62        ixd.dx.rb = wrt_dum(pdum,ndum) ;
63                                       /* set up free block list */
64                                       /* start it after dummy blocks */
65        make_free( ((RECPOS) (MAX_LEVELS+1)) * IXB_SIZE, filesize) ;
66        closeix(&ixd) ;                /* close file updating desc. info */
67        return( IX_OK ) ;              /* successful creation */
68    }
69
70
71    RECPOS wrt_dum(pdum,ndum)         /* write index block for each level */
72    ENTRY *pdum ;                      /* dummy entry */
73    int ndum ;                         /* size of dummy entry */
74
75        BLOCK b ;
76        int l ;
77        RECPOS r ;
78
79        pdum->rptr = NULLREC ;
80        r = 0 ;
81        for( l=0 ;l < MAX_LEVELS  ; l=l+1)
82          { r = r + IXB_SIZE ;
83            mover(&b.entries,pdum,ndum); /* put dummy in block */
84            b.lvl = l ;
85            b.bend = ndum ;            /* block contains one entry */
86            write_block(r,&b) ;        /* write the block */
87            pdum->rptr = r ;
88          }
89        return( r ) ;
90    }
91
92
93
94    int removeix(name)                /* delete an index file */
95    char name[] ;                      /* name of the file */
96    {
97        unlink(name) ;
98    }
```

permanent descriptor data from the index file and places it in the descriptor data
structure supplied by the calling function. The addresses of the compare and entry
size functions to be used for this index file are also stored in the descriptor. openix
calls init_bio to clear the cache buffers and go_first to establish a valid current
position.

closeix is called where the application finishes using an index. It updates the
permanent data in the index file and then closes the file.

creatix creates a new index file. It sets up the initial structure with a single
entry using the dummy key supplied by the calling function. A call to make_free
allocates space for and links a list of free index blocks. It calls closeix to write the
permanent descriptor data in the file and close it.

removeix deletes an index file. It hides the way we implemented an index file
from the application.

bt_first.c

The go_first and go_last functions in Figure 6.18 set the current position in an
index file to the beginning or end of the file. Both functions start at the root block
and work down to the leaf level. The recursive functions, first_ix and final_ix,
set the position. This organization—a small function for interface to the application and a recursive function to do the work—is shared by other BTREE functions.
Storing the address of the descriptor structure in the global variable pci is also common to many BTREE functions called from the application program.

The index file contains a dummy entry at the end. Thus, go_last and
final_ix set the current position in front of this dummy entry.

bt_get.c

Figure 6.19 shows the get_next and get_previous functions that move forward
or backward in an index file. These functions use the recursive functions next_ix
and last_ix to do the work. They are similar, so we discuss next_ix only.

Unlike the first_ix and final_ix functions just discussed, next_ix starts at
the leaf level. If there is a next entry in the leaf level block, the process is finished. If
we are at the end of the block, we use next_ix to find the next entry at the index level
above the current one. This entry contains the record pointer for the new current
block, and next_ix returns it. next_ix keeps advancing the position at higher
levels until we can get a next entry at some level or until we get to the end of the
root block. The last_ix function works in a similar way: it just looks for the
previous entry instead of the next one.

Both get_next and get_previous copy the entry at the new current position
to the address supplied as an input argument. Both functions must accommodate
exception cases when the index file is positioned at the beginning or end of
the file. Note that get_next avoids moving past the dummy entry at the end of the
file. For get_previous, the beginning-of-file exception is signaled by the last_ix's

Figure 6.18   bt_first.c

```
1    /* bt_first.c - position at start/end of index */
2    #include "stdio.h"
3    #include "btree.h"
4    #include "bt_macro.h"
5
6    extern IX_DESC *pci ;          /* global variable for current pix */
7
8    int go_first(pix)             /* go to first entry in index */
9     IX_DESC *pix ;               /* points to an index descriptor */
10    {
11        BLOCK b ;
12
13        pci = pix ;
14                                  /* start at root level and */
15        first_ix(pci->dx.nl-1,pci->dx.rb,&b) ; /* set at first entry */
16        return( IX_OK ) ;         /* success code */
17    }
18
19
20    int first_ix(l,r,pb)          /* set curr. pos. to first entry */
21     int l ;                      /* at this and lower levels */
22     RECPOS r ;                   /* curr. block for level l */
23     BLOCK *pb ;
24    {
25
26        CB(l) = r ;               /* set curr. block */
27        CO(l) = 0 ;               /* and offset */
28        retrieve_block(l,CB(l),pb,CURR); /* get the block */
29
30        if( l > 0 )               /* set lower levels too */
31          first_ix(l-1,ENT_ADR(pb,0)->rptr,pb) ;
32    }
33
34
35
36    int go_last(pix)              /* go to last index entry (dummy) */
37     IX_DESC *pix ;               /* points to an index descriptor */
38    {
39        BLOCK b ;
40
41        pci = pix ;
42        final_ix(pci->dx.nl-1,pci->dx.rb,&b) ; /* start at root */
43                                  /* position at last entry */
44        return( IX_OK ) ;         /* success return code */
45    }
46
47
48    int final_ix(l,r,pb)          /* set curr. pos. to first entry */
49     int l ;                      /* at this and lower levels */
50     RECPOS r ;                   /* curr. block for level l */
51     BLOCK *pb ;
52    {
53        int off ;
54
55        CB(l) = r ;                       /* set curr. block */
```

Figure 6.18 bt_first.c (continued)

```
56          retrieve_block(l,r,pb,CURR);/* get the block */
57          off = last_entry(pb);        /* curr. offset = last entry */
58          CO(l) = off ;
59          if( l > 0 )                  /* set lower levels too */
60            final_ix(l-1,ENT_ADR(pb,off)->rptr,pb) ;
61      }
```

function returning a NULLREC value (when last_ix is called with l equal to pci->dx.nl).

bt_block.c

We are finally in sight of the find, insert, and replace functions that are the main purpose of the BTREE module. Figure 6.20 shows functions that support those operations on a single block.

The find_block function searches a single block for a specified key value. It stops when the end of the block is reached or when an entry is found with a key greater than or equal to the search value. The result of the last compare operation is returned with the offset in the block where the search stopped.

ins_block inserts an entry into a block. It moves the entries from the insertion point to the end of the block upward to make room and copies the new entry into the block. The bend field is adjusted for the increased size of the block.

The del_block function removes an entry from a block. It moves entries downward to fill the hole and adjusts the bend field downward.

combine merges two blocks. It makes room for and copies the contents of the left block to the front of the right block. The bend field is the total of the two original sizes.

The moveup and movedown functions shuffle part of a block up to create a hole or down to fill one. They support the insertion, deletion, and combining functions just described.

bt_find.c

The find_ix function in Figure 6.21 searches an index file for a specified key value. In the process, it establishes a new current position in the index file. If the search was successful, this position is at the first entry whose key matches the search value. If the search did not find a match, the current position will be at the first entry whose key is greater than the search value. This current position can be used for subsequent insertions or deletions.

Figure 6.19   bt_get.c

```
1    /* bt_get.c - get_next , previous entries */
2    #include "stdio.h"
3    #include "btree.h"
4    #include "bt_macro.h"
5
6    extern IX_DESC *pci ;          /* global variable for current pix */
7    RECPOS next_ix() ;
8    RECPOS last_ix() ;
9
10   int get_next(pe,pix)          /* get next index entry */
11    ENTRY *pe ;                   /* put the entry here */
12    IX_DESC *pix ;                /* points to an index descriptor */
13   {
14       BLOCK b ;
15
16       pci = pix ;
17                                  /* check for dummy entry at end-of-ix */
18       copy_current(0,pe) ;
19       if( call(pci->pcomp)(pe,& pci->dx.dume) == 0 )
20           return( EOIX ) ;
21
22       if( next_ix(0,&b) !=NULLREC)/* got next leaf entry ? */
23           { copy_current(0,pe);    /* copy it   */
24             return( IX_OK ) ;      /* and return success */
25           }
26       else return( EOIX ) ;
27   }
28
29   RECPOS next_ix(l,pb)           /* get next entry on a level */
30    int l ;                       /* level number */
31    BLOCK *pb ;
32   {
33       int off ;
34       RECPOS newblk ;
35
36       if( l >= pci->dx.nl )       /* above top level ? */
37           return( NULLREC ) ;     /*    yes - failure */
38
39       retrieve_block(l,CB(l),pb,CURR) ; /* get current block */
40       off = next_entry(pb,CO(l)); /* move to next entry in block */
41       if( off >= 0)               /* past end of the block */
42           CO(l) = off ;           /*  no - record new position */
43       else                        /* yes - move to next index block */
44           {
45               newblk =next_ix(l+1,pb);/*    next block on this level */
46               if( newblk != NULLREC ) /*    check for Begin of index */
47                 { CB(l) = newblk ;    /*    make this current block */
48                   retrieve_block(l,CB(l),pb,CURR) ; /* put into memory */
49                   CO(l) = 0 ;         /*    at first entry */
50                 }
51               else return( NULLREC ) ; /*   at begin. of index - can't */
52           }
53       return( ENT_ADR(pb,CO(l))->rptr ) ; /* block no. lower level */
54   }
```

Figure 6.19   bt_get.c (continued)

```
55
56
57
58    int get_previous(pe,pix)          /* get previous index entry */
59     ENTRY *pe ;                       /* put the entry here */
60     IX_DESC *pix ;                    /* points to an index descriptor */
61    {
62        BLOCK b ;
63
64        pci = pix ;
65        if( last_ix(0,&b) !=NULLREC)/* got next leaf entry ? */
66           { copy_current(0,pe);       /*    yes - return it */
67             return( IX_OK ) ;         /*         and success code */
68           }
69        else return( EOIX ) ;          /*    no - at BOF. return failure */
70    }
71
72    RECPOS last_ix(l,pb)               /* get previous entry for a level */
73     int l ;                           /* level number */
74     BLOCK *pb ;                       /* space for a block */
75    {
76        int off ;
77        RECPOS newblk ;
78
79        if( l >= pci->dx.nl )
80            return( NULLREC ) ;
81
82        retrieve_block(l,CB(l),pb,CURR) ; /* get current block */
83        off = prev_entry(pb,CO(l)) ;        /* back up one entry */
84        if( off >= 0 )                 /* past beginning of block */
85            CO(l) = off ;              /*   no - record new offset */
86        else
87           { newblk =last_ix(l+1,pb);/*   yes - get previous block */
88             if( newblk != NULLREC ) /*      check for Begin of index */
89               { CB(l) = newblk ;     /*    make this the current block */
90                 retrieve_block(l,CB(l),pb,CURR) ; /* put into memory */
91                 CO(l)=last_entry(pb); /* offset = last entry */
92               }
93             else return( NULLREC ) ;/*         at begin. of index - */
94           }                          /*              can't back up */
95                                      /* record ptr in curr. entry */
96        return( ENT_ADR(pb,CO(l))->rptr ) ;
97    }
98
99
100
101   int get_current(pe,pix)           /* get current index entry */
102    ENTRY *pe ;                       /* put the entry here */
103    IX_DESC *pix ;                    /* points to an index descriptor */
104   {
105       pci = pix ;
106       copy_current(0,pe) ;           /* copy it */
107   }
```

Figure 6.20   bt_block.c

```
 1     /* bt_block.c - block level stuff */
 2     #include "stdio.h"
 3     #include "btree.h"
 4     #include "bt_macro.h"
 5
 6     extern IX_DESC *pci ;
 7     BLOCK *retrieve_block() ;
 8
 9
10     int find_block(pe,pb,poff,comp_fun)
11                                     /* look for a key in a block */
12     ENTRY *pe ;                     /* contains the target key */
13     BLOCK *pb ;                     /* look in this block */
14     int *poff ;                     /* store offset where we stop here */
15     int (*comp_fun) () ;            /* address of the compare function */
16     {                               /* returns the compare result */
17         int i ;                     /* offset */
18         int ret ;                   /* result of last comparison */
19         ENTRY *p ;
20
21         i = 0 ;
22         while( i < pb->bend )        /* repeat until end of block */
23           { p = ENT_ADR(pb,i) ;      /* get entry address */
24                                      /* compare to target key */
25             ret = call(comp_fun)( pe , ENT_ADR(pb,i) )  ;
26             if( ret <= 0 )           /* quit when the target is */
27                 break ;              /* <= the current entry */
28             i = next_entry(pb,i) ;   /* move to next entry */
29           }
30         *poff = i ;                 /* store offset where we stopped */
31         return( ret ) ;             /* result of last compare */
32     }
33
34
35
36
37     int ins_block(pb,pe,off)         /* add an entry to a block */
38     BLOCK *pb ;                      /* the block */
39     ENTRY *pe ;                      /* the entry to insert */
40     int off ;                        /* the offset where we insert it */
41     {
42         int ne ;
43
44         ne = ENT_SIZE(pe) ;          /* how big is the new insert ? */
45                                      /* move everything to end of block */
46         moveup( pb,off,ne) ;         /* make room for new entry */
47         copy_entry(ENT_ADR(pb,off),pe) ; /* move it in  */
48         pb->bend = pb->bend + ne ;   /* adjust block size */
49     }
50
```

Figure 6.20   bt_block.c (continued)

```
51
52     int del_block(pb,off)              /* remove an entry from a block */
53     BLOCK *pb ;                        /* the block to work on */
54     int off ;                          /* where to remove the entry */
55     {
56         int ne ;
57
58         ne = ENT_SIZE( ENT_ADR(pb,off) ) ; /* get entry size */
59         movedown(pb,off,ne) ;     /* move entries above curr. one down */
60         pb->bend = pb->bend - ne ; /* adjust number of bytes used */
61     }
62
63
64     int moveup(pb,off,n)               /* move part of a block upward */
65     BLOCK *pb ;                        /* the block */
66     int off ;                          /* place to start moving  */
67     int n ;                            /* how far up to move things */
68     {
69         ENTRY *p ;
70
71                                        /* move entries */
72         mover(  ENT_ADR(pb,off+n),     /* to here */
73                 ENT_ADR(pb,off) ,      /* from here */
74                 pb->bend - off) ;      /* rest of the block */
75     }
76
77
78     int movedown(pb,off,n)             /* move part of a block downward */
79     BLOCK *pb ;                        /* the block */
80     int off ;                          /* place to start moving  */
81     int n ;                            /* how far down to move things */
82     {
83         ENTRY *p ;
84
85                                        /* move entries */
86         mover(ENT_ADR(pb,off),         /* to here */
87               ENT_ADR(pb,off+n),       /* from here */
88               pb->bend - (off+n)) ;    /* rest of the block */
89     }
90
91
92     int combine(pl,pr)                 /* combine two blocks */
93     BLOCK *pl ;                        /* add left block */
94     BLOCK *pr ;                        /* to right block */
95     {
96         moveup(pr,0,pl->bend) ;        /* make room for left block */
97                                        /* move in left block contents */
98         mover(ENT_ADR(pr,0),ENT_ADR(pl,0),pl->bend) ;
99         pr->bend = pr->bend + pl->bend ; /* adjust block size */
100    }
```

Figure 6.21   bt_find.c

```
 1    /* bt_find.c - find function */
 2    #include "stdio.h"
 3    #include "btree.h"
 4    #include "bt_macro.h"
 5    extern IX_DESC *pci ;
 6
 7    int find_ix(pe,pix)              /* find first entry with a key */
 8     ENTRY *pe ;                     /* points to key to be matched */
 9                                     /* store the rec. loc. here */
10     IX_DESC *pix ;                  /* points to index descriptor */
11     {                               /* returns success=1 , failure=0 */
12        int ret ;
13        ENTRY tempe ;
14
15        pci = pix ;
16                                     /* be sure target is < dummy */
17        if( call(pci->pcomp) (pe,&pci->dx.dume) >= 0 )
18           { go_last(pix) ;          /*    no - position at end */
19             return( 1 ) ;           /* and return not equal */
20           }
21
22        ret = find_level(pci->dx.nl-1,pe,pci->dx.rb) ;
23        if( ret == 0 )                /* if an entry was found, */
24           { copy_current(0,&tempe); /*    store its record ptr. */
25             pe->rptr=tempe.rptr ;
26           }
27        return( ret ) ;
28     }
29
30
31    int find_level(l,pe,r)          /* find a key within a level */
32     int l ;                        /* the level */
33     ENTRY *pe ;                    /* the target entry */
34     RECPOS r ;                     /* block to look in */
35     {
36        BLOCK b ;
37        int ret , off ;
38
39        retrieve_block(l,r,&b,CURR);/* get current block */
40                                    /* look for the key there */
41        ret = find_block(pe,&b,&off,pci->pcomp) ;
42        CB(l) = r ;                  /* make this the current block */
43        CO(l) = off ;                /* and offset in the block */
44
45        if( l > 0 )                  /* now search lower levels */
46           ret = find_level(l-1,pe,ENT_ADR(&b,off)->rptr) ;
47        return( ret ) ;
48     }
```

find_ix first checks to ensure that the search key is not greater than that of the dummy entry at the end of the index. This is a simple way of ensuring that we do not leave the current position past the dummy entry. find_ix calls find_level to start at the root level. At each level find_level searches the block whose record pointer was an input argument. This establishes the current offset on this level. The record pointer from the current entry supplies the record pointer to be used in a call to find_level for the next lower level.

Note that the scratch block, b, is a local variable. A separate copy is allocated for each level.

bt_ins.c

Figure 6.22 lists the insert_ix function that inserts new entries and the functions that support it. insert_ix calls ins_level to insert the entry at the leaf level. If there is room in the current block, the entry is inserted and the block updated. But if there is no room to insert the entry in the block, split is called to split the block into two blocks.

split copies the current block into an oversize scratch block (allocated in line 69) and inserts the new entry. Then it finds the offset where the block must be split. A new block is allocated in the file to hold the first half of the scratch block's contents. The current block will contain the right half of the scratch block's contents.

Before we carry out the split, we call ins_level to insert a new entry in the higher-level index pointing to the new block. If this step fails, we exit from the split function without finishing the split. This leaves the index file as it was before insert_ix was called. If the call to ins_level was successful, the right and left blocks are formed and updated.

Splitting the current block requires adjusting the current position; what to

Figure 6.22 bt_ins.c

```
1    /* bt_ins.c - insert function */
2    #include "stdio.h"
3    #include "btree.h"
4    #include "bt_macro.h"
5
6
7
8    extern IX_DESC *pci ;
9    extern int split_size ;          /* threshold for splitting a block */
10   extern BLOCK spare_block ;
11
12   int insert_ix(pe,pix)            /* find first entry with a key */
13     ENTRY *pe ;                    /* points to key to be matched */
14                                    /* store the rec. loc. here */
15     IX_DESC *pix ;                 /* points to index descriptor */
```

Figure 6.22   bt_ins.c (continued)

```
16    {                                /* returns success=1 , failure=0 */
17        int ret ;
18        BLOCK b ;
19
20        pci = pix ;
21        ret = ins_level(0,pe,&b) ;  /* insert entry at leaf level */
22
23        if( ret ==IX_OK)            /* if the insertion worked */
24            next_ix(0,&b) ;         /*    move past entry inserted */
25
26        return( ret ) ;             /* return success / failure */
27    }
28
29
30    int ins_level(l,pe,pb)          /* insert an entry at */
31    int l ;                         /* this level */
32    ENTRY *pe ;                     /* points to the entry */
33    BLOCK *pb ;
34    {
35        RECPOS r ;
36        int ret ;
37
38        if( l >= pci->dx.nl )       /* do we need a new level ? */
39            return( IX_FAIL ) ;     /*    yes - overflow */
40
41        retrieve_block(l,CB(l),pb,CURR) ;
42                                    /* does it fit into the block ? */
43        if( (pb->bend + ENT_SIZE(pe)) <= split_size )
44            { ins_block(pb,pe,CO(l)); /*    yes - put entry into block */
45            update_block(pb) ;
46            ret = IX_OK ;
47            }
48        else ret = split(l,pe,pb);  /*    no - split the block */
49
50        return( ret ) ;
51    }
52
53
54    int split(l,pe,pb)              /* split a block into two */
55    int l ;
56    ENTRY *pe ;
57    BLOCK *pb ;
58    {
59        int half , ins_pos , last , ret ;
60        BLOCK *pbb  ;
61        ENTRY e ;
62
63        ins_pos = CO(l) ;           /* remember where insert was */
64
65        if( (l+1) >= pci->dx.nl )    /* check for top level */
66            return( IX_FAIL ) ;     /* (can't split top level block) */
67
68                                    /* allocate a big block */
69        pbb = (BLOCK *) calloc(sizeof(BLOCK)+sizeof(ENTRY),1) ;
70        if( pbb == NULL )           /* did allocation fail ? */
```

Figure 6.22   bt_ins.c (continued)

```
71              return( IX_FAIL ) ;        /*    yes - exit */
72
73                                          /* do insert in big block */
74       pbb->bend = 0 ;
75       combine(pb,pbb);                   /* copy contents of old buffer */
76       ins_block(pbb,pe,CO(1));           /* insert new entry */
77
78                                          /* now find where to split */
79                                          /* no more than 1/2 in left block */
80       last =   scan_blk(pbb, pbb->bend/2 ) ; /* start of last entry */
81                                          /* in left half of big block */
82       half = next_entry(pbb,last);/* end of left half */
83
84                             /* allocate disk space for left block */
85       if( get_block(1,pbb) == IX_FAIL )   /* check for failure */
86         { free(pbb) ;
87           return( IX_FAIL) ;
88         }
89                                   /* make an entry for the new block */
90                                   /* on the upper level */
91       copy_entry(&e,ENT_ADR(pbb,last) ) ;
92       e.rptr = pbb->brec ;        /* point entry to our left block */
93
94       ret=ins_level(1+1,&e,pb);  /* inserting new index entry  */
95                                  /* for left block at higher level */
96                                  /* (this makes the l+1 position */
97                                  /*  point to the left block) */
98        if( ret != IX_OK )        /* check for higher level failure */
99           { free(pbb) ;          /*    yes - free big block area */
100            put_free(pbb) ;       /*          free new index block */
101            return( ret ) ;       /*          return failure code */
102         }
103
104                                  /* use pb for right block */
105      mover(ENT_ADR(pb,0),ENT_ADR(pbb,half),pbb->bend-half) ;
106      pb->bend = pbb->bend - half ;
107      pb->brec = CB(1) ;          /* restore block's location */
108      pb->lvl  = 1 ;              /* and its level */
109      update_block(pb) ;          /* and update it */
110
111                                  /* fix up left block */
112      pbb->bend = half ;          /* size = left half */
113                                  /* entries already in place */
114      update_block(pbb) ;         /* update left block */
115
116                                  /* adjust current position */
117      if( ins_pos >= half )       /* is curr. entry in left or right? */
118         { CO(1) = CO(1)-half ;   /*   right - adjust offset   */
119           next_ix(1+1,pb);       /*            upper level pos. */
120         }
121      else CB(1) = e.rptr ;       /*   left - make left block current */
122      free(pbb) ;                 /* free the big scratch block */
123
124      return( ret ) ;
125    }
```

adjust depends on whether the new position is in the left or right block. Lines 117 to 121 perform this adjustment. ins_level and split leave the current position at the entry just inserted. This is what we want for higher levels, but insert_ix advances the final position so that it is after the entry inserted. Thus, a series of insertions leave the entries in the order of insertion.

The recursive function, find_level (Figure 6.21), declares a local variable to store the current block each time it is called. The insertion functions use a different strategy: They use a single memory area for all levels. But since a split at one level may require further splits at higher levels, each call to split allocates its own oversize scratch block.

insert_ix is a very low-level function. It is up to the calling program to ensure that the index file is positioned where the entry belongs. The find_ins function discussed later searches for the right position before inserting an entry. It is safer and would normally be used.

bt_del.c

The source file in Figure 6.23 shows several functions that implement entry deletion. The application program calls delete_ix to delete an entry at the current position. delete_ix calls del_level to delete the current entry at the current level. If the current block is more than half-full, delete_ix updates the block. But if the block is empty after the deletion, the block is returned to the free list, and the upper-level entry that points to the block is deleted (by calling del_level). Since the current block has been deleted, the current position at this level and below must be re-established. Figure 6.24 shows this situation before such a deletion and after.

If a block is not empty but less than half-full, the compress function tries to combine it with a neighboring block on the left or right. This requires that the neighbor block exist and that the contents of both blocks fit in one block.

Lines 78 to 89 in Figure 6.23 combine the current block with its left neighbor, while lines 91 to 101 combine it with its right neighbor. The two cases are similar but there are some differences. In both cases we place the combined contents into the right of the two blocks and remove the left block. The left block is freed and the higher-level entry that pointed to it is deleted by calling del_level. The current position is adjusted after combining blocks; the adjustment needed differs for the two cases.

Deleting entries has lots of complicated exception cases to be handled. If the last entry in a block is deleted, the key value in the higher-level entry that points to the block must be replaced by that of the new last entry. Figure 6.25 shows an example: deleting the DOT entry from the tree in Figure 6.24a. The fix_last and replace_entry functions implement this replacement. Since the new key may be different in length from the old value, the process is like a deletion followed by an insertion. A relation exception occurs when a deletion leaves the current position at the end of a block. Lines 58 and 59 in Figure 6.23 check for this condition and, if

Figure 6.23 *bt_del.c*

```
1    /* bt_del.c - delete function */
2    #include "stdio.h"
3    #include "btree.h"
4    #include "bt_macro.h"
5    extern int split_size ;          /* split block threshold */
6    extern IX_DESC *pci ;
7    extern int comb_size ;           /* threshold for combining blocks */
8    BLOCK *neighbor() ;
9
10
11   int delete_ix(pix)               /* delete current entry */
12    IX_DESC *pix ;                  /* points to index descriptor */
13    {                               /* returns success=1 , failure=0 */
14       ENTRY tempe ;
15       BLOCK b ;
16       int ret ;
17
18       pci = pix ;
19                                    /* check for dummy entry at end-of-ix */
20       copy_current(0,&tempe) ;
21       if( call(pci->pcomp)(&tempe,& pci->dx.dume) == 0 )
22           return( IX_FAIL ) ;
23                                        /* not at end - delete it */
24       ret = del_level(0,&b) ;
25
26       return( ret ) ;
27    }
28
29
30   int del_level(l,pb)              /* delete entry within the level */
31    int l ;
32    BLOCK *pb ;
33    {
34       RECPOS r ;
35       int ret ;
36       ENTRY tempe ;
37
38       ret = IX_OK ;
39       retrieve_block(l,CB(l),pb,CURR) ; /* get current block */
40       del_block(pb,CO(l)) ;       /* delete the entry in the block */
41
42       if( pb->bend == 0 )         /* block now empty? */
43          { put_free(pb) ;         /* yes - free the block */
44            ret = del_level(l+1,pb);/* delete entry for empty block */
45            copy_current(l+1,&tempe) ;/* get new curr. block ptr. */
46            first_ix(l,pb,tempe.rptr);/* reset pos. for lower levels */
47            return( ret ) ;
48          }
49       if( CO(l) >= pb->bend )      /* last entry in block deleted ? */
50          {                        /* yes - correct upper index */
51            fix_last(l,pb->brec,ENT_ADR(pb,last_entry(pb))) ;
52          }
53       if( pb->bend < comb_size)    /* less than half full ? */
54            ret = compress(l,pb) ;  /* yes - try combine with neigh. */
55       else update_block(pb) ;
```

Figure 6.23 bt_del.c (continued)

```
56
57          retrieve_block(1,CB(1),pb,CURR) ; /* get our block again */
58          if( CO(1) >= pb->bend )     /* is position past end of block? */
59              first_ix(1,pb,next_ix(1+1)) ;/* yes - move to next block */
60          return( ret ) ;
61      }
62
63
64      int compress(1,pb)                  /* combine a block with a neighbor */
65      int l ;
66      BLOCK *pb ;                         /* the block to be combined */
67      {
68          int nb ;
69          BLOCK *pt ;
70          ENTRY tempe ;
71
72
73          if( (1+1) == pci->dx.nl )    /* is this the root level ? */
74              { update_block(pb) ;     /*     yes - update the block */
75                return( IX_OK ) ;      /*            and return */
76              }
77
78          pt = neighbor(1,LEFTN) ;     /* get left neighbor block */
79          if(    (pt != NULL)
80              && (pt->bend +pb->bend <= IXB_SPACE) )
81              { combine(pt,pb) ;            /* combine blocks */
82                update_block(pb) ;          /* update right block */
83                put_free(pt) ;              /* free the left index block */
84                                            /* CB(1) is OK as is */
85                CO(1) = CO(1) + pt->bend ; /* adjust our curr. pos. */
86                last_ix(1+1,pb) ;           /* point higher level to left blk. */
87                del_level(1+1,pb) ;     /* delete ptr. to left block */
88                return( IX_OK ) ;
89              }
90
91          pt = neighbor(1,RIGHTN) ;   /* get right neighbor block */
92          if(    (pt != NULL)
93              && (pt->bend +pb->bend <= IXB_SPACE) )
94              { combine(pb,pt) ;            /* combine blocks */
95                update_block(pt) ;          /* update right block */
96                CB(1) = pt->brec ;          /* right block is curr. one now */
97                                            /* CO(1) is ok as is */
98                put_free(pb);               /* free the left block */
99                del_level(1+1,pb) ;     /* delete ptr. to left block */
100               return( IX_OK ) ;
101             }
102
103         update_block(pb) ;              /* can't combine - just update blk. */
104         return( IX_OK ) ;
105     }
106
107
108
109     int fix_last(1,r,pe)                /* fix higher level index */
110     int l ;                             /* level we are on */
```

Figure 6.23   bt_del.c (continued)

```
111     RECPOS r ;                          /* rptr for higher level entry */
112     ENTRY *pe ;                         /* entry with new key */
113     {
114         ENTRY tempe ;
115                            /* last entry in a block deleted/replaced */
116                            /* update higher level index */
117         copy_entry(&tempe,pe) ;          /* copy key */
118         tempe.rptr = r ;                 /* put in the record pointer */
119         return( replace_entry(1+1,&tempe) ) ; /* replace the entry */
120     }
121
122
123     int replace_entry(l,pe)             /* replace current index entry */
124      int l ;                             /* at this index level */
125     ENTRY *pe ;                          /* new entry */
126     {
127         BLOCK b ;
128         int ret ;
129
130         retrieve_block(l,CB(l),&b,CURR) ;   /* get the index block */
131         if( CO(l) == last_entry(&b))/* is this the last entry ? */
132             fix_last(l,CB(l),pe) ;  /*     yes - fix up higher lvl */
133
134         del_block(&b,CO(l)) ;           /* remove the current entry */
135                                         /* room to insert the new entry */
136         if( (b.bend + ENT_SIZE(pe)) <= split_size )
137           { ins_block(&b,pe,CO(l)) ;/*    yes - insert in the block */
138             update_block(&b) ;      /*           and update the block */
139             ret = IX_OK ;
140           }
141         else ret = split(l,pe,&b) ; /*    no - split the block */
142         return(ret));
143     }
```

found, reset the position to be at the first entry in the next block. The call to next_ix advances the higher-level position and returns the record pointer to the new current block. Calling first_ix sets the current position to the first entry in this block and also sets the position of lower levels down to the leaf level.

Like insert_ix, the delete_ix function requires that the current position in the index file be established before it is called. The find_del function searches for the entry first to set the current position and then calls delete_ix.

bt_low.c

The neighbor function in Figure 6.26 looks for the left or right neighbor of the current block. It first retrieves the current block for the next higher level and checks for the presence of a neighbor block. If the requested neighbor block exists, it is

Figure 6.24   Deleting the only entry in a block

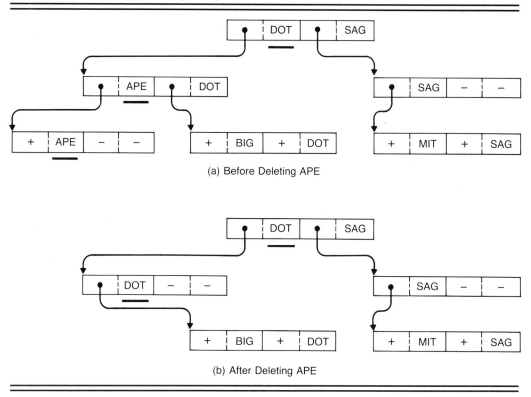

(a) Before Deleting APE

(b) After Deleting APE

Figure 6.25   deleting the last entry in a block

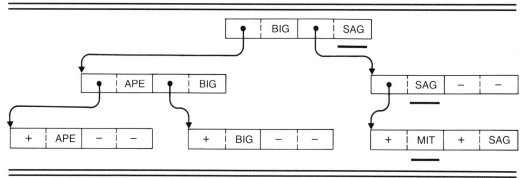

Figure 6.26   bt_low.c

```
1    /* bt_low.c - low level functions for BTREE module */
2    #include "stdio.h"
3    #include "btree.h"
4    #include "bt_macro.h"
5
6    extern IX_DESC *pci ;
7    extern BLOCK spare_block ;
8
9    BLOCK *neighbor(l,direction)     /* get block to right of curr. one */
10     int l ;                        /* level to fetch neighbor on */
11     int direction ;                /* left or right neighbor */
12     {
13         RECPOS rnext ;
14         int off ;
15         BLOCK *pb ;
16
17         pb = & spare_block ;
18         l = l + 1 ;                 /* look in higher level index */
19         retrieve_block(l,CB(l),pb,CURR) ;
20                                     /* get offset on next/prev. entry */
21         if( direction == RIGHTN )
22             off = next_entry(pb,CO(l));/* get offset of next entry */
23         else
24             off = prev_entry(pb,CO(l));
25                                     /* get offset of previous entry */
26         if( off < 0 )               /* at end or beginning ? */
27             return( NULL ) ;
28         rnext = ENT_ADR(pb,off)->rptr ;    /* neighbor's block no. */
29                                     /* read it into memory */
30         retrieve_block(l-1,rnext,pb,NOT_CURR) ;
31         return( pb ) ;       /* return its address */
32     }
33
34
35   int copy_current(l,pe)          /* copy current index entry */
36     int l ;                        /* at this level */
37     ENTRY *pe ;                    /* to this address */
38     {
39         BLOCK *pb ;
40
41         pb = & spare_block ;
42         retrieve_block(l,CB(l),pb,CURR);/* get curr. block */
43                                     /* copy current entry */
44         copy_entry(pe,ENT_ADR(pb,CO(l) ) ) ;
45         return( IX_OK ) ;
46     }
```

retrieved and placed in the spare block structure. An input argument specifies the left or right neighbor block.

The copy_current function gets the entry at the current position on a specified level. It first retrieves the current block and then copies the entry at the current offset.

bt_top.c

The functions discussed also provide the capabilities we need for managing index files. However, they are rather low level and dangerous. For example, when using insert_ix, if the current position is not set correctly, then index entries may get out of order. The functions in Figure 6.27 are more convenient to use and safer.

find_exact searches for the presence of an entry in an index file. It uses find_ix to get to the first entry whose key matches the search value. Calls to get_next retrieve subsequent entries until the key field no longer matches the search value. The search may also stop when an entry is found with the same record pointer value as well as the same key value. Like find_ix, find_exact serves two purposes: It checks for the presence of an entry and sets the current position. If the search entry was not found, the find_exact function sets the current position after all entries with the search key.

find_ins uses find_exact to verify that the entry to be inserted is not already present. If not, the new entry is inserted at the current position that find_exact set.

find_del checks for the presence of an entry using find_exact and, if it is found, calls delete_ix to delete it.

6.6 Analyzing BTREE

□ The operation of the BTREE module is complex, and it is not obvious how well it performs. This section lists some important questions about the way BTREE uses RAM memory and the amount of disk I/O it performs. The answers are derived from analyzing the source code.

Q. How much RAM memory does BTREE require to store blocks?

Different functions allocate space for blocks differently so the requirement is different for each function. find_ix requires one block per tree level, or 4 Kbytes. insert_ix requires 1 Kbyte with 1.1 Kbyte for each of the three level splits, or 4.3 Kbytes. delete_ix requires 1 Kbyte with 1 Kbyte for replace_entry on three levels—a total of 4 Kbytes. The spare_block variable is allocated statically so it is always present. The cache buffers require 4 Kbytes per open index file. The total is 5 Kbytes plus 4 Kbytes per open index, or 9 Kbytes for a single index.

Figure 6.27   bt_top.c

```
1    /* bt_top.c - find_exact, find_ins find_del functions */
2    #include "stdio.h"
3    #include "btree.h"
4    #include "bt_macro.h"
5    extern IX_DESC *pci ;
6
7    int find_exact(pe,pix)          /* find entry with same key & rptr */
8    ENTRY *pe ;                     /* put the entry here */
9    IX_DESC *pix ;                  /* points to an index descriptor */
10   {
11       int ret ;
12       ENTRY e ;
13
14       pci = pix ;
15       copy_entry(&e,pe) ;         /* make copy for find call */
16       ret = find_ix(&e,pix);      /* get first entry that matches key */
17
18       while( ret == 0 )           /* keep going until keys don't match */
19           { if( e.rptr==pe->rptr)    /* compare rec. ptrs */
20                 return( 0 ) ;        /* return if they match */
21                                      /* ptrs. not same - continue */
22             if( get_next(&e,pix) == EOIX ) /* get next entry */
23                 return( 1 ) ;        /*   at end-of-index - not found */
24             ret = call(pci->pcomp) (&e,pe) ; /* compare keys */
25           }
26       return( ret ) ;             /* not found - non-zero code */
27   }
28
29
30   int find_ins(pe,pix)            /* find position, insert an entry */
31   ENTRY *pe ;                     /* the entry */
32   IX_DESC *pix ;                  /* points to an index descriptor */
33   {                               /* returns IX_FAIL if entry present */
34       int ret ;
35       ENTRY tempe ;
36
37       if(find_exact(pe,pix) == 0) /* look for the entry */
38           return( IX_FAIL ) ;     /*    already there - failure */
39                                   /* the find set the curr. pos. */
40       return(insert_ix(pe,pix)) ; /* do the insertion */
41   }
42
43
44   int find_del(pe,pix)            /* find position, delete an entry */
45   ENTRY *pe ;                     /* the entry */
46   IX_DESC *pix ;                  /* points to an index descriptor */
47   {                               /* returns IX_FAIL if not found */
48       int ret ;
49       ENTRY tempe ;
50
51       if(find_exact(pe,pix) !=0)  /* look for the entry */
52           return( IX_FAIL ) ;     /*    not there - failure */
53                                   /* the find set the curr. pos. */
54       return(delete_ix(pix)) ;    /* delete the current entry */
55   }
```

Q. What is the effect of forcing the tree to be of maximum height?

A maximum of 3 Kbytes of disk space is wasted for small index files that actually need only one level. The cost in RAM space is 1 Kbyte plus 1 Kbyte per open index file for each extra level in the tree. Since nontrivial index files would have at least two levels, the cost would be 4 Kbytes at most with a single index file open.

Performance is not affected much. Those tree levels that are not really needed have a single index block that stays in the cache buffer. Thus, there is little extra disk I/O.

Q. The functions seem to call retrieve_block **a number of times.**
For example, calls to copy_current **retrieve a block that**
has already been retrieved in another function.
Doesn't this hurt performance?

BTREE was designed with maximum separation of its parts so functions make minimal assumptions about what has already been retrieved. This approach relies heavily on the cache scheme to avoid actual disk I/O on the extra calls to retrieve_block.

Q. How many disk I/O operations are needed for common
operations such as find_ix, find_ins, **and** find_del?

Assume that the index file has two levels with more than one index block. Then find_ix would require two disk reads. In the common case, an insertion or deletion does not require splitting or combining blocks. So find_ins or find_del require the same two read operations and a single write operation. (This also assumes that the key value occurs in only a few entries.) A call to get_next, get_previous, or get_current does not require any disk I/O in the normal case since the current block is in the cache for each level.

Q. The linear search used to find a match for a key in a
block is not very sophisticated. Would a fancier
algorithm like a binary search speed BTREE up much?

The important bottleneck is in disk I/O operations. The effect of a faster method of searching a block would be minimal. BTREE does make lots of function calls, and that seems to add perhaps half a second to the response time for an operation. In practice, single insertion and deletions and searches seem to take a second or two even with the index file on a floppy disk.

6.7   Testing BTREE

□   The BTREE module is larger and more complex than the programs presented in earlier chapters. The methods we presented also apply to testing BTREE and are even more important. The complexity and size of the BTREE module makes it vital to structure BTREE in a modular way and to test each function thoroughly.

There are many exception conditions to be tested—for example, insertions that cause blocks to split and deletions that require combining a block with its neighbor. If we test the BTREE module as a whole without testing each module, it is very difficult to force the occurrence of exception conditions. Creating index files for each case can be a nightmare. When we test functions individually, we can use dummy I/O functions and force the conditions we want. Thus, thorough unit tests are the first step.

Testing the module as a whole is still necessary. When we create and update real index files, we can use the FILEDUMP program from Chapter 4 to examine the index file. Finding out exactly what is in the file after an update is important, not just checking to see if listing the contents seems to produce the expected result. It takes a lot of data to fill 1,024-byte index blocks, and building large test files to test exception conditions is very difficult. But we can set the split_size and comp_size variables to force exception conditions to occur for much smaller files.

Several functions in the BTREE module are recursive. It is often useful to track how many times such functions are called by inserting a printf statement at the beginning of the function. For example, the following statement was used in the ins_level function:

```
printf(" called ins_level − l = %d  pe = %x  pb = %x \ n",1,pe,pb);
```

6.8   BTREE Enhancements

□   Some limitations and simplifications were necessary to keep the BTREE module small enough to list and simple enough to discuss. This section discusses removing those limitations along with other enhancements.

Removing Limitations

BTREE manages free space for index blocks in a static way. We specify the size of the index file when it is created. A more flexible approach would be to allow BTREE to extend the index file when the free list was empty. This would reduce the space needed for small index files since they could grow later.

BTREE does not allow the index tree to grow in height or shrink. This also makes the index file larger than necessary for small numbers of entries. Removing this limitation requires code in bt_ins.c to split the root block and create a new index level. Support for shrinking the height of the index tree would be required in bt_del.c as well.

We used a dummy entry with a key value greater than any allowed for a normal entry. This might be inconvenient for some types of keys. Removing the need for a dummy entry requires support for more exceptions like inserting an entry at the end of the index.

Better Error Handling

BTREE needs more error checking to make it really bulletproof. Disk file read and write operations may produce errors; BTREE should check for them and recover gracefully. Index files may be corrupted so that the format of index blocks is invalid. For example, the file may be missing the dummy entry; the size field, bend, in a block may be invalid; the data in the descriptor block may be invalid. The pointers in index blocks may be scrambled so that two upper-level index blocks point to the same block. An index block may be pointed to by an upper-level block and also be on the free list. BTREE should validate everything it reads from an index file.

Since index files are created and used only through the BTREE module, you may wonder why we need to validate its contents. But the index file may be corrupted through misuse of DOS commands or through bugs in DOS or another program as well as in the BTREE module. A common reason for inconsistencies is that a power failure occurred while an update was in process (or the user turned off the computer before exiting from a program).

Utilities

Since index files may become corrupted, we need some utilities to help with the problem. A standalone program that can quickly check the integrity of an index file is good for peace of mind. A repair program that can restore a damaged index file to consistency is another worthwhile utility.

The key to checking for and restoring data integrity is redundancy in the information stored. We recorded the level number within each block so we could interpret the use of each block without any other source of information. That redundancy could be used to restore an index using only the leaf-level blocks.

Better Use of Storage

Our caching scheme is simple and adequate for one or a few indexes. But if a number of indexes were to be open at the same time, a common pool of buffers for caching would be more efficient in using RAM memory. Another way to reduce the amount of RAM required is to work with the cache buffers directly. We separated working space for blocks from the cache buffers to make the module easier to understand and debug. After the module works and we understand it well, optimizing it at the expense of simplicity is a reasonable next step.

Coupling BTREE with Data Record Management

Most B-TREE file management modules handle both the index and storage of the associated data records. As a result, they lack flexibility to handle the most interesting problems. Our BTREE module handles only the index and does it at a fairly low level. This makes it a flexible tool for a variety of applications. You may wish to build a module that uses BTREE to provide integrated management of the index and the data record.

Key Compression

In some applications, the size of an index file may be reduced by a factor of two or more by storing key values in a compressed form. One method used with character string keys is to store the difference between a key and the one that precedes it in an index block. The part of the key that is the same is replaced by a count of characters that are equal. For example:

Keys	*Stored as*
Kettle	0 Kettle
Key	2 y
Kidney	1 idney
Lion	0 Lion

This compression scheme can be very effective on large files where successive keys differ little. The keys can also be truncated to the minimum needed to distinguish them from their neighbors at the expense of retrieving the data record to compare a search value to the full key.

A File Manager Application

Chapter 5 developed a merge program that accepts the description of record type and sort key type when the program is run. We could develop a file manager that accepts a similar description of record and key type. This single program could be used to scan and update a number of files with different applications.

A number of file manager programs are available that work this way. But

Figure 6.28   Document index application

Name

doccreat, docindex, docscan—programs to index documents by name of addressee, date sent, and subject

Function

These programs build and maintain an index of correspondence documents. The documents are not stored by the programs, just their file names. doccreat creates a new document index. docindex adds new documents to the index. docscan locates documents based on a search value for the addressee, date, or subject attribute. docscan lists all document references that match the specified criteria. A partial value may be specified for the search. All documents whose attribute matches the search value are displayed.

Usage

    a>doccreat docs 15000   creates a document index named
                                       docs with a 15,000 byte index file

    A>docindex docs   executes the docindex program
       doc . . . name : abc.let
       addressee : smith, fred
       date sent (yy/mm/dd) : 84/08/05
       subject : widget sales
       doc . . . name :
    A>

docindex prompts for a document's name and its attributes. Pressing return (and entering a null document name) ends execution.

    A>docscan docs
       which field to scan ?
       a = addressee / d = date / s = subject : s
       value to look for: widget

       document file name: abc.let
       addressed to: smith, fred
       date sent: 84/08/05
       subject : widget sales

       document file name: weekly.rep
       addressed to: jones, sam
       date sent: 84/08/07
       subject : widget production
       . . .
    A>

Notes

1. Dates must be entered in the form shown: year then month then day. Each part must be two digits with slashes between them.
2. All letters should be entered as lower case. The programs distinguish uppercase and lowercase.
3. No attempt is made to verify dates, document names, or the field type for docscan.

even if you do not need to write your own program, our BTREE module should show you what is involved.

6.9   A Simple Application: Indexing Correspondence

□   Our discussion of the BTREE module is not complete without a concrete example of its use. We could build a simple mailing list program that indexed records by name and zip code (or some other filing application with structured records), but such applications are rather common. Instead we present a set of programs to index correspondence documents. The manual page in Figure 6.28 describes the document index programs.

The programs do not store documents; they just record the document's name indexed by the addressee's name, the date sent, and the subject. Figure 6.29 shows a data structure describing a document. The document's name and its attributes are stored as character strings.

Separate programs—doccreat, docindex, and docscan—create the document index files, add document references, and scan for documents on a specified subject, date, or addressee. The doccreat program shown in Figure 6.30 creates two files: an index file and a data file. Since the BTREE module allocates free blocks for the index file when the file is created, doccreat prompts for and accepts a file size value.

The docindex program shown in Figure 6.31 adds new document references to the index. For each document, a record is appended to the data file with the document's name, addressee, date sent, and subject. The single index file contains three entries for each document—one for each field indexed.

The loop in lines 43 to 52 collects input for each document, records it in the data file, and then adds index entries. The input function in lines 58 to 74 prompts for each field in the document record. The getstr function from Chapter 1 collects

Figure 6.29   document.h

```
 1    /* document.h - defines document data structure */
 2
 3                           /* lengths of document fields */
 4    #define NAME_LEN 65
 5    #define ADR_LEN  40
 6    #define DATE_LEN 10
 7    #define SUBJ_LEN 40
 8
 9    typedef struct
10      { char dname[NAME_LEN] ;        /* document file name */
11        char addressee[ADR_LEN] ;     /* person document sent to */
12        char date[DATE_LEN] ;         /* date the document was sent */
13        char subject[SUBJ_LEN] ;      /* subject of the document */
14      } DOCUMENT ;
```

Figure 6.30   doccreat.c

```
 1    /* doccreat.c - creat a document index and data file */
 2    #include "stdio.h"
 3    #include "cminor.h"
 4    #include "btree.h"
 5    #include "bt_macro.h"
 6
 7    #define WR_MODE  1                    /* write access for open */
 8
 9    extern ENTRY dume ;
10    extern int ndum ;
11
12    main(argc,argv)
13     int argc ;
14     char *argv[] ;
15     {
16        int ret ;
17        char fn[65] ;
18        RECPOS fs ;
19
20        if( argc < 3 )
21          {  printf(" USAGE - doccreat doc-file-name file_size \n");
22             exit(5) ;
23          }
24
25        add_str(fn,argv[1],".idx") ;
26
27        ret = sscanf(argv[2],"%ld",&fs) ;
28        if( (ret == 0) || (fs < 0) )
29          {  printf(" bad file size specification \n");
30             exit(6) ;
31          }
32
33        if( creatix(fn,fs,&dume,ndum) < 0 )
34          {  printf(" can't create the index file \n");
35             exit(10) ;
36          }
37
38        add_str(fn,argv[1],".dat") ;
39        ret = gcreat(fn,WR_MODE,BIN_MODE) ;
40        if( ret < 0 )
41          {  printf(" can't create the data file \n");
42             exit(12) ;
43          }
44        close(ret) ;
45     }
```

Figure 6.31   docindex.c

```
1     /* docindex.c - index a new document */
2     #include "stdio.h"
3     #include "cminor.h"
4     #include "document.h"
5     #include "btree.h"
6     #include "bt_macro.h"
7
8     int compf() ;
9     int sizef() ;
10    #define RW_MODE 2              /* read & write allowed */
11    #define EOF_REL 2              /* seek relative to End-Of-File */
12    long lseek() ;
13
14    main(argc,argv)
15     int argc ;
16     char *argv[] ;
17     {
18       int ret , datfile ;
19       char fn[65] ;
20       RECPOS fs , r ;
21       IX_DESC ixd ;
22       DOCUMENT doc ;
23
24       if( argc < 2 )
25         { printf(" USAGE - docindex doc-file-name \n");
26            exit(5) ;
27         }
28
29       add_str(fn,argv[1],".idx") ;
30       if( openix(fn,&ixd,compf,sizef) < 0 )
31         { printf(" can't open the index file \n");
32            exit(10) ;
33         }
34
35       add_str(fn,argv[1],".dat") ;
36       datfile = gopen(fn,RW_MODE,BIN_MODE) ;
37       if( datfile < 0 )
38         { printf(" can't open the data file \n");
39            closeix(&ixd) ;
40            exit(12) ;
41         }
42
43       while( 1 )                     /* collect and index doc. names */
44         { if( input(&doc) <= 0 )    /* get input for next doc. */
45              break ;                 /* exit if at end */
46           r = lseek(datfile,0L,EOF_REL) ;/* append the doc. record */
47           ret = write(datfile,&doc,sizeof(DOCUMENT) ) ; /* at EOF */
48           if( indexit(&doc,r,&ixd) < 0 )    /* index the document */
49              { printf(" indexing failed \n");
50                break ;
51              }
52         }
53
54       closeix(&ixd) ;
55       close(datfile) ;
```

Figure 6.31   docindex.c (continued)

```
56      }
57
58      int input(pdoc)                    /* get input describing a document */
59        DOCUMENT *pdoc ;
60        {
61          int ret ;
62
63          printf("\n document name (return to quit): ");
64          ret = getstr(pdoc->dname,NAME_LEN-1) ;
65          if( ret <= 0 )
66              return( -1 ) ;
67          printf(" addressed to: ");
68          getstr(pdoc->addressee,ADR_LEN-1) ;
69          printf(" date sent (yy/mm/dd): ");
70          getstr(pdoc->date,DATE_LEN-1) ;
71          printf(" subject: ");
72          getstr(pdoc->subject,SUBJ_LEN-1) ;
73          return( 1 ) ;
74        }
75
76      indexit(pdoc,r,pix)                 /* index the document */
77        DOCUMENT *pdoc ;
78        RECPOS r ;
79        IX_DESC *pix ;
80        {
81          ENTRY e ;
82
83          e.rptr = r ;
84          add_str(e.key,"A*",pdoc->addressee) ;
85          if( find_ins(&e,pix) != IX_OK )
86              return( -1 ) ;
87          add_str(e.key,"D*",pdoc->date) ;
88          if( find_ins(&e,pix) != IX_OK )
89              return( -1 ) ;
90          add_str(e.key,"S*",pdoc->subject) ;
91          if( find_ins(&e,pix) != IX_OK )
92              return( -1 ) ;
93          return( 0 ) ;
94        }
```

a line of console input for each field. A null string for the document name is interpreted as the signal to exit the program.

Lines 46 to 51 append the document record to the end of the data file. A check is made to see if the operation was successful.

The indexit function in lines 76 to 94 constructs index entries and inserts them in the index file. The first two characters of the index key field distinguish the different types of entries. Since we are not inserting entries in order by key value, we use the find_ins function to establish the position in the index first.

Figure 6.32 lists the docscan program. The scan_input function in lines 65 to 80 prompts for the type of field for which we want to scan and a value for the

Figure 6.32   docscan.c

```
1     /* docscan.c - scan indexed documents */
2     #include "stdio.h"
3     #include "ctype.h"
4     #include "cminor.h"
5     #include "document.h"
6     #include "btree.h"
7     #include "bt_macro.h"
8
9     #define BOF_REL   0            /* seek relative to Begin. Of File */
10    #define RW_MODE   2            /* read & write access */
11    int compf() ;
12    int sizef() ;
13
14    main(argc,argv)
15     int argc ;
16     char *argv[] ;
17     {
18        int ret , datfile , line ;
19        char fn[65] ;
20        RECPOS fs ;
21        IX_DESC ixd ;
22        ENTRY e , e2 ;
23        DOCUMENT doc ;
24
25        if( argc < 2 )
26          { printf(" USAGE - docscan doc-file-name \n");
27             exit(5) ;
28          }
29
30        add_str(fn,argv[1],".idx") ;
31        if( openix(fn,&ixd,compf,sizef) < 0 )
32          { printf(" can't open the file \n");
33             exit(11) ;
34          }
35
36        add_str(fn,argv[1],".dat") ;
37        datfile = gopen(fn,RW_MODE,BIN_MODE) ;
38        if( datfile < 0 )
39          { printf(" can't open the data file  \n");
40             closeix(&ixd) ;
41             exit(12) ;
42          }
43
44        scan_input(e.key) ;
45        ret = find_ix(&e,&ixd) ;
46        get_current(&e2,&ixd) ;      /* find out where we are */
47        line = 0 ;
48        while( cmp_part(e.key,e2.key) == 0 )
49          { lseek(datfile,e2.rptr,BOF_REL) ; /* retrieve the data */
50             read(datfile,&doc,sizeof(DOCUMENT)) ;
51             if( line >= 20 )
52               { printf("\n press a key for more \n") ;
53                  getkey() ;
54                  line = 0 ;
55               }
```

Figure 6.32   docscan.c (continued)

```
56              display_doc(&doc) ;
57              line = line + 5 ;
58              if( get_next(&e2,&ixd)   == EOIX )
59                  break ;
60          }
61      closeix(&ixd) ;
62  }
63
64
65  int scan_input(s)
66    char s[] ;
67    {
68        char ans[81] ;
69
70        printf(" which field to scan ? \n");
71        printf(" a = Addressee / d = Date / s = Subject :");
72        getstr(ans,80) ;
73        s[0] = toupper(ans[0]) ;
74        s[1] = '*' ;
75        s[2] = '\0' ;
76
77        printf(" value to look for: ");
78        getstr(ans,ADR_LEN-1) ;
79        strcat(s,ans) ;
80    }
81
82
83  int display_doc(pdoc)               /* display one document record */
84    DOCUMENT *pdoc ;
85    {
86        printf("\n document file name: %s \n",pdoc->dname);
87        printf(" addressed to: %s \n",pdoc->addressee);
88        printf(" date sent: %s \n",pdoc->date) ;
89        printf(" subject: %s \n",pdoc->subject) ;
90    }
```

field. It constructs a search key with the type of field—A, D, or S at the front of the key.

The loop in lines 48 to 60 fetches consecutive entries until an entry fails to match the search key. For each entry, we read the corresponding document record and display it. The find_ix function positions the index file at the first entry less than or equal to the search key. Since find_ix does not provide the entry where the search stopped, we call current entry to get this entry. Calls to get_next advance our position and retrieve subsequent entries.

This loop resembles that in the find_exact function. But we use a partial compare function to determine if we should accept the entry. This is a practical requirement because we may not remember the full name of an addressee or the entire subject name of a document. This *generic key* capability of searching an index for all keys that begin with the search value is often useful. While we did not provide it in the BTREE module, our design allows it to be constructed easily.

Figure 6.33   doc_util.c

```
1      /* doc_util.c - utilities for document index programs */
2      #include "stdio.h"
3      #include "ctype.h"
4
5      int cmp_part(s1,s2)             /* compare all chars in s1 to s2 */
6       char s1[] ;                    /* first string */
7       char s2[] ;                    /* second string */
8       {
9          int i , n , ret ;
10
11         n = strlen(s1) ;
12         for(i=0 ; i<n ;i=i+1)       /* compare no chars in s1 */
13            { ret = tolower(s1[i]) - tolower(s2[i]) ;
14               if( ret != 0 )
15                  break ;
16            }
17         return( ret ) ;
18      }
19
20
21      int add_str(result,s1,s2)       /* concatenate two strings */
22       char result[] ;               /* put the completed result here */
23       char s1[] ;                   /* first string */
24       char s2[] ;                   /* second string   */
25       {
26          strcpy(result,s1) ;
27          strcat(result,s2) ;
28      }
```

Figure 6.33 shows the partial comparison function, **cmp.part**, and the **add_str** function used to combine character strings. Figure 6.34 shows compare and entry size functions for character string keys.

Our document index application is quite simple. We omitted features and error checking to keep it short. Better verification of input and better checking for errors would be useful improvements. Allowing dates to be entered in the natural mm/dd/yy form with single digits for month and day would make the programs easier to use as would ignoring uppercase and lowercase in searches. A facility for deleting old document records would be necessary in a real application, but our simple application should give a useful example of using BTREE.

6.10   Summary

□   We have presented a usable module for building and maintaining index files. Our BTREE module provides a low level of support; it is a tool for building applications that require keyed access to data records. The low-level primitives allow you to tailor your application.

Figure 6.34   varsize.c

```
1
2      /* compare and size functions - char[16] keys */
3      #include "stdio.h"
4      #include "btree.h"
5      #include "bt_macro.h"
6
7      #define KEY_SIZE   16              /* max length of a key */
8
9      int ndum = 20 ;                    /* length of dummy entry */
10
11     ENTRY dume =                       /* dummy entry with high key */
12        { NULLREC , { 0xff , 0xff , 0xff , 0xff ,
13                      0xff , 0xff , 0xff , 0xff ,
14                      0xff , 0xff , 0xff , 0xff ,
15                      0xff , 0xff , 0xff , 0x0 } } ;
16
17
18     int compf(p1,p2)
19       ENTRY *p1 , *p2 ;
20       {
21            return( strcmp(& p1->key,& p2->key) ) ;
22       }
23
24     int sizef(p1)
25       ENTRY *p1 ;
26       {
27            return( strlen(p1->key) + 1 + sizeof(RECPOS) ) ;
28       }
29
30
```

While we had to introduce some limitations, the BTREE module does provide some powerful features. It handles duplicate keys, multiple entries that point to the same data record, multiple indexes in use, variable-length keys, and sequential movement through an index. In addition, it allows variable-length keys of any data type. Since the application supplies the compare function, ascending or descending order can be arranged as can compound keys.

You should get three things out of this chapter: (1) The BTREE module should allow you to concentrate on the application and use BTREE as a tool for indexing data records. (2) The BTREE module should also provide a good base for enhancements. It is feasible to develop your own module starting from BTREE even if you would not build one from scratch. (3) Our discussion should remove the mystery from keyed file access.

7
A Low-level Toolkit
for IBM PC Specific Tools

The applications presented in earlier chapters are useful with whatever C compiler we use. Most are useful in environments other than the IBM PC and PC-DOS. And most of the C source files presented in those chapters require no changes for other environments. But those C programs also made use of low-level, system-dependent functions. In this chapter we develop a toolkit containing the nonportable functions we need to produce quality applications.

Writing programs that are completely portable is a noble goal. However, it is often necessary to use the features of the operating system and the computer hardware to produce good performance and smooth operation. The C language provides no special features for access to the PC's hardware or to the operating system. The C standard library does use operating system facilities to implement I/O functions, but it does not provide any services tailored to the PC's capabilities. Our toolkit supplements the standard C library with the tools we need to make full use of the IBM PC's hardware and of the PC-DOS operating system. Once we have written a library of functions to access the PC's hardware and its operating system, we can use these functions as easily as we use C library functions.

The functions developed in this chapter are specific to the IBM PC family and to PC-DOS. They also apply to PC look-alikes and in part to other Intel 8086/8088/80186/80286-based MS-DOS environments. But an equivalent toolkit would be useful in another environment, and our methods for developing it would still apply.

We develop a variety of tools in this chapter. We start by developing a foundation of low-level functions for basic access to PC hardware and system software. Then we develop modules for keyboard input, screen output, and other functions based on these low-level functions. Finally, we show the implementation of generalized file opening functions that hide differences in C standard I/O library functions between different C compilers.

The low-level functions are written in assembler language. While C is quite versatile, there are cases where assembler language functions are needed. We neither explain the 8088 instruction set nor machine language since many books discuss these subjects in detail. Our purpose is to show when and how to apply assembler language. Several available C compilers support more than one *memory model*. Our assembler functions are developed for the small memory model that is supported by all PC-DOS C compilers. Appendix C explains memory models and the layout of C programs in RAM memory.

This chapter focuses on some key skills for C programmers. You are not really a complete programmer until you know how to make full use of the capabilities of your computer and its operating system. You will not need all the functions presented in every program that you write, but you will often need at least one in each serious program.

7.1 Assembler Language Tools

□ Writing and testing assembler language software is slow, tedious work; most programmers use it only when they must. There are situations where assembler language is necessary, and by writing a few assembler functions, we make the whole toolkit possible. Once the assembler functions are written and tested, we can use them as easily as functions written in C.

If you program in C you will not need to write entire programs in assembler language. However, you should be able to write small functions in assembler to handle low-level needs like access to the operating system or the computer's hardware. You may not need to modify the assembler language functions in this chapter, but they also serve as examples of using assembler language with C. Each assembler function we present performs an essential function and illustrates a common use for assembler language. As we discuss each function, we explain why we wrote it in assembler.

Port I/O

The PC's 8088 processor provides special instructions for input and output. These instructions, in and out, can address any of 64K different *ports*. Many of the PC's hardware capabilities are controlled through these I/O ports. Since there are no C statements to generate in and out instructions and no such standard library functions either, we develop two functions, inport and outport, to perform the 8088 in and out instructions. A manual page for the two functions is shown in Figure 7.1.

Our assembler functions are short and simple; we can adopt a standard format that can be copied in each source file. We can also avoid many of the complicated features of the IBM Macro Assembler language. The following outline shows our standard format for assembler language source files:

Figure 7.1   Port I/O description

Name

> inport –read in a byte from an 8088 I/O port.
> outport–write a byte to an 8088 I/O port.

Usage

> unsigned port_no ;   /* 8088 port number */
> char b ;   /* store the byte read here */
>
> b = inport (port_no) ;
> outport(b,port_no);

Function

> inport( ) performs an 8088 instruction
>
> in al,dx

using the port number specified by the caller. The byte value read is returned in **ax**. The value returned is between 0 and 255.

> outport ( ) performs an 8088 instruction
> out dx,al

using the port number and byte value specified by the caller.

Registers DS, ES, SS, SP, BP, SI, and DI are preserved. The other register values are destroyed.

Examples

Using inport to read the configuration switch values on the PC system unit board:

> int pc_switch ;
> . . .
> pc_switch = inport (0x62) ;   /* read PC sys. unit switches */
> printf (" PC system unit switches %x \n",pc_switch) ;

Using outport to turn on the PC speaker:

> int port_value ;
> . . .
> port_value = inport (0x61) ;
> outport (port_value ¦ 0x01, 0×61) ;

References

IBM PC Hardware Technical Reference Manual.

comments describing the contents of the file

statements defining the data area
    declarations of data variables
statements to end the data area

statements defining the code area
    1st Function
        instructions for the 1st function
    2nd Function
        instructions for the 2nd function

   . . .
statements to end the code area

The statements required to define data and code areas vary, depending on the C compiler and the assembler we use. But whatever the compiler and assembler used, the same statements can be used in every assembler source file. Most assemblers support an *include* statement (like the #include statement in C) that we can use to incorporate these standard statements. Figures 7.2a–d show include files appropriate for Lattice C (using the small memory model). Most of the time, we can use whatever statements the compiler documentation tells us to use.

Many of the statements in an assembler source file correspond to C statements. The following C function is analogous to the real inport function. (Since C has no provisions for addressing inport ports, we fake it with the array ports.) We can relate the assembler function to this C function piece by piece.

```
extern char ports[ ] ;
int inport(iport)        /* C analogy to inport */
 int iport ;
 {
   char c ;
   c = ports[iport] ;
   return( c ) ;
 }
```

Figure 7.3 shows the assembler source file containing the inport and outport functions. Lines 4, 5, 8, and 49 include the statements defining data and code areas. Lines 19 and 20 declare the function name inport. In C, function names are global in scope by default. In assembler, names that are to be known by other source files must be declared as public. K&R states that external names may be significant to only 8 characters. But since some compilers actually truncate external names to 7 characters, we use names no longer than 7 characters.

Lines 14 to 18 define the arguments to be passed to inport. These arguments are passed on the 8088's stack, and this declaration defines their position relative to the top of the stack in inport. The struc statement defines a data structure much

Figure 7.2a   begdata.ha

```
 1    ;          assembler declarations before data section
 2    ;          Lattice C version
 3
 4    Pgroup  group    prog
 5    Dgroup  group    data
 6            assume   cs:pgroup,ds:dgroup
 7    dstart  equ      dgroup
 8    Data    segment word public 'DATA'
 9
10    ;          end of Lattice C version
```

Figure 7.2b   enddata.ha

```
 1    ;          assembler declarations after data section
 2    ;          Lattice C version
 3    Data    ends
 4    ;          end of Lattice C version
```

Figure 7.2c   begcode.ha

```
 1    ;          assembler declarations before code section
 2    ;          Lattice C version
 3
 4    Prog    segment byte public 'PROG'
 5
 6    ;          end of Lattice C version
```

Figure 7.2d   endcode.ha

```
 1    ;          assembler declarations after code section
 2    ;          Lattice C version
 3
 4    Prog    ends
 5
 6    ;          end of Lattice C version
```

Figure 7.3 portio.asm

```
 1    ;           portio.asm - 8088 port I/O functions
 2
 3    ;           start data section
 4                include begdata.ha
 5                include enddata.ha
 6
 7    ;           start code section
 8                include begcode.ha
 9
10    ;           inport - read a byte from an 8088 port
11    ;
12    ;           usage:  byte_value = inport(port_number) ;
13    ;
14    inport_args struc                  ; input arguments
15                dw      0              ; saved BP value
16                dw      0              ; return address
17    iport       dw      0              ; port number to read
18    inport_args ends
19                public  inport
20    inport:
21                push    bp
22                mov     bp,sp                  ;set our arg pointer
23                mov     dx,word ptr iport[bp] ; set up port address
24                in      al,dx
25                xor     ah,ah
26                pop     bp
27                ret
28
29    ;           outport - write a byte to an 8088 port
30    ;
31    ;           usage:  outport(byte_value,port_number) ;
32    ;
33    outport_args struc                 ; input arguments
34                dw      0              ; saved BP value
35                dw      0              ; return address
36    byte_value      dw      0                  ; value to write
37    oport       dw      0              ; write to this port number
38    outport_args ends
39                public  outport
40    outport:
41                push    bp
42                mov     bp,sp                  ;set our arg pointer
43                mov     dx,word ptr oport[bp] ; get port address
44                mov     ax,word ptr byte_value[bp]
45                out     dx,al
46                pop     bp
47                ret
48
49                include endcode.ha
50                end
```

like the C **struct** keyword. The data declarations following the struc statement to the matching ends statement define the inport_args data type.

To address these arguments, lines 21 and 22 save the current value of the BP register and make BP point to the top of the stack. The same instructions will form a standard *prologue* at the beginning of each function. Any other registers that need to be preserved will also be saved. Lines 26 and 27 form a matching *epilogue*, restoring registers and returning to the function that called inport. This epilogue is also standard.

Lines 23 and 24 get the port number into the DX register and execute the in instruction, reading the data into the AL register. The calling program expects an integer result to be returned in the AX register so line 25 clears the high-order 8 bits of AX.

The outport function in lines 29 to 47 is similar. Lines 43 and 44 load the port number into DX and the data value into AX. The OUT instruction in line 45 writes the data byte to the specified port.

Accessing All the PC's Memory

We have assumed that the C compiler generates programs with the small memory model—separate 64K-byte areas for code and data areas. Most C compilers in the IBM PC environment support this memory model, and it is adequate for most of our needs. But the IBM PC can address up to 1 Mbyte, and sometimes we need to access parts of that address space outside our program. We can alleviate the limitations of the small memory model with a few functions written in assembler language. A manual page for our memory access functions is shown in Figure 7.4. peek and poke functions let us read and write single bytes while lmove moves a number of bytes between two locations specified by 8088 segmented addresses.

The assembler source file is shown in Figure 7.5. The peek and poke functions resemble the inport and outport functions just discussed. One difference is that the I/O port address was a single number placed into the DX register, while the segmented address is two numbers placed into the ES segment register and the BX register.

The lmove function requires two segmented addresses—source and destination—and a byte count as arguments. The byte count is placed into the CX register and the segmented addresses into ES:SI (source) and DS:DI registers. The bytes are transferred by the instruction and prefix

```
rep movsb
```

The movsb instruction moves a single byte and advances the SI and DI register values. The rep prefix repeats the movsb instruction until the count in CX is reduced to 0. This line is analogous to the C code fragment

Figure 7.4 Memory access description

Name

```
peek -get a byte from a memory address.
poke -store a byte at a memory address.
lmove-move bytes from one memory address to another.
```

Usage

```
#include "asmtools.h"
unsigned seg_adr ;    /* 8088 segment address */
unsigned off_adr ;    /* 8088 offset within a segment */
char b ;              /* store the byte value here */
b = peek(seg_adr,off_adr) ;
poke(b,seg_adr,off_adr) ;

unsigned from_seg ;      /* get data from here-seg. */
unsigned from_off ;      /* get data from here-offset */
unsigned to_seg ;        /* put data here-seg. */
unsigned to_off ;        /* put data here-offset */
int nbytes ;             /* number of bytes to move */
lmove(to_seg,to_off,from_seg,from_off,nbytes) ;
```

Function

peek( ) lets you get the contents of any memory location in the PC. poke( ) lets you store data anywhere in memory. lmove( ) moves a specified number of bytes between any two memory locations in the PC. All functions expect 8088 segmented addresses.

Registers DS, ES, SS, SP, BP, SI, and DI are preserved. The other register values are destroyed.

Example

To get the first character on the PC screen (mono adapter):

```
b = peek(0xb000,0) ;   /* char only */
```

To write an X as the first character on the PC screen (mono adapter):

```
poke ('X,'0xb000,0) ;     /* write char only */
```

To copy a new screenful of data from an array:

```
unsigned screen_seg = 0xb000 ; /* mono adapter */
unsigned seg_adr ;
char image[4000] ;      /* a screen image */
seg_adr = get_ds( ) ;
lmove(screen_seg,0,seg_adr,image,4000) ;
```

Figure 7.5   memory.asm

```
 1     ;          memory.asm - memory access functions
 2     ;          start data section
 3                include begdata.ha
 4                include enddata.ha
 5     ;          start code section
 6                include begcode.ha
 7
 8     ;          peek - get a byte from another segment
 9     ;
10     ;          usage:  byte_value =peek(segment_address,offset_address);
11     ;
12     peek_args struc                        ; input arguments
13            dw         0                    ; saved BP value
14            dw         0                    ; return address
15     peek_seg dw       0                    ; segment part of address
16     peek_off dw       0                    ; offset part of the address
17     peek_args ends
18            public    peek
19     peek:
20            push      bp
21            mov       bp,sp               ;set our arg pointer
22            push      es
23            mov       ax,word ptr peek_seg[bp] ; load segmented addr.
24            mov       bx,word ptr peek_off[bp]
25            mov       es,ax
26            mov       al,es:byte ptr [bx]
27            xor       ah,ah
28            pop       es
29            pop       bp
30            ret
31
32     ;          poke - store a byte in another segment
33     ;
34     ;          usage:  poke(byte_value,segment_address,offset_address) ;
35     ;
36     poke_args struc            ;          input arguments
37            dw         0                    ; saved BP value
38            dw         0                    ; return address
39     poke_byte        dw        0                    ; byte value to store
40     poke_seg dw       0                    ; segment part of address
41     poke_off dw       0                    ; offset part of the address
42     poke_args ends
43            public    poke
44     poke:
45            push      bp
46            mov       bp,sp               ;set our arg pointer
47            push      es
48            mov       ax,word ptr poke_seg[bp] ; load segmented addr.
49            mov       bx,word ptr poke_off[bp]
50            mov       es,ax
51            mov       ax,word ptr poke_byte[bp] ; load the data value
52            mov       es:byte ptr [bx],al       ; write it to the port
53            pop       es
54            pop       bp
```

Figure 7.5   memory.asm (continued)

```
55              ret
56
57      ;       lmove - move data between segemnts
58      ;
59      ;       usage:  lmove(dest_offset,dest_segment,source_offset,
60      ;               source_segment,number_bytes) ;
61      ;
62      lmove_args struc                    ;           input arguments
63              dw      0           ; saved BP value
64              dw      0           ; return address
65      destseg dw      0           ; destination segment address
66      doff    dw      0           ; destination offset address
67      srcseg  dw      0           ; source segment address
68      soff    dw      0           ; source offset address
69      mbytes  dw      0           ; number of bytes to move
70      lmove_args      ends
71              public  lmove
72      lmove:
73              push    bp
74              mov     bp,sp               ;set our arg pointer
75              push    ds
76              push    es
77              push    si
78              push    di
79              cld
80              mov     ax,word ptr destseg[bp]  ; load dest. address
81              mov     es,ax
82              mov     di,word ptr doff[bp]
83              mov     ax,word ptr srcseg[bp]   ; load source address
84              mov     ds,ax
85              mov     si,word ptr soff[bp]
86              mov     cx,word ptr mbytes[bp]   ; load the byte count
87              rep movsb                        ; move the data
88              pop     di
89              pop     si
90              pop     es
91              pop     ds
92              pop     bp
93              ret
94
95      ;       get_cs - get CS segment address
96      ;       USAGE:  cs_value = get_cs() ;
97              public  get_cs
98      get_cs: mov     ax,cs
99              ret
100
101     ;       get_ds - get DS segment address
102     ;       USAGE:  ds_value = get_ds() ;
103             public  get_ds
104     get_ds: mov     ax,ds
105             ret
106
107             include endcode.ha
108             end
```

```
while( mbytes > 0 )
  { *to = *from ;
    to = to + 1 ;
    from = from + 1 ;
    mbytes = mbytes − 1 ;
  }
```

The movsb instruction can increment or decrement the address offsets in SI or DI, depending on the setting of the direction flag maintained by the 8088. Line 79 clears this direction flag to ensure that the offsets are incremented as we intend.

The special 8088 instructions rep and movsb are quite fast for moving data. Even if our compiler supports a large memory model for accessing all memory from C, the lmove function would be a faster way of moving large blocks of data. Assembler functions are frequently needed to make full use of special features of a computer's instruction set.

When we use the lmove function, we need to specify segment addresses for both source and destination locations. Special locations like the video display buffer have fixed segment addresses (0xB000 for the monochrome display adapter, for example). But the segment address of an array in our C program may vary, depending on the version of DOS used and many other variables. The assembler functions get_ds and get_cs in Figure 7.5 provide segment addresses of data and code areas for programs using the small memory model.

Generating Software Interrupts

Using PC-DOS and BIOS services requires executing a software interrupt instruction. Neither the C language nor the standard library provides a mechanism for generating such an instruction, so we need an assembler function to do it. The software interrupt instruction includes an interrupt number; most DOS function calls are accessed through one number, while each type of BIOS service has its own interrupt number. We develop a simple function (vidint) for accessing the BIOS VIDEO_IO service and then extend the technique to produce a general purpose function to execute any software interrupt (swint).

Figure 7.6 shows a manual page for two functions, vidint and swint. Both DOS and BIOS services receive input arguments in 8088 registers and return information in those registers. The header file, asmtools.h, in Figure 7.7 defines the data structure, REGS, that vidint and swint use to store register values.

Figure 7.8 shows the assembler source file for the vidint and swint functions. Its structure is much like that of the other assembler functions discussed in earlier sections. Lines 6 to 19 define the REGS data structure in assembler language just as the asmtools.h file defines it in C.

The vidint function follows the same sequence we saw in other assembler functions. A standard prologue saves BP and other registers and sets up a new BP

Figure 7.6   Software interrupt generation

Name

swint   perform a specified software interrupt
vidint   perform a BIOS Video_IO s/w interrupt

Usage

```
#include "asmtools.h"
int    int_no  ;      /* number of interrupt to perform */
int    fun_no  ;      /* number of Video_IO function to perform */
REGS sreg      ;      /* register values input to s/w int */
REGS dreg      ;      /* register values returned */
int    ret     ;      /* return value (status flags) */
ret = swint(int_no,&sreg,&dreg) ;
vidint(fun_no,&sreg,&dreg) ;
```

Function

swint sets the 8088 registers (all but CS, SS, SP, and BP) to the values in sreg. It then performs an **int** instruction with the number of the interrupt supplied by the caller. The values of the registers (except CS, SS, SP, and BP) on return from the interrupt are stored in dreg.

vidint performs an **INT 16** instruction to access the BIOS VIDEO_IO functions. Its first argument is the function number requested. Like swint, the second and third arguments point to structures for input and returned registers; only registers AX to DX are set up or returned by vidint.

Registers DS, ES, SS, SP, BP, SI, and DI are preserved. The other register values are destroyed. swint( ) expects SP to be the same on return from the **int** instruction as before executing the instruction.

The 8088 status flag register is returned in AX (the normal return value expected by C functions).

Example

Setting the cursor position with a *ROM BIOS* call:

```
sreg.ax = 0x0200 ;   /* set cursor position function */
sreg.dx = (row > > 8) + col ; /* new cursor row and column */
ret = swint (0x10,&sreg,&dreg) ; /* do a BIOS Video_IO int */
```

Notes

The swint function is quite general. It can be used for PC-DOS function calls or for ROM BIOS calls. The swint function should not be used for software interrupts 0x25 and 0x26. These absolute disk I/O services leave a status flag value on the stack when they return. This would cause swint to return to the wrong point in the program.

The register structure REGS is defined in asmtools.h. PC-DOS function codes are defined in dosfun.h.

Figure 7.7   asmtools.h

```
1    /* asmtools.h - header (include) file for ASMTOOLS module */
2
3    typedef struct
4       { word16
5             ax , bx , cx , dx ,
6             si , di , bp , sp ,
7             ds , es , ss , cs ;
8       } REGS ;
9
10   typedef struct
11      { char al , ah ,
12             bl , bh ,
13             cl , ch ,
14             dl , dh ;
15      } BYTE_REGS ;
16
17   /* flag bit definitions */
18   #define   ZF_FLAG  0x40
19   #define   AF_FLAG  0x10
20   #define   PF_FLAG  0x04
21   #define   CF_FLAG  0x01
22   #define   TF_FLAG  0x0100
23   #define   SF_FLAG  0x0080
24   #define   IF_FLAG  0x0200
25   #define   DF_FLAG  0x0400
26   #define   OF_FLAG  0x0800
27
28
29   #define   DOS_CALL    0x21        /* s/w interrupt no. for DOS call */
30
31   /* absolute disk read and write interrupt numbers */
32   #define   ABS_READ    0x25
33   #define   ABS_WRITE   0x26
```

Figure 7.8   swint.asm

```
1    ;    swint.asm - software interrupt function
2
3    ;    structure for register values is
4    ;         struct regval{ unsigned ax,bx,cx,dx,si,di,ds,es;};
5    ;    the following defines the offsets for use in the asm. functions
6    regs     struc
7    reg_ax   dw        0              ; ax value
8    reg_bx   dw        0              ; bx value
9    reg_cx   dw        0              ; cx value
10   reg_dx   dw        0              ; dx value
11   reg_si   dw        0              ; si value
12   reg_di   dw        0              ; di value
13   reg_bp   dw        0              ; bp value
14   reg_sp   dw        0              ; sp value
15   reg_ds   dw        0              ; ds value
```

Figure 7.8 swint.asm (continued)

```
16      reg_es   dw      0                       ; es value
17      reg_ss   dw      0                       ; ss value
18      reg_cs   dw      0               ; cs value
19      regs     ends
20
21      ;       start data section
22              include begdata.ha
23              include enddata.ha
24
25      ;       start code section
26              include begcode.ha
27
28      ;       execute an ROM BIOS s/w int 10H with registers ax-dx set up
29      ;
30      ;       typedef struct
31      ;       { word16 ax,bx,cx,dx,si,di,sp,bp,ds,es,ss,cs;} REGS ;
32      ;       REGS   sregs , /* input register values */
33      ;              dregs ; /* values returned in regs */
34      ;       int    fun_no  ;         /* number of function to execute */
35      ;
36      ;       ax_value = vidint(fun_no,&input_regs,&return_regs);
37      vid_args         struc          ; input arguments
38              dw      0               ; saved BP value
39              dw      0               ; return address
40      fun_no  dw      0               ; specific function requested (AH value)
41      vid_sreg dw     0               ; address of input reg. values
42      vid_dreg dw     0               ; store returned reg. values here
43      vid_args ends
44              public  vidint
45      vidint:
46              push    bp
47              mov     bp,sp           ;set our arg pointer
48              push    si
49              push    di
50              mov     bx,word ptr vid_sreg[bp] ;get input reg. val. addr.
51              mov     ax,word ptr reg_ax[bx] ; place values in registers
52              mov     cx,word ptr reg_cx[bx]
53              mov     dx,word ptr reg_dx[bx]
54              mov     bx,word ptr reg_bx[bx]
55              mov     ah,byte ptr fun_no[bp]
56              int     16              ; VIDEO I/O ROM BIOS call
57              mov     di,word ptr vid_dreg[bp] ;get return reg. area addr.
58              mov     word ptr reg_ax[di],ax ;store register values there
59              mov     word ptr reg_bx[di],bx
60              mov     word ptr reg_cx[di],cx
61              mov     word ptr reg_dx[di],dx
62              pop     di
63              pop     si
64              pop     bp              ; restore registers
65              ret
66
67
68      ;       execute an s/w function call with all registers set up
69
70      ;       typedef struct
```

Figure 7.8 swint.asm (continued)

```
71     ;                { word16 ax,bx,cx,dx,si,di,sp,bp,ds,es,ss,cs;} REGS ;
72     ;           REGS   sregs , /* input register values */
73     ;                  dregs ; /* values returned in regs */
74     ;           int status ;  /* 8088 status flags returned by the INT call
75     ;
76     ;           status = swint(fun_code,&input_regs,&return_regs);
77     swint_args struc              ; input arguments
78             dw       0            ; saved BP value
79             dw       0            ; return address
80     int_no  dw       0            ; number of software interrupt to issue
81     sw_sreg dw       0            ; address of input reg. values
82     sw_dreg dw       0            ; store returned reg. values here
83     swint_args ends
84             public   swint
85     swint:
86             push     bp
87             mov      bp,sp              ;set our arg pointer
88             push     ds                 ; save ds as a local variable
89             push     es
90             push     si
91             push     di
92             mov      al,byte ptr int_no[bp] ; insert int. no into instr.
93             mov      cs:byte ptr int_instr[1],al
94             mov      bx,word ptr sw_sreg[bp] ;get input reg. values addr.
95             mov      ax,word ptr reg_ax[bx] ; place values in registers
96             mov      cx,word ptr reg_cx[bx]
97             mov      dx,word ptr reg_dx[bx]
98             mov      si,word ptr reg_si[bx]
99             mov      di,word ptr reg_di[bx]
100            mov      es,word ptr reg_es[bx]
101            mov      ds,word ptr reg_ds[bx]
102            mov      bx,ss:word ptr reg_bx[bx]
103    int_instr:
104            int      32             ; dummy int. (no. filled in on each use)
105            mov      bp,word ptr sw_dreg[bp] ; get & dreg structure
106            mov      word ptr reg_ax[bp],ax ; store register values
107            mov      word ptr reg_bx[bp],bx ; in return reg. structure
108            mov      word ptr reg_cx[bp],cx
109            mov      word ptr reg_dx[bp],dx
110            mov      word ptr reg_si[bp],si
111            mov      word ptr reg_di[bp],di
112            mov      word ptr reg_ds[bp],ds
113            mov      word ptr reg_es[bp],es
114            pushf                    ; return flags
115            pop      ax              ; in ax
116            cld                      ; make sure D flag is cleared on return
117            pop      di
118            pop      si
119            pop      es
120            pop      ds              ; restore registers
121            pop      bp
122            ret
123
124            include endcode.ha
125            end
```

value for addressing input parameters. The address of the structure containing input register values is loaded into the BX register, and the AX to DX register values are loaded. The software interrupt instruction is then executed with the interrupt number 16 (**10 Hex**). After the BIOS finishes executing the VIDEO_IO service, control returns to the next instruction. The address of the structure for returned register values is then loaded into the DI register, and the contents of registers AX to DX are stored in that structure.

The swint function is a little more complicated. The number of the interrupt is an input argument. Since the 8088 **int** instruction includes the interrupt number, line 93 in Figure 7.8 writes this number into the instruction. Since swint is a general purpose function, it sets up more registers and returns more register values than vidint. In addition, some software-interrupt-based services return information in one of the 8088 status flags, so swint returns the complete 8088 flag value in AX.

Not all the registers listed in the REGS data structure are set up (or returned) by vidint or even in swint. But defining them all in REGS makes it more generally useful with little extra cost. Using the same structure for vidint and for swint reduces the effort to develop the functions and makes them easier to use.

Note

There are several possible objections to our way of executing a specified software interrupt. swint modifies itself, which makes it nonreentrant and invalid for a ROM-based program. In addition, a processor that prefetched many instructions might not execute the **int** instruction as it was before it was altered. None of these objections is important to the IBM PC environment, and our implementation is fast and easy to explain.

7.2   Testing Assembler Functions

□   Testing assembler functions presents some new problems. When we write functions in assembler language, we have the freedom to write any sequence of instructions, whether or not it makes any sense. But that freedom means that the assembler cannot help much in locating bugs. Since we have to specify everything in much greater detail in assembler than we do in C, there are many more opportunities for errors. Each line we write in assembler language may contain several bugs; I have found six bugs in one line. Bugs in assembler language can be quite subtle; they may affect parts of a program seemingly unrelated to the function they perform. Finally, if writing assembler functions is a new experience to you, then testing them must seem a frightening prospect.

This list of difficulties sounds discouraging, and it is valid in part. It makes no sense to write assembler functions where functions in C would serve the same purpose. But when assembler functions are needed, good testing techniques can make testing them a routine process. We illustrate that technique on the swint function.

When we test a C function, we treat it as a black box. We feed it the expected input arguments, observe its action (such as writing data to a file), and check the return value and other outputs. By varying the inputs to such a function, we can verify its action for all distinct cases.

C provides some assurance that the function will not alter variables not declared in the function or passed as parameters. (Invalid use of pointers and array subscripts can affect unrelated variables, but we can check for those problems where pointers and array subscripts are used.) Assembler language provides no such assurance. If we want to be confident that an assembler function is correct, we must verify that each instruction does what we intended and nothing else.

The freedom that assembler language provides also makes testing somewhat dangerous. While bugs in C functions may occasionally lock up the computer (crash it) or corrupt the operating system's operation, assembler functions are much more likely to do so. Before testing an assembler function, back up any files stored on a ram disk. If you work a floppy-disk-based system, remove the disk containing your source files (or open the drive door on that drive). If you have a hard disk, set the current directory to point to a dummy subdirectory. Making things safe before you start testing is a good habit to cultivate.

Figure 7.9a shows a test program for the swint function. We prompt for input parameters, call swint, and display the results of calling swint. testswi.c resembles programs that we have developed for testing C functions. However, there is a difference in how we use testswi.

Figure 7.9b lists two functions that support our testing. The showadr function called in line 15 of testswi.c (Figure 7.9a) displays a function address and then waits for input. This allows us to abort execution at this point by pressing the **Control–Break** keys.

The PC-DOS debugger is the key tool for testing swint. It provides commands for executing a program one step at a time or until a specified address is reached (a breakpoint). It also allows us to display and modify the contents of memory or of the 8088's registers. Our testing session uses the following debugger commands:

Purpose of Command	Form of Command
Execute the program to completion	g
Execute the program until the instruction at cs:36A is reached	g 36A
Execute a single 8088 instruction	t
Display memory from 7370:ff96 to 7370:ff9f in hexadecimal and ASCII format	d 7370:ff96 ff9f

Figure 7.9a   testswi.c

```
1     /* testswi.c - test swint function */
2     #include "stdio.h"
3     #include "cminor.h"
4     #include "asmtools.h"
5
6     int swint() ;
7
8
9     main()
10      {
11        unsigned ret , int_no ;
12        REGS  sreg , dreg ;
13
14        printf("\n testing swint \n");
15        showadr("swint",swint);
16        printf(" & sreg = %x    & dreg = %x \n",& sreg, & dreg);
17
18        printf("\n int_no (Hex): \n");
19        scanf("%x",&int_no) ;
20        getregs("input regs. ",&sreg) ;
21        getregs("return regs. ",&dreg) ;
22        ret = swint(int_no,&sreg,&dreg);
23        printf("\n swint returns -%x \n",ret);
24        prtregs("input regs. ",&sreg);
25        prtregs("return regs. ",&dreg);
26        dispflag(ret) ;
27      }
28
29    int prtregs(name,p)
30     char name[] ;
31     REGS *p ;
32      {
33        printf(" %s values \n",name) ;
34        printf(" ax bx cx dx %x %x %x %x \n",p->ax,p->bx,p->cx,p->dx);
35        printf(" si di bp sp %x %x %x %x \n",p->si,p->di,p->bp,p->sp);
36        printf(" ds es ss cs %x %x %x %x \n",p->ds,p->es,p->ss,p->cs);
37      }
38
39
40    int getregs(name,p)
41     char name[] ;
42     REGS *p ;
43      {
44        printf(" enter %s values ax bx cx dx si di bp sp ds es ss cs \n",
45          name) ;
46        scanf("%x %x %x %x",& p->ax,& p->bx,& p->cx,& p->dx);
47        scanf("%x %x %x %x",& p->si,& p->di,& p->bp,& p->sp);
48        scanf("%x %x %x %x",& p->ds,& p->es,& p->ss,& p->cs);
49      }
```

Figure 7.9b   showadr.c

```
1    /* showadr.c - display the address of a function and pause */
2    #include "stdio.h"
3    #include "cminor.h"
4    #include "asmtools.h"
5
6    #define END_OF_LINE '\n'
7
8    int showadr(name,fun_adr)        /* display a function addr & pause */
9     char name[] ;                   /* name of function */
10    int (*fun_adr) () ;             /* address of a function */
11    {
12        printf("\n & %s = %4x ",name,fun_adr) ;
13        printf("  press return twice \n");
14        while( getchar() != END_OF_LINE )
15            { ; }
16        while( getchar() != END_OF_LINE )
17            { ; }
18    }
19
20
21    int dispflag(flags)              /* display state of each 8088 flag */
22     int flags ;
23    {
24      char s[40] ;
25
26      if( (flags & OF_FLAG) == 0) strcpy(s,"NV ");
27          else strcpy(s,"OV ");
28      if( (flags & DF_FLAG) == 0) strcat(s,"UP ");
29          else strcat(s,"DN ");
30      if( (flags & IF_FLAG) == 0) strcat(s,"DI ");
31          else strcat(s,"EI ");
32      if( (flags & SF_FLAG) == 0) strcat(s,"PL ");
33          else strcat(s,"NG ");
34      if( (flags & ZF_FLAG) == 0) strcat(s,"NZ ");
35          else strcat(s,"ZR ");
36      if( (flags & AF_FLAG) == 0) strcat(s,"NA ");
37          else strcat(s,"AC ");
38      if( (flags & PF_FLAG) == 0) strcat(s,"PO ");
39          else strcat(s,"PE ");
40      if( (flags & CF_FLAG) == 0) strcat(s,"NC ");
41          else strcat(s,"CY ");
42      printf(" flags= %s \n",s) ;
43    }
44
```

Purpose of Command	Form of Command
Display memory from CS:36A as 8088 instructions (Displays 16 lines. Another u command will display the next 16 lines.)	u 36A
Exit from the debugger and return to the DOS	q

The addresses in the commands are 8088 segmented addresses, with the number before the colon representing a segment value and the second part the offset part of the address. The debug program does not recognize symbolic names for variables or functions; we have to supply numeric addresses. Fortunately, we can write a test program that will display the addresses of variables and functions in the program.

The listing in Figure 7.9c documents one session testing swint. We begin by locating the start of the swint function in the test program. Once we know that address we can execute the assembler function one instruction at a time using the debugger. Our strategy is to verify that each instruction does what we intended and nothing else. The testing session produced lots of output. We removed material not needed for the discussion, and these omissions are marked by ellipses.

Line 1 executes the debugger and tells it to load the test program testswi.exe. Line 2 executes the program to completion. After displaying the address of the swint function, the program waits for console input. At this point we interrupt the program by pressing the **Control–Break** keys. This gives control to the debugger, and we type **Q** to return to DOS. Now that we know the address of swint, we are ready to start testing. Lines 11 and 12 run the debugger again and start executing the test program with a breakpoint at the start of the swint function. This time we press the return key twice when the showadr function pauses.

The program prompts for values for the input to swint. We specify values for all the members of the input register data structure—even if they are not needed for the particular software interrupt we specify. This will allow us to verify that swint does set up all the input register values we specify. We also specify distinctive values for the return register data structure (dreg). This specification allows us to verify that all the register values returned by the software interrupt handler are stored in the dreg structure by swint.

When all this input has been typed, the program continues executing until it reaches the breakpoint at the swint function. The program stops executing and the debugger regains control. It displays the register values present when the breakpoint was encountered. Before we continue, we examine the stack to see that the input arguments were passed successfully. Line 27 displays the data at the top of the stack. The first value is the return address, and the next three 16-bit words are the expected arguments int_no (0x0010), &sreg (0xffa4), and &dreg (0xffbc). The addresses of sreg and dreg were displayed by testswi in line 15.

Figure 7.9c testswi.fig

```
 1    D>debug testswi.exe
 2    -g
 3    & swint =   36A   press return twice
 4    ^C
 5
 6    AX=3F00 BX=0000 CX=0200 DX=0830 SP=FF5E BP=FF5E SI=044C DI=0000
 7    DS=7370 ES=7370 SS=7370 CS=706B IP=0D82  NV UP EI PL ZR NA PE NC
 8    706B:0D82 7305          JNB     0D89
 9    -Q
10
11    d>debug testswi.exe
12    -g 36A
13
14     testing swint
15     & sreg = FFA4    & dreg = FFBC
16     & swint =   36A   press return twice
17
18     int_no (Hex): 10
19     enter input regs.  values ax bx cx dx si di bp sp ds es ss cs
20    0941 07 30 4 5 6 7 8 9 a b c
21     enter return regs.  values ax bx cx dx si di bp sp ds es ss cs
22    f1 f2 f3 f4 f5 f6 f7 f8 f9 fa fb fc
23
24    AX=FFA4 BX=0000 CX=0000 DX=0000 SP=FF96 BP=FF9E SI=01C0 DI=01EA
25    DS=7370 ES=7370 SS=7370 CS=706B IP=036A  NV UP EI NG NZ AC PE NC
26    706B:036A 55            PUSH    BP
27    -d 7370:ff96 ff9f
28    7370:FF96   B6 01-1- 00 A4 FF BC FF 00 00         6...$.<...
29
30    -u 36A
31    706B:036A 55            PUSH    BP
32    706B:036B 8BEC          MOV     BP,SP
33    706B:036D 1E            PUSH    DS
34    706B:036E 06            PUSH    ES
35    706B:036F 56            PUSH    SI
36    706B:0370 57            PUSH    DI
37    706B:0371 8A4604        MOV     AL,[BP+04]
38    706B:0374 2E            CS:
39    706B:0375 A29403        MOV     [0394],AL
40    706B:0378 8B5E06        MOV     BX,[BP+06]
41    706B:037B 8B07          MOV     AX,[BX]
42    706B:037D 8B4F04        MOV     CX,[BX+04]
43    706B:0380 8B5706        MOV     DX,[BX+06]
44    706B:0383 8B7708        MOV     SI,[BX+08]
45    706B:0386 8B7F0A        MOV     DI,[BX+0A]
46    706B:0389 8E4712        MOV     ES,[BX+12]
47    -u
48    706B:038C 8E5F10        MOV     DS,[BX+10]
49    706B:038F 36            SS:
50    706B:0390 8B5F02        MOV     BX,[BX+02]
51    706B:0393 CD20          INT     20
52    706B:0395 8B6E08        MOV     BP,[BP+08]
53    706B:0398 894600        MOV     [BP+00],AX
54    706B:039B 895E02        MOV     [BP+02],BX
55    706B:039E 894E04        MOV     [BP+04],CX
```

Figure 7.9c   testswi.fig (continued)

```
56    706B:03A1 895606          MOV      [BP+06],DX
57    706B:03A4 897608          MOV      [BP+08],SI
58    706B:03A7 897E0A          MOV      [BP+0A],DI
59    706B:03AA 8C5E10          MOV      [BP+10],DS
60    -u
61    706B:03AD 8C4612          MOV      [BP+12],ES
62    706B:03B0 9C              PUSHF
63    706B:03B1 58              POP      AX
64    706B:03B2 5F              POP      DI
65    706B:03B3 5E              POP      SI
66    706B:03B4 07              POP      ES
67    706B:03B5 1F              POP      DS
68    706B:03B6 5D              POP      BP
69    706B:03B7 C3              RET
70    706B:03B8 55              PUSH     BP
71    ...
72    -t
73    AX=FFA4 BX=0000 CX=0000 DX=0000 SP=FF94 BP=FF9E SI=01C0 DI=01EA
74    DS=7370 ES=7370 SS=7370 CS=706B IP=036B  NV UP EI NG NZ AC PE NC
75    706B:036B 8BEC            MOV      BP,SP
76    -t
77    AX=FFA4 BX=0000 CX=0000 DX=0000 SP=FF94 BP=FF94 SI=01C0 DI=01EA
78    DS=7370 ES=7370 SS=7370 CS=706B IP=036D  NV UP EI NG NZ AC PE NC
79    706B:036D 1E              PUSH     DS
80    -t
81    ...
82    -t
83    AX=FFA4 BX=0000 CX=0000 DX=0000 SP=FF8C BP=FF94 SI=01C0 DI=01EA
84    DS=7370 ES=7370 SS=7370 CS=706B IP=0371  NV UP EI NG NZ AC PE NC
85    706B:0371 8A4604          MOV      AL,[BP+04]            SS:FF98=10
86    -t
87    AX=FF10 BX=0000 CX=0000 DX=0000 SP=FF8C BP=FF94 SI=01C0 DI=01EA
88    DS=7370 ES=7370 SS=7370 CS=706B IP=0374  NV UP EI NG NZ AC PE NC
89    706B:0374 2E              CS:
90    706B:0375 A29403          MOV      [0394],AL            CS:0394=20
91    d 706B:393 397
92
93    706B:0393   CD 20 8B 6E ...n
94    -t
95
96    AX=FF10 BX=0000 CX=0000 DX=0000 SP=FF8C BP=FF94 SI=01C0 DI=01EA
97    DS=7370 ES=7370 SS=7370 CS=706B IP=0378  NV UP EI NG NZ AC PE NC
98    706B:0378 8B5E06          MOV      BX,[BP+06]            SS:FF9A=FFA4
99    d 706B:393 397
100
101   706B:0393   CD 10 8B 6E ...n
102   ...
103   -t
104
105   AX=0941 BX=0007 CX=0030 DX=0004 SP=FF8C BP=FF94 SI=0005 DI=0006
106   DS=0009 ES=000A SS=7370 CS=706B IP=0393  NV UP EI NG NZ AC PE NC
107   706B:0393 CD10            INT      10
108   -g 395
109   AAAAAAAAAAAAAAAAAAAAAAAAAAAAAAAAAAAAAAAAAAAAAAAAAAAA
110   AX=0741 BX=0007 CX=0030 DX=0004 SP=FF8C BP=FF94 SI=0005 DI=0006
```

Figure 7.9c   testswi.fig (continued)

```
111   DS=0009 ES=000A SS=7370 CS=706B IP=0395   NV UP EI NG NZ AC PE NC
112   706B:0395 8B6E08          MOV     BP,[BP+08]                SS:FF9C=FFBC
113   -t
114   ...
115
116   AX=F296 BX=0007 CX=0030 DX=0004 SP=FF96 BP=FF9E SI=01C0 DI=01EA
117   DS=7370 ES=7370 SS=7370 CS=706B IP=03B7   NV UP EI NG NZ AC PE NC
118   706B:03B7 C3             RET
119   -g
120
121    swint returns -F296
122    input regs.  values
123    ax bx cx dx 741 7 30 4
124    si di bp sp 5 6 F7 F8
125    ds es ss cs 9 A FB FC
126    return regs.  values
127    ax bx cx dx 741 7 30 4
128    si di bp sp 5 6 F7 F8
129    ds es ss cs 9 A FB FC
130    flags= NV UP EI NG NZ AC PE NC
131
132   Program terminated normally
133   -Q
134   D>
```

Before we execute the **swint** function, we display it with the unassemble command (**u**). Each **u** command displays the next sixteen lines of instructions. We keep displaying until we find the **return** instruction (**RET**) at the end of the **swint** function. While the instruction syntax used by the debugger differs somewhat from that of the Microsoft Macro Assembler (MASM), the **u** command gives us a roadmap of the **swint** function to follow as we execute each instruction.

swint should preserve the values of at least some of the registers when it returns to its caller. When we get to the end of **swint**, we will compare the register values at that point to those present when **swint** was entered.

Now we start executing **swint** one instruction at a time with the trace command, **t**. After each instruction is executed, we check register values and relevant memory locations to see that the instruction did what we expected. While this may seem unnecessary and tedious, it is our only way to verify that the function does not alter unrelated memory locations or perform other undesired actions. While we are testing, we want to lay aside our belief that the function works and verify its operation by tests independent of our belief.

The instruction displayed in line 85 of Figure 7.9c and executed by the following trace command loads the interrupt number into register AL (the low-order byte of the AX register). We can verify the instruction's effect by comparing the values for the AX register displayed before and after executing the instruction. The next instruction stored this value in the **INT** instruction, turning it into an **INT 10H** instruction. We display the contents of memory in that area before and after executing the instruction. Note that we display values of bytes before and after the byte we expect to see altered. This verifies that only the relevant byte of memory is changed.

Even before an instruction is executed, we can check its effect. The debugger displayed the address and contents of the memory location (if any) affected by the next instruction. Thus, we can check to see that the instruction will not have a catastrophic effect like corrupting DOS.

We have skipped forward to the point where the INT 10H instruction is the next instruction to be executed. We can now check all the register values to verify that they correspond to the values in sreg. (Note that the values of CS, IP, SS, and SP do not agree. Although sreg contains values for those registers, the swint function does not make use of them.)

We do not want to follow the execution of the software interrupt handler with the trace command, so we execute the program with a breakpoint at the instruction after the INT 10H. The software interrupt we specified is a BIOS VIDEO_IO function to display forty-eight As, and we can see its effect in line 109. We note the values in the registers at this point; we will expect to find them in the dreg structure when swint is finished. The 8088 status flags are displayed by the debugger in a symbolic form (the letters NV through NC at the end of the line). The DOS debugger manual describes the abbreviations used for flag values.

We wrote the swint function with the expectation that the software interrupt handler would preserve the SS and SP register values (the stack would be as it was before executing the INT 10H instruction). We check that assumption to be sure that the interrupt handler works as we expected.

We continue executing swint one instruction at a time with the trace command until the ret instruction is reached. There we compare register values to those present when we entered swint. In the example, our swint function was supposed to preserve the SI, DI, BP, DS, ES, SS, and SP registers, and it does. As we pointed out earlier, it is especially important that the stack pointer (SS:SP) be preserved.

Now that we have stepped through swint, we execute the program to completion with the g command in line 119. The main function displays the value returned by swint and the values in sreg and dreg. We check to see that nothing in the input register data structure (sreg) has been altered and that the return register structure (dreg) contains the register values returned by the interrupt handler. The value returned by swint is the 8088 status flag register value returned by the interrupt handler. Line 130 displays this value in the same form as that used by the debugger.

This session is typical for a first execution of swint. Once the operation of each instruction has been verified, we can skip the single instruction tracing. We have tested swint with a real software interrupt handler—one that was safe and had an observable effect. However, it used only a few input register parameters and returned no useful information. To complete the testing, we might check out swint with other interrupts that use other input and return registers. We have not shown any further testing since the same techniques apply.

The standard debugger that is provided with DOS is not a pleasant or efficient tool for testing. It has some of its own bugs, and its operation is poorly documented. Its lack of support for symbolic addresses creates extra work. As the sample testing session indicates, however, the standard debugger, despite its drawbacks, is a useful and necessary tool for testing assembler functions. More elaborate debugger programs are available with more features and some support for symbolic variable and function names. These programs may make the testing process easier and faster, but the methods we illustrated still apply.

7.3   Adapting the Toolkit for Other Compilers and Assemblers

□   We illustrated the assembler functions in our toolkit in a form appropriate for the Lattice C compiler. Some changes that are required for use with other C compilers depend on the C compiler used and on the assembler program as well. If the Microsoft/IBM Macro Assembler is used, only minor changes are required.

For example, the header files that describe the data and code areas must be tailored to the C compiler used. Figures 7.10a–d list header files with statements appropriate for a number of C compilers. You must edit these files, selecting the version for your compiler, then rename the files to **begdata.ha** and so on.

Some C compilers (Manx Aztec C and Mark Williams C, for example) alter names of functions and global variables in object files by appending an underscore.

Figure 7.10a   c:begdata.hax

```
 1
 2     ;         magic words for asm functions
 3     ;         this goes before the data section
 4     ;         edit this file deleting all the lines except those
 5     ;         for your compiler
 6     ;         all versions apply to the small memory model
 7
 8
 9     ;         *** start CI-C86 magic        ***
10     ;         this applies to Version 1.33 and earlier
11     code      segment byte public
12     code      ends
13     data      segment word public
14     dstart    equ     data
15               assume  cs:code,ds:data,es:data,ss:data
16     ;         ***     end v1.xx CI-C86 magic  ***
17
18     ;         *** start CI-C86 magic        ***
19     ;         this applies to Version 2.00 and earlier
20     @bigmodel EQU 0           ; selects small model
21               Include prologue.h
22     @code     ends
```

Figure 7.10a   c:begdata.hax (continued)

```
23   @datab   segment para public 'DATAB'
24   ;        ***      end v2.xx CI-C86 magic   ***
25
26   ;        ***        start Lattice C magic    ***
27   ;        (for both Lattice, Inc. and Lifeboat Versions)
28   ;        also for C Ware with .obj option
29   ;        and Microsoft C version 2.0 or earlier
30   pgroup   group    prog
31   dgroup   group    data
32   dstart   equ      dgroup
33   Data     segment word public 'DATA'
34            assume   cs:pgroup,ds:dgroup
35   ;        ***      end of Lattice magic   ***
36
37   ;        ***        start of C-Ware magic   (for ASM88) ***
38   ;        also change include statement to include "begcode.ha"
39            CSEG
40   ;        ***      end of C-Ware magic    ***
41
42   ;        ***        start of Manx Aztec C magic   ***
43   ;        (use with IBM/Microsoft Assembler or the Manx assembler)
44   Cg       group    CODESEG
45   CODESEG segment byte public 'code'
46   CODESEG ends
47   Dg group STATICS
48   dstart   equ Dg
49   STATICS segment word public 'data'
50    assume cs:Cg,ds:Dg,es:Dg,ss:Dg
51   ;        ***      end of Manx magic     ***
52
53   ;        ***        start of C-Systems magic       ***
54   cseg     segment byte public
55   cseg     ends
56   dgrp     group    data
57   dstart   equ  dgrp
58   data     segment word public
59            assume   cs:cseg,ds:dgrp,es:dgrp,ss:dgrp
60   ;        ***      end of C-Systems magic  ***
61
62   ;        ***        start of Digital Research magic ***
63   dgroup   DATA
64   dstart   equ dgroup
65   DATA     dseg
66   ;        ***      end of Digital Research magic    ***
67
68   ;        *** start Mark Williams version   ***
69   ;        for use with the IBM/Microsoft Assembler
70   Cgroup   group    code
71   Dgroup   group    data
72            assume   cs:cgroup,ds:dgroup,es:dgroup,ss:dgroup
73   dstart   equ      dgroup
74   Data     segment word public 'DATA'
75   ;        ***   end of Mark Williams  C version
76
77   ;        No Whitesmith's C version. See Appendix D.
```

Figure 7.10b   enddata.hax

```
 1
 2    ;           magic file for asm functions - goes after data declarations
 3    ;           edit this file deleting all the lines except those
 4    ;           for your compiler
 5    ;           this applies to the small memory model
 6
 7    ;           *** start Computer Innovations - C86   ***
 8    ;           for version 1.33 and earlier
 9    data    ends
10    ;           ***       end Computer Innovations - C86 magic    ***
11
12    ;           *** start Computer Innovations - C86   magic   ***
13    ;           for version 2.00 and later
14    @datab  ends
15    ;           ***       end Computer Innovations - C86 magic    ***
16
17
18    ;           *** start Lattice C version   ***
19    ;           (for Lattice, Inc, Microsoft and Lifeboat Versions)
20    ;           also for C Ware compiler with .obj option
21    Data    ends
22    ;           end of Lattice C version
23
24
25    ;           ***     start of C-Ware magic (ASM88)    ***
26    ;           ***     end of C-Ware magic       ***
27
28
29    ;           ***     start of Manx magic     ***
30    ;           (use with IBM/Microsoft Assembler or the Manx assembler)
31    STATICS ends
32    ;           ***     end of Manx magic        ***
33
34
35    ;           ***     start of C-Systems magic       ***
36    data    ends
37    ;           ***     end of C-Systems magic   ***
38
39    ;           ***     start of Digital Research magic ***
40    ;           ***     end of Digital Research magic    ***
41
42    ;           ***   start of Mark Williams C  version   ***
43    Data    ends
44    ;           ***     end of Mark Williams C version    ***
45
46    ;           No Whitesmith's C version. See Appendix D.
```

Figure 7.10c   begcode.hax

```
 1
 2     ;         magic words for asm functions - goes before code section
 3     ;         edit this file deleting all the lines except those
 4     ;         for your compiler
 5     ;         all versions apply to the small memory model
 6
 7     ;         *** start Computer Innovations - C86 version    ***
 8     ;         this applies to Version 1.33 and earlier
 9     code      segment byte public
10     ;         ***     end v1.xx CI-C86 magic   ***
11
12     ;         *** start Computer Innovations - C86 version    ***
13     ;         this applies to Version 2.00 and later
14     @code     segment byte public 'CODE'
15     ;         ***     end v2.xx CI-C86 magic   ***
16
17
18     ;         start Lattice C version
19     ;         (for both Microsoft and Lifeboat Versions)
20     Prog      segment byte public 'PROG'
21     ;         end of Lattice C version
22
23     ;         ***     start of C-Ware magic   ***
24     ;         also change include statement to include "begcode.ha"
25               CSEG
26     ;         ***     end of C-Ware magic      ***
27
28
29     ;         ***     start of Manx Aztec C magic   ***
30     ;         (use with IBM/Microsoft Assembler or the Manx assembler)
31     CODESEG   segment byte public 'code'
32     ;         ***     end of Manx magic        ***
33
34     ;         ***     start of C-Systems magic        ***
35     cseg      segment public
36     ;         ***     end of C-Systems magic   ***
37
38     ;         ***     start of Digital Research magic ***
39     code      cseg
40     ;         ***     end of Digital Research magic    ***
41
42
43     ;         ***   start Mark Williams version    ***
44     code      segment byte public 'CODE'
45     ;         ***    end of Mark Williams  version    ***
46
47     ;         No Whitesmith's C version. See Appendix D.
```

Figure 7.10d   endcode.hax

```
 1
 2    ;           magic file for asm functions
 3    ;           this goes after the code section (instructions)
 4    ;           edit this file deleting all the lines except those
 5    ;           for your compiler
 6    ;           this applies to the small memory model
 7
 8
 9    ;           *** start CI-C86 version                    ***
10    ;           for version 1.33 and earlier
11    code    ends
12    ;           ***      end CI-C86 version       ***
13
14
15    ;           *** start CI-C86 version  ***
16    ;           for version 2.00 and later
17    @code   ends
18    ;           ***      end CI-C86 version       ***
19
20
21    ;           ***      start Lattice C magic    ***
22    ;           (for Lattice, Inc., Microsoft and Lifeboat Versions)
23    prog    ends
24    ;           ***      end of Lattice magic    ***
25
26
27    ;           ***      start of C-Ware magic    ***
28    ;           ***      end of C-Ware magic      ***
29
30
31    ;           ***      start of Manx magic      ***
32    ;           (use with IBM/Microsoft Assembler or the Manx assembler)
33    CODESEG ends
34    ;           ***      end of Manx magic        ***
35
36    ;           ***      start of C-Systems magic        ***
37    cseg    ends
38    ;           ***      end of C-Systems magic  ***
39
40    ;           ***      start of Digital Research magic ***
41    ;           ***      end of Digital Research magic   ***
42
43
44    ;           ***      start  Mark Williams C version   ***
45    code    ends
46    ;           ***      end of Mark Williams C version   ***
47
48    ;           No Whitesmith's C version.  See Appendix D.
```

If your compiler does this, you must edit the *.asm files, appending the underscore character to each PUBLIC or EXTRN name.

If another assembler is used, more editing may be required. Appendix B points out changes needed for several compilers.

The assembler functions were written with some assumptions about sizes of data types and the mechanism for executing function calls. These assumptions are valid for all the compilers listed in Appendix B, but they should be stated:

Small memory model is used.

Integers, unsigned and pointer values are 16 bits long.

Function arguments are pushed on the stack, right-most one first and left-most one last.

The calling function removes arguments from the stack after the called function returns.

16-bit values are returned in the AX register.

Only DS, ES, SP, BP, SI, DI registers need be saved.

7.4 Using Other Memory Models

□ The functional specifications for our toolkit functions are valid for any memory model. Our assembler functions were developed for use with the small memory model, but we can modify them for other memory models. There are too many possibilities to discuss in full, but we point out where changes are required. We use the large memory model as supported by Lattice C to give a concrete example.

First, the magic words in begdata.ha and the other header files must be revised. Changing memory models requires different instructions to the assembler and linker about how the source file relates to the rest of the program. The documentation for your compiler should show what statements are required for each memory model supported.

Second, the form of label and public statements must be changed. Our format for assembler functions,

```
swint:
    . . .
        ret
```

is convenient since it is recognized by most assemblers. It specifies swint as a near address (16-bit) and the return instruction as a near return (16-bit). For large memory models where far addresses and returns are required, the following format is required:

```
swint proc far
        public swint
        . . . ( body of swint )
        ret
swint endp
```

The IBM/Microsoft MASM Assembler recognizes the PROC and ENDP statements we use. Other assemblers may require different statements.

Third, the size of return addresses and C pointer values varies with the memory model. This affects the structures such as swint_args that define input arguments. In the large memory model, as supported by the Lattice C and CI-C86 compilers, return addresses and pointers are 32 bits long—a 16-bit offset and a 16-bit segment address:

```
swint_args struc      ; large model version
        dw    0     ; saved BP value
        dd    0     ; return address—32-bit double word
int_no dw 0      ; number of interrupt to execute
sw_sreg dd 0     ; 32-bit address of source reg. values
sw_dreg dd 0     ; 32-bit address of returned reg. values
swint_args ends
```

Finally, since C pointer values may be different in length and have a different interpretation for other memory models, the instructions that use those pointer values must be changed. The following examples from the swint function show typical changes:

From	*To*
mov bx,word ptr sw_sreg[BP]	les bx,dword ptr sw_sreg[BP]
mov bp,word ptr sw_dreg[BP]	les bx,dword ptr sw_dreg[BP]

Note that these new statements load two 8088 registers: The offset goes into the BX register, and the segment value goes into the ES register. Since the pointer values occupy more registers, some extra statements are needed in swint to preserve the value of ES returned by the interrupt handler.

7.5   Supporting swint

□   When we want to call the swint function, we fill out the REGS data structure with input register values. For characters and integer values this is straightforward, but for addresses of variables and functions that are to be passed to swint, some extra support is required. We can get the address of a variable or a function easily enough in C. However, the relation of such a C address to the 8088 segmented addresses expected by DOS and BIOS functions varies with the C compiler we use and the memory model we select. We can hide those differences with two functions that convert C addresses into 8088 segmented addresses. Figure 7.11 describes functions get_dads for addresses of data variables and get_fads for addresses of functions.

Figure 7.12 shows the implementation of these functions for a small memory model. The functions get_cs and get_ds are defined in the memory.asm source file. If we change the memory model used, we have to revise these functions, but the programs that use get_dads and get_fads need not be altered.

Figure 7.11   Convert to/from segemented address

Name

```
get_dads -translate C data pointer into segmented address
get_fads -translate C function pointer into segmented address
```

Usage

```
char msg[ ] = "error 10 $" ;
int strcmp ( ) ;
word16 seg ;      /* segment part of address */
word16 off ;      /* offset part */
. . .
get_dads(msg,&seg,&off) ;
get_fads (strcmp,&seg,&off) ;
```

Function

get_dads translates a C pointer to data into an 8088 segmented address. This translation is different for different memory models and compilers; get_dads and get_fads hide these differences. get_dads( ) expects three arguments: a C pointer to data of some kind and addresses where the segment and offset parts of the address will be stored.

get_fads performs a similar translation for pointers to functions.

The word16 data type is declared in cminor.h.

Example

```
char msg[ ] = "error 10 $" ;
int strcmp( ) ;
word16 seg , off ;
REGS sreg,dreg ;      /* defined in asmtools.h */
get_dads(msg,&sreg.ds,&sreg.dx) ;
dos2call (DISP_STRING,&sreg,&dreg) ;
get_fads(strcmp,&seg,&off) ;
printf(" & strcmp = %x:%x \n",(int) seg,(int) off) ;
```

Notes

1. As the example suggests, get_dads is used to set up arguments for DOS calls.

2. The segment and offset values are defined as 16-bit words by the 8088 architecture. We define them as word16 to ensure that the C compiler allocates 16-bit variables.

7.6   Accessing DOS

□   Now that we have a function for executing software interrupts, we can use DOS services directly. Since this is a common and important need, we build a function to make it more convenient. Most DOS calls require some common steps:

1. A single software interrupt (0x21) is used for most DOS calls. We specify this interrupt number automatically.

Figure 7.12 get_dads.c

```
1    /* get_dads.c - convert C pointer to 8088 segmented address */
2    /* this implementation is appropriate for a small memory model */
3    #include "stdio.h"
4    #include "cminor.h"
5
6    word16 get_ds() ;              /* returns the DS segment value */
7    word16 get_cs() ;              /* returns the CS segment value */
8
9    int get_dads(p,pseg,poff)      /* convert data pointer to seg. adr. */
10    char *p ;                      /* pointer value */
11    word16 *pseg ;                 /* place segment value here */
12    word16 *poff ;                 /* place offset value here */
13    {
14        *pseg = get_ds() ;
15        *poff = (word16) p ;
16    }
17
18
19    int get_fads(pfun,pseg,poff)/* convert fun. pointer to seg. adr. */
20    int (*pfun) () ;               /* pointer value */
21    word16 *pseg ;                 /* place segment value here */
22    word16 *poff ;                 /* place offset value here */
23    {
24        *pseg = get_cs() ;
25        *poff = (word16) pfun ;
26    }
```

2. The service requested is specified by a function number in register AH (high-order byte of register AX). We make this function number one of the arguments to the DOS call function.
3. Many DOS calls signal an error condition by setting the carry flag on return. If it is set, the AX register contains an error code. The DOS call function will check the carry bit, returning 0 if no error has occurred or −1 if an error has occurred. (For DOS calls that do not follow this convention, the return code can be ignored.)

Figure 7.13 shows a manual page for the dos2call function that fits our description. Figure 7.14a shows its implementation. dos2call places the DOS function number into the source register data structure and calls swint to perform the software interrupt. It tests the status flag value returned by swint to see whether an error occurred. The dosfun.h header file in Figure 7.14b defines constants for DOS function numbers to make dos2call easier to use.

The dos2call function is useful for most DOS calls. There are a few exceptions: DOS provides services for reading and writing raw disk sectors. These services are accessed via software interrupts, 0x25 and 0x26. The EXEC DOS call is accessed via the 0x21 software interrupt, but there are two other problems: (1) It does not preserve the SS and SP registers as assumed by the swint function, and (2) it uses memory locations in the segment pointed to by the ES segment register for

Figure 7.13   dos2call description

Name

> dos2call – perform a DOS function call

Usage

```
int    fun_no ;        /* DOS function number */
REGS sreg    ;        /* register values to pass to DOS */
REGS dreg    ;        /* register values returned by DOS */
int    ret     ;        /* return value 0=normal , −1= error */
ret = dos2call (fun_no,&sreg,&dreg) ;
```

Function

dos2call performs a DOS function call (a software interrupt 0x21). The function code supplied is placed in register AH and the input registers' values set based on the contents of the source register structure (**sreg** in the usage section). When the DOS call returns, the register values are stored in the destination register structure (**dreg** in the usage section).

dos2call checks the carry flag returned by DOS. If it is set, the value in register AX is interpreted as an error code and saved in the global variable, dos_err. dos2call returns 0 if no error was detected and −1 if an error was detected. This error checking is appropriate for DOS calls using the carry flag to signal errors. dos2call can be used for DOS calls that do not signal errors in this way; just ignore the value dos2call returns.

The header file **dosfun.h** defines symbolic constants for DOS function codes.

The functions **get_dads** and **get_fads** translate C data and function pointers into the segmented address form that DOS expects.

Examples

```
extern int dos_err ;        /* holds last DOS error code */
REGS sreg , dreg ;
char newdir[128] ;
get_dads(newdir,&sreg.ds,&sreg.dx) ; /* translate address */
if( dos2call(CHDIR,&sreg,&dreg) != 0 ) /* change directory */
   printf (" error code = %d \n",dos_err) ;

sreg.dx = 7 ;      /* BEL char */
dos2call (0x02,&sreg,&dreg) ; /* output it to the console */

dos2call (GET_DRIVE,&sreg,&dreg) ; /* get current dir. name */
printf(" drive = %d \n",tochar(dreg.ax) ) ;
```

Limitation

A DOS bug in the **EXEC** call (0x4B) may cause problems.

Figure 7.14a   dos2call.c

```
1   /* dos2call.c - does dos 2.0 calls checking carry flag on return */
2   #include   "stdio.h"
3   #include   "cminor.h"
4   #include   "asmtools.h"
5
6   unsigned dos_err ;              /* record error code here */
7   unsigned dos_flags ;           /*        and flag values here */
8
9   dos2call(fun_no,pin,pout)      /* do a DOS function call */
10   int    fun_no ;               /* function number */
11   REGS   *pin   ;               /* points to input reg. structure */
12   REGS   *pout  ;               /* points to output reg. structure */
13   {
14                                 /* set up function code in AH */
15      ( (BYTE_REGS *) pin) ->ah = fun_no ;
16      dos_flags = swint(DOS_CALL,pin,pout) ; /* do the dos call */
17      if((dos_flags&CF_FLAG) != 0)/* check for an error return */
18         { dos_err = pout->ax ;  /*    yes - record error code */
19            return( -1 ) ;       /*         and return error value */
20         }
21      else
22         { dos_err = 0 ;         /*    no error - clear error code */
23            return( 0 ) ;        /*              return normal value */
24         }
25   }
```

scratch space. Thus, supporting the **EXEC** call correctly requires changes to the **swint** function.

Making DOS Calls

The *IBM DOS Technical Reference Manual* describes how the DOS services work: what values they expect in 8088 registers as input and what information DOS returns in those registers. In theory, making DOS calls should be a cookbook operation: Just fill out the register values in the **REGS** structure as directed by the manual. Unfortunately, the descriptions in the manual are often unclear and incomplete, but careful experiments can yield the missing information. To provide a start, Figure 7.14c gives examples of making DOS calls using **dos2call**.

The **get_drive** function illustrates how we get information back from DOS. DOS puts the default drive number in the AL register, the **dos2call** function stores it in the **ax** member of the **dreg** data structure, and **get_drive** extracts it and makes it the return value. Since the drive number is specified as being in AL, the lower 8 bits of the AX register, **get_drive** forces the high-order bits to be 0 in the returned value.

The **set_drive** function passes a new default drive number to DOS through the **dx** member of the **sreg** structure. **dos2call** will place this value into the 8088

Figure 7.14b   dosfun.h

```
 1    /* dosfun.h - header file to define DOS function call values */
 2
 3    #define   CON_OUTPUT    0x02
 4    #define   CON_RAWIN     0x07
 5    #define   INPUT_STATUS  0x0b
 6    #define   CON_INPUT     0x08
 7    #define   DISP_STRING   0x09
 8    #define   SELECT_DISK   0x0e
 9    #define   CURR_DISK     0x19
10    #define   SET_DTA       0x1a
11    #define   GET_CURR_FAT  0x1b
12    #define   GET_FAT       0x1c
13    #define   SET_INT       0x25          /* install an interrupt vector */
14    #define   GET_DATE      0x2a
15    #define   SET_DATE      0x2b
16    #define   GET_TIME      0x2c
17    #define   SET_TIME      0x2d
18    #define   GET_DTA       0x2f
19    #define   GET_DOS_VER   0x30
20    #define   KEEP_PROC     0x31
21    #define   GET_INT       0x35          /* return an interrupt vector */
22    #define   DISK_FREE     0x36
23    #define   MKDIR         0x39
24    #define   RMDIR         0x3a
25    #define   CHDIR         0x3b
26    #define   CREAT_FILE    0x3c
27    #define   OPEN_FILE     0x3d
28    #define   CLOSE_FILE    0x3e
29    #define   READ_FILE     0x3f
30    #define   WRITE_FILE    0x40
31    #define   UNLINK_FILE   0x41
32    #define   LSEEK_FILE    0x42
33    #define   CHMOD_FILE    0x43
34    #define   IOCTL_FILE    0x44
35    #define   GET_DIR       0x47
36    #define   ALLOC_MEM     0x48
37    #define   FREE_MEM      0x49
38    #define   EXEC_PGM      0x4b
39    #define   EXIT_PROC     0x4c
40    #define   FIND_FIRST    0x4e
41    #define   FIND_NEXT     0x4f
42    #define   RENAME_FILE   0x56
43    #define   DATE_FILE     0x57
44
```

Figure 7.14c   c:usedos.c

```
1      /* usedos.c - examples of using DOS services */
2      #include "stdio.h"
3      #include "cminor.h"
4      #include "asmtools.h"
5      #include "dosfun.h"
6
7      int get_drive()                  /* get default drive number */
8      {                                /* returns 0=A: , 1=B: , 2=C: etc */
9          REGS sreg , dreg ;
10
11         dos2call(CURR_DISK,&sreg,&dreg) ;
12         return( dreg.ax & 0xff ) ;
13                                  /* return what DOS left in AL register */
14     }
15
16
17     int set_drive(dno)               /* set default drive */
18      int dno ;                       /* new drive number 0=A: , 1=b: etc */
19     {
20         REGS sreg , dreg ;
21
22         sreg.dx = (word16) dno ;
23         dos2call(SELECT_DISK,&sreg,&dreg) ;
24     }
25
26
27     int get_cd(dno,dname)            /* get name of current directory */
28      int dno ;                       /* on this drive 0=default, 1=a: 2=b: */
29      char dname[] ;                  /* put the directory name here */
30     {
31         REGS sreg , dreg ;
32
33         sreg.dx = (word16) dno ;
34         get_dads(dname,&sreg.ds,&sreg.si) ;
35         return(dos2call(GET_DIR,&sreg,&dreg) ) ;/* return success(0) */
36     }                                           /* or failure(-1)    */
37
38
```

DX register before making the DOS call. **get_cd** shows how we pass an address to DOS in the DS and SI registers. We use the **get_dads** function discussed earlier to convert the C address into the 8088 segmented address that DOS expects. This function also demonstrates how we can sense an error return from DOS. The GET_DIR DOS call signals errors via the 8088 carry flag. **dos2call** checks for this convention and returns 0 for a successful DOS call and −1 for a failure. **get_cd** can just pass the **dos2call** return value back to its caller.

7.7   Keyboard Input

□   The C library provides several functions for keyboard input. For example, the **getchar** and **get(stdin)** functions get a single character. However, most implementations of these functions are inappropriate for interactive programs. They may collect an entire line of input before returning a single character. They may also echo the character before returning. Finally, they may suppress inputs corresponding to special characters such as cursor control or function keys. The solution is to build our own functions—a KEYIO module. The function getkey, documented in Figure 7.15, returns a single character without echoing it or waiting for an entire line. Another function, keypress, documented in the same figure, checks to see if a character is waiting.

getkey returns an integer value; for ASCII characters this is like the value returned by getchar—a number between 0 and 0xff. For keys that do not correspond to an ASCII character, getkey returns a number greater than 0xff. The header file, keyio.h, in Figure 7.16 defines some ASCII control characters and non-ASCII keys.

Figure 7.17a shows a BIOS-based implementation of getkey and keypress. The BIOS status call returns with the 8088 zero flag set if no keystrokes are available. It returns with that flag not set if any input is available. Line 23 generates a software interrupt and tests the zero flag bit returned. Lines 25 to 27 set keypress's returned value based on that flag's value.

The getkey function uses the swint function to get a single keystroke with the ASCII code in AL and the scan code in AH. Line 41 extracts the ASCII code from AX, and if that value is 0, line 43 uses the scan code (+ 256) instead.

We can use getkey and keypress as the basis for additional keyboard functions. Figure 7.17b shows the waitcr and keyflush functions. waitcr calls getkey and discards keyboard input until a carriage return is typed. keyflush checks for and discards keyboard input until keypress indicates that no keyboard input is waiting. The following fragments show possible uses of these functions:

```
printf("press return when ready to continue \ n");
waitcr ( ) ;
```

and

```
keyflush( ) ; /* flush old input */
printf("delete file? (y/n) \ n");
if( getkey ( ) = = 'y' )
        { /* delete the file */
        . . .
```

Our KEYIO module gets input from the same source as the C library functions for the conosole input (getchar and scanf, for example). If you want to use both KEYIO and C library functions for console input in the same program, be careful to experiment with the interactions.

Figure 7.15   KEYIO description

Name

```
getkey   – get one keystroke from the keyboard
keypress – check for waiting keystroke
keyflush – discard any waiting keystroke input
waitcr   – discard keyboard input until CR pressed
```

Usage

```
int getkey( ) ;
int c , input_waiting ;
c = getkey( ) ;
input_waiting = keypress( ) ;
keyflush( ) ;
waitcr( ) ;
```

Function

getkey waits for the next keystroke from the keyboard. It returns an ASCII code (0 to 127) for keys corresponding to ASCII characters and values from 256 up for special keys such as function keys or cursor control keys. These are returned as (256 + extended code) using the extended code described in the PC technical reference manual.

The include file keyio.h defines symbolic constants for the values returned for many special keys.

keypress returns a zero value if no keyboard input is waiting and a nonzero value if some input is waiting. keyflush checks for keyboard input using keypress and discards it using getkey until no more input is waiting. waitcr uses keypress and getkey to discard input until the return key is pressed.

Keyboard input is not echoed by any of these functions. Input is available as soon as a single key is pressed; it is not queued until an entire line has been typed.

Examples

```
if( getkey( ) = = UPARROW )
  { /* start scrolling up */
    keyflush( ) ;
    printf(" press a key to stop scrolling \n");
    while( keypress( ) = = 0 )
        { scroll_up( ) ; }
  }
. . .
printf(" press return to continue \n");
waitcr( ) ;
```

References

IBM PC Technical Reference Manual, Appendix A: BIOS Listing.
Character codes and extended codes.

Figure 7.16   keyio.h

```
 1
 2      /* keyio.h  - definitions of values returned by getkey() */
 3
 4    /* keypress return values */
 5    #define NO_INPUT    0
 6    /* non-zero return means there is input waiting */
 7
 8      /* ASCII control characters */
 9
10    #define   ASCNUL      (256+3)
11    #define   ASCBEL         7
12    #define   ASCBS          8
13    #define   ASCTAB         9
14    #define   ASCLF       0xA
15    #define   ASCFF       0xC
16    #define   ASCCR       0xD
17    #define   ASCESC      0x1B
18    #define   ASCDEL      0x7F
19    #define   ASCSPACE    0x20
20
21      /* special keys for IBM PC */
22
23    #define   HOMEKEY     (256+71)
24    #define   BACKTAB     (256+15)
25    #define   UPARROW     (256+72)
26    #define   LEFTARROW   (256+75)
27    #define   RIGHTARROW  (256+77)
28    #define   ENDKEY      (256+79)
29    #define   DOWNARROW   (256+80)
30    #define   PGUPKEY     (256+73)
31    #define   PGDNKEY     (256+81)
32    #define   INSERTKEY   (256+82)
33    #define   DELETEKEY   (256+83)
34    #define   CTLPRTSC    (256+114)
35    #define   CTLLARROW   (256+115)
36    #define   CTLRARROW   (256+116)
37    #define   CTLEND      (256+117)
38    #define   CTLPGDN     (256+118)
39    #define   CTLHOME     (256+119)
40    #define   CTLPGUP     (256+132)
41
42    /* function key codes */
43    #define   F1KEY       (256+59)
44    #define   F11KEY      (256+84)
45    #define   F21KEY      (256+94)
46    #define   F31KEY      (256+104)
47
48    /* alt-key + number key (top row) */
49    #define   ALT1KEY     (256+120)
```

Figure 7.17a   *keyio1.c*

```
1     /* keyio1.c - getkey() and keypress() functions */
2     /* system dependent part of the keyboard input module */
3     /* this version uses BIOS function calls */
4     #include "stdio.h"
5     #include "cminor.h"
6     #include "asmtools.h"
7     #include "dosfun.h"
8     #include "keyio.h"
9
10                           /* constants for BIOS calls */
11    #define KEYIO_CALL  0x16 /* software interrupt number */
12    #define CHK_STAT 0x0100 /* function code for check input status */
13    #define GET_CHR  0x0000 /* function code for getting a char */
14
15
16    int keypress()          /* check for keyboard input waiting */
17    {
18       int stat ;
19       REGS sreg , dreg ;
20
21                           /* do BIOS call to check status */
22       sreg.ax = CHK_STAT ;
23       stat = swint(KEYIO_CALL,&sreg,&dreg) & ZF_FLAG  ;
24
25       if( stat == 0 )
26           return( 1) ;       /* input is waiting */
27           else return(0) ;  /* no input waiting */
28    }
29
30
31    /* getkey - waits for and returns the next keystroke input */
32    /* keystrokes that the Rom-BIOS describes with extended codes */
33    /* are returned as integers > 255 */
34    int getkey()            /* get the next key input  */
35    {
36       int c ;
37       REGS sreg , dreg ;
38
39       sreg.ax = GET_CHR ;
40       swint(KEYIO_CALL,&sreg,&dreg) ;
41       c = dreg.ax  & 0xff ;          /* get ASCII code */
42       if (c == 0)             /* is it a non-ASCII extended code */
43           c = 0x100 + (dreg.ax >> 8)  ;/* yes - use 256 + scan code */
44       return(c) ;
45    }
46
```

Figure 7.17b   keyio2.c

```
1    /* keyio2.c - keyflush() and waitcr() functions */
2    /* system-independent part of the keyboard input module */
3    #include "stdio.h"
4    #include "keyio.h"
5
6
7    int keyflush()                    /* discard any waiting console input */
8      {
9                                        /* repeat */
10        while( keypress() != 0 )       /* check for input */
11          { getkey() ; }               /* and discard if found */
12      }
13
14
15
16   int waitcr()                      /* wait until a cr is typed. */
17     {
18        while( getkey() != '\r' )      /* discard input until CR found */
19          { ; }
20     }
```

Note

These keyboard I/O functions can be implemented using PC-DOS services or BIOS services. Using PC-DOS services allows our functions to be used on any computer running PC-DOS or MS-DOS. If we use DOS calls that check for control–Break, we will be able to abort a program when it calls getkey or keypress. And using DOS calls minimizes the risk that our program will conflict with other software such as keyboard enhancers or print spoolers. Finally, using a DOS function or input allows us to copy console output to the printer by pressing Ctrl–PrtSc. But there are disadvantages also: Some PC-DOS calls dedicate keystrokes such as control-P and others to control echoing console output to the printer. Version 2.0 and earlier versions of PC-DOS also misinterpret some non-ASCII key inputs.

The BIOS approach has particular advantages: Keyboard input is passed to our function without interpretation. And the BIOS functions provide the scan code for each key input as well as its ASCII code.

The disadvantage is that our function is limited to IBM-PC-compatible computers. Our solution is to define the functions so that either implementation could be chosen. This gives us the freedom to change the implementation without affecting the programs that use getkey and keypress.

7.8 VIDEO Output Functions

□   The vidint function we developed gives us access to the video output services in the PC's ROM BIOS. But we can make these functions somewhat easier to use. The functions described in Figure 7.18 hide the details of register assignments and

Figure 7.18   VIDEO I/O module description

Name

VIDEO - Module for Access to Rom BIOS video_IO Services

Function

The various functions in the VIDEO module provide access to the VIDEO output services in the PC ROM BIOS. The header function, video.h, defines symbolic constants for VIDEO modes, screen attributes, and I/O addresses. Since these functions use BIOS services, they are fairly portable but have rather poor performance for displaying large numbers of characters.

Individual functions are described below. See the *IBM PC Technical Reference Manual* for further information.

A few assumptions are made to simplify the functions. Page 0 is selected and an 80 column per line width is assumed.

Function Descriptions

int vid_init(new_mode)

initializes BIOS video support to a new mode. Modes are defined in video.h.

int ncols ;
int vid_state(& ncols)

returns the current video mode. The number of columns per line is stored in the integer location whose address is passed. Modes are defined in video.h.

vid_set_cur(row,col)

sets the cursor position on the display. Page 0 of the display is assumed.

vid_get_cur(&row,&col)

gets the row and column numbers of the current cursor position. Page 0 of the display is assumed.

vid_clr_scn(from_row,thru_row)

clears the screen from the first row number through the second. Page 0 and 80 columns per line are assumed.

vid_up(nrows,from_row,thru_row)

Figure 7.18   VIDEO I/O module description (continued)

scrolls part of the screen (defined by the second and third arguments) upward by nrows. Page 0 and 80 columns per line are assumed.

vid_down(nrows,from_row,thru_row)

scrolls part of the screen (defined by the second and third arguments) downward by nrows. Page 0 and 80 columns per line are assumed.

vid_blank(n,a)

writes *n* blank characters (with attribute a) at the cursor position. Page 0 is assumed. Attributes are defined in video.h.

vid_wca(c,a)

writes the character c with the attribute a at the cursor position. The cursor is not advanced. No special characters such as carriage return or line feed are recognized.

char c , a ;
vid_gca(&c,&a)

gets the character and the attribute at the cursor position. Note that addresses of character variables—not integers—should be passed. The cursor is not advanced.

vid_tc(c)

writes the character c at the cursor position. The cursor is advanced. Special characters such as carriage return, line feed, bel, and backspace are recognized. The attribute at the cursor location is unchanged. This is the normal TTY output used by DOS for console output. Page 0 is assumed.

vid_tca(c,a)

writes the character c with the attribute a at the cursor position. Both vid_wca and vid_tc are used.

vid_ts(s)

Figure 7.18   VIDEO I/O module description (continued)

writes the character string s at the cursor position. The cursor is advanced. The vid_tc function is used to output each character.

vid_tsa(s,a)

writes the character string s with the attribute a at the cursor position. The cursor is advanced. The vid_tca function is used to output each character.

References

IBM PC Technical Reference Manual, Appendix A: BIOS Listing.

provide a different function for each BIOS service. The video.h header file in Figure 7.19 defines constants needed within the VIDEO module and by functions that use the module.

Figures 7.20a–c list the basic VIDEO output functions. Most of the functions in the module correspond directly to a BIOS service, but there are a few additions. The vid_clr_scn function in lines 7 to 11 of Figure 7.20b clears part or all of the screen using a special case feature of the scroll up function. The vid_blank in lines 39–47 of Figure 7.20b function blanks a number of positions that we specify along with the screen attribute to be used. Lines 21 and 22 and 34 and 35 of Figure 7.20b set up row and column numbers for the 16-bit CX and DX registers. A faster but less readable way to perform line 22 would be

```
( (BYTE_REGS *) &sreg.dx) − >dh = thru−row ;
( (BYTE_REGS *) &sreg.dx) − >dl = 79 ;
```

The BYTE_REGS data structure is defined in asmtools.h. It is convenient for setting up values in al-dh.

The functions in Figure 7.21 illustrate how we can use the basic VIDEO functions to build higher-level functions. The ROM BIOS does not provide any services for outputting C strings, but we can easily implement them using the single character functions, vid_wca and vid_tc. Functions to insert and delete characters can be written in a similar way using the vid_gca and vid_set_ cursor functions.

The ROM BIOS functions are well standardized. All IBM PC models and PC compatibles support them. Many other MS-DOS systems also support these functions. Even systems with nonstandard display adapters respond properly to these BIOS calls. When it is feasible, you should use these functions for screen output. However, their performance sometimes makes them unsatisfactory.

The following table shows times for writing 1,000 characters (with and

Figure 7.19   video.h

```
1    /* video.h - define constants for Video_IO module */
2
3    /* screen attributes */
4    #define   NON_DISPLAY       0x00
5    #define   UNDERLINE         0x01
6    #define   NORMAL_DISPLAY    0x07
7    #define   REVERSE_VIDEO     0x70
8    /* combine the following with the above values */
9    #define   HI_INTENSITY      0x08
10   #define   BLINK_BIT         0x80
11
12   /* video modes (as defined by the Rom BIOS */
13   #define   BW40_MODE              0
14   #define   CO40_MODE              1
15   #define   BW80_MODE              2
16   #define   CO80_MODE              3
17   #define   CO320_MODE             4
18   #define   BW320_MODE             5
19   #define   BW640_MODE             6
20   #define   MONO_MODE              7
21
22   /* Rom BIOS function values */
23   /* (put one of these values into sreg.ah before calling */
24   /* the VIDEO_IO services in the Rom BIOS) */
25   #define   V_INIT            0
26   #define   V_CTYPE           1
27   #define   V_SET_CUR         2
28   #define   V_GET_CUR         3
29   #define   V_SETPAGE         5
30   #define   V_SCRLUP          6
31   #define   V_SCRLDOWN        7
32   #define   V_GCA             8
33   #define   V_WCA             9
34   #define   V_WC             10
35   #define   V_WTTY           14
36   #define   V_STATE          15
```

without scrolling the screen after each 80-character line). This performance level is satisfactory for writing a few characters, but the delay is noticeable when the entire screen is updated. For this reason, most commercial programs that are highly interactive perform screen output in a more direct but less portable way. The next section develops a SCREEN module for much faster screen output.

	Time to Write 1,000 Characters	
Function	*No Scroll*	*With Scroll*
vid__tc	1.2	1.5
vid__tca	1.8	2.1

Figure 7.20a   video1.c

```
1     /* video1.c - basic Rom BIOS calls for Video_IO   */
2     #include "stdio.h"
3     #include "cminor.h"
4     #include "video.h"
5     #include "asmtools.h"
6
7     int vid_init(new_mode)            /* initialize display mode */
8      int new_mode ;                   /* (See video.h for modes ) */
9      {
10       REGS sreg,dreg ;
11
12       sreg.ax = new_mode & 0x07 ;   /* force mode to be <= 7 */
13       vidint(V_INIT,&sreg,&dreg) ;
14      }
15
16    int vid_state(pcol)               /* get current state info */
17     int *pcol ;                      /* store number of columns here*/
18     {                                /* return the current mode value */
19       REGS sreg , dreg ;
20
21       vidint(V_STATE,&sreg,&dreg) ;
22       *pcol = ( (BYTE_REGS *)&dreg)->ah ;
23       return( dreg.ax & 0xff) ;
24      }
25
26    int vid_page(new_page)            /* set display page */
27     int new_page ;                   /* new page number */
28     {
29       REGS sreg,dreg ;
30
31       sreg.ax = new_page & 0x07 ;   /* force new page to be <= 7 */
32       vidint(V_SETPAGE,&sreg,&dreg) ;
33      }
34
35    int vid_set_cur(row,col)          /* set cursor position */
36     int row ;                        /* new row number */
37     int col ;                        /* new column number */
38     {
39       REGS sreg , dreg ;
40
41       ((BYTE_REGS *) &sreg) ->dh = row ;
42       ((BYTE_REGS *) &sreg) ->dl = col ;
43       sreg.bx = 0 ;
44       vidint(V_SET_CUR,&sreg,&dreg) ;
45      }
46
47    int vid_get_cur(prow,pcol)        /* get current cursor position */
48     int *prow ;                      /* store row number here */
49     int *pcol ;                      /* store column number here */
50     {
51       REGS sreg , dreg ;
52
53       sreg.bx = 0 ;
54       vidint(V_GET_CUR,&sreg,&dreg) ;
55       *prow = ( (BYTE_REGS *)&dreg)->dh ;
56       *pcol = ( (BYTE_REGS *)&dreg)->dl ;
57      }
```

Figure 7.20b   video2.c

```
1    /* video2.c - basic Rom BIOS calls for Video_IO  */
2    #include "stdio.h"
3    #include "cminor.h"
4    #include "video.h"
5    #include "asmtools.h"
6
7    int vid_clr_scn(from_row,thru_row)  /* clear part/all of screen */
8     int from_row , thru_row ;        /* top and bottom row to clear */
9     {
10        vid_up(0,from_row,thru_row) ; /* special case of scroll */
11    }
12
13   int vid_up(nrows,from_row,thru_row) /* scroll part/all screen up */
14    int nrows ;                         /* number of rows up */
15    int from_row , thru_row ;        /* start and end here */
16    {
17       REGS sreg , dreg ;
18
19       sreg.ax = nrows ;
20       ( (BYTE_REGS *)&sreg)->bh = NORMAL_DISPLAY ;
21       sreg.cx = from_row << 8 ;           /* ch=from_row , cl=0  */
22       sreg.dx = (thru_row << 8) | 79 ;  /* dh=thru_row , dl=79 */
23       vidint(V_SCRLUP,&sreg,&dreg) ;
24    }
25
26   int vid_down(nrows,from_row,thru_row) /* scroll screen down */
27    int nrows ;                          /* number of rows up */
28    int from_row , thru_row ;        /* start and end here */
29    {
30       REGS sreg , dreg ;
31
32       sreg.ax = nrows ;
33       ( (BYTE_REGS *)&sreg)->bh = NORMAL_DISPLAY ;
34       sreg.cx = from_row << 8 ;           /* ch=from_row , cl=0  */
35       sreg.dx = (thru_row << 8) | 79 ;  /* dh=thru_row , dl=79 */
36       vidint(V_SCRLDOWN,&sreg,&dreg) ;
37    }
38
39   int vid_blank(n,a)        /* write n blanks */
40    int n ;                  /* no. blanks to write */
41    char a ;                 /* use this attribute */
42    {
43       REGS sreg , dreg ;
44
45       sreg.bx = a & 0xff ;   sreg.ax = ' ' ;   sreg.cx = n ;
46       vidint(V_WCA,&sreg,&dreg) ;
47    }
```

Figure 7.20c   video3.c

```
1    /* video3.c - char output calls for Video_IO   */
2    /* note that vid_wca() and vid_gca() do not advance the cursor */
3    #include "stdio.h"
4    #include "cminor.h"
5    #include "video.h"
6    #include "asmtools.h"
7    #include "keyio.h"
8
9    int vid_wca(c,a)              /* display char and attribute */
10    int c  ;                     /* char to display */
11    int a ;                      /* attribute */
12    {
13      REGS sreg , dreg ;
14
15      sreg.bx = a & 0xff ;
16      sreg.ax = c & 0xff ;
17      sreg.cx = 1 ;              /* count of chars to display =1 */
18      vidint(V_WCA,&sreg,&dreg) ;
19    }
20
21    int vid_gca(pc,pa)           /* get char and attribute at cursor */
22    char *pc  ;                  /* store char here */
23    char *pa ;                   /* store attribute here */
24    {
25      REGS sreg , dreg ;
26
27      sreg.bx = 0 ;
28      vidint(V_GCA,&sreg,&dreg) ;
29      *pc = ( (BYTE_REGS *) &dreg)->al ;
30      *pa = ( (BYTE_REGS *) &dreg)->ah ;
31    }
32
33    int vid_tc(c)                /* output one char with TTY write */
34    int c  ;                     /* char to write */
35    {
36      REGS sreg , dreg ;
37
38      sreg.bx = 0 ;
39      sreg.ax = c & 0xff ;
40      vidint(V_WTTY,&sreg,&dreg) ;  /* write char & advance cur. */
41    }
```

7.9   Direct Screen Output

□   Fortunately, we can bypass the ROM BIOS VIDEO I/O services and write characters on the screen directly. While this is specific to the PC's hardware architecture, it provides adequate performance. Since our purpose is to support interactive applications with high-speed screen output, we provide only the basic functions: writing single characters and character strings and reading back characters and attributes. Other functions control the position on the screen and the current video attribute.

Figure 7.21   video4.c

```
 1    /* video4.c - higher level char and string output */
 2    #include "stdio.h"
 3    #include "cminor.h"
 4    #include "video.h"
 5    #include "keyio.h"
 6
 7    int vid_tca(c,a)                    /* output char with attribute */
 8     int c  ;                           /* char value */
 9     int a ;                            /* attribute value */
10     {
11                                        /* don't write attribute if */
12        if(    (c != ASCBEL)            /* it is a special char */
13           && (c != ASCCR ) && (c != ASCLF)
14           && (c != ASCBS ) )
15           vid_wca(c,a) ;               /* write out the attrib. */
16        vid_tc(c) ;                     /* now write char & advance cur. */
17     }
18
19    int vid_ts(s)                       /* output a string with TTY write */
20     char *s  ;                         /* the string to output */
21     {
22        while( *s != '\0' )             /* repeat until end of string */
23           { vid_tc(*s) ;               /* output current char */
24             s = s + 1 ;                /* point to next char */
25           }
26     }
27
28    int vid_tsa(s,a)                    /* output string with attribute */
29     char *s  ;                         /* the string to output */
30     int a ;                            /* the attribute */
31     {
32        while( *s != '\0' )             /* repeat until end of string */
33           { vid_tca(*s,a) ;            /* output curr. char & attribute */
34             s = s + 1 ;                /* point to next char */
35           }
36     }
```

Several features of the BIOS functions can be eliminated to improve performance. Scrolling the screen when the cursor reaches the bottom is not required in many interactive applications. Our screen output functions will not check for the end of the screen and will not recognize special characters such as carriage return, line feed, bel, or backspace (those services can be added at a higher level). Updating the position of the visible cursor after each character is written slows output and causes distracting movement on the screen; we do not update the cursor position with our screen output functions. To keep the module simple (and performance high), we always use text mode with 80 columns and page 0 of display memory.

Figure 7.22 describes the SCREEN module. All the functions use a structure that records where the next character will be written on the screen and the display attribute to be used. This structure keeps all the context we need to output

Figure 7.22   SCREEN I/O module description

Name

SCREEN – Module for Direct Output to CRT Screen

Function

The SCREEN module provides fast console output by writing directly to the CRT screen. It writes/reads characters during horizontal retrace intervals to avoid screen interference (called snow). Functions for writing characters and strings are included with utility functions for controlling position on the screen and the display attribute of characters written.

Some symbolic constants such as display attribute values are defined in video.h. The scn.h header file defines the data structure that contains current screen position and display attribute.

SCREEN does not provide scrolling or recognize special control characters such as carriage return and line feed. Use the VIDEO module for scrolling and cursor positioning. SCREEN makes direct use of hardware addresses for the screen buffer memory and for other addresses. This makes SCREEN specific to IBM PCs and to PC compatibles.

Individual functions are described following. See the *IBM PC Technical Reference Manual* for further information.

Function Descriptions

```
SCN_DATA sc ;
int scn_init(& sc)
```

initializes the SCREEN data structure. The current position is set at the beginning of the screen and the display attribute to that for normal display. The screen buffer and status port addresses appropriate for the display adapter in use are also stored in the data structure. An 80-column text mode (with display page 0) is forced if not already selected.

```
scn_pos(&sc,row,col)
```

sets the current position on the screen. The position of the visible cursor is not affected.

```
char attrib ;
scn_attrib (&sc,attrib)
```

sets the display attribute to be used when characters are written. See video.h for attribute values.

```
char c , a ;
scn_gca(&c,&a,&sc)
```

gets the character and the attribute at the current screen position. Note that addresses of character variables—not integers—should be passed. The current screen position is advanced.

Figure 7.22   SCREEN I/O module description (continued)

```
char c ;
scn_wc(c,&sc)
```

writes the character c at the cursor position. The current position is advanced. Special characters such as carriage return, line feed, bel, and backspace are not recognized. The current display attribute is written with the character value at the current screen position.

```
char s[10] ;
scn_ws(s,&sc)
```

writes the character string s at the cursor position. The current screen position is advanced. The current display attribute is written with each character. The null character ('\0') marks the end of the string, but no other special character values are recognized.

characters. If we want to create separate output areas in different parts of the screen, we can create a different structure for each area.

Design

The characters displayed on the screen and their attributes are stored in memory locations that can be read or written by the 8088 processor, so outputting characters just requires writing them to special memory locations. There are some details that complicate our job, however.

Two types of display adapters are used in the IBM PC. They differ in the address of the screen buffer and in the I/O port addresses used for control and status functions. In addition, the monochrome adapter supports a single mode—25-line by 80-column text—while the color graphics adapter supports a variety of modes—text and graphics. Our SCREEN module must determine which adapter is in use and use the appropriate set of addresses.

The layout of characters and display attributes in memory varies with the video mode in use. We eliminate the differences by forcing the display to be in an 80-column text mode. The color graphics adapter also supports more than one display page; for simplicity we force the use of page 0. With these limitations, the following memory layout applies to either adapter and any 80-column video mode. The three diagrams show the organization of lines of text in the buffer, of columns of text within a line, and of the character and attribute for each column.

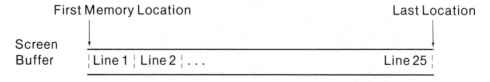

Line N	Col 1	Col 2	. . .	Col 40/80

Line N	Char	Attribute	Char	Attr.	. . .

--Column 1---- --Column 2-- . . .

Characters and attributes each occupy one byte of memory. Characters are stored as normal ASCII values (32 to 126 for ASCII graphic characters). Attribute byte values are defined in the video.h header file.

If we use the 8088 small memory model, as discussed earlier in the chapter, we cannot address these memory locations with C pointers. But could we use the poke functions developed earlier in this chapter? The following fragment is an example of how we might use poke:

```
poke(c,scn_seg,scn_off) ;
poke(attrib,scn_seg,scn_off + 1) ;
```

If we try this with a monochrome display adapter, it works fine, but on a color graphics adapter it produces distracting flashes on the screen. This is a hardware limitation of the color graphics adapter; if we write to the screen buffer while the CRT monitor is being updated, this flashing occurs. We can avoid the problem if we wait for *horizontal retrace* intervals when the display adapter has just finished updating a line on the CRT screen. Our functions monitor a status port on the display adapter to detect the horizontal retrace condition.

Implementing SCREEN

The header file, scn.h, in Figure 7.23 defines a structure for the SCREEN module. This structure keeps track of our current position on the screen and the display attribute being used. Each function in the SCREEN module uses a pointer to such a structure. The structure also contains the segment address of the screen buffer and the I/O port address of the status port.

The source file in Figure 7.24a contains several housekeeping functions. The scn_init function initializes the SCN_DATA structure. It checks the current video mode to ensure that an 80-column text mode will be used. It also forces page 0 to be the active page of display memory. A call to the scn_addr function sets the screen buffer address and the status port address.

The scn_attrib function sets the current display attribute to be used when characters are written with the SCREEN module. scn_pos sets the current screen position in the same way. Note that this position is stored as an offset relative to the start of the screen buffer. This representative makes scn_pos slower but allows

Figure 7.23   scn.h

```
1
2     /* scn.h - defines data and control values for screen module */
3
4     typedef struct scn_data
5       { unsigned cpos ;        /* current position on screen */
6                                 /* (offset relative to scn_seg) */
7         unsigned scn_seg ;     /* segment address of screen memory */
8         unsigned cattrib ;     /* current screen attribute */
9         unsigned stport  ;     /* CRT status I/O port address */
10        int      ncols   ;     /* number of columns on screen */
11      } SCN_DATA ;
12
13    /* segment addresses for screen memory */
14    #define   MONO_SEG        0xb000
15    #define   CG_SEG          0xb800
16
17    /* Control and status port addresses */
18    #define   MONO_BASE       0x3b0
19    #define   COLOR_BASE      0x3d0
20    /* combine the following port addresses w/ the above base values */
21    #define   M6845_INDEX        4
22    #define   M6845_DATA         5
23    #define   CRT_CTRL           8
24    #define   CRT_STATUS      0x0a
25
26    /* definitions for display attributes are in video.h */
```

the functions for writing data to be very fast. The assumption behind this trade-off is that writing data will be more frequent than changing the screen position.

The **scn_type** function in Figure 7.24b determines the type of display adapter in use based on the equipment determination BIOS call. This method uses the same information that the BIOS **VIDEO_IO** calls use for maximum compatibility. The **scn_addr** function sets the screen buffer segment address and the CRT status port address based on the type of adapter.

Figure 7.24c lists the Assembler functions for writing a single character (**scn_wc**), writing a character string (**scn_ws**), and reading a single character. The structure of the source file is the same as we described earlier for the **asm.tools** file. Lines 6 to 12 define the **SCN_DATA** structure in assembly language format. Each function has another structure that defines its input arguments.

Lines 21 to 48 define the **scn_wc** function. It sets up the character, attribute, screen buffer address (segment and offset), and the status port address in registers and calls the **scn_0** routine (lines 50 to 64) to wait for horizontal retrace and write the character. The form of this routine is dictated by the short retrace time interval.

The **scn_ws** function in lines 66 to 108 writes each of a string of characters. It uses the same routine **scn_0** to write each character as did **scn_wc**. The

Figure 7.24a   scn1.c

```
1     /* scn1.c - initialize for screen I/O */
2     #include "stdio.h"
3     #include "video.h"
4     #include "scn.h"
5
6
7     int scn_init(pscn)
8       SCN_DATA *pscn ;    /* points to screen data area to init */
9       {
10        int cols ;
11
12                                    /* check video mode and reset */
13                                    /* if not 80 col. text */
14        switch( vid_state(&cols) & 0x07 )
15          {
16          case BW80_MODE :
17          case CO80_MODE :
18          case MONO_MODE :
19            break ;
20          default :
21            vid_init(BW80_MODE) ;
22            break ;
23          }
24
25        scn_addr(pscn) ;            /* set up screen addresses */
26        vid_page(0) ;              /* force page zero */
27
28        pscn->cpos = 0 ;            /* current position on screen */
29        pscn->cattrib = NORMAL_DISPLAY ; /* use normal video attr. */
30        vid_state(& (pscn->ncols) ); /* get no. columns per line */
31      }
32
33    int scn_attrib(pscn,a)          /* set screen attribute */
34      SCN_DATA  *pscn ;
35      int a ;
36      {
37        pscn->cattrib = a ;
38      }
39
40    int scn_pos(pscn,row,col)      /* set current position on screen */
41      SCN_DATA *pscn ;
42      int row ;
43      int col ;
44      {
45        pscn->cpos = (row*(pscn->ncols) + col) << 1 ;
46      }
47
```

Figure 7.24b   scn3.c

```
1    /* scn3.c - utilities for setting up screen I/O */
2    #include "stdio.h"
3    #include "cminor.h"
4    #include "video.h"
5    #include "asmtools.h"
6    #include "scn.h"
7
8    #define EQUIP_DET   0x11    /* software int no. for Equipment */
9                               /* Determination */
10   #define DISP_BITS   0x30    /* mask for display type bits */
11   #define BW_DISP     0x30    /* value of above bits for mono disp. */
12   #define CG_USED     1       /* screen type = color/graphics */
13   #define MONO_USED   0       /* screen type = monochrone adapter */
14
15   int scn_type()             /* get type of display adapter used */
16     {
17       REGS sreg,dreg ;
18
19       swint(EQUIP_DET,&sreg,&dreg) ;
20       dreg.ax=dreg.ax & DISP_BITS; /* isolate display type */
21       if( dreg.ax != BW_DISP )      /* is it mono adapter type ? */
22            return( CG_USED ) ;      /*  no - return Color Gr. in use */
23       else return( MONO_USED ) ;    /*  yes - return MONO in use */
24     }
25
26   int scn_addr(pscn)         /* set display addresses */
27     SCN_DATA *pscn ;         /* address of screen control block */
28     {
29       if( scn_type() == MONO_USED )
30         { pscn->scn_seg = MONO_SEG ;
31           pscn->stport  = MONO_BASE + CRT_STATUS ;
32         }
33       else
34         { pscn->scn_seg = CG_SEG ;
35           pscn->stport  = COLOR_BASE + CRT_STATUS ;
36         }
37     }
38
```

scn_gca function in lines 111 to 139 reads the character and attribute at the screen position. The routine in lines 141 to 154 is analogous to scn_0 except that after waiting for the retrace interval, it reads the character and attribute from SCREEN memory.

All three functions update the current screen position for each character written or read. This is normally desirable and, as the listing shows, can be incorporated with little extra overhead. A single instruction—stosw or lodsw—writes or reads character and attribute and also advances the buffer offset in the SI or DI register. Another instruction stores the updated offset back into the SCN_DATA structure before leaving the function. Since two bytes are written for each

Figure 7.24c   scn2.asm

```
 1    ;          scn2.asm - asm functions for fast screen I/O
 2
 3    ;          structure for screen data
 4    ;          defines the offsets for use in the assembler functions
 5    ;          (see scn.h for C structure definition)
 6    scn_data struc
 7    cpos     dw      0                  ; current offset
 8    scn_seg dw       0                  ; screen segment value
 9    cattr    dw      0                  ; current screen attrib.
10    stp      dw      0                  ;  "    "    "     "  "  stat. "
11    ncols    dw      0                  ; number of columns on screen
12    scn_data ends
13
14    ;        put data here
15             include begdata.ha
16             include enddata.ha
17
18    ;        start code
19             include begcode.ha
20
21    ;        scn_wc - write char to screen
22    ;
23    ;        usage:  scn_wc(char,p_scn_data) ;
24    ;
25    scn_wc_args struc                    ; input arguments
26             dw      0                   ; saved BP value
27             dw      0                   ; return address
28    schar    dw      0                   ; character to write
29    pswc     dw      0                   ; pointer to scn_data
30    scn_wc_args ends
31             public  scn_wc
32    scn_wc:
33             push    bp
34             mov     bp,sp              ;set our arg pointer
35             push    es
36             push    di
37             cld
38             mov     bx,word ptr [pswc+bp]    ; get ptr to scn data
39             les     di,dword ptr [cpos+bx]   ; get offset & seg. address
40             mov     cl,byte ptr [schar+bp]   ; save the char
41             mov     ch,byte ptr [cattr+bx]   ; and the attribute in cx
42             mov     dx,word ptr [stp+bx]     ; get status port address
43             call    scn_0       ; actually write the char
44             mov     word ptr [bx],di ; update position on screen
45             pop     di
46             pop     es
47             pop     bp
48             ret
49
50    scn_0:  ; internal routine - writes one char
51    ;        wait for horizontal retrace
52    scn_1:
53             in      al,dx              ; wait until non in retrace
54             test    al,1               ; test horizontal retrace bit
55             jnz     scn_1
```

Figure 7.24c   scn2.asm (continued)

```
56              cli
57      scn_2:
58              in      al,dx               ; wait until retrace starts
59              test    al,1                ; test retrace bit
60              jz      scn_2
61              mov     ax,cx               ; bring back data
62              stosw                       ; and write it to screen
63              sti                         ; now allow interrupts again
64              ret
65
66      ;       scn_ws - write string to screen
67      ;
68      ;       usage:  scn_ws(string,p_scn_data) ;
69      ;
70      scn_ws_args struc                   ; input arguments
71              dw      0                   ; saved BP value
72              dw      0                   ; return address
73      sstr    dw      0                   ; address of string to write
74      psws    dw      0                   ; pointer to scn_data
75      scn_ws_args ends
76              public  scn_ws
77      scn_ws:
78              push    bp
79              mov     bp,sp               ;set our arg pointer
80              push    es
81              push    di
82              push    si
83              cld
84              mov     si,word ptr [sstr+bp]   ; get the string pointer
85              mov     bx,word ptr [psws+bp]   ; get ptr to scn data
86              les     di,dword ptr [cpos+bx]  ; get offset & seg. address
87              mov     cl,byte ptr [schar+bp]  ; save the char
88              mov     ch,byte ptr [cattr+bx]  ;   and the attribute in cx
89              mov     dx,word ptr [stp+bx]    ; get status port address
90
91      sscn_0:
92              lodsb                           ; get next char in string
93                                              ; (and advance pointer)
94              or      al,al                   ; is it null ?
95              jz      sscn_3                  ;   y - exit
96              mov     cl,al                   ;   n - save it
97              call    scn_0                   ;       write the char
98      ;       written one char - repeat loop
99              jmp     short sscn_0
100
101     sscn_3: ; end of string reached - exit
102             mov     bx,word ptr [psws+bp] ; get ptr to scn data
103             mov     word ptr [bx],di ; update screen position
104             pop     si
105             pop     di
106             pop     es
107             pop     bp
108             ret
109
110
```

Figure 7.24c   scn2.asm (continued)

```
111     ;            scn_gca - get char and attrib from screen
112     ;
113     ;            usage:  c = scn_gca(&attrib,p_scn_data) ;
114     ;
115     scn_gca_args struc                  ; input arguments
116             dw      0                   ; saved BP value
117             dw      0                   ; return address
118     pattr   dw      0                   ; store attribute here
119     psgca   dw      0                   ; pointer to scn_data
120     scn_gca_args ends
121             public  scn_gca
122     scn_gca:
123             push    bp
124             mov     bp,sp               ;set our arg pointer
125             push    si
126             cld
127             mov     bx,word ptr [psgca+bp] ; get ptr to scn data
128             mov     dx,word ptr [stp+bx]    ; get status port address
129             push    ds
130             lds     si,dword ptr [cpos+bx] ; get offset & seg. address
131             call    scn_rd0             ; get the char and attribute
132             pop     ds
133             mov     word ptr [bx],si ; update position on screen
134             mov     si,word ptr pattr[bp] ; get address to store attrib
135             mov     byte ptr [si],ah ; store the attribute
136             xor     ah,ah               ; clear ah so that ax = char
137             pop     si
138             pop     bp
139             ret
140
141     scn_rd0: ; internal routine - reads one char and attribute
142     ;       wait for horizontal retrace
143     scn_rd1:
144             in      al,dx               ; wait until signal is low
145             test    al,1
146             jnz     scn_rd1
147             cli
148     scn_rd2:
149             in      al,dx               ; wait until high
150             test    al,1
151             jz      scn_rd2
152             lodsw
153             sti
154             ret
155
156             include endcode.ha
157             end
```

character—the character and the attribute—this offset is incremented by two for each character written or read.

Measuring SCREEN's Speed

Now that the SCREEN module is developed, we can check its performance. The following table compares times for writing 1,000 characters with the VIDEO function vid_tc and with the SCREEN functions. Direct screen output is over six times as fast as using the BIOS functions. (Reading characters from the screen is the same speed as writing them with scn_wc.)

Function	Time to Write 1,000 Characters (seconds)
vid_tc (no scroll)	1.2
scn_wc	0.19
scn_ws	0.10

The SCREEN module uses very detailed information about the IBM PC architecture. This may seem to be bad programming practice to write such nonportable functions. However, since such direct screen output techniques are necessary for good performance, they are used in most high-quality commercial software. Thus, the screen buffer address and status port address have become part of the PC architecture standardized in various IBM models and in products compatible with the IBM PC.

7.10 An Elapsed Time Function

□ Many of the performance measurements in previous chapters were timed by hand with a stopwatch. However, we can use the Time-of-Day call provided by the ROM BIOS to implement an elapsed time function, timer. Figure 7.25 describes this timer function.

The source code for timer is listed in Figure 7.26. timer uses the swint function to perform the Time-of-Day software interrupt, returning a time-of-day value. Line 17 assembles this time value returned in registers CX and DX into a single long variable. Line 18 gets the time difference since the last call to timer. Lines 19 and 20 correct the time difference if the time-of-day value rolled over to a new day since the last call. The last time-of-day value (stime) is updated before leaving timer.

Figure 7.25   timer function description

Name

   timer   get elapsed time since last call

Usage

```
int timer( ) ;
int t ;
t = timer( );
```

Function

timer returns the number of ticks since the last time it was called. (There are about 18.2 timer ticks per second.) The ROM BIOS Time-of-Day service is the basis for the timer function.

   Since the value returned by timer is an integer, it cannot record elapsed times greater than one hour. timer does correct for the rollover in the BIOS tick value at the end of a day.

Example

```
timer( ) ;
for(i=0 ; i< 20000 ; i=i+1)
   { vid_tc('A') ; }
printf(" %6.2f Seconds \n", ( (float) timer( ) ) / 18.2) ;
```

References

IBM PC Technical Reference Manual, Appendix A; the ROM BIOS Time-of-Day software interrupt (1A Hex).

The following fragment shows how timer can be used. The first call sets the starting time (stime), and a call later gets the time difference. The elapsed time value is returned as an integer value; this limits the timer function to differences of 30 minutes or less. This limitation makes timer a little easier to use; you can change timer to return a **long** value if you prefer.

```
int t ;
timer( ) ;
/* event to be timed */
t = timer( ) ;
printf(" elapsed time – %d Ticks or %6.2 Secs. \ n",
    t ,    (float) t) / 18.2 ) ;
```

The time interval used by the BIOS function and by timer is an odd one. But since the floating point division needed to convert it into seconds is fairly slow, we leave the conversion out of the timer function.

Figure 7.26   timer.c

```
 1    /* timer.c - use BIOS time-of-day interrupt */
 2    #include "stdio.h"
 3    #include "cminor.h"
 4    #include "asmtools.h"
 5
 6    long stime ;                    /* store time-of-day from last call */
 7    #define TOD_INT   0x1A          /* BIOS time-of-day interrupt */
 8
 9    int timer()                     /* count ticks since last call */
10      {
11        REGS sreg , dreg ;
12        long etime , delta ;
13
14        sreg.ax = 0 ;                    /* get time count */
15        swint(TOD_INT,&sreg,&dreg); /* get current  count */
16                                    /* assemble 32-bit time-of-day value */
17        etime = ( ((long) dreg.cx) << 16 ) + dreg.dx ;
18        delta = etime - stime ;
19        if( (dreg.ax & 0xff) != 0)   /* new day since last call? */
20            delta = delta + 0x01800B0L ; /* yes - add 1 day in ticks */
21        stime = etime ;             /* save time-of-day for next call */
22        return( (int) delta ) ;          /* return as an integer */
23      }
```

7.11   Generalized File I/O Library Functions

□   The toolkit functions developed have added new capabilities based on environment-dependent functions. The functions in this section serve a different purpose: They hide differences between different C compiler libraries. In Chapter 2 we discussed differences in handling ASCII/binary file types between C compilers and gave manual page descriptions for the gfopen, gopen, and gcreat generalized functions to hide compiler library differences. Several programs presented in the intervening chapters have used one of these functions. This section presents their implementation.

Figures 7.27 and 7.28 show implementations for several C compilers. Each source file contains versions of the functions for several popular C compilers. Before compiling and using these functions, you must edit them, removing all versions of the functions except the one appropriate for your compiler.

The gfopen, gopen, and gcreat functions do not add any new capabilities; they just isolate compiler-dependent source code into a few easily modified source files.

7.12   Using and Modifying the Toolkit

□   The toolkit functions we have discussed are ready to be used. You can type them into your editor and edit them for your compiler. Then you can compile them and build an object module library. But the available program diskette makes the

Figure 7.27   gfopen.cx

```
 1    /* gfopen.c - generalized buffered file open function */
 2    /*              allows either Binary or ASCII treatment */
 3    /*              (if the compiler supports it)           */
 4    /*              edit the file removing all versions     */
 5    /*                except that for your compiler         */
 6    #include "stdio.h"
 7    #include  "cminor.h"
 8    FILE *fopen() ;
 9
10    /* Lattice C/Microsoft C version */
11    extern int _fmode ;   /* global binary/ASCII flag */
12    FILE *gfopen(fn,fmode,ft)
13     char fn[] ;
14     char fmode[] ;
15     int  ft ;
16     {
17         int tmode ;
18         FILE *tfd ;
19
20         tmode = _fmode ;          /* save the flag value */
21         if( ft == BIN_MODE )
22             _fmode = 0x8000 ;  /* open in binary mode */
23         else _fmode = 0 ;      /* "    "  ASCII  mode */
24         tfd = fopen(fn,fmode) ; /* open the file */
25         _fmode = tmode ;   /* restore the flag value */
26         return( tfd ) ;
27     }
28    /* end of version */
29
30
31    /* Computer Innovations & Mark Williams version */
32    FILE *gfopen(fn,fmode,ft)
33     char fn[] ;
34     char fmode[] ;
35     int  ft ;
36     {
37         char mode_string[20] ;
38
39         strcpy(mode_string,fmode) ;   /* copy input mode string */
40         if( ft == BIN_MODE )
41            strcat(mode_string,"b");
42         return( fopen(fn,mode_string) ) ;
43     }
44    /* end of version */
45
46
47    /* Digital Research version */
48    FILE *fopenb() ;
49
50    FILE *gfopen(fn,fmode,ft)
51     char fn[] ;
52     char fmode[] ;
53     int  ft ;
54     {
55        if( ft == BIN_MODE )
56             return( fopenb(fn,fmode) ) ;
```

Figure 7.27   gfopen.cx (continued)

```
57        else return( fopena(fn,fmode) ) ;
58    }
59   /* end of version */
60
61
62   /* version for C-Ware, Manx Aztec C, Whitesmith's and C-Systems */
63   /* (They do not allow a choice of modes) */
64   FILE *gfopen(fn,fmode,ft)
65    char fn[] ;
66    char fmode[] ;
67    int  ft ;
68    {
69        return( fopen(fn,fmode) ) ; /* ignore ASCII/Binary type */
70    }
71   /* end of version */
```

job much easier. It contains object module libraries ready for use for several popular C compilers. You copy the appropriate object library file to your floppy or hard disk and set up a batch file to include this library when you link C programs.

The program diskette also contains the toolkit source files. If the diskette does not include an object library for your compiler or if you need to alter toolkit functions, you can start with these source files. Versions are included for a number of compilers. The diskette includes instructions on unpacking the files you need.

7.13   Summary

□ Developing toolkit functions requires understanding lots of low-level detail about how the computer hardware and operating system work. Understanding the computer's instruction set and the interface between C functions and functions written in Assembler are also necessary. Testing toolkit functions is a tedious, time-consuming task. In spite of the difficulty and effort involved, we had several reasons for discussing the toolkit functions.

Flexibility and Quality of Applications

Without services such as single-key input, fast screen output, and DOS access, most of the applications would be compromised in design or in execution speed. Our aim has been to show how to implement applications right, and a good toolkit is essential to that aim.

Some C compiler libraries may implement the standard C library functions well and may provide useful system-specific functions. But such libraries rarely provide everything required or implement everything well enough. Having a

Figure 7.28   gopen.cx

```
1     /* gopen.c - generalized file open and creat functions */
2     /* Select the version to be used and delete other versions. */
3     #include "stdio.h"
4     #include "cminor.h"
5
6     /* Lattice/Microsoft C version. */
7     /* Change BIN_BIT define for CI-C86, C-ware, Manx, C-systems */
8
9     /* define File Mode bit for Binary Mode */
10    #define BIN_BIT  0x8000        /* Lattice C  binary mode */
11    /* #define BIN_BIT   4 */ /* CI-C86  binary mode */
12    /* #define BIN_BIT   0 */ /* C-WARE, Manx, C-systems binary mode */
13
14    int gopen(fn,fmode,ft)              /* generalized version of open */
15     char fn[] ;                       /* file name */
16     int  fmode ;                      /* file mode read/write */
17     int  ft ;                         /* file type ASCII/binary */
18    {
19        unsigned tmode ;
20
21        tmode = fmode ;
22        if( ft == BIN_MODE )
23            tmode = tmode +  (unsigned) BIN_BIT ;
24        return( open(fn,tmode) ) ;
25    }
26
27    int gcreat(fn,fmode,ft)            /* generalized version of creat */
28     char fn[] ;                       /* file name */
29     unsigned  fmode ;                 /* file mode read/write */
30     int  ft ;                         /* file type ASCII/binary */
31    {
32        unsigned tmode ;
33
34        tmode = fmode ;
35        if( ft == BIN_MODE )
36            tmode = tmode +  (unsigned) BIN_BIT ;
37        return( creat(fn,tmode) ) ;
38    }
39    /* end of version */
40
41
42    /* Digital Research  version */
43    int gopen(fn,fmode,ft)             /* generalized version of open */
44     char fn[] ;                       /* file name */
45     int  fmode ;                      /* file mode read/write */
46     int  ft ;                         /* file type ASCII/binary */
47    {
48        if( ft == BIN_MODE )
49            return( openb(fn,fmode) ) ;
50        else return( open(fn,fmode) ) ;
51    }
52
53    int gcreat(fn,fmode,ft)            /* generalized version of creat */
54     char fn[] ;                       /* file name */
55     int  fmode ;                      /* file mode read/write */
```

Figure 7.28   gopen.cx (continued)

```
56      int  ft ;                              /* file type ASCII/binary */
57      {
58          if( ft == BIN_MODE )
59              return( creatb(fn,fmode) ) ;
60          else return( creat(fn,fmode) ) ;
61      }
62  /* end of version */
63
64  /* Whitesmiths version (based on version 2.2) */
65  int gopen(fn,fmode,ft)              /* generalized version of open */
66   char fn[] ;                        /* file name */
67   int  fmode ;                       /* file mode read/write */
68   int  ft ;                          /* file type ASCII/binary */
69   {
70       return( open(fn,fmode,ft) ) ;
71   }
72
73  int gcreat(fn,fmode,ft)             /* generalized version of creat */
74   char fn[] ;                        /* file name */
75   int  fmode ;                       /* file mode read/write */
76   int  ft ;                          /* file type ASCII/binary */
77   {
78       return( creat(fn,fmode,ft) ) ;
79   }
80  /* end of version */
81
82  /* Mark Williams  version - no support for low-level I/O */
83  int gopen(fn,fmode,ft)              /* generalized version of open */
84   char fn[] ;                        /* file name */
85   int  fmode ;                       /* file mode read/write */
86   int  ft ;                          /* file type ASCII/binary */
87   {
88       return( -1 ) ;                 /* no low level fun. in library */
89   }
90
91  int gcreat(fn,fmode,ft)             /* generalized version of creat */
92   char fn[] ;                        /* file name */
93   int  fmode ;                       /* file mode read/write */
94   int  ft ;                          /* file type ASCII/binary */
95   {
96       return( -1 ) ;                 /* no low level fun. in library */
97   }
98  /* end of version */
```

toolkit that you define and implement frees you from many of the limits of the C compiler and its library. Without a toolkit, the quality of your applications is determined in part by those limitations.

Portability

Some C compiler libraries implement some of the functions in our toolkit. If we want to write portable applications, however, we need to standardize our toolkit functions to be usable with any compiler. By collecting the functions dependent on the hardware, operating system, or C compiler in one library that we implement, we can keep the work of transporting software to another environment to an acceptable level.

Most of the applications discussed in other chapters would be useful in very different environments such as UNIX, the Apple Macintosh, or an 8-bit CP/M-80 system. Some of the toolkit modules such as KEYIO and SCREEN could be reimplemented to the same functional specification. For others such as dos2call and timer, a different but functionally equivalent definition is required. The toolkit still provides an effective way to control the use of system-specific functions in an application.

Developing Skills

You may not understand all the ideas presented in this chapter. You may not feel at home writing or even reading assembler functions. You may not be able to follow the descriptions in the IBM technical reference manuals either. You may even question the value of such skills since newer and better environments will replace the IBM PC and PC-DOS. However, acquiring these skills is an important part of being a competent programmer. You may never write an assembler function to access computer hardware directly, but you will be a better programmer if you understand how your C programs work. Our discussion should give you good examples of what to do with assembler language and how to do it.

The material we presented was checked with several C compilers. New releases of those compilers contain some changes that affect our toolkit functions. Appendix B discusses some C compilers for the IBM PC PC-DOS environment and the versions of the compilers that we examined.

8
A Terminal
Emulation Program

The subject of this chapter is terminal emulation programs. These programs allow you to use an IBM PC as a dumb ASCII terminal to talk to another computer via an RS-232 cable or a modem and a phone line. We start with a very bare-bones program that illustrates the basic requirements of the problem and then introduce improvements.

Like program editors, terminal emulator programs are widely available. However, no product may fit your needs completely. The programs developed here can serve as the basis for your own custom-tailored program.

A terminal emulator program is an example of a *real-time* program—one that communicates with the outside world and must meet absolute deadlines for handling input or producing some output. Our programs illustrate techniques such as polling, priority-driven scheduling, interrupts, and input buffering commonly used in real-time programs.

As in the previous chapter, there are many low-level details: It is necessary to use the PC hardware directly to produce satisfactory results. The programs we present have lots of references to I/O port addresses and control and status bit assignments. We explain what we are doing but not why the PC hardware works as it does. If the details of the PC's hardware and of asynchronous communications are a mystery to you, read this chapter along with appropriate references from Appendix D. There are a number of books discussing how the IBM PC's hardware works; our purpose is to show how to use that information to do something useful.

8.1 What Terminal Emulation Programs Do

☐ The basic functions of a terminal emulation program are simple. When we type a character, the program transmits it to the other computer. When we receive a character from the other computer, the program displays the character on the PC's screen. These are the basic functions of an ASCII CRT terminal; our program emulates such a terminal. To be genuinely useful, a TTY program needs to do more than this, but we start with a program that does only these functions.

Our TTY program uses asynchronous communications, or *async*, to send and receive characters. A PC can communicate with the outside world in many ways, but the terminals we emulate talk async so that is what we must use.

We do not describe the historical and technical reasons why async is used or explain how it works; the references in Appendix D contain good discussions. We list here some terms needed to discuss the TTY program and their definitions.

Asynchronous communications: This communication method sends characters one bit at a time (serially) rather than with all bits sent at one time in parallel. *Synchronous communication* is another related method, but asynchronous communication is more widely used on PCs. Both methods have advantages and applications in which they are appropriate. The choice is usually made on a practical basis; one method is supported by the other computer for the application you want to do.

Communications methods are like human languages because both parties in the conversation must agree to speak the same language to get anything done. Such agreements are called *protocols*, whether they specify the way a single character is transmitted or the way to interpret those characters as whole messages.

Some terminals use synchronous communications, and we could write a program to emulate them. But the problem our TTY program solves is emulating an async terminal so we will be concerned with asynchronous communication exclusively.

Async adapter: The hardware needed in an IBM PC for async communication is an asynchronous communications adapter. IBM supplies plug-in boards that perform this single function; multifunction boards from other vendors may perform additional functions. The function of these boards and the I/O addresses they use and commands they accept are well standardized.

8250 UART chip: The heart of the async adapter is a single chip—an INS8250 asynchronous communications element or its equivalent. Chips that transmit and receive characters serially for async communications are called UARTS (Universal Asynchronous Receiver-Transmitters). The 8250 is only one of many UART chips, but it is the standard for async communications in IBM PCs. Just remember the number 8250 and the acronym UART as names for the chip that transmits and receives characters in async protocol.

RS-232: The async adapter connects to the outside world through an RS-232 connector. RS-232 is the name of a standard for async and synchronous communications. It covers the size and shape of connectors, the number of pins in those connectors and their use, and the voltage levels used for signaling. Two voltage levels, high and low, are used to encode information.

Two devices communicating with async protocol may be connected directly through an RS-232 cable or via phone lines. *Modems* translate the RS-232 voltage levels into tones the phone lines can transmit successfully. Some of the pins in an RS-232 connector allow a device to sense a modem's status and to control the modem. We refer to the cable or modems (and phone line) that connect two computers as an *RS-232 line.*

Break signals: In addition to transmitting characters, we can transmit a special signal called *break.* Think of it like whistling; if you wanted to get the attention of a crowd, a loud whistle is an alternative to talking. Like the whistle, it does not convey much information. The RS-232 standard defines a break signal as being a low-voltage level held for at least 200 milliseconds.

Baud rate: Baud rate describes the speed at which data are transmitted. A rate of 300 baud is 30 characters per second, while 1,200 baud and 9,600 baud correspond to approximately 120 and 960 characters per second. The baud rate is the number of bits sent; two overhead bits are sent with each 8-bit character. At 110 baud, 3 overhead bits are normally used, making a rate of 10 characters per second.

8.2 A Basic Terminal Emulation Program

□ Figure 8.1 shows a simple terminal emulation program. It has no options or extra features but illustrates the nature of terminal emulators. The loop in lines 16 to 27 is the heart of the program. It repeatedly checks for either keyboard input or a character received from the communication line. When a character is received from the RS-232 line, it is displayed. When keyboard input is available, it is transmitted on the RS-232 line (if it is an ASCII character).

TTY1 uses the KEYIO and VIDEO modules from Chapter 7 for console input and ouput. The RS-232 functions comm_init, chk_rcy, rcv_char, chk_xmt, and xmt_char are in the async1.c module to be discussed in the next section.

Async I/O Support

The TTY1 program requires some support for serial I/O to the async hardware on the IBM PC. It needs functions to receive and transmit characters and to check receive and transmit status. The PC's ROM BIOS does provide these services, but with poor performance and no flexibility. We implement an ASYNC module that bypasses the BIOS and uses the PC's async I/O hardware directly.

Figure 8.2 shows the source file for this module. The module performs port input and output operations to control the async hardware; Figure 8.3 lists port addresses and control and status bit values for those ports. Two async ports, COM1: and COM2:, are supported by the PC's BIOS and by PC-DOS. For each async port, there is a range of I/O ports for control, status checking, and receiving and transmitting data. The async.h file defines this range of addresses. The comm_init function in lines 21 to 39 (Figure 8.2) determines which set of port addresses is to be used.

Figure 8.1   tty1.c

```
1     /* tty1.c - bare-bones tty emulation program */
2     #include "stdio.h"
3     #include "cminor.h"
4     #include "keyio.h"
5     #include "async.h"
6
7     #define   CARD    COM2            /* which RS-232 port to use */
8     #define   THRU_KEY  F1KEY         /* define key for exiting pgm */
9
10    main()
11    {
12        int c ;
13
14        comm_init(CARD) ;            /* set up for RS-232 use */
15        c = ' ' ;                    /* force execution the first time */
16        while( c != THRU_KEY )
17          {
18            if( chk_rcv() != 0 )     /* check for rcvd data */
19              { c = rcv_char() ;     /*    yes - get it */
20                vid_tc(c) ;          /*          and display it */
21              }
22            else if(keypress() != 0)/* check for keybd. input */
23              { c = getkey() ;       /*    yes - get it */
24                if( c < 0x100 )      /*          and transmit if ASCII */
25                    send_char(c) ;
26              }
27          }
28    }
```

The ROM BIOS maintains a table relating the COM1: and COM2: ports to I/O ports. comm_init uses the card number supplied as an index into this table. The result is checked to see that it corresponds to one of the async ports supported by the PC.

The chk_rcv function in lines 42 to 48 checks a status port to determine whether a received character is available. The rcv_char function in lines 51 to 60 collects that character from the receive data port. Several types of errors may occur—for example, the character may have overwritten a previously received character; the received character may have a parity error (one or more bits in error); a break signal may have been received. The rcv_data function reads a status port to check for these conditions. If an error has occurred, a –1 error value is returned. Otherwise, the received character (a value between 0 and 0xff) is returned.

The xmt_char function in lines 71 to 75 writes a character to the transmit data port. The corresponding status function, chk_xmt, tests the status port to see that the hardware is ready to accept another character. The final function, send_char, combines chk_xmt and xmt_char to wait until the async hardware is ready before transmitting a character.

Figure 8.2 async1.c

```
1     /* async1.c - basic async I/O module */
2     #include "stdio.h"
3     #include "cminor.h"
4     #include "async.h"
5
6     typedef struct
7       { int base_port ;              /* 1st I/O port for this async card */
8         int int_no ;                 /* associated interrupt level */
9       } ASY_ADRS ;
10
11    #define BIOS_DATA    0x40        /* segment address of BIOS data area */
12    int  rs232card ;                 /* save card number here */
13    int iobase ;                     /* 1st port address of async card */
14    int iasync ;                     /* index into aadr table */
15
16    ASY_ADRS aadr[2] =
17      { PRIMARY , PRI_INT ,          /* primary async adapter (COM1:) */
18        SECONDARY , SEC_INT          /* seconadry adapter (COM2:) */
19      } ;
20
21    int comm_init(card)
22      int card ;                     /* card number for RS232 I/O */
23      {
24          rs232card = card ;         /* save card number */
25                                     /* get the corresponding port */
26                                     /* address from the BIOS data seg. */
27          iobase = peek(BIOS_DATA,card*2) |
28              ( peek(BIOS_DATA,card*2+1) << 8 ) ;
29          switch( iobase )           /* check for valid I/O address */
30            {
31            case PRIMARY    : iasync = 0 ; break ;
32            case SECONDARY : iasync = 1 ; break ;
33            default :
34              printf(" unrecognizable RS232 card address - %x \n",
35              iobase) ;
36              exit(10) ;
37              break ;
38            }
39      }
40
41
42    int chk_rcv()                    /* check for received char */
43      {
44          int s ;
45
46          s = inport(iobase + LINE_STATUS) ; /* get line status */
47          return( s & DTA_RDY ) ;
48      }
49
50
51    int rcv_char()                         /* get a received char */
52      {
53          int s , c ;
54                                          /* check status for errors */
55          s = inport(iobase + LINE_STATUS) & RCV_ERRS ;
```

Figure 8.2   async1.c (continued)

```
56          c = inport(iobase + RCV_DATA) ; /* get the char itself */
57          if( s == 0 )
58               return( tochar(c) ) ;   /* no errors return char */
59          else return( -1 ) ;          /* error - return (-1)   */
60      }
61
62  int chk_xmt()                        /* check to see if ready */
63      {                                /* to transmit next char */
64          int s ;
65
66          s = inport(iobase + LINE_STATUS) ; /* get line status */
67          return( s & XMT_RDY ) ;
68      }
69
70
71  int xmt_char(c)                      /* transmit a char */
72   int c ;                             /* char to be transmitted */
73      {
74          outport(c, iobase + XMT_DATA) ;
75      }
76
77
78  int send_char(c)                     /* check Xmt status and then */
79   int c ;                             /* transmit this char */
80      {
81          while( chk_xmt() == 0 )      /* wait until ok to xmt char */
82              { ; }
83          xmt_char(c) ;                /* transmit the char */
84      }
```

8.3   How TTYl Performs

□   Although TTY1 is too simple to be very useful, we can learn something from measuring its performance. Figure 8.4 shows a program that transmits a continuous stream of characters at the full baud rate. The stream is a series of lines of ASCII characters, with each line being one character longer than the previous one. Figure 8.5a shows a sample of the stream. To run the test we need two IBM PCs connected by an RS-232 cable. If we execute the PERFTTY1 program in one PC and run TTY1 in the other PC, we should see the pattern shown. If the TTY1 program loses any characters, the change in the pattern should be apparent.

Figures 8.5b and 8.5c show the results at 1,200 baud and at 9,600 baud, respectively. At 1,200 baud, the TTY1 program receives most of the characters correctly, but it drops the character immediately after a line feed control character. At 9,600 baud, TTY1 loses so many characters that the pattern is completely altered. While TTY1's performance at 9,600 baud is obviously unsatisfactory, the loss of even a few characters at 1,200 baud makes it useless at that speed, too.

When TTY1 receives a line feed character, the entire screen is scrolled up-

Figure 8.3   async.h

```
1    /* async.h - defines constants for async I/O */
2
3    /* async port names */
4    #define COM1    0
5    #define COM2    1
6
7    /* software interrupt number for Rom BIOS async support */
8    #define  RS232_IO    0x14
9
10   /* service codes for rom BIOS calls (put in AX) */
11   #define   RS_INIT       0x0000
12   #define   RS_XMT        0x0100
13   #define   RS_RCV        0x0200
14   #define   RS_STATUS     0x0300
15
16   /* bit definitions for BIOS status returns */
17   #define   TIM_OUT_BIT     0x8000
18   #define   XMT_RDY_BIT     0x2000
19   #define   BRK_DET_BIT     0x1000
20   #define   FRM_ERR_BIT     0x0800
21   #define   PAR_ERR_BIT     0x0400
22   #define   OVR_RUN_BIT     0x0200
23   #define   DTA_RDY_BIT     0x0100
24   #define   CAR_DET_BIT     0x0080
25   #define   RNG_IND_BIT     0x0040
26   #define   DSR_BIT         0x0020
27   #define   CTS_BIT         0x0010
28
29   /* mask for receive error conditions */
30   /*  (TIM_OUT_BIT|FRM_ERR_BIT |PAR_ERR_BIT |OVR_RUN_BIT) */
31   #define   RCV_ERR_BIT   0x8E00
32
33
34   /* the following are parms for the RS232_init service */
35   /* choose one from each group and combine (+ or |) */
36   /* and put into REGS.AX (with service code) */
37
38   /* baud rates   */
39   #define   BAUD_110          0x00
40   #define   BAUD_300          0x40
41   #define   BAUD_1200         0x80
42   #define   BAUD_4800         0xc0
43
44   /* parity settings   */
45   #define   PAR_NONE          0x00
46   #define   PAR_ODD           0x08
47   #define   PAR_EVEN          0x18
48
49   /* number of stopbit settings */
50   #define   STOP_1            0x00
51   #define   STOP_2            0x04
52
53   /* data word length settings */
54   #define   DATA_7            0x02
55   #define   DATA_8            0x03
```

Figure 8.3   async.h (continued)

```
56
57   /* I/O port offsets for async card */
58   /* (add the base address for the card being used) */
59   #define RCV_DATA        0
60   #define XMT_DATA        0
61   #define INT_ENABLE      1
62   #define INT_ID          2
63   #define LINE_CTRL       3
64   #define MODEM_CTRL      4
65   #define LINE_STATUS     5
66   #define MODEM_STATUS    6
67
68   /* Line Status Register Bits */
69   #define  XMT_RDY     0x20        /* 1 = ok to transmit */
70   #define  BRK_DET     0x10        /* 1 = break rcvd */
71   #define  FRM_ERR     0x08        /* 1 = framing error detected */
72   #define  PAR_ERR     0x04        /* 1 = parity error detected */
73   #define  OVR_RUN     0x02        /* 1 = rcv overrun   */
74   #define  DTA_RDY     0x01        /* 1 = rcvd data ready */
75   #define  RCV_ERRS    0x1E        /* all rcv error bits above */
76
77   /* Modem Status Register bits */
78   #define  CAR_DET     0x80
79   #define  RNG_IND     0x40
80   #define  DSR         0x20
81   #define  CTS         0x10
82
83
84
85   /* various control register bits */
86   #define SET_BRK_BIT      0x40
87   #define INT_PENDING      0x01
88   #define ENABLE_RCV_INT   0x01
89   #define OUT2             0x08   /* in MCR. = 1 to allow ints. */
90
91   /* 1st I/O port addresses for com1: and com2: */
92   #define PRIMARY          0x3f8
93   #define SECONDARY        0x2f8
94
95   /* corresponding interrupt numbers */
96   #define PRI_INT          4
97   #define SEC_INT          3
```

ward. This requires so much time that the next character received is overwritten before we finish scrolling the screen. Although TTY1 may handle received characters at an average rate of more than 1,200 baud, it fails to meet the *worst case* test of handling every character in 1/120 second or less.

We can also test to see how well TTY1 handles keyboard input while receiving data at the full baud rate. We can run the test and hold down a key; this produces keyboard input at the rate of 10 to 15 characters a second. If TTY1 fails to

Figure 8.4   perftty1.c

```
1    /* perftty1.c - generate a character stream for TTY pgm */
2    #include "stdio.h"
3    #include "cminor.h"
4
5    main()
6      {
7        int i , j , imax ;
8
9        comm_init(1) ;                    /* set up for RS-232 use */
10
11
12       printf("max line length: \n");
13       scanf("%d",&imax) ;
14       printf("press a key to quit \n");
15       while( keypress() == 0 )
16         {
17           for(i= 0 ; i < imax ; i=i+1)
18             {
19               for(j=0 ; j<i ; j=j+1)
20                 { send_char('0'+j) ; }
21               send_char('\r');
22               send_char('\n');
23             }
24         }
25     }
```

Figure 8.5   perftty1.fig

```
1
2    A) Display from TTY1 at 300 Baud
3
4    ...
5    012345
6    0123456
7    01234567
8    012345678
9
10   0
11   01
12   012
13   0123
14   01234
15   012345
16   0123456
17   01234567
18   012345678
19
20   0
21   01
22   ...
```

Figure 8.5   perftty1.fig (continued)

```
23
24
25
26    B) Display from TTY1 at 1200 Baud
27
28    ...
29    12345
30    123456
31    1234567
32    12345678
33
34
35    1
36    12
37    123
38    1234
39    12345
40    123456
41    1234567
42    12345678
43
44
45    1
46    12
47    ...
48
49    C) Display from TTY1 at 9600 Baud
50
51    ...
52    0134
53
54    0134
55
56    0134
57
58     0234
59
60    0145
61
62    01345
63    ...
```

collect keyboard input fast enough, the BIOS keyboard support software will sound a warning beep to indicate that input has been lost.

We can already see in TTY1 some characteristics of real-time programs in general. The following sections discuss these characteristics.

Polling

The *polling loop* in TTY1.C is a common structure in real-time programs. We cannot predict which type of input will be received next and wait for it. Instead, we check the *status* for each input until something is received.

There are two problems with waiting for a single type of input. First, the PC provides a limited amount of storage for keyboard and RS-232 inputs. If we wait for the next keyboard input and ten characters arrive over the RS-232 port, some of those characters will be lost. But even if the PC could buffer all ten characters, we would not see them displayed until we typed a character. So whatever provisions our computer and operating system make for buffering input, we need to accept and process any inputs promptly.

Priority-Driven Scheduling

The program also illustrates the concept of *priority-driven scheduling*. Checking for and handling input on the RS-232 line has priority over handling keyboard input. Keyboard input arrives at a slow rate (about 10 to 20 keystrokes per second at most), and the BIOS support provides a sixteen-entry buffer. The async hardware provides a 2-character buffer, and at 1,200 baud the RS-232 input rate may be a maximum of 120 characters per second. Thus, giving higher priority to RS-232 input is a good design decision.

Analyzing the Problem

Our example illustrates another characteristic of real-time problems: Good analysis of the input rates and the processing deadlines is vital to producing good real-time programs.

Performance

Our performance works fine at 300 baud (30 characters per second). When we use it at 1,200 baud, however, it loses a few received characters. This illustrates another characteristic of real-time programs: If the program is not fast enough, input is lost (or some equivalent misfortunate occurs). Poor performance might make programs presented in Chapters 1 to 7 less pleasant to use, but it makes TTY work incorrectly. While good average performance is satisfactory for ordinary programs, real-time programs must have good *worst case* performance.

8.4 Improving TTYI's Performance

□   The IBM PC hardware and the ROM BIOS keyboard support provide *buffering* or *queueing* of keyboard input. When a key is pressed, a hardware interrupt occurs, and code in the BIOS is executed. This interrupt-handling code collects the keyboard input and places it into a buffer (normally sixteen keystrokes). Keystroke data are removed from this buffer on demand in the order entered. The interrupt handler must still act promptly to collect each keystroke, but the application program (such as TTY1) may fall behind occasionally.

Without interrupts and buffering, any application program must handle each keystroke before the next one arrives. But with these aids, the program need only keep the buffer from overflowing. This requires handling sixteen keystrokes in any interval in which sixteen keystrokes arrive. A similar strategy using hardware interrupts and a buffer is a way to improve TTY1's performance. We develop these techniques in the following sections.

Interrupts are a foreign concept to many programmers. The following analogy may help show the purpose of interrupts and how we can use them.

The TTY1 program is like a phone-order business run by one clerk with a one-track mind. When the clerk receives a call, he writes up the order. After hanging up the phone, the clerk then finishes filling the order. If a phone call comes in while the order is being filled, the clerk ignores it. Unless our clerk works at superhuman speed, he will lose some orders. A more flexible clerk would stop to answer the phone immediately. After the order has been taken, the clerk goes back to what he was doing. Phone calls can preempt the other work, but the clerk remembers where he left off. Since the clerk may receive several orders before the current one has been processed, he or she must store a list of orders not yet filled.

Applying these ideas to the TTY program requires several new elements:

1. We need to make the async hardware preempt our current activity when a character arrives. The IBM PC provides hardware interrupts that we can use; we just have to initialize the async adapter to generate them and the PC to accept them. Part of that initialization is to specify the address of an interrupt handler to be executed when the interrupt occurs.

2. When the interrupt occurs and our interrupt handler begins execution, its first job is to preserve register values and anything else we will need to return to the activity interrupted. The last thing the interrupt handler does is to restore this context information and return control to the activity interrupted.

3. The interrupt handler must collect the received character from the async adapter and store it in a queue.

4. The interrupt handler must tell the async adapter and the PC hardware that the interrupt has been handled. In the case of our phone-order analogy, answering the phone makes it stop ringing.

5. The TTY program must regularly check the queue for characters that have been received. It must remove characters at the same average rate at which they are added by the interrupt handler. The queue allows the program to fall behind temporarily without losing characters. The larger the queue, the farther we can fall behind. If we have a 100-character buffer, the performance constraint is that we must remove 100 characters for every interval in which 100 characters are added to the buffer.

The ideas involved apply to many real-time programming problems. To get better performance we split a task into a small part accomplished by an interrupt handler and a larger part that involves a less stringent time constraint. A storage buffer provides communication between the two parts. This programming solution does not improve the average performance of the program, but it improves the worst case performance by relaxing the time constraint for most of the work.

8.5 Specifying the TTY Program

□ Now that we understand the lessons of the TTY1 program, we can specify what the next TTY program is to do. First, TTY1 had a few omissions in the emulation of a dumb terminal: The keyboard input did not allow us to send an ASCII null character or to send a break signal. In addition, we want commands to record received data to a disk file or to replay (send) an existing data file. Figure 8.6 describes our next TTY program.

It is a good practice to initialize the async adapter hardware completely before use. Setting baud rate, parity, and other communications parameters are a part of the initialization process. To keep TTY small and easy to discuss, we use the DOS MODE command to initialize the async adapter and to set the communications parameters. The batch file in Figure 8.7 packages the MODE command with the TTY2 program. This TTY2 program does the rest of the TTY function; its implementation is discussed in the next section.

8.6 TTY2 Source Files

□ The following sections discuss source files that make up the TTY2 program. In addition, the async.h and async1.c files are part of the TTY2 program.

The structure of function calls in the TTY2 program is shown in the following printout. Note that the interrupt handler, gotint, is executed as a result of a hardware interrupt rather than by being called from another function. To keep the diagram to a manageable size, we have omitted the names of toolkit functions such as keypress, getkey, inport, and outport.

```
main
    comm_init
    start_rcv
        initq
        en_asy
            get_fads
            install
            en8259
    chk_asy
        intsoff
```

Figure 8.6   TTY description

Name

TTY – Terminal Emulation Program

Function

TTY emulates a dumb async terminal (a teletype, or TTY, terminal). It can be used to communicate with another computer over an async RS-232 line. This connection may be via async modems or an RS-232 cable.

ASCII characters typed on the keyboard are sent out on the RS-232 line, and characters received are displayed on the screen. Carriage return, line feed, backspace, and bell control characters are interpreted as display commands, and other control characters are displayed as ^ c, where c is a printable ASCII character whose value is 0x40 plus the value of the control character.

TTY can record received data in a disk file or transmit data from an existing data file. Baud rate, parity, and number of data bits are specified on the command line when TTY is executed.

Keyboard Input

Keyboard input is interpreted as ASCII characters or as input commands. Control characters are input with the control key and an alphanumeric key. Control-@ is interpreted as the ASCII NULL character. The following input commands are recognized:

F1 key	–	Exit to DOS.
F10 key	–	Start/stop recording received data (TTY will prompt for a file name).
Shift F10 key	–	Start/stop replaying an existing file. The contents will be transmitted on the RS-232 line (TTY will prompt for a file name).
Alt – B	–	Send an RS-232 Break sequence on the RS-232 line.

Usage

A > tty 1200 n 8 specifies 1200 baud , no parity and 8 data bits
A > tty 300 e 7   specifies 300 baud , even parity and 7 data bits

Notes

1. TTY has limited features; it is a basis for expansion by the reader.
2. TTY operates correctly for 300 or 1,200 baud. At faster speeds it loses some data.
3. Baud rate and other parameters are as described for the DOS MODE command.

Figure 8.7   tty.bat

```
1    mode com%1:%2,%3,%4
2    tty2
```

```
            chkq
            intson
        get_asy
            intsoff
            getq
            intson
        disp_char
        rec_char
        get_kbd
        exec_cmd
            record
                end_record
                    disp_msg
            replay
                end_replay
                    disp_msg
                send_brk
                    xmt_brk
                    end_brk
            chk_xmt
            rep_char
                    end_record
            xmt_char
            stop_rcv
                dis_asy
            end_record
            end_replay

    (hardware interrupt occurs)
        gotint
            rcv_int
                rcv_char
                    putq
```

Header Files for TTY2

Figures 8.8 and 8.9 show two header files for the TTY2 program. tty2cmds.h defines the keyboard input commands recognized by TTY2. tty2parm.h defines status bits for a global state variable.

tty2.c

The main function for the TTY2 program is shown in Figure 8.10. Lines 14 to 17 initialize parts of the program, and lines 38 to 40 clean up before returning to DOS.

Figure 8.8 tty2cmds.h

```
1
2      /* tty2cmds.h - define keyboard input commands */
3
4      #define   NOCMD           0
5      #define   ASCIICMD        1
6      #define   EXITCMD         2
7      #define   RECCMD          3
8      #define   REPCMD          4
9      #define   BRKCMD          5
10
11     /* return codes for exec_cmd */
12     #define   NOT_THRU        0
13     #define   THRU            1
```

Figure 8.9 tty2parm.h

```
1      /* tty2parm.h - defines some parms & constants for TTY2 program */
2
3      /* bit definitions for state variable */
4      #define REC_BIT    0x0001    /* on if we are recording rcvd data */
5      #define REP_BIT    0x0002    /* on if we are replaying  a file */
6
```

The polling loop in lines 19 to 37 is similar to that in the TTY1 program, but since the program is much larger, calls to functions keep the main function small and uncluttered. The loop enforces the same priority as did TTY1: Received data have priority over keyboard input.

Support for recording has been added to the handling of received data in lines 24 and 25. Lines 31 to 36 provide similar support for replaying an existing file. Note that this activity is lowest in priority and that transmit status is checked before transmitting a character so that the program never waits for the transmit hardware to be available.

tty2get.c

The get_kbd function in Figure 8.11 collects the next keystroke and translates it into a command. Keystrokes corresponding to ASCII characters are classified as ASCII commands, including the control-@ keystroke. Some non-ASCII keys are identified as valid commands; a keystroke that is not recognized is classified as the null command—NOCMD.

get_kbd stores the command type where the pcmd argument specifies. It also returns the character value (or its replacement in the case of control-@).

Figure 8.10 tty2.c

```
1    /* tty2.c - second tty emulation program */
2    #include "stdio.h"
3    #include "async.h"
4    #include "tty2parm.h"
5    extern int nrerr , nrqo ;        /* receive error counters */
6    int adapter    = COM2 ;          /* which async adapter to use */
7    int state ;                      /* records current state */
8                                     /* bits defined in ttyparm.h */
9
10   main()
11     {
12       int c , cmd , thru ;
13
14       comm_init(adapter) ;         /* set up for using comm. port */
15       start_rcv() ;
16       thru = 0 ;
17       state = 0 ;                  /* not recording or replaying */
18
19       while( thru  == 0 )          /* scan for input until thru */
20         {
21         if( chk_asy() != 0 )       /* check for rcvd. data */
22            { c = get_asy() ;       /*    data waiting - get it */
23              disp_char(c) ;
24              if((state & REC_BIT) != 0) /*Are we capturing data?*/
25                  rec_char(c) ;     /*    yes -put char into file */
26            }
27         else if(keypress() !=0) /* check for keybd. input */
28            { c = get_kbd(&cmd); /*    data waiting - get it */
29              thru=exec_cmd(cmd,c) ;
30            }
31         else if( ((state & REP_BIT) != 0) /* sending a file ? */
32              && (chk_xmt() !=0))/* if so and XMT ready */
33            { c = rep_char() ;    /* get next char from file */
34              if( c != EOF )
35                xmt_char(c) ;       /*    send next char from file */
36            }
37         }
38       stop_rcv() ;                 /* shut down async rcv */
39       end_record() ;              /* stop recording */
40       end_replay() ;              /* stop replaying */
41       printf(" %d receive errors \n %d buffer overflows \n",
42         nrerr , nrqo ) ;
43     }
```

get_kbd is called only when keyboard input is available. Thus getkey always returns immediately with a keystroke.

tty2exec.c

Figure 8.12 lists the exec_cmd function that executes input commands. A **switch** statement provides an action for each command, including the null command,

Figure 8.11   tty2get.c

```
1    /* tty2get.c - get keyboard input */
2    #include "stdio.h"
3    #include "keyio.h"
4    #include "tty2cmds.h"
5
6                                      /* define special keys */
7    #define   ALT_B   (256+48)        /* 48 is scan code for Alt-B */
8    #define   CTRL_AT  (256+3)        /*  3 is scan code for Ctrl-@ */
9    #define   F10KEY  (F1KEY+9)       /* F10 */
10   #define   F20KEY  (F11key+9)      /* Shift-F10 */
11
12   int get_kbd(pcmd)
13    int *pcmd ;                     /* store the command type here */
14    {
15       int c ;
16
17       c = getkey() ;
18       if( c == F1KEY )             /* F1 = Exit */
19           *pcmd = EXITCMD ;
20       else if( c == (ALT_B) )      /* ALT B = Send Break */
21           *pcmd = BRKCMD ;
22       else if( c == F10KEY )       /* F10 = Record input */
23           *pcmd = RECCMD ;
24       else if( c == F20KEY )       /* Shift-F10 = Replay a File */
25           *pcmd = REPCMD ;
26       else if( c == CTRL_AT )      /* Ctrl-@ = ASCII Null char */
27         { c = 0 ;                  /* convert to null char */
28           *pcmd = ASCIICMD ;
29         }
30       else if( c <= 127 )          /* ASCII char */
31           *pcmd = ASCIICMD ;
32       else                         /* not a recognized key  */
33           *pcmd = NOCMD ;
34       return( c ) ;
35    }
```

NOCMD. The value returned by **exec_cmd** determines whether the program continues or exits (when the **EXITCMD** is typed).

tty2disp.c

The **disp_char** and **disp_msg** functions in Figure 8.13 display single characters and strings. Both functions use ROM BIOS services via the VIDEO module from Chapter 7.

The **disp_char** function displays each character received on the RS-232 line. It treats some ASCII control characters as display commands: carriage return, line feed, backspace, and bell. Other control characters are displayed in the form ^c, where c is a printable character with a value **0x40** higher than the control

Figure 8.12   tty2exec.c

```
1    /* tty2exec.c - execute a keyboard command */
2    #include "stdio.h"
3    #include "tty2cmds.h"
4
5    extern unsigned state ;
6
7    int exec_cmd(cmd,c)
8     int cmd ;              /* type of command */
9     int c ;                /* char input (if asciicmd) */
10    {
11       int ret ;
12
13       ret = NOT_THRU ;
14       switch( cmd)
15          {
16          case NOCMD :                       break ;
17          case ASCIICMD : send_char(c);  break ;
18          case RECCMD : record() ;          break ;
19          case REPCMD : replay() ;          break ;
20          case BRKCMD : send_brk() ;        break ;
21          case EXITCMD : ret = THRU ;       break ;
22          }
23       return( ret ) ;
24    }
25
```

character. For example, the control character 0x03 is displayed as ^C (C has the value 0x43). The rubout control character (0x7f) is displayed as ^r.

Line 10 sets the high-order bit in the character to 0 before displaying it; characters with values from 0x80 through 0xff are displayed as normal ASCII characters with values 0x00 through 0x7f.

The disp_msg function displays messages originated by the TTY2 program. It uses the vid_ts function to display the characters without any special formats.

tty2rec.c

The source file in Figure 8.14 implements functions to record received data in a disk file and to transmit the contents of an existing file.

The record function is called when a record command is typed. It checks to see whether the TTY2 program is already recording data. If not, it prompts for a file name and opens the file. If recording is already underway, record ends recording and closes the file. A bit in the global variable state records whether we are currently recording received data.

The rec_char function is called to record each character received. end_record, called by record and by the main function before it exits to DOS,

Figure 8.13   tty2disp.c

```
1    /* tty2disp.c - display chars */
2    /* uses VIDEO module functions (BIOS I/O funs.) */
3    #include "stdio.h"
4    #include "cminor.h"
5    #include "keyio.h"
6
7    int disp_char(c)                   /* display one character */
8     int c ;                           /* the character */
9     {
10        c = toascii(c) ;
11        if(    isgraphic(c)            /* printable char ? */
12           ||(c==ASCCR) ||(c==ASCLF)/* or CR , LF , BS , BELL */
13           || (c==ASCBEL)|| (c==ASCBS) )
14              vid_tc(c) ;
15        else if ( c == 0x7f )
16           {   vid_tc('^') ;
17               vid_tc('r') ;
18           }
19        else
20           {   vid_tc('^') ;          /* other control char */
21               vid_tc( c + '@' ) ;    /* display as ^printable char */
22           }
23     }
24
25    int disp_msg(s)                    /* display a message */
26     char s[] ;                        /* message char string */
27     {
28         vid_ts(s) ;
29     }
```

closes the recording file if it is open and turns off the record status bit in the variable state.

The functions replay, rep_char, and end_replay perform corresponding roles for replaying an existing file. A replay status bit in the variable state tracks the current status of replaying a file.

Recording characters may involve delays of 500 to 1,000 milliseconds to perform disk reads and writes. During this time, additional characters may be received. If interrupts were not used to handle these characters, characters could be overwritten in the async hardware and lost. The receive interrupt function will continue to collect these characters and to place them into the queue for received data. So this queue must be able to store all the data received for a 500-to-1,000-millisecond period. Prompting for a file name and opening a file may take much longer; TTY2 provides about 80 seconds of buffering, but the program's user may wait even longer to type a file name.

These record and replay functions hide the details of file I/O from the rest of the TTY2 program. Our implementation used C library functions for buffered I/O; we could change it to use other I/O functions without disturbing the rest of TTY2.

Figure 8.14   tty2rec.c

```
1    /* tty2rec.c - disk file record/replay functions  */
2    #include "stdio.h"
3    #include "cminor.h"
4    #include "tty2parm.h"
5
6    extern unsigned state ;
7    char rec_name[65] ;              /* store name of record file here */
8    char rep_name[65] ;              /* store name of replay file here */
9    FILE *rec_file ;
10   FILE *rep_file ;
11
12   FILE *get_file() ;
13   FILE *gfopen() ;
14
15   int record()                     /* start/stop recording */
16   {
17      if( (state & REC_BIT) == 0) /* are we already recording? */
18         {                           /* no - open capture file */
19           rec_file = get_file("record",rec_name,"a") ;
20           state = state | REC_BIT ;
21           disp_msg("\r\n ** Starting File recording ** \r\n ") ;
22         }
23      else end_record() ;         /* already recording. So stop */
24   }
25
26   int end_record()                 /* stop recording & close file */
27   {
28      if( (state & REC_BIT) != 0 )
29         { fclose(rec_file) ;        /*     yes - close it */
30           disp_msg("\r\n ** File recording completed ** \r\n\07 ") ;
31         }
32         fclose(rec_file) ;
33      state = state & ( ~REC_BIT);/* turn off record flag */
34   }
35
36   int rec_char(c)                  /* record a char */
37    int c;
38   {
39      fputc(c,rec_file) ;           /* put char into the file */
40   }
41
42
43   int replay()                     /* start replaying a file */
44   {
45      if( (state & REP_BIT) == 0) /* are we already replaying ? */
46         {                           /*  no - open replay file */
47           rep_file = get_file("replay",rep_name,"r") ;
48           state = state | REP_BIT ;
49           disp_msg("\r\n ** Starting File Replay ** \r\n ") ;
50         }
51      else end_replay() ;         /*   yes - file open. close it */
52   }
53
54   int end_replay()                 /* stop replay and close file */
55   {
```

Figure 8.14 tty2rec.c (continued)

```
56          if( (state & REP_BIT) != 0) /* is the replay file open ? */
57              { fclose(rep_file) ;         /*    yes - close it */
58                disp_msg("\r\n ** File replay completed ** \r\n\07 ") ;
59              }
60          state = state & ( ~REP_BIT);/* turn off the flag */
61      }
62
63
64   int rep_char()                    /* get next char from replay file */
65      {
66          int c ;
67
68          c = fgetc(rep_file) ;      /* get next char */
69          if( c == EOF )             /* check for end-of-file */
70              end_replay() ;
71          return( c ) ;             /* return char or EOF */
72      }
73
74   FILE *get_file(prompt,name,fmode) /* get name of file & open it */
75   char prompt[] ;                   /* display this prompt */
76   char name[] ;                     /* store file name here */
77   char fmode[] ;                    /* file open mode */
78      {
79          FILE *rfile ;
80
81          get_name(prompt,name) ;
82          rfile = gfopen(name,fmode,BIN_MODE) ;
83          while( rfile == NULL )
84              {
85                  printf(" can't open the file. Try again \n");
86                  get_name(prompt,name) ;
87                  rfile = gfopen(name,fmode,BIN_MODE) ;
88              }
89          return( rfile ) ;
90      }
91
92   int get_name(prompt,name)         /* prompt for & collect file name */
93   char prompt[] ;
94   char name[] ;
95      {
96          printf(" %s file name:",prompt) ;
97          getstr(name,64) ;
98      }
```

tty2brk.c

The send_brk function in Figure 8.15 transmits a break signal—a low level on the RS-232 line that lasts for approximately 200 milliseconds. send_brk implements the 200-millisecond timing; it calls the functions xmt_brk and end_brk to start and stop transmitting the RS-232 low-voltage level.

xmt_brk and end_brk manipulate the PC's async hardware and are specific to that hardware. send_brk is not specific to the hardware but implements the

Figure 8.15   tty2brk.c

```
1     /* tty2brk.c - send a break on the async line */
2     #include "stdio.h"
3
4     #define brk_length  4          /* break length in timer ticks */
5
6     int send_brk()                 /* start transmitting break */
7     {
8         int t ;
9
10        xmt_brk() ;                /* start sending break */
11        t = brk_length ;           /* set up a timer count */
12
13        while( t > 0 )             /* wait until timer count runs out */
14          { t = t - timer() ; }
15
16        end_brk() ;                /* stop sending break */
17     }
18
```

200-millisecond timing of the break signal in a particular way. If we wanted to adapt TTY2 for different hardware, we would change the async1.c and async2.c modules that interface to the async hardware. If we wanted to change the implementation of the 200-millisecond timing so the program did not wait in a delay loop, we would change the tty2brk.c source file.

send_brk uses the timer function from Chapter 7 to produce a 200-millisecond delay. During this delay, buffering the received data prevents losing characters. The timer function is another feature that would be much more difficult to implement without interrupts and buffering of received data.

tty2rcv.c

The tty2rcv.c source file in Figure 8.16 handles the details of receiving data. The start_rcv function, called by main during initialization, sets up the receive queue and calls en_asy to enable interrupts for received characters. An assembler function—gotint—is installed to handle async interrupts.

When a character is received, the gotint function is executed. It calls the rcv_int function in lines 31 to 42. rcv_int calls rcv_char (in Figure 8.2) to collect the character and then places it in the receive queue. If a receive error is detected or if the queue is full, an error counter is incremented and nothing is added to the queue.

The chk_asy and get_asy functions are used by the main polling loop to check for and collect received characters (from the queue). While we could call chkq and getq directly, our approach isolates the rest of TTY2 from the details of buffering received data.

Figure 8.16   tty2rcv.c

```
1    /* tty2rcv.c - handle rcving chars */
2    #include "stdio.h"
3    #include "cminor.h"
4    #include "queue.h"
5
6    int nrerr ;                         /* count of rcv. errors */
7    int nrqo ;                          /* count of rcv Q overflows */
8    QUEUE rq ;                          /* queue for rcving chars */
9    #define RQS    10000                /* size of rcv queue */
10   char rd[ RQS ] ;                    /* store rcvd chars here */
11
12   int gotint() ;                      /* interrupt handler code */
13
14   int start_rcv()                     /* setup async rcv */
15     {
16       int int_no ;
17       word16 iseg , ioff ;            /* segmented addr. of gotint() */
18
19       nrerr = 0 ; nrqo = 0 ;          /* zero error counters */
20       initq(&rq,rd,RQS) ;             /* setup queue for rcvd data */
21
22       en_asy(gotint) ;                /* enable int. on async board */
23     }
24
25
26   int stop_rcv()                      /* shut down async rcv */
27     {
28       dis_asy() ;                     /* disable int. on async board */
29     }
30
31   int rcv_int()                       /* called by gotint when a rcv. */
32     {                                 /* data interrupt occurs */
33       int c ;
34
35       c = rcv_char() ;                /* get the char */
36       if( c == (-1) )                 /* check for rcv error */
37           nrerr = nrerr + 1 ;         /*    error - bump counter */
38       else
39         { if( putq(c,&rq) == (-1) ) /* no error - put char into Q */
40              nrqo = nrqo + 1 ;       /*    Q overflow - bump counter */
41         }
42     }
43
44   int chk_asy()                       /* check for a received char */
45     {
46       int ret ;
47
48       intsoff() ;                     /* turn off ints while we   */
49       ret = chkq(&rq) ;               /* look at rcv Q - empty ? */
50       intson() ;                      /* now turn ints back on    */
51       return( ret ) ;
52     }
53
54
55   int get_asy()                       /* get next char from rcv Q */
```

Figure 8.16   tty2rcv.c (continued)

```
56     {
57         int ret ;
58
59         intsoff() ;           /* turn ints. off while we  */
60         ret = getq(&rq) ;     /* get next char from rcv Q */
61         intson() ;            /* now turn ints. back on   */
62         return( ret ) ;
63     }
```

queue.c

Buffers that keep data in a first come, first served order are often called *FIFO queues,* for first in, first out. These queues are useful building blocks in many programming problems. In the TTY2 program, we need one queue for a specific purpose—buffering received characters. However, it is easy and sensible to design a tool for more general use. Before we show the queue source code, we discuss how queues work and how they can be implemented. The following drawing shows how we might think of a FIFO queue—a long, elastic tube with data going in at the right and out at the left. Inside the data stay in order so the first item entered is the first removed.

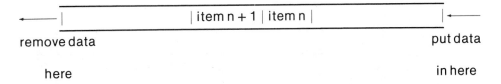

remove data   put data

    here   in here

    This picture works fine for expressing the concept of a FIFO queue, but it does not tell us how to implement one. We can come closer to that goal with a picture of a queue as a circle. Two pointers—a head and a tail pointer—keep track of where we should remove or add the next item. When the head and tail point to the same place, the queue is empty. As we add and remove data, the head pointer chases the tail pointer around the ring (Figure 8.17).

    One change gives us a model that we can implement. We cut the circle so that it is a linear area of storage of fixed size. When one of the pointers reaches the end of the area, we reset it to point to the beginning of the area.

FIFO queue as linear array

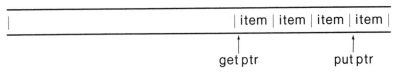

    get ptr   put ptr

Figure 8.17

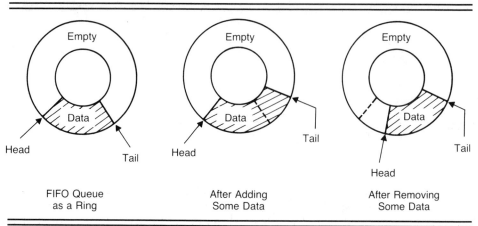

FIFO Queue
as a Ring

After Adding
Some Data

After Removing
Some Data

After adding an item

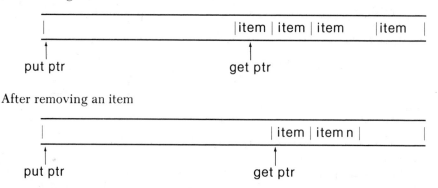

put ptr

get ptr

After removing an item

put ptr

get ptr

The header file in Figure 8.18 defines a data structure to keep track of the state of a queue. The actual data storage area is outside the queue structure; the queue structure contains pointers to the beginning and end of the data area and head and tail locations. Figure 8.19 lists the functions that make up the QUEUE module.

The initialization function, initq, is called before a queue is used. The area where characters are stored is separate from the queue structure; the address of this area and its size are supplied as arguments to initqueue. This organization allows the data area to be allocated statically or dynamically as appropriate for the program as a whole. Since the QUEUE module expects the address of the queue structure as an input argument, it can be used for a single queue or for a number of queues.

The putq function stores one character in a queue. After it stores the character, it updates the queue's tail pointer, checking for the end of the data area

Figure 8.18   queue.h

```
1     /* queue.h - header file for queue module */
2
3     /* return codes */
4     #define  Q_SUCCESS     0
5     #define  Q_FAIL       (-1)
6     #define  Q_EMPTY       0
7     #define  Q_FULL        1
8
9     /* queue data structure */
10    typedef struct
11    { char *head ;                    /* get next char from here */
12      char *tail ;                    /* put next char here */
13      char *bbuf ;                    /* beginning of data area */
14      char *ebuf ;                    /* end of data area */
15    } QUEUE ;
```

Figure 8.19   queue.c

```
1     /* queue.c - general purpose FIFO queue module */
2     #include "stdio.h"
3     #include "queue.h"
4
5     initq(pq,buf,nbuf)            /* initialize a queue */
6      QUEUE *pq ;                  /* address of a Q structure */
7      char buf[] ;                 /* use this to store the chars */
8      int nbuf ;                   /* size of the buffer */
9     {
10       pq->head = buf ;           /* point head and tail to start */
11       pq->tail = buf ;           /* of buffer. (Q empty) */
12       pq->bbuf = buf ;           /* store starting & ending addresses */
13       pq->ebuf = buf + nbuf ;
14    }
15
16
17    int getq(pq)                  /* get a char from a Q */
18     QUEUE *pq ;                  /* address of a Q structure */
19    {                             /* returns first char in Q or -1 */
20       register char *p ;
21       char c ;
22
23       p = pq->head ;
24       if( p != pq->tail )        /* is the Q empty ? */
25         { c = *p ;               /*    no - get first char */
26           p = p + 1 ;            /*        advance head ptr */
27           if( p == pq->ebuf )    /*        check for end of buffer */
28             p = pq->bbuf ;       /*            yes - set to buf. start*/
29           pq->head = p ;         /*        store updated head ptr */
30           return(tochar(c)) ;    /*        return the char */
31         }
32       else return( Q_FAIL ) ;    /*    yes - Q empty, return fail code */
33    }
```

Figure 8.19   queue.c (continued)

```
34
35     int putq(c,pq)                    /* put a char into a Q */
36      char c ;                         /* char to store */
37      QUEUE *pq ;                      /* address of a Q structure */
38      {
39        register char *p ;
40
41        p = pq->tail ;
42        *p = c ;                        /* store the char */
43        p = p + 1 ;                     /* advance the tail ptr */
44        if( p == pq->ebuf )             /* check for end of buffer */
45            p = pq->bbuf ;              /*    yes - set to buf. start */
46        if( p != pq->head )             /* check for Q overflow */
47          { pq->tail = p ;              /*    no - store updated tail ptr */
48            return( Q_SUCCESS ) ; /*          and return success code */
49          }
50        else return( Q_FAIL ) ;  /*    yes - don't update tail ptr */
51      }                               /*          and return failure code */
52
53     int chkq(pq)                     /* check for data in a Q */
54      QUEUE *pq ;                      /* address of a Q structure */
55      {
56        if( pq->tail == pq->head ) /* compare head and tail pointers */
57            return( Q_EMPTY ) ;  /*    equal - Q empty */
58        else return( Q_FULL ) ;  /*    not equal - Q not empty */
59      }
60
61
```

and for overflow (the tail pointer overtaking the head pointer). This points up a small trade-off: To keep things simple, we interpret a queue with the pointers at the same position as being empty. So we can only put (N−1) characters into a queue with an N-byte buffer.

The getq function removes one character from a queue and updates the queue's head pointer, checking for the end of the data area. getq also checks for an empty queue, returning a special value in that case. The chkq function checks for data in the queue without removing the character.

We can think of a queue as connecting two independent parts of a program—a producer who puts data in the queue and a consumer who removes it. The producer calls putq, advancing the tail pointer and examining but not changing the head pointer. The consumer calls getq and chkq, advancing the head pointer and examining but not changing the tail pointer. This separation of function in the QUEUE module prevents subtle time-dependent bugs in interrupt handlers and makes debugging much easier.

async2.c

The **async1.c** source file presented earlier (Figure 8.2) provided basic support for sending and receiving characters. The **async2.c** file in Figure 8.20 adds functions for transmitting a break signal and for setting up interrupts for received data.

The **xmt_brk** function in lines 20 to 26 sets a bit in a control port to start

Figure 8.20   async2.c

```
1    /* async2.c - async I/O rcv interrupts and xmt break */
2    #include "stdio.h"
3    #include "cminor.h"
4    #include "async.h"
5
6    typedef struct
7     { int base_port ;            /* 1st I/O port for this async card */
8       int int_no ;              /* associated interrupt level */
9     } ASY_ADRS ;
10
11   #define BIOS_DATA   0x40      /* BIOS data segment address */
12   extern int  rs232card ;      /* save card number here */
13   extern int iobase ;          /* 1st async io port to be used */
14   extern ASY_ADRS aadr[]   ;
15   extern int iasync ;          /* index into aadr table */
16
17   #define VECSTART   8          /* interrupt no. of 1st H/W int. */
18   word16 ssave , osave ;        /* save address of old handler here */
19
20   int xmt_brk()                 /* start transmitting break */
21   {
22       int ctl ;
23
24       ctl = inport(iobase+LINE_CTRL) | SET_BRK_BIT ;
25       outport( ctl , iobase+LINE_CTRL);
26   }
27
28   int end_brk()                 /* stop transmitting break */
29   {
30       int ctl ;
31
32       ctl = inport(iobase+LINE_CTRL) & ( ~ SET_BRK_BIT ) ;
33       outport( ctl , iobase + LINE_CTRL);
34   }
35
36
37   int en_asy(pfun)              /* setup async rcv int */
38    int (*pfun) () ;             /* address of int. handler */
39   {
40       int int_no , t ;
41       word16 iseg , ioff ;
42
43       int_no = aadr[iasync].int_no; /* get int. level no. */
44                                /* install our int. handler */
```

Figure 8.20 async2.c (continued)

```
45          get_fads(pfun,&iseg,&ioff) ;
46          install(int_no + VECSTART,iseg,ioff,&ssave,&osave) ;
47          en8259(int_no) ;            /* enable int. in 8259 */
48                                      /* turn on 8250 enable */
49       outport(ENABLE_RCV_INT,iobase+INT_ENABLE) ;
50              /* rcvd data only - turn on async board enable */
51       t = inport(iobase+MODEM_CTRL) | OUT2 ;
52       outport(t,iobase+MODEM_CTRL) ;
53       }
54
55   int dis_asy()                    /* turn off async rcv int */
56       {
57       int t , int_no , temp ;
58
59       int_no = aadr[iasync].int_no; /* get int. level no. */
60       dis8259(int_no) ;            /* disable int. in 8259 */
61                                    /* turn off async board enable */
62       t = inport(iobase + MODEM_CTRL) & (~ OUT2) ;
63       outport(t,iobase + MODEM_CTRL) ;
64                                    /* turn off 8250 enable */
65       outport(0,iobase+INT_ENABLE) ; /* all 8250 ints off */
66       dis8259(int_no) ;           /* disable int. in 8259 */
67                                    /* restore old int. handler */
68       install(int_no+ VECSTART,ssave,osave,&temp,&temp) ;
69       }
70
71   /*  functions for manipulating the 8259 interrupt controller */
72   #define MASK_PORT   0x21       /* interrupt enable register */
73   #define EOI_PORT    0x20       /* clear int. here */
74   #define EOI_CMD     0x20       /* write this value to clear int. */
75
76   int en8259(int_no)            /* enable an interrupt in the 8259 */
77    int int_no ;                 /* interrupt number to enable */
78    {
79       unsigned t ;
80
81       t = inport(MASK_PORT) ;
82       t = t & ~ (1 << int_no) ;
83       outport(t,MASK_PORT) ;
84    }
85
86   int dis8259(int_no)           /* disable an interrupt in the 8259 */
87    int int_no ;                 /* interrupt number to disable */
88    {
89       unsigned t ;
90
91       t = inport(MASK_PORT) ;
92       t = t | (1 << int_no) ;
93       outport(t,MASK_PORT) ;
94    }
95
96   int clr_int()                 /* clear an interrupt from the 8259 */
97    {
98       outport(EOI_CMD,EOI_PORT) ;
99    }
```

transmitting the break signal. The en_brk function clears that bit to stop transmitting the break signal.

The en_asy function sets up the PC hardware for received data interrupts. First, the function address passed as an input argument is converted to a segmented address and installed as the interrupt vector for the interrupt. Then the interrupt is enabled at several levels: in the 8250 UART chip, on the async adapter, and in the PC's 8259 interrupt controller. Note that the interrupt vector is installed first so an interrupt occurring immediately will be handled correctly.

When the TTY2 program finished execution, interrupts from received data must be disabled. Leaving this interrupt enabled would produce a dramatic crash as the interrupt handler function is overwritten by part of the next program being executed. Thus, the dis_asy function reverses the actions of en_asy, disabling received data interrupts at all levels. The original interrupt vector for this interrupt is replaced as the last action in the function.

Two functions, en8259 and dis8259, turn on and off a single interrupt in the PC's 8259 interrupt controller. To avoid disturbing settings for other interrupt levels, the functions read the current value of the interrupt mask and alter the bit for the specified interrupt level.

The interrupt level to be used is related to the communications port addresses: The primary async port at I/O port 0x3f8 uses level 4, while the secondary async port uses level 3. The aadr table shows this relationship, and the iasync index set by com_init selects the values we should use. Hardware interrupt levels 0 to 7 correspond to PC interrupt vectors 8 to 0x0f so we add the VECSTART constant in specifying the interrupt vector we are installing.

install.c

The install function in Figure 8.21 sets up a specified interrupt vector. It first gets and saves the current interrupt vector so it can be replaced later. Then it installs the new interrupt vector address.

The original vector address is stored where the calling function specifies. Later install can be recalled to reinstall this original address.

tty2int.c

To handle interrupts we need some assembler code. This assembler code must save all the register values and set up the environment that a C program expects. It can then call a function written in C to service the interrupt. When this C function finishes executing, it returns control to the assembler code. The original register values are restored and a return from interrupt instruction executed.

The assembler function in Figure 8.22 follows this outline. Lines 26 to 40 save the original registers on input, and lines 50 to 64 restore the original register values. Lines 35 to 46 set up the environment expected by the C function, rcv_int:

Figure 8.21   install.c

```
 1    /* install.c - install/remove interrupt vectors */
 2    #include "stdio.h"
 3    #include "cminor.h"
 4    #include "asmtools.h"
 5    #include "dosfun.h"
 6
 7
 8    int install(vecno,iseg,ioff,save_seg,save_off)
 9     int vecno ;                       /* number of interrupt vector */
10     WORD16 iseg ;                     /* new seg. address */
11     WORD16 ioff ;                     /* new offset address */
12     WORD16 *save_seg ;                /* save old seg. address here */
13     WORD16 *save_off ;                /* save old offset here */
14    {
15        REGS sreg , dreg ;
16
17                                       /* first save old vector */
18        sreg.ax = vecno & 0xff ;       /* vector number */
19        dos2call(GET_INT,&sreg,&dreg) ;
20        *save_seg = dreg.es ;
21        *save_off = dreg.bx ;
22
23        sreg.ax = vecno & 0xff ;       /* int. number in AL */
24        sreg.ds = iseg ;               /* setup full address in DS:DX */
25        sreg.dx = ioff ;
26        dos2call(SET_INT,&sreg,&dreg) ; /* now install it */
27    }
28
```

1. The CS register already points to the code segment of the program.
2. Segment registers DS, ES, and SS point to the data segment of the program.
3. The stack pointer is pointed to the top of an area to be used as a stack. The TTY2 program uses another area for a stack when executing normally. Since the interrupt routine may be executed at any time, we need to provide a separate stack area for it. The 512-byte area we provide should be adequate.
4. Set the BP register to the same value as SP. Some C compilers may expect BP to have such a value on entry to a function.
5. Clear the direction flag. At least one C compiler expects this flag to be cleared on entry to a C function.

Whenever an interrupt occurs and the interrupt handler is executed, further hardware interrupts are disabled. To prevent delays in servicing other interrupts, our function enables interrupts before calling rcv_int. Note that we ensure that interrupts are always disabled before we change the stack address (SS and SP registers). An interrupt occurring after SS was changed and before SP was also changed would use an invalid stack address (new SS value and old SP value). While

Figure 8.22   c:tty2int.asm

```
 1   ;          intcode.asm - assembler prologue/epilogue for interrupt
 2   ;          handler written in C
 3
 4   ;          definitions for 8250 interrupt controller
 5   EOI_PORT EQU   20H              ; write to this I/O port to clear int.
 6   EOI_CMD  EQU   20H              ; value to write to clear int.
 7
 8   ;          data section
 9          include begdata.ha
10   save_ss dw       3412H          ; save entry stack ss:sp here
11   save_sp dw       0AA55H
12   istack  dw 256 dup (0)          ; stack for interrupt routine
13   topstk  dw 0                    ; end of the stack
14   astack  dw       topstk        ; store the address of the stack top
15   marker  db       '0123456789'   ; pattern for the debugger
16          include enddata.ha
17
18   ;          code section
19          include begcode.ha
20   extrn   rcv_int:near            ; the C function we call
21
22   ;          prologue/epilogue for an interrupt handling function in C
23   ;          set the interrupt vector to point to gotint
24          public  gotint
25   gotint:
26          push    ax               ; save the current register values
27          push    bx
28          push    cx
29          push    dx
30          push    si
31          push    di
32          push    bp
33          push    ds
34          push    es
35   ;          change to our data segment and our interrupt stack
36          mov     ax,dstart    ; make DS = our
37          mov     ds,ax        ; data segment (or group)
38          mov     es,ax
39          mov     word ptr Save_ss,ss ; save current stack
40          mov     word ptr Save_sp,sp
41                               ; can assume ints. still off
42          mov     ss,ax        ; point to our int. stack - SS
43          mov     sp,astack    ; and then SP
44          sti                  ; now allow ints again
45          mov     bp,sp        ; point bp to top of stack
46          cld                  ; direction flag = forward
47          call    rcv_int      ; call C function
48   ;          restore the stack we had on entry
49          cli                  ; turn off ints. during change
50          mov     ss,cs:word ptr save_ss
51          mov     sp,cs:word ptr save_sp
52          mov     dx,EOI_PORT  ; clear int from 8259 controller
53          mov     ax,EOI_CMD
54          out     dx,al
55                               ; let iret enable ints again
```

Figure 8.22   c:tty2int.asm (continued)

```
56              pop     es              ; restore registers
57              pop     ds
58              pop     bp
59              pop     di
60              pop     si
61              pop     dx
62              pop     cx
63              pop     bx
64              pop     ax
65              iret                    ; and exit
66
67      ;       intson - enable 8088 interrupts
68      ;
69      ;       USAGE -  intson() ;
70      ;
71              public intson
72      intson: sti
73              ret
74
75      ;       intsoff - disable 8088 interrupts
76      ;
77      ;       USAGE -  intsoff() ;
78      ;
79              public intsoff
80      intsoff: cli
81              ret
82
83              include endcode.ha
84              end
```

newer 8086 family chips prevent interrupts at this point, some older 8088 chips allowed interrupts between these instructions. After rcv_int returns control, lines 52 to 54 clear the interrupt in the PC's 8259 interrupt controller.

C functions may also need to enable and disable interrupts. The functions intson and intsoff in lines 67 to 81 provide these capabilities.

8.7   Compiling, Testing, and Measuring TTY2

□   Some of the C functions in TTY2 are executed from an interrupt handler. This may require special options for compiling. For example, the Lattice C compiler normally performs checks on stack usage as each C function is called. This produced error messages when the interrupt handler called rcv_int. To prevent this condition, the source files were compiled with the −v option in the second pass (LC2).

Testing TTY2 presents several problems. Real-time programs are sensitive to the volume of input and to the exact timing of events. Bugs may be very subtle and hard to duplicate. The first defense against the problem is to design out time-dependent bugs. The modular construction and unit testing we have stressed throughout the book are more important than ever here. Even functions executed inside an interrupt handler such as rcv_int, rcv_char, and putq can be thoroughly tested in a normal environment. The assembler function, gotint, that is executed when a received data interrupt occurs can be checked with the debugger. The queue data structure that connects the interrupt handler with the rest of TTY2 is designed to eliminate bugs.

Another problem is that we need a terminal or another computer to test the TTY2 program fully. There is no cure for this; you need something to transmit characters to TTY2 and to display what TTY2 transmits. Once TTY2 as a whole has been tested, small modifications can often be tested without another computer. But if you work with communications programs, a second computer is just a cost of doing business.

Section 8.3 discussed measuring the performance of TTY1. The same program, perftty1.c, listed there is useful for testing TTY2 and measuring its performance. That program illustrates two requirements for testing real-time programs: a way to generate a worst case load and a mechanism for spotting incorrect behavior. When we measure TTY2 we find some improvement relative to TTY1.

At 1,200 baud with lines of one to ten characters long, no characters are lost. Recording and replaying data work correctly, and no keyboard input is lost. (The limitations of the IBM PC still cause problems with pathological cases like a stream of line feed characters. The PC cannot scroll the screen upward 120 times per second.)

TTY2 makes direct use of the async hardware and of the interrupt system of the PC. You may wonder how much this limits the systems on which it can operate. It operates successfully on IBM PCs, XTs and ATs, and compatible computers with IBM async adapter cards or functional equivalents. It has not been tested on a PC jr but should work within the limitations of that computer. (The PC jr cannot support async interrupts while disk I/O is in progress and cannot support keyboard input with async interrupts at speeds above 1,200 baud.)

8.8   Enhancements

□   We have concentrated on performance issues rather than on features. The techniques we developed for using buffering and interrupts makes it straightforward to add features without disrupting the TTY program. The list of useful features is potentially endless; we mention a few common ones here.

Usage Parameters

TTY2 relies on the other computer to echo keyboard input. This is appropriate in some cases, but we need an option to make TTY2 echo keyboard input. Other options might include translating characters (adding a line feed after each carriage return, for example) or stripping unwanted control characters such as control-Z or the ASCII bel char.

Setting Communications Parameters

Our program relies on the DOS MODE command for setting the baud rate, the parity setting, and the number of data bits in a word. It would be much more convenient to be able to set these from within TTY.

TTY2 treats received characters as full 8-bit values. If the mode command has initialized the 8250 UART for 7 data bits and even parity, the rcv_char function should strip the high-order bit:

```
if( /* using even parity */ )
    c = toascii(c) ;
```

Dialing Phone Numbers

A session with TTY usually starts with dialing the phone number of the computer with which we will talk. Smart modems that can accept commands and dial the number for us are common. We could extend TTY to prompt for a phone number, build a dialing command, and send it to the modem. When the modem at the other end answers the phone, TTY would announce the fact and then perform normal data transfers.

Implementing this feature requires adding modes to TTY. When it is in the dialing mode, it handles input differently from its actions in the data transfer state.

Dialing Directory

The same phone numbers will be called on a regular basis. A directory storing a list of names and phone numbers would save typing a phone number for each session. This directory could also specify communications parameters for each phone number. The directory would be stored in a file and read by TTY when it was executed.

Reporting Status and Errors

We keep track of errors in receiving data with the counters nrerr and nrqo. However, it would be more useful to signal them on the screen. When TTY is used with a modem, it is important to monitor the modem's status to tell when the modem at the other end answers the phone or when it hangs up. The modem status register of the 8250 UART supplies this information; TTY2 needs to examine it periodically to display changes.

Error-Checking Protocols

TTY2 can send and receive data files, but we do not have any protection against losing or garbling characters. A protocol for ensuring correct transmission and reception of files is an important feature for a terminal emulation program. The elements of such a protocol are (1) the file must be transmitted in short packets (of 50 to 150 bytes) with an accompanying *checksum* that verifies correct reception; (2) positive (and perhaps negative) acknowledgments of correct reception; (3) timeouts on arrival of the next packet or acknowledgment; (4) retransmission of data not acknowledged or negatively acknowledged.

Since the same protocol must be used by both computers, your choice of a protocol is governed by what is supported by the computers that will communicate.

Emulating Specific CRT Terminals

Many applications of terminal emulation require that the program emulate a specific model CRT terminal. For example, if we want to talk to a DEC VAX system, we would emulate a DEC VT-52 or VT-100 terminal. Talking to a Hewlett-Packard computer might require emulating some Hewlett-Packard terminal.

Most CRT terminals support special commands for moving the cursor position, inserting or deleting characters, and doing other functions. The newer the terminal, the longer the list of features to be emulated. Unfortunately, the commands that control these features vary from one terminal model to another.

Documentation of terminal features is often inadequate, and the terminal's performance often differs from its specifications in subtle but significant ways. Many of these features are blunders by the original programmers, but once committed, they are faithfully reproduced by generations of compatible terminals and emulation programs.

Bulletin Board Systems

Our program emulates a terminal and lets us talk to a mini- or mainframe computer. A bulletin board system emulates a computer so people with terminals or PCs can call up and get messages or files from our system.

Bulletin board systems are passive; that is, they wait for someone to call and then respond to commands from the caller. In a sense, such systems are the complement of terminal emulation programs. A really complete program might combine both roles.

More Speed

TTY2 is fast enough for 1,200 baud but not for higher speeds. Rewriting the rcv_int, rcv_char, and putq functions is one possibility. Using the SCREEN module for displaying characters is another possibility. Still another approach is to combine functions to reduce the number of function calls (rcv_int and rcv_char, for example). A careful analysis of TTY2's current performance to identify the real bottlenecks is a good first step.

8.9 Summary

□ We have presented a terminal emulation program as an example of a real-time program. We introduced techniques for buffering input and for using interrupts. The TTY2 program is short on features but has good performance and provides a good basis for enhancement. In addition, its components can be used for related programs like bulletin board systems.

The chapter should also prepare you to understand other real-time problems. The same themes—polling, worst case performance, buffering, and using interrupts—will be useful in attacking many real-time problems.

The TTY2 program is filled with I/O port addresses and definitions of bits in control and status ports. Those details may seem difficult and foreign to you. The references listed in Appendix D should help somewhat. One lesson you should absorb from this chapter is that the low-level programming we have done is not really harder than more system-independent programming. The main difficulty is finding out how the hardware really works.

9
Loose Ends
and Final Thoughts

The C source files in Chapters 1 to 8 did not use most of the unique features in C. We review some programming techniques for using these features and examine the benefits and costs of using them. Handling errors was another topic often neglected in previous chapters; we present interrupt handlers that give control of control-Break and critical error conditions.

9.1 Using the Rest of C: Optimization

☐ The programs in this book were written in a subset of C. Many of the features that are unique to C were not used at all, and other features were used in a restricted way. Producing clear, readable programs was stressed over speed, but we paid a penalty for this choice. This section looks at some advanced features in C and measures their effect on performance.

Many of the features we did not use have something in common: They allow you to give hints to the compiler about what you really mean. For example, instead of the line

```
i = i + 1 ;
```

we can use the increment operator (+ +):

```
i + + ;    or    + + i ;
```

This means the same thing but it tells the compiler that we are putting the result back where we got it. We can use the increment operator inside expressions as shown in the following printout. In an expression, + + does two things: It increments the value in a variable, and it has a value that is used in the rest of the expression. Placed in front of a variable, + + means increment the variable and then get its value. Placed after a variable, + + means get the value of a variable and then increment the variable. The following examples show both uses:

```
i = i + 1;
sum = sum + a[i];        or     sum = sum + a[ ++i ];
```

```
tot = tot + a[i];        or     tot = tot + a[ i++ ];
i = i + 1;
```

The decrement operator (− −) is analogous: It subtracts rather than adds.

C also provides *assignment operators* for more general cases. Instead of

```
a = a + b;
```

we can write

```
a + = b;
```

This tells us and the compiler that we are adding the value of b to that of a and storing the result back in a. Other operators such as minus (−), multiply (∗), divide (/), BitOr (|), and BitAnd (&) can be combined with the assignment operator.

Assignments can be placed inside expressions. The following example condenses a loop for reading characters from a file:

```
c = getchar ();
while( c ! = EOF )
   { n = n + 1;
     c = getchar ();
   }
```

or

```
while( (c = getchar ()) ! = EOF )
   { n = n + 1; }
```

Pointers can often be used instead of array subscripts. This is most appropriate when the program steps through the array one element at a time. The following example shows how the technique works:

```
sum = 0;
for(i = 0 ; i< n ; i = i + 1)
   { sum = sum + a[i]; }
```

or

```
sum = 0 ;
pa = a ;
for(i = 0; i <n ; i = i + 1)
    { sum = sum + *pa++ ; }
```

It is possible to combine these techniques to produce very compact source files. Such source files look as though the program should run much faster, but this is rarely true. Unfortunately, such programs also are harder to read, enhance, and maintain.

Several of these optimization techniques were used in modifying the integer quicksort function from Chapter 5. The original function was shown in Figure 5.2, and the modified version is shown in Figure 9.1. The modified version is 1.08 times as fast using the Lattice C compiler (Version 2.0) and 1.26 times as fast for the C-Ware DeSmet C compiler. While these differences are measurable, they are minor compared to the difference between the quicksort and insertion sort algorithms (23 times as fast).

It seems our hints or shortcuts should save more time. Good compilers are fairly effective at analyzing expressions and generating effective programs. A compiler that does little or no optimization and generates poor code might benefit greatly from our hints. But if your compiler is reasonably efficient, it makes more sense to write straightforward programs that can be enhanced with better algorithms. Rewriting local bottlenecks to make full use of C's features is a valid optimization technique, but the payoff is often a small one.

Writing compact source files that make full use of C's shortcut operators has been a test of manhood for many C programmers. Many C hackers and even some authors of C books will tell you that you have to use all of C's features and write compact but unreadable source files. This is not true: Writing obscure, tricky programs is good for a hacker's ego but unnecessary and dangerous in serious programming projects.

9.2 Handling Control-Break Conditions

□ DOS provides simple default handling when control-Break (or control-C) is typed. It displays ^C on the screen at the current cursor position and then returns control to command.com (the DOS command interpreter). Files may not be closed properly, and the disk directory and file allocation tables may be left in an inconsistent state. In addition, the application program is not able to tidy up its files or restore default interrupt vectors.

Since this action is not satisfactory for most applications, we need to avoid it. One way is to bypass DOS (and the C library standard I/O functions) for all console I/O and use BIOS calls instead (or the SCREEN module). If this method is not practical, we can install our own control-Break handler.

When DOS detects that control-Break has been typed, it displays the ^C

Figure 9.1   c:qsorti2.c

```
1    /* qsorti2.c - performs a quicksort on an array of integers */
2    #include "stdio.h"
3    #include "cminor.h"
4
5    int qsort(a,na)
6      int a[] ;                    /* array of integers to be sorted */
7      int na  ;                    /* number of elements to be sorted */
8      {
9        int i , j ;                /* indices for loops */
10       int temp ;                 /* temporary storage for element */
11       int nr ;                   /* number elements in right partition */
12       int part ;                 /* element chosen as partition value */
13       int *pi , *pj ;            /* pointer style indices */
14       if( na < 2  )
15           return ;
16
17       part = a[na/2] ;           /* pick middle element for partition */
18
19       pi = & a[0] -1 ; pj = & a[na] ;
20       while( 1 == 1 )
21         { /* find first element to move right */
22           do { pi ++ ; } while( *pi < part ) ;
23
24           /* find first element to move left */
25           while( * --pj > part ) { ; }
26
27           if( pi >= pj )              /* have the boundaries met ? */
28               break ;                 /*   yes - through partitioning */
29
30           /* swap i and j elements */
31           temp = *pi ;  *pi = *pj ; *pj = temp ;
32         }
33
34       i = pi - & a[0] ;
35       nr = na - i ;
36       if( i < (na/2) )               /* now deal with each partition */
37         { qsort( a , i ) ;           /* sort left side  */
38           qsort( &(a[i]),nr);        /* sort right side */
39         }
40       else
41         { qsort( &(a[i]),nr);        /* sort right side */
42           qsort( a , i ) ;           /* sort left side  */
43         }
44     }
```

message on the screen and then executes a software interrupt instruction (INT 23H). We can handle control-Break exceptions ourselves by replacing the default interrupt vector for **INT 23H** with the address of our own handler. The set_brk function in Figure 9.2 installs our handler using the **install** function developed in Chapter 8.

The rm__brk function in this source file restores the original interrupt vector so that the default handler again functions. It might be called if we want to stop handling control-break interrupts and restore the default handler.

Figure 9.2   c:set_brk.c

```
1    /* set_brk.c - install / remove our handler for Control-Break */
2    #include "stdio.h"
3    #include "cminor.h"
4
5    #define BRK_INT    0x23          /* number of s/w int. for CTL-BRK */
6
7    int got_brk() ;                  /* the handler we will install */
8    int16 brkflag ;                  /* flag to record Control-Break */
9
10   static WORD16 oseg,ooff ;        /* save address of old handler here */
11
12   int set_brk()                    /* set up our Ctl-Break Handler */
13   {
14       WORD16 iseg,ioff ;           /* form segmented address here */
15       int n ;
16
17                                    /* get segmented addr. of handler */
18       get_fads(got_brk,&iseg,&ioff) ;
19
20       install(BRK_INT,iseg,ioff,&oseg,&ooff) ;
21       brkflag = 0 ;                /* no Break yet so clear flag */
22   }
23
24
25   int rm_brk()                     /* remove our Ctl-Break Handler */
26   {
27       WORD16 iseg , ioff ;
28
29       install(BRK_INT,oseg,ooff,&iseg,&ioff) ;
30   }
31
32
33   int chk_brk()                    /* check Control-Break flag */
34   {
35       return( brkflag ) ;
36   }
37
38
39   int clr_brk()                    /* clear Control-Break flag */
40   {
41       brkflag = 0 ;
42   }
```

Our interrupt handler is shown in Figure 9.3. It simply sets a flag variable and returns. This allows us to test the value of this flag variable after each DOS call and take whatever action is appropriate. The chk_brk and clr_brk functions in Figure 9.2 check and clear this flag variable.

Figure 9.4 shows an experimental program that uses our break handler. It illustrates installing and removing the handler and checking the flag variable. You should compile and try this program with your compiler to find out exactly how your library functions interact with the DOS control-Break handling.

Figure 9.3   c:handbrk.asm

```
 1    ;            handbrk.asm - intercept control-Break (and Ctl-C)
 2    ;
 3    ;            this function is not called from the program
 4    ;            it is invoked by DOS when a Control-Break is detected
 5    ;            by DOS.
 6    ;            See the discussion of INT 23H in the DOS 2.0 Manual
 7    ;            or in the DOS Technical Reference Manual (2.1 or Later)
 8
 9
10    ;            start data section - use compiler specific include file
11                 include begdata.ha
12
13    ;            brkflag is defined in another source file
14    ;            It is set to 1 when Control_Break is detected
15                 extrn    brkflag:word
16    ;            Your compiler may require brkflag_ or _brkflag instead
17                 dw       0
18                 include enddata.ha
19
20    ;            start code section
21                 include begcode.ha
22
23    ;            got_brk - handle control-C or Ctl-Break
24                 public   got_brk,got_brk_,_got_brk
25    got_brk:
26    got_brk_:
27    _got_brk:
28                 push     ax
29                 push     ds
30                 mov      ax,dstart
31                 mov      ds,ax
32                 mov      word ptr brkflag,1
33                 pop      ds
34                 pop      ax
35                 iret
36
37                 include endcode.ha
38
39                 end
```

9.3   Handling Critical Errors

□   Handling data errors is an unpleasant fact of life in real-world programs. The diskette on which we want to write a file may be unformatted or write-protected; we may find a bad sector in reading a file. DOS reports some errors to the application via an error return code. For example, if a write operation fails because the disk runs out of free space, an error return notifies the program. But many serious errors are handled in a different way: DOS executes a software interrupt (INT 24H). The default error handler that DOS provides for this interrupt displays the message

Abort, Retry or Ignore

Figure 9.4   c:testbrk.c

```
1    /* testbrk.c - test Control_Break handling */
2    #include "stdio.h"
3    #include "cminor.h"
4
5    main()
6      {
7        int n , i , c ;
8        char s[512] ;
9
10       set_brk() ;                      /* install our break handler */
11
12       printf(" enter a number: \n");
13       scanf("%d",&i) ;
14       if( chk_brk() != 0 )
15         { printf(" BREAK typed - continuing \n") ;
16           clr_brk() ;
17         }
18       printf(" the number entered was %d \n",i) ;
19
20       printf(" enter a another number: \n");
21       scanf("%d",&i) ;
22       if( chk_brk() != 0 )
23         { printf(" BREAK typed - exiting \n") ;
24           exit(10) ;
25         }
26       printf(" the number entered was %d \n",i) ;,
27
28       c = getchar() ;                  /* flush rest of input line */
29       while( (c != '\n') && (c != '\r') )
30         { c = getchar() ; }
31
32       printf(" enter a line of text: \n");
33       c = getchar() ;
34       n= 0 ;
35       while( (c != '\n') && (c != '\r') )
36         { s[n] = c ;
37           n = n + 1 ;
38           c = getchar() ;
39         }
40
41       if( chk_brk() != 0 )
42         { printf(" BREAK typed - continuing \n") ;
43           clr_brk() ;
44         }
45
46       printf(" the characters typed were \n") ;
47       for(i=0 ; i<n ; i=i+1)
48         { printf(" %02x",tochar(s[i]) ) ; }
49
50       rm_brk() ;                       /* restore default handler */
51       printf("\n default handler restored \n") ;
52       printf(" enter a another number: \n");
53       scanf("%d",&i) ;
54       printf(" the number entered was %d \n",i) ;
55     }
```

and offers a chance to abort the program, retry the operation, or ignore the error. This is rarely a satisfactory solution for an application program. Programs that are used for important work must respond to such error conditions in a way that makes sense for the application. Fortunately, we can install our own handler for critical errors.

Figures 9.5 and 9.6 show a module for handling critical errors. It simulates a DOS error return so our program can respond to the error in the context of the action that failed.

The set_err function in Figure 9.5 installs our interrupt vector. It calls the storvec function to make the address of the default handler known to our handler. The rm_err function restores the default handler, while chk_err checks for an error and clr_err clears the error flag. chk_err returns a zero value if no error occurs and a nonzero error code (based on the DI register value passed by DOS to the error handler) if there is an error. Since the error code DOS returns may be zero, the return value is doctored to force it to be nonzero if an error occurred.

The error handler is shown in Figure 9.6. Both disk-related and other errors are passed to the critical error handler. We can handle the disk-oriented errors ourselves and use the default handler for non-disk-oriented errors. DOS detects errors during a DOS function call. Our error handler sets an error flag and then returns control to the application program that called DOS. It simulates a DOS error return, setting the carry flag and returning an error code in the AX register with an error return. This notifies the application that the DOS call did not work and allows that application to take an appropriate recovery action.

Lines 66 to 106 make up the error handler code. The AX register is first tested to determine whether the error is disk-related. If not, the jump instruction in line 73 passes control to the default error handler. Lines 76 to 106 handle disk errors. Register values containing error information are saved, and the error flag is set. The stack contains the return address (and 8088 flag register contents) left by the INT 24H instruction that invoked the error handler. So the error handler discards these values from the stack. It then sets the carry bit in the flag register and places an error code in the AX register. This simulates a DOS-2-style error return. The register values from the original application program are then restored, and the handler executes a return from interrupt instruction to return to the application.

The storvec function in lines 50 to 64 stores the address of the default error handler so we can pass control to it if necessary. storvec is called by set_err during installation of our handler.

Figure 9.7 gives an example of using the error handler with the unbuffered read/write library I/O functions; you can use it to experiment with error handling in the environment of your compiler's library functions. The easiest way to cause a disk-related critical error is to open the door of a floppy disk drive before the program performs an I/O operation. Another way is to apply a write-protect tab to the diskette before writing to it.

The correct response to an error depends on the type of error as well as the action in progress. A disk write that fails because the disk drive door is open requires a different reaction than a write that fails because of a bad sector. The following

Figure 9.5   c:set_err.c

```
1    /* set_err.c - setup / remove our critical error handler */
2    #include "stdio.h"
3    #include "cminor.h"
4
5    #define ERR_INT    0x24        /* number of s/w int for crit. err. */
6
7    int got_err() ;
8
9                                   /* variables used by error handler */
10   int16  errflag ;              /* =1 if error occurred */
11   int16 err_ax ;               /* register value with error info */
12   int16 err_di ;               /*    "    */
13   int16 err_bp ;               /*    "    */
14   int16 err_si ;               /*    "    */
15   int16 ecode ;                /* error code returned by handler */
16
17   static WORD16 oseg,ooff ;    /* save address of old handler */
18
19   int set_err()                /* setup our critical error handler */
20   {
21       WORD16 iseg,ioff ;
22
23                                   /* get segmented address of handler */
24       get_fads(got_err,&iseg,&ioff) ;
25       install(ERR_INT,iseg,ioff,&oseg,&ooff) ;
26       storvec(oseg,ooff) ;
27       errflag = 0 ;               /* no errors yet */
28   }
29
30   rm_err()                      /* remove our error handler */
31   {
32       WORD16 iseg,ioff ;
33
34                                   /* install old error handler */
35       install(ERR_INT,oseg,ooff,&iseg,&ioff) ;
36   }
37
38
39   int chk_err()                 /* check Critical Error flag */
40   {
41       if( errflag == 0 )
42           return( 0 ) ;
43       else return( (err_di & 0xff) | 0x100 ) ;
44   }
45
46   int clr_err()                 /* clear Critical Error flag */
47   {
48       errflag = 0 ;
49   }
```

Figure 9.6   c:handerr.asm

```
 1    ;          handerr.asm - intercept critical errors
 2    ;
 3    ;          this function is not called from the program
 4    ;          it is invoked by DOS when a Critical Error is detected
 5    ;          by DOS.
 6
 7    ;          See the discussion of INT 24H in the DOS 2.0 Manual
 8    ;          or in the DOS Technical Reference Manual (2.1 or Later)
 9
10
11    ;          start data section - use compiler specific include file
12               include begdata.ha
13               dw      0
14
15    ;          data variables defined in other source files
16    ;          err_flag -  =1 if a disk-related error occurred
17
18    ;                    the next four variables store error info
19    ;          err_ax   - AX value passed to handler
20    ;          err_di   - DI value passed to handler
21    ;          err_bp   - BP value passed to handler
22    ;          err_si   - SI value passed to handler
23
24    ;          ecode    - use this value as a DOS-type return code
25
26               extrn   errflag:word
27               extrn   err_ax:word
28               extrn   err_di:word
29               extrn   err_bp:word
30               extrn   err_si:word
31               extrn   ecode:word
32    ;          Your compiler may require an underscore before or after
33    ;          each of these names
34
35    ;          declare arguments for storvec
36    args       struc
37               dw      0          ; saved BP value
38               dw      0          ; return address
39    old_seg dw      0          ; segment address of old handler
40    old_off dw      0          ; offset address of old handler
41    args       ends
42
43               include enddata.ha
44
45    ;          start code section
46               include begcode.ha
47
48    saveold dd      0              ; save address of old error handler here
49
50    ;          storvec(old_seg,old_off)
51    ;          store the address of the old error handler
52    ;          then got_err can call it if necessary
53               public  storvec,storvec_,_storvec
54    storvec:
55    storvec_:
56    _storvec:
```

Figure 9.6   c:handerr.asm (continued)

```
57                  push    bp
58                  mov     bp,sp
59                  mov     ax,old_seg[bp]
60                  mov     cs:word ptr saveold[2],ax
61                  mov     ax,old_off[bp]
62                  mov     cs:word ptr saveold,ax
63                  pop     bp
64                  ret
65
66      ;           got_err - handle Critical Error
67                  public  got_err,got_err_,_got_err
68      got_err:
69      got_err_:
70      _got_err:
71                  test    al,128          ; disk error ?
72                  jz      de              ;   yes - handle it ourselves
73                  jmp     cs:dword ptr saveold ; no - use old handler
74
75      de:
76                  push    ds
77                  push    ax
78                  mov     ax,dstart
79                  mov     ds,ax
80                  pop     ax
81                  mov     word ptr errflag,1
82                  mov     word ptr err_ax,ax
83                  mov     word ptr err_di,di
84                  mov     word ptr err_bp,bp
85                  mov     word ptr err_si,si
86                  pop     ds
87
88                  pop     ax              ; discard DOS registers on stack
89                  pop     ax              ; ( IP , CS , FLAGS )
90                  pop     ax
91
92      ;           the iret below pops flags register from the stack
93      ;           so we set the carry bit in that word on the stack
94                  mov     bp,sp
95                  or      word ptr [bp+22],1  ; set carry flag
96
97                  pop     ax              ; restore application program registers
98                  mov     ax,word ptr ecode      ; fake DOS 2 error code
99                  pop     bx
100                 pop     cx
101                 pop     dx
102                 pop     si
103                 pop     di
104                 pop     bp
105                 pop     ds
106                 pop     es
107
108                 iret
109
110                 include endcode.ha
111
112                 end
```

Figure 9.7   c:testerr.c

```
1     /* testerr.c - test Critical Error handling  */
2     /*     using the write I/O function */
3     #include "stdio.h"
4     #include "cminor.h"
5
6     main()
7      {
8         int n , i , out ;
9         char buffer[512] ;
10
11        set_err() ;
12        for(i=0;i<512 ; i=i+1)
13          { buffer[i] = 32 + (i % 96) ; }
14
15        printf(" press a key to open file \n");
16        getkey() ;
17
18        out = creat("b:test.dat",0x8001) ;
19        printf(" out=%d chk_err=%x \n",out,chk_err() ) ;
20        if( chk_err() != 0 )
21          { printf(" error detected - exiting \n");
22            exit(7) ;
23          }
24        if( out < 0 )
25          { printf(" creat failed - exiting \n");
26            exit(6) ;
27          }
28
29        printf("file b:test.dat created -press key for each write \n");
30        printf("press q to stop writing \n");
31        n = 0 ;
32        while( getkey() != 'q' )
33          { n = n + 1 ;
34            printf(" %4d ret=%d \n",n , write(out,buffer,512) ) ;
35            printf(" chk_err=%x \n",chk_err() ) ;
36          }
37
38        printf(" chk_err=%x \n",chk_err() ) ;
39        if( chk_err() != 0 )
40          { printf(" error detected - continuing \n");
41            clr_err() ;
42          }
43
44        printf(" replacing old handler \n");
45        rm_err() ;                  /* restore default handler */
46        printf(" press a key to close file \n");
47        getkey() ;
48        close(out) ;
49        printf(" file closed \n" ) ;
50      }
```

table lists error codes returned by chk_err for some common errors. These codes and the other information that we needed to implement the error handler are documented in the *DOS Technical Reference Manual.*

Error Code	Meaning
0x100	Write-Protected Diskette
0x101	Drive Not Ready (Drive door open or no diskette in the drive)
0x102	Bad CRC checksum. (Data no longer readable)

The error handler is very low-level programming; it requires a lot of understanding of how DOS and the 8088 work. The discussion of error handling in the DOS manuals is fragmentary and hard to follow, but good programs need to handle error gracefully. Our error handler provides a basic tool and an example from which to learn.

9.4 Summary

□ Our objective in this book has been to open some doors for you. Chapters 3 to 8 discussed important algorithms and techniques in a realistic context. The information we discussed has genuine usefulness, and we provided a practical tool to allow immediate use of the information.

Developing good tools once and then using them many times in a variety of programs was our main theme. Programming is hard, unproductive work when you do everything from scratch. The programs and toolkit functions in the book can give you a head start; they are large and complicated enough to do something interesting. You can make useful modifications to them to get quick results for a minimum of effort.

We have also described the process of creating programs. The main message is to break problems up into small parts and work through them in bite-sized chunks. If you do not understand the problem completely, explore it with small experiments. Do simple prototype programs before you add all the bells and whistles the final solution requires. Organize programs into a number of small modules—each with a single clear function. Test all the modules before you put the entire program together. Look for good tools that can be applied to other problems.

You may find parts of the book hard to understand at first. That is natural since we picked topics that are not trivial and tried to cover them in useful depth. In choosing material for the book, we had to balance simplicity and clarity against depth and content. We opted for more depth and tougher topics than most authors choose. Our chief fear was that the book would not contain enough material to make it worth reading, so if there is enough material for a second reading, think of it as added value.

Programmers often learn by reading each other's work. Most working programmers have benefited greatly from contact with their colleagues. This book attempts to give you another shoulder to look over, another set of program listings to explore. We tried to make the view over that shoulder unique.

Appendix A
Compiling
and Executing
the Programs

Many of the programs in this book require header or include files. You should collect these header files and place them on the default drive before compiling the programs. (A batch file to transfer all these header files to the default drive is a useful timesaver.) Some C compilers accept a command line parameter to specify where to find header files; such options are especially useful with a hard disk.

The low-level tools in Chapter 7 are needed in a number of programs. You should compile or assemble these source files before linking programs in other chapters.

Most of the programs in this book consist of a number of source files. Linking a large number of object files can require a lot of typing. Here are some remedies:

1. Put tools into an object library as soon as they are compiled and checked out. Specifying the name of an object library is easier than typing the names of six to twelve object files. Most C compiler products now include a librarian to build and maintain object libraries. In the following examples, we assume that a library named *tools* have been created and is located on the default drive.

2. Construct a general purpose batch file for linking C programs. The following batch file (l.bat) is for Lattice C, but a similar one could be constructed for other compilers. It specifies names of object files and libraries that do not change and allows up to nine object files to be named in the command line.

```
link cs %1 %2 %3 . . . %9,%1,nul,tools c: \ lc \ s \ lc
```

3. When you write a program, create a batch file that specifies the names of all the files that must be linked. The file shown (linkview.bat) applies to the VIEW program and uses the general purpose batch file from the previous remedy:

l view viewget viewexec viewpos viewdisp viewfind viewio

4. DOS restricts command lines typed or in batch files to 128 characters maximum, this restricts the number of file names that the linker can accept. You can create an automatic response file to specify more file names. The following example of such a file (linkview.arf) is equivalent to the linkview.bat file:

```
cs +
view viewget viewexec viewpos +
viewdisp viewfind viewio
view.exe
nul
tools c: \ lc \ s \ lcs
```

Lines 1 to 3 specify object files and lines 4, 5, and 6 specify the name of the .exe file, the listing file, and the libraries to be searched. The + character at the end of lines 1 and 2 tells the linker that the next line in the file contains more object file names. To link the program you would type the command

link @linkview.arf

This method allows a large number of files to be specified.

The program diskette to be used with this book makes modifying the programs much easier and quicker. Source files are ready for compiling or modification, and object librarians are provided for the Lattice C, C Ware, and Computer Innovations C86 compilers.

General Suggestions on Developing C Programs

1. Keep the tools you need on-line. Even in a floppy-disk-based system, you should be able to keep the editor, compiler, linker, and object libraries ready for use without changing diskettes. The C Ware DeSmet C compiler is compact enough and compiles fast enough for use with floppy disks; if you are going to use other C compilers, you should get a ramdisk or a hard disk.

2. Using the EDLIN line editor is senseless punishment. Any of the following choices changes editing from pain to pleasure: WordStar (nondocument mode), Vedit, P-Edit (SSI), Brief (Solution Systems), or PC-Write (Quicksoft).

3. Short source files produce quick compile times, and that makes programming endurable. Think of a one-page source file as the normal size. Short files can often be created, compiled, and tested without producing paper listings.

4. You can usually locate and correct syntax errors using the line numbers the compiler displays on the screen. Keep in mind that syntax errors confuse the compiler; after the first few syntax errors, it may report errors that do not really exist.

5. You should use some caution when debugging and testing C programs. Copy altered files from a ramdisk to a floppy disk or hard disk before running tests. Crashes that lock up the PC do happen, but if you play safe, they just cause a delay while you restart the PC. The IBM PC does not provide memory protection so your bugs can overwrite the program and even corrupt DOS. Using the small memory model minimizes the risk and is a good idea even when the final program will use a large memory model.

Appendix B
C Compilers for the IBM PC Environment

We checked our programs with a number of C compilers for use on an IBM PC under PC-DOS. Several compilers (C Ware, Manx, and C-Systems) did not support a choice of ASCII or binary mode for buffered file I/O. Since all supported binary mode, the programs in Chapters 3 to 9 are not affected. This appendix comments on program changes required for each compiler. The version evaluated is also listed for each compiler.

Lattice C

☐ Version 2.00 was used for examples of compiling and linking and for performance measurements. Some testing was done with Version 2.13.

Versions 1.00 to 1.04 buffered console output until a newline character ('\n') was output. Some programs that prompt with a printf statement before accepting input need a newline character added to the character string that is displayed.

Starting with Version 2.00, the Lattice C library contains a function named movedata. It expects different arguments and performs different functions than the movedata function defined in Chapter 2. The following examples 1 and 2 show ways to force the use of our function, while example 3 shows how to get the Lattice movedata function:

1. link cs test movedata,test,,c: \ ls \ s \ lcs
2. link cs test,test,, tools c: \ ls \ s \ lcs
3. link cs test,test,, c: \ ls \ s \ lcs

These examples assume that the Lattice library is named lcs, that it is located in the c:\ls\s subdirectory, and that our library tools contain the movedata.obj file.

Versions 2.10 to 2.13 use RAM memory in an awkward way, reserving a fixed amount of memory for the stack. The default stack size of 8 Kbytes is inadequate for many programs in this book; stack overflow error messages result. A stack overflow message indicates that a larger stack size parameter is required while an insufficient memory message indicates that the stack size is too large to allow room for the static data.

You may specify a stack size on the command line when you execute a C program:

```
A>view = 30000 sample.txt
```

You may also change the value by compiling the following C file and including the object file when you link C programs:

```
/* bigstack.c - set stack size */
int_stack = 30000 ;
```

Unfortunately, no single stack size will work for all programs. This problem may be fixed in later versions of Lattice C.

Microsoft C

□ Through Version 2.03, Microsoft C was the same as Lattice C. The toolkit functions in Chapter 7 apply to these versions. Version 2.03 was tested.

Starting with Version 3.0, Microsoft C is different from Lattice C. This new version was not available when the book was completed, but the program diskette contains up-to-date information on using the new version of Microsoft C.

Computer Innovations C86

□ No changes are required to the Assembler source files. Version 2.10 was tested.

C Ware DeSmet C

□ The compiler is compact, compiles fast, and is a terrific bargain when cost matters. The following list shows changes to Assembler source files for the DeSmet assembler:

MASM	DeSmet
include fn.ext	include "fn.ext"
funname :	funname_ :
mov ax,word ptr [bx]	mov ax,word [bx]
mov ax,wrd ptr reg_ax[di]	mov ax,word [reg_ax + di]
struc	
reg_ax dw 0	reg_ax EQU 0
reg_bx dw 0	reg_bx EQU 2
. . .	. . .
ends	

Version 2.4 of the compiler can produce **.obj** files, allowing the Micro-soft/IBM Assembler to be used. No changes to the assembler source files are required when the Microsoft assembler is used.

Version 2.3 of the DeSmet compiler was examined.

Mark Williams C

□   The assembler provided with the compiler requires extensive changes to the assembler files in this book, but the Microsoft/IBM Assembler can also be used. Assembler source files modified for the Mark Williams assembler are included on the program diskette. The following list shows changes required for this assembler:

MASM	Mark Williams
; comment	/ comment
include fn.ext	no include statement
xor ah,ah	xorb ah,ah
funname:	funname_ :
public name	.globl name_
struc	
reg_ax dw 0	reg_ax = 0
reg_bx dw 0	reg_bx = 2
. . .	. . .
ends	
name EQU 2	name = 2
var db CDH	var: .byte 0xCD
mov bx,ss:reg_bx[bx]	.byte 0x36
	mov bx,reg_bx(bx)

When the Microsoft Assembler is used, a single change is required to *.asm source files: An underscore must be appended to names of functions and public

variables. Thus, instead of name, as used in this book, you would use name_:.
Version 2.0 was examined.

C-Systems C

□ No changes to assembler source files are required. Version 1.18 was used.

Manx Aztec C

□ An underscore must be appended to function names and public variables, as shown for the Mark Williams C. We used version 1.05L.

Digital Research C

□ The compiler must be used with the assembler and linker supplied in the product. The following few syntax changes are required to assembler source files:

```
struc
  reg_ax dw 0                    reg_ax = 0
  reg_bx dw 0                    reg_bx = 2
  . . .                          . . .
ends

mov ax,word ptr [reg_ax + di]    mov ax,word ptr reg_ax[di]
```

Version 1.1 was examined.

Whitesmith's C

□ The default option for the compiler expects the BX register to be preserved across function calls. A compiler option can change this to agree with our assumption.

The assembler format required is very different from that used in this book. Changes required to assembler source files parallel those for the Mark Williams assembler with the following differences:

MASM	*Whitesmith's C*
; comment	/ comment
include fn.ext	no include statement
xor ah,ah	xor .b ah,ah (.w for word)
funname:	__funname :
public name	.public __name
struc	
reg__ax dw 0	reg__ax = 0
reg__bx dw 0	reg__bx = 2
. . .	. . .
ends	
name EQU 2	name = 2
var db CDH	var: .byte 0xCD
mov bx,ss:reg__bx[bx]	.sseg
	mov bx,reg__bx(bx)

Version CDOS 2.2 was used. The program diskette for this book documents changes to source files needed for each compiler.

Chapters 1 and 2 gave some examples of commands required for compiling and linking with Lattice C. There is little value in listing such commands for every compiler because the commands needed can change with each new release of a compiler. The documentation provided with the compiler should describe how to compile and link programs with that compiler. We can list the questions you want to answer when you read the compiler documentation:

1. What command name do I type to compile a program? Compiling often requires executing several programs, but a single batch file or executive program is often provided to let you type a single command to do the whole compilation.

2. What command name do I type to execute the linker program? This might be the LINK (the DOS linker) or a special linker provided with the compiler. The linker provided with the C Ware DeSmet compiler is called BIND, for example. Even if LINK is used, a batch file may be included to specify object files and libraries needed.

3. What special .obj files and libraries are required when I link programs? Where are they specified on the command line? How can I specify additional libraries when I link programs?

4. What restrictions are there on the placement of the compiler program and library files? What assumptions are made about the default drive and the PATH that is searched for command names? Where does the compiler place .obj files? Where does the linker place .exe files?

Appendix C
IBM PC Architecture
and C Memory Models

The 8086 family of processors used in the IBM PC computers can address up to 1 Mbyte of memory. The 80286 processor used in the PC AT can address even more memory in the protected mode. Under PC-DOS 3.0, the AT operates in real address mode and is limited to 1 Mbyte. Since registers and address fields in instructions are only 16 bits long (and thus can specify only 64 Kbytes directly), some trickery is required to address the whole 1-Mbyte range. In addition to its general purpose registers, the processor has four segment registers—code, data stack, and extra segment registers. When an instruction references memory, it specifies a 16-bit effective address—either directly or through a register value and an offset. This 16-bit value is combined with one of the four segment register values as follows:

full address = effective_address + 16 * segment_value

The four-segment registers allow a program to reference four different 64-Kbyte areas. Segment register values can be changed by a program, but there is a penalty in terms of program size and execution speed. There are several different strategies (called *memory models*) for using segment registers in a program:

8080 model: All four segment registers are set to point to the same 64-Kbyte area when the program begins execution and is left unchanged. This model is simple and has no overhead for changing segment registers but is limited to a total of 64 Kbytes.

Small Model: The code segment register points to an area containing the program's instructions, and the other segment registers point to a separate area for data. The segment registers are not changed during execution. Code and data areas may be up to 64 Kbytes each with no overhead for changing segment registers.

Medium Model: The code segment register is changed when function calls are made. The other segment registers point to a data area and are unchanged. This allows up to 1 Mbyte for code and a separate 64 Kbytes for data. The penalty in code size and execution speed is modest.

Large Model: The code segment register is changed during function calls. In addition, the data and extra segment registers are changed as needed to address up to 1 Mbyte of data. The cost in extra execution time may be 25 percent or more.

The small memory model is supported by all the C compilers evaluated. Since implementation differences are fairly small, this model is a natural choice for our programs. For this small model, a C program might fit into the PC's memory, as shown in Figure C.1. Some versions of the Lattice C compiler may place the heap area above the stack. Data allocated with `calloc` and `malloc` are located in the heap area.

A C compiler translates source files into computer instructions, but this pro-

Figure C.1   PC memory map for small model

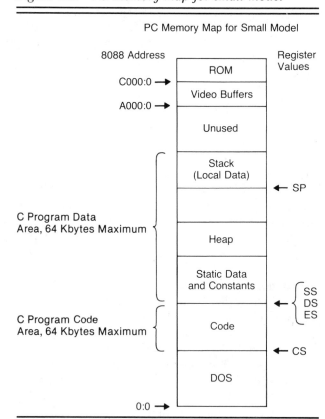

duces only part of a complete program. The linker combines one or more .obj files from the compiler with other object code stored in libraries. When the linker glues object files together to form a program, it needs some guidance in grouping instructions, static data, and local data (the stack) to produce the memory layout shown in the figure. The C compiler normally supplies this information, but we have to provide it for assembler source files.

Two levels of groupings are recognized by the linker: segments and groups. All data and variables in the same segment are contiguous in the program. All segments in the same group are contiguous as well. Each C compiler uses different segment and group names; our assembler files must specify segment and group names that match those of the compiler we use. That is the reason for the include files, *.ha, discussed in Chapter 7.

Appendix D
Reference Materials

Chapters 1 and 2: Books on C

☐ *The C Primer*, Les Hancock and Morris Krieger (New York: McGraw-Hill Byte Books, 1982). This is a well-written primer on C. Some topics such as file I/O are barely covered.

C Programming Guide, Jack Purdum (Indianapolis: Que Corporation, 1983). It is not as well written as the Hancock and Krieger book but covers all parts of C. The chapter on common mistakes is quite good.

The C Programming Language, Brian Kernighan and Dennis Ritchie (Englewood Cliffs, N.J.: Prentice-Hall, 1978). This book serves as the de facto standard of the C language. The C standard library is not fully discussed here.

UNIX Programmer's Manual, vols 1 and 2 (New York: Holt, Rinehart & Winston, 1983). The UNIX implementations of C complement Kernighan and Ritchie's book in defining C. Standard library functions are documented in Section 3 of the manual.

This is not a complete list of books on C or even the best books on C. You are on your own with the rest.

Chapters 5 and 6: Sorting and Searching

☐ *Algorithms + Data Structures = Programs*, Niklaus Wirth (Englewood Cliffs, N.J.: Prentice-Hall, 1976). Algorithms are presented in Pascal with less analysis than in Knuth's book.

The Art of Computer Programming, vol. 3, *Sorting and Searching*, Donald Knuth (Reading, Mass.: Addison-Wesley, 1973). Sorting and searching algorithms used to be popular topics for computer science research. This book is the standard work on the subject. Thorough mathematical analysis of running times is the unique feature of this book.

Data Structures and Program Design, Robert L. Krause (Englewood Cliffs, N.J.: Prentice-Hall, 1984). Textbooks on data structures and algorithms are plentiful, but this one has a more practical flavor than most.

Software Tools in Pascal, B.W. Kernighan and P.J. Plauger (Reading, Mass.: Addison-Wesley, 1981). A chapter on sorting covers the same ground as our Sections 5.1 to 5.7.

Chapter 7: Toolkit

□   *Assembler Language Programming for the IBM Personal Computer*, David J. Bradley (Englewood Cliffs, N.J.: Prentice-Hall, 1984). The discussion of the Assembler language—instructions and pseudo-operations—is much easier to understand than that in the *Microsoft/IBM Macro Assembler Manual*.

IBM PC Technical Reference Manual. (IBM Corporation, 1981). New versions of the manual are issued for new IBM PC models (PC jr, PC XT, and PC AT). Add-on devices are now documented in a separate manual as well. This is the definitive guide to IBM hardware and to the ROM BIOS. The listings of BIOS code are very useful in understanding how to use the PC hardware.

IBM Disk Operating System Technical Reference Manual. (IBM Corporation, 1984). Versions are issued for each new release of PC-DOS. This one documents DOS function calls and the format of directory information.

Chapter 8: Terminal Emulation Programs

□   *8088 Assembler Language Programming: The IBM PC*, David C. Willin and Jeffrey I. Krantz (Indianapolis: Howard W. Sams and Co., Inc., 1983). The discussion of using the IBM PC hardware, DOS, and the BIOS from Assembler language is good.

The IBM Personal Computer from the Inside Out, Murray Sargent and Richard Shoemaker (Reading, Mass.: Addison-Wesley, 1984). This is a somewhat rambling guide to the IBM PC's hardware. The discussions of asynchronous communications, modems, and interrupts contain more material than those in most other books.

Interfacing to the IBM Personal Computer, Lewis C. Eggebrecht (Indianapolis: Howard W. Sams and Co., Inc., 1983). The PC's hardware is discussed in great detail. Programming the 8259 Interrupt Controller chip is discussed thoroughly.

"Interrupts and the IBM PC, Parts 1 and 2," *PC Tech Journal* 1 (November 1983 and January 1984), pp. 173–179, 144–186. All the steps needed to use interrupts on the IBM PC are discussed with the async adapter as an example. Part 2 gives concrete examples, with I/O port numbers and bit definitions detailed. I strongly recommend this as the best material on async interrupts on the IBM PC.

Index to Programs and Illustrations

This index is a quick guide to program listings and illustrations. It does not include every file; for example, many output files that directly follow their coding are not listed. Program descriptions are quick summaries of the programs and may not match the description in the first line of the code.

Chapter 3

Chapter 4

Chapter 5

Chapter 6

Chapter 7

Chapter 8

Chapter 9

Index

Throughout the index, figures are cited as F.1, F.2, and so on. Page numbers are not indicated.

Program Disk Order Form

☐ All the C and assembler language source code from *The C Toolbox* is available on a disk ready for use. The disk also contains additional source files on reading DOS directories as well as updates on using the source files with recent releases of various C compilers.

To order, send your name and address with a check or money order for $20 per copy ($30 for orders outside the U.S.) to the address shown below. Checks must be in U.S. funds and be drawn on a U.S. bank or on a U.S. branch of a foreign bank.

> William James Hunt
> C Toolbox Disk
> P.O. Box 271965
> Concord, CA 94527

Your name and address:

_____

_____

_____

_____

_____

Which C compiler do you use?_____

System requirements: An IBM PC or other computer that runs PC-DOS or MS-DOS (version 2.00 or later) and can read standard 5-1/4-inch floppy disks in a 40 track, 9 sectors per track, two-sided PC-DOS format.

Lattice C Users' Group

☐ If you liked *The C Toolbox* and use the Lattice, Microsoft, or IBM compilers, you may want to join the Lattice C Users' Group. I write the 16-page LCUG newsletter six times a year with the same practical approach as in this book. Membership is $30 a year ($40 in Canada and Europe, $45 elsewhere.)

To join, send your name and address with a check or money order payable to the Lattice C Users' Group to the address below. Checks must be in U.S. funds drawn on a U.S. bank or a U.S. branch of a foreign bank.

> Lattice C Users' Group
> P.O. Box 271965
> Concord, CA 94527